D1349186

# Sociological Human Ecology

## Contemporary Issues and Applications

edited by
**Michael Micklin** and **Harvey M. Choldin**

ERRATA

Sociological Human Ecology: Contemporary Issues and Applications

edited by Michael Micklin and Harvey M. Choldin

Please note that there has been an error made in the pagination of this book. The pages now numbered 412-413 belong between pages now numbered 418 and 419. (The correct sequence is then 411, 414-418, 412-413, 419.)

4/30/84

# Sociological Human Ecology

# Sociological Human Ecology: Contemporary Issues and Applications

edited by Michael Micklin
and Harvey M. Choldin

Westview Press / Boulder and London

Copyright © 1984 by Westview Press, Inc.

Published in 1984 in the United States of America by Westview Press, Inc., 5500
Central Avenue, Boulder, Colorado 80301; Frederick A. Praeger, President and
Publisher

Library of Congress Catalog Card Number: 83-51576
ISBN: 0-86531-670-8
ISBN: 0-86531-671-6 (pbk.)

Composition for this book was provided by the editors
Printed and bound in the United States of America

5  4  3  2  1

# Contents

*Preface*..........................................................vii
*Acknowledgments*..............................................  xi
*About the Contributors*.....................................xiii

Prologue:  Sociological Human Ecology: Past,
           Present, and Future, *Amos H. Hawley*...............1

Part I:    THE FOUNDATIONS OF ECOLOGICAL KNOWLEDGE

           Introduction, *the Editors*.......................17

        1. Human Ecology and Ecology, *Paul M. Siegel*........21

        2. The Ecological Perspective in the Social
           Sciences: A Comparative Overview,
           *Michael Micklin*..................................51

        3. Sociological Human Ecology: Theoretical and
           Conceptual Perspectives, *Dudley L. Poston, Jr.,
           W. Parker Frisbie, and Michael Micklin*...........91

        4. Data and Methods in Human Ecology,
           *W. Parker Frisbie*..............................125

Part II:   THE THEORY AND SUBSTANCE OF ECOLOGICAL KNOWLEDGE

           Introduction, *the Editors*......................179

        5. A Human Ecological Theory of Organizational
           Structuring, *John D. Kasarda and
           Charles E. Bidwell*..............................183

        6. Subcommunities: Neighborhoods and Suburbs
           in Ecological Perspective, *Harvey M. Choldin*....237

        7. The City, *Avery M. Guest*........................277

        8. Regional Ecology: A Macroscopic Analysis of
           Sustenance Organization, *Dudley L. Poston, Jr.*...323

vi

Part III:  THE APPLICATION OF ECOLOGICAL KNOWLEDGE

Introduction, *the Editors*......................383

9. Human Ecology and Social Policy,
*William R. Catton, Jr*.........................385

Epilogue:  Research and Policy Issues in Sociological
Human Ecology: An Agenda for the Future,
*Michael Micklin and Harvey M. Choldin*..........427

*Author Index*..................................................437
*Subject Index*.................................................445
*About the Book and Editors*...................................455
*Other Titles of Interest from Westview Press*.............456

# Preface

This volume grew out of concerns raised by the contributors and a few others over the current status of human ecology within the field of sociology. The year 1975 marked the twenty-fifth anniversary of the publication of Amos Hawley's highly influential *Human Ecology: A Theory of Community Structure*. The following year, at the annual meeting of the Population Association of America, a group of sociologist-demographers met informally to discuss recent developments in sociological human ecology. All those present had serious interests in the topic and most were conducting ecological research. The meeting, attended by John Kasarda, Dudley Poston, Paul Siegel, David Sly, Howard Hammerman, Michael Micklin, and Harvey Choldin (chair), produced a lively discussion. We agreed that Hawley's book represented a major turning point in the field and that no volume of equivalent scope had been published in the intervening years. Moreover, the discussion identified numerous issues regarding the theory, methods and relevance of the ecological perspective. At the end of the session we resolved to conduct an assessment of ecological knowledge within the discipline of sociology.

Over the next two years several meetings were held in which we identified the ground rules for our assessment of the state of the field and developed a division of labor for accomplishing this task. We agreed that one of the distinguishing features of the ecological perspective is its focus on characteristics of aggregates, and decided to give only limited attention to approaches that incorporate the individual as a unit of ecological analysis. We also shared the view that while spatial relationships are an important component of ecological organization, earlier approaches to sociological human ecology that were limited to describing spatial distributions of social phenomena should be ignored. In short, our definition of the field was shaped by the writings and teaching of those sociologists commonly identified with "organizational ecology"--especially Amos Hawley, Leo Schnore, Otis Dudley Duncan, Jack Gibbs and Walter Martin.

As the project developed from these early discussions to draft papers, the composition of the group changed. Hammerman and Sly dropped out and several new members were added, including Charles Bidwell, William Catton, Parker Frisbie, and Avery Guest. Preliminary versions of the chapters in this book were presented at a seminar held at the University of Illinois, Urbana, in the spring of 1977. The final papers were presented and discussed at a conference held at the Battelle Seattle Research Center in the fall of that year. Apart from the authors of the papers contained in this volume, the Battelle Conference also included a number of social scientists, listed in the Acknowledgements, who served as discussants. In addition, Amos Hawley provided an overview of sociological human ecology which is printed as the Prologue to this volume.

The original essays contained in this book are designed to review and assess the current state of knowledge in the field. The book is divided into three sections. Part I summarizes the conceptual, theoretical and methodological underpinnings of sociological ecology. Paul Siegel reviews the connections between the ecological perspective in sociology and the broader field of general ecology. Michael Micklin describes the similarities and differences between sociological ecology and ecological approaches developed in other social science disciplines. Dudley Poston, Parker Frisbie, and Micklin evaluate the theoretical bases of the major ecological paradigms used by sociologists. Concluding Part I, Frisbie assesses the data and methods available for ecological analysis.

In Part II, attention is directed to the substantive issues addressed in sociological ecology. These chapters are organized in terms of the varying types of aggregates which serve as the unit of ecological analysis. John Kasarda and Charles Bidwell present an ecological theory of formal organizations, a topic that has only recently attracted the attention of social ecologists. Harvey Choldin analyzes the ecological organization of subcommunities. In the next chapter Avery Guest reviews current ecological understanding of the city, perhaps the most frequently employed unit of analysis in this field. Finally, Dudley Poston examines the sustenance organization of subnational regions.

Part III contains but a single chapter. William Catton reviews the bearing of ecological knowledge on social policy, showing how understanding of national and global issues of human welfare can be improved through use of an ecological frame of reference. In addition to the chapters mentioned above and Hawley's Prologue, the book contains an Epilogue by the editors that suggests some fruitful directions for future work in the field.

The contributors to this volume feel strongly that the principal aims of sociology--the description, prediction and explanation of social organization--can be advanced through greater and more imaginative use of ecological concepts, theories, and methods. We hope that the essays presented in this volume provide an impetus in that direction.

*Michael Micklin*
*Harvey M. Choldin*

# Acknowledgments

Publication of this volume is truly a collective accomplishment. The editors and contributors have received encouragement, suggestions, and assistance from many individuals and several organizations. We thank all those mentioned below for their roles in making this book possible. Grants from the American Sociological Association's Committee on Problems of the Discipline, and the Graduate School of the University of Illinois supported a workshop at the University where early drafts of the papers were outlined. The penultimate versions of these papers were presented and discussed at a conference funded by the National Science Foundation (Grant Number SOC-77-08-747) and held at the Battelle Seattle Research Center. In addition to the contributors to this volume, participants in the conference included Richard N. Adams (University of Texas), John W. Bennett (Washington University), Brian J. L. Berry (Harvard University), Donald J. Bogue (University of Chicago), William R. Burch (Yale University), Glen V. Fuguitt (University of Wisconsin), Michael T. Hannan (Stanford University), Albert D. Hunter (Northwestern University), Samuel Z. Klausner (University of Pennsylvania), Walter T. Martin (University of Oregon), Charles Perrow (State University of New York at Stony Brook), Leo F. Schnore (University of Wisconsin), Gideon Sjoberg (University of Texas), G. Edward Stephan (Western Washington University), George A. Theodorson (Pennsylvania State University), Gary Wallace (National Science Foundation), and Basil G. Zimmer (Brown University). The aforementioned persons served as discussants of the conference papers and contributed to several open forums on sociological human ecology. Their comments and suggestions were invaluable in revising these papers for publication.

The editors and contributors owe a special debt of gratitude to Adeline Dinger, secretary extraordinaire at Battelle's Health and Population Study Center. Mrs. Dinger typed the entire manuscript in its numerous versions and facilitated communications among ten geographically dispersed contributors.

Any opinions, findings, and conclusions or recommendations in this publication are those of the contributors and do not necessarily reflect the view of the National Science Foundation.

# About the Contributors

CHARLES E. BIDWELL is Professor of Sociology and Education and Chairman of the Department of Education at the University of Chicago and has served as Editor of the <u>American Journal of Sociology</u>. He and John Kasarda continue their work on an ecological theory of formal organizations. He also is interested in the political economy of schooling. *THE ANALYSIS OF EDUCATIONAL PRODUCTIVITY,* of which he is coeditor, was published by the Ballinger Publishing Company in 1980.

WILLIAM R. CATTON, Jr., is Professor of Sociology at Washington State University. He has taught at colleges and universities in various parts of the United States and in Canada and New Zealand. He served as a member of New Zealand's Committee on Man in the Biosphere and was subsequently elected to chair the American Sociological Association's Environmental Sociology Section. His latest book is *OVERSHOOT: THE ECOLOGICAL BASIS OF REVOLUTIONARY CHANGE* (University of Illinois Press, 1980).

HARVEY M. CHOLDIN is Professor of Sociology at the University of Illinois, Urbana campus. His research explores social change in metropolitan communities at the local level. He is the author of *CITIES AND SUBURBS* (McGraw-Hill, forthcoming).

W. PARKER FRISBIE is Associate Professor of Sociology and Research Associate at the Population Research Center at the University of Texas at Austin. His areas of special interest are human and urban ecology and the demography of racial and ethnic groups. Among his publications is a coedited volume, the *DEMOGRAPHY OF RACIAL AND ETHNIC GROUPS*. His current research examines metropolitan interdependence, technological change, and U.S. migration trends.

AVERY M. GUEST, Associate Professor of Sociology at the University of Washington, teaches and does research in the areas of urban sociology and historical population patterns. Most of his published work focuses on the comparative spatial development of American metropolitan areas. He is currently studying the nature of attachment to urban neighborhoods and the American fertility transition in the late 19th century.

AMOS H. HAWLEY is Kenan Professor Emeritus at the University of North Carolina at Chapel Hill. He has served as President of the Population Association of America and of the American Sociological Association. Among his publications are *HUMAN ECOLOGY: A THEORY OF COMMUNITY STRUCTURE* (Ronald, 1950) and *URBAN SOCIETY: AN ECOLOGICAL APPROACH*, rev. ed. (Wiley, 1980).

JOHN D. KASARDA is Professor and Chairman, Department of Sociology, University of North Carolina at Chapel Hill. In addition to articles in numerous professional journals, he is coauthor of *CONTEMPORARY URBAN ECOLOGY* and currently is working with Charles Bidwell on a book developing ecological models of organizational structuring.

MICHAEL MICKLIN is Director of the Population and Development Policy Program at the Battelle Human Affairs Research Centers in Washington, D.C. Prior to joining Battelle he was on the faculty of Tulane University. He has conducted demographic and sociological research in several Latin American countries. His publications include *POPULATION, ENVIRONMENT, AND SOCIAL ORGANIZATION* (Dryden, 1973) and the coedited *HANDBOOK OF APPLIED SOCIOLOGY* (Praeger, 1981).

DUDLEY L. POSTON, Jr., is Professor of Sociology and Director of the Population Research Center at the University of Texas at Austin. He is coauthor of *CENSUS '80: CONTINUING THE FACTFINDER TRADITION* (U.S. Government Printing Office, 1980) and coeditor of *THE POPULATION OF THE SOUTH* (University of Texas Press, 1981). His current research deals with ecological models of migration and international patterns of childlessness.

PAUL M. SIEGEL is Chief of the Education and Social Stratification Branch of the Population Division, U.S. Bureau of the Census. When this volume was being prepared, he was a member of the Department of Sociology and an Associate Director of the Population Studies Center at the University of Michigan. He has taught a version of human ecology which stresses its roots in biological principles of organization since 1967.

# PROLOGUE
# Sociological Human Ecology: Past, Present, and Future

*Amos H. Hawley*

It is now some sixty-odd years ago that the ecological point of view was first introduced into sociology.[1] Thus, it is appropriate to take stock and to inquire into the future of human ecology. Indeed, the question of the future of the subject has been asked so often of late that one wonders what lies behind the question. However that may be, it is a legitimate question which might be, and probably should be, asked of all theoretical persuasions within a discipline. Certainly, one answer would be the same in all instances, that is, the future will be determined by the quality of research that issues from the theory under discussion.

---

[1] *In his 1916 essay on "The City: Suggestions for the Investigation of Human Behavior in an Urban Environment"* American Journal of Sociology, *xx(1916):577-612), R. E. Park says that the city has been recently studied "from the point of view of its ecology." I have been unable to find any such studies antedating Park's work.*

If the question addressed to human ecology implies some uncertainty as to whether it has a future, then one should give some thought to its lineage. Human ecology is an heir to a tradition that reaches back through the "Chicago School" to Halbwachs, Durkheim, Marx, Spencer, Darwin, Bagehot, Malthus, Montesquieu, and beyond. While not all of these individuals subscribed to the naturalistic theme common to many of them, all agreed that the complexities of human life arise from the exigencies of obtaining a livelihood from available resources. That so persistent an intellectual heritage should perish in the foreseeable future seems most improbable. The problem treated grows more acute and also more difficult of formulation with each passing year. The demands for understanding grow apace.

Certain specific dividends have been drawn from the intellectual capital of that tradition to form the rudiments of the human ecologist's point of view. There is, in the first place, a very elementary notion that social phenomena occur in a space-time universe. Hence, they are manifested as territorially based systems. Second, the social system is regarded as a mechanism by which a population adapts to its environment. Thus, the environment-population system interaction is the central concern. Third, adaptation is an irreversible process of cumulative change in which a system is moved from simple to complex forms. Fourth, it is in the environmental relationship that the organizing principle of the system and its sub-systems is generated. Finally, since adaptation is a collective achievement, a system cannot be explained in terms of the internal processes of its parts. Human ecology, therefore, is committed to a holistic and macro-level mode of analysis.

The several elements of the ecological paradigm not only give the point of view its identity, they also are responsible for the possible loss of that identity. There are two reasons for the latter possibility. One of these is that the paradigm describes a distinctively sociological perspective. What could be more sociological than the assumption that human being deal with their life problems through collective action? There is thus a tendency for the two approaches to blend into one. The second reason for the possible blurring of the field lies in the comprehensiveness of its conception. Environment, population, and social system pretty well exhaust the content of the phenomenal realm. A reach of that scope cannot be very specific. In consequence of its sociological essence and its inclusiveness, human ecology always threatens to lead the student into the labyrinthine byways of all of life's complexities. Some have described the field as a transdisciplinary focus. While that may be defensible, it presumes too much. Unless the ecologist keeps a tight mental grip on his paradigm, he is apt to attempt everything and accomplish nothing.

It is the first of these sources of "identity crisis" that concerns me here. Not only does the human ecologist deal with what is essentially a sociological problem, non-ecological sociologists often wander into the problem areas of ecology sometimes without knowing where they are and sometimes with an apology for descending to an ecological level. In short, I think there has been a great deal of convergence between human ecology and the parent discipline. Whether that is to be regarded as fortunate or not depends on how one views the objectives of social science. Let us see where and to what extent convergence has occurred.

I will come back to the paradigm in a moment, but first it should be pointed out that human ecology with its sociological coloration has drifted apart from many of the current uses of the term ecology. That is contrary to what was expected in earlier days. It was then thought that human ecology was an extension to bio-ecology and that there might be a fruitful exchange of ideas (Hawley, 1944). That has not occurred in any marked degree for reasons that are obscure. Perhaps a circumstance of some relevance in this connection is the rise of ethology which seems to have removed much of the sociological content from general ecology. There is the further fact that the term "ecology" has become increasingly identified with policy and action in the solution of environmental problems such as pollution, wildlife preservation, and resource and energy conservation. As a consequence, the term is commonly used interchangeably with environment. The disjunction might also be due to the failure of human ecology to develop its theory sufficiently in fruitful directions. Whatever may be the explanation, the continuity between human ecology and general ecology seems to have been lost, for the moment at least.

To return to the paradigm, the first element mentioned is the focus of attention upon territorially based systems. Human ecology begins with the obvious fact that human life is lived on the ground, so to speak, and that it is all mixed up with soil, tools, food, raw materials, buildings, and other material externalities. A social system is reared upon these profane foundations and it is never disassociated from them, not even in its more rarefied moral and sacred aspects. Human ecology had its inception as a promising way of accounting for certain structural features of a particular manifestation of territoriality, namely, the urban community. Soon, it was recognized that the high visibility of the compact city does not encompass all that is involved in the urban system. Functional boundaries, it was observed, lie well beyond the corporate limits of cities, and of other settlement units as well, and the ecologist found himself dealing with centers and tributary zones, or entities sometimes described as trade areas, service areas, and metropolitan areas. And now it is beginning to appear that even the most inclusive of these, the metropolitan area, is insufficiently bounded, for urban characteristics are being diffused through the entire society. In the meantime, however, ecologists became aware of the fact that urban centers, i.e., cities, carry on differentiated functions relative to one another. The units thus form what is in effect a system of cities or city-centered areas. Although this idea was introduced formally as central place theory by economic geographers, it was left to ecologists and location theorists in economics to point out that in an industrial, as distinguished from an agrarian, society the urban hierarchy is cast in functional rather than in spatial relations. While the urban hierarchy has been studied with cities as units (Duncan, 1960; Vance and Smith, 1954), it has also been investigated with respect to inter-city linkages operated by special institutions such as administrative offices (Pappenfort, 1959) and as banking (Lieberson, 1961). But sociologists who do not regard themselves as ecologists, notably, Roland Warren (1972) and Herman Turk (1970), have dealt with the same phenomenon in their work on vertical relations among organizations.

Ecologists have been less attentive to the international dimension of territorially based systems than to the intranational scope. McKenzie's early essay on "Dominance and World Organization" (1927), set a precendent for a broader view, but the suggestion was not vigorously pursued, perhaps because of the relative lack of comparative data before the establishment of the United Nation's statistical services. Now we find that Wallerstein (1974), Richard Rubinson (1976), and others are interested in much the same problem as that treated by McKenzie. I think one can say with some confidence that this problem will occupy an increasing amount of the attention of sociologists and of all social scientists, for that matter. It has become all too apparent that what happens in local communities, regions, and nations is critically affected by events occurring beyond their respective boundaries (i.e., in the environment). Yet, although a social system of world scope is rapidly maturing, we have the seeming anomaly of ethnic and regional separatist movements springing up in widely removed places. A comparable development is the rising demand in large urban

areas for some degree of neighborhood administrative autonomy. Evidently, there has been a tendency toward over-
centralization. The phenomenon is theoretically intriguing
and, from a policy standpoint, demanding of attention.

The second component of the ecological paradigm I mentioned is the environment-population-social system interaction in which adaptation is accomplished, if and when it
is accomplished. Environment has been a preoccupation of
human ecologists from the beginning. But, since the earliest
applications of ecology to human life was in reference to
the city, environment was conceived abstractly as space
alone, though later some attention was given to the time
dimension. The reasoning underlying that treatment might be
paraphrased as follows: Under any given transportation
regime, locally accessible space is limited in supply,
hence, increase in number of people and activities leads to
competition for location from which a predictable pattern in
space takes form. This syllogism gave rise to a great out-
pouring of descriptive research on spatial distributions, so
much in fact, that human ecology became identified with the
study of spatial relations. Gradients were plotted, concentric zones were delineated, ethnic and socioeconomic subareas were charted, correlations of social-psychological
events with physical features of cities were computed, and
various other aspects of spatial distributions were recorded. This concentration of interest might be explained, I
suppose, partly because it lent itself to dissertation-scale
research, partly because it touched upon a number of practical problems, and partly because it made very slight
demands upon the theoretical imagination. In any event,
virtually no contribution to theory resulted from either the
producers of the work or the critics of the product. Human
ecology seemed to stagnate on a concern with spatial patterns. In fact, that conception of the field has become so
embedded in the sociological literature that, as with a
grammatical error in a family line, its excision may require
three generations or more. Parenthetically, most of the
empirical and the theoretical support for our early notions
about spatial patterns have disappeared with technological
change. I refer to the Burgess (1926) model of concentric
zones. It is no longer true that urban growth increments
enter a place at a single point and distribute their effects
centrifugally from that point. Increments now enter at many
points and at peripheries as often as not. But, while the
old idea is obsolete, we have no local scale model with
which to replace it.

That environment involves more than mere space and the physical structures imposed upon it is implied, of course, in the adaptation assumption. If that were not apparent in the spatial emphases of the urban researcher, it became so as thought shifted to the relation of the city and of other settlement units to their hinterlands. The obviously dependent status of such units underscored the importance of the sustenance concern and of the source of requisite materials. But sustenance is a matter not only of materials, it consists also of services, information, and mutual assistance arrangements. Environment is defined by the thing environed. In the modern era, given the facility of movement, we must think in terms of an inclusive environment comprising social as well as physical components. The two segments are now so intertwined that they cannot be untangled; virtually all of our experience with the physical environment is filtered through a social environment. This has not made life easier for the student who wishes to use environment as a variable, for the points of contact are so numerous, so unequal in value, and so indirectly mediated that it defies measurement. The problem is further complicated by the unstable character of environment. Yet, an understanding of the principles of adaptation, whether as equilibrium maintenance or as growth, requires that we find a workable operationalization of the concept. The ecologist cannot ignore the task. How he handles it will have much to do with the future of his field of study.

While the issue of how to deal with the system-environment relationship is of great moment to ecologists, it has interested a very small number of sociologists. The influence of environment at the individual level is generally recognized, i.e., as in socialization, but it has been only casually appreciated at the system level. I suppose one might hold the prestige of functional theory responsible for that state of affairs, though there has been a grudging admission among functionalists recently that there is an environment. The notion of a closed system has yielded a little bit more of late with the growth of interest in causal modelling and its acknowledgment of exogenous factors. But its built-in commitment to the notion of a recursive model misses the main point.

A somewhat different situation obtains with reference to population. To the ecologist, population is of major concern, for inasmuch as adaptation is a collective enterprise, the social system is the property, as it were, of a population. In trying to explain his specialty to a demographer, the ecologist is apt to say that it is concerned with discovering the organizational implications of population.

Thus, ecologists have devoted a great deal of effort to ascertaining the effects of population size, composition, and distribution on social structure and, conversely, the effects of social structural changes on population parameters. The social and psychological correlates of density have been the focus of attention in several disciplines. But, to human ecology, a more pertinent, though as yet only partly explored, line of investigation concerns density requirements of organizations and the possibility of determining optimal densities for different types of systems.

Population, as indicated already, is not the private preserve of ecologists. In its very nature, the subject is relevant to every social science concern. It is noteworthy in this connection that, in the United States, sociology has provided the disciplinary home to demography down to quite recent years. Sociologists of many different persuasions have shown some interest in population. When that has gone beyond its use as a control variable, it has usually taken the form of an inquiry into the proportion of administrative personnel to size of group or institution. That work has also been affected by boundary problems, due partly to the existence of systems within systems, but also to differing characteristics of subsystems. That is, some groups have their entire clienteles within their memberships, while others have only external clienteles. Population has also entered into the considerations of urban sociologists as a measure of the size or extent of urbanization. It cannot be said, however, that sociologists in general have shown much enthusiasm for the subject.

The third element of the paradigm, the conception of the environment-population-social system interaction as a development process, touches upon a basic aspect of the field. Those of us who are familiar with the history of the subject will recall that the initial conception of the development process was borrowed from plant ecology as succession. This term connotes a discontinuous and cumulative process in which change and equilibrium alternate until finally a climax stage or steady-state equilibrium is reached. Thereafter, no further change takes place without a significant environmental shift. Thus, succession is a sort of ontogenetic version of evolution. While succession has been refined by the bioecologists and used to account for ecosystem formation, it has had a somewhat short-lived utility in human ecological studies, perhaps because of difficulties encountered in operationalizing the equilibrium concept. Although that concept is retained for certain expository and analytical purposes, it has faded from view as an element in ecological theorizing about change. A theory of expansion has very largely replaced succession theory. By the term expansion, we refer to a process of cumulative change in which environmental inputs modify system structure and processes, involve various redistributions of parts, and bring about increases in population and territorial scope. In this idea, the equilibrium concept has not figured prominently, though the emergence of some clearer notions regarding asymptotic properties in systems may bring it into the foreground once again.

Sociologists have had a long-standing interest in change. In fact, it has been a major focus of attention. Even so, it has seldom received any systematic treatment. For the most part, sociologists have dealt with very specific changes or very particular features of change. A notable exception is the late growth of interest in modernization and development. And still more recently, there has been a revival of evolutionary thought owing largely to the scholarship of Leslie White (1949) in anthropology and G. E. Lenski (1970) in sociology. But sophisticated as modern evolutionary theory is, it still seems to me to be mainly a description of chronological series of social system types viewed as stages. What happens between stages, or how the movement from stage to stage occurs, is not made explicit. That should present an opportunity for a useful cooperation between evolutionary and ecological thought. That is, the ecological concept of expansion might very well be used to account for interstage transitions.

Of interest, it seems to me, is that an essentially ecological theory of change, the demographic transition theory, arose not from the work of ecologists but from the thoughts of demographers with backgrounds in sociology and economics: Thompson (1929) and Notestein (1945). Having missed that opportunity, ecologists should not fail to exploit another open to it, namely, a demonstration of how fertility decline results from social system changes that remove the functional imperative for reproduction. Some work has been done on that hypothesis (Kasarda, 1971), but as better data become available, more refined analyses will be possible. In any event, the interaction of population and development processes is a problem ecologists share with other disciplines.

A fourth part of the paradigm is that the organizing principle of a system arises from the environmental relationship. First, a system begins to appear as such with the emergence of specialization in conducting or mediating the environmental relationship. Second, the function specialized in obtaining environmental inputs sets the main conditions under which all other functions operate, hence, it occupies a dominant position in the system. Third, other functions are scaled and rated, that is, their powers are diminished, in accordance with their degrees of removal from direct involvement in the generation of environmental inputs. The amount of control over system processes varies directly with position in a functional chain. What is true of the system as a whole is true also of its subsystems. The principle of hierarchy as hinged upon the environmental relationship has a general application. It underlies the stratification of functionally differentiated individuals; it accounts for the ordering on an ordinal scale of groups or subsystems; and it is the key to the ascendancy pattern observed in sets of cities. Not all of the implications of this line of reasoning have been extracted, but it seems to be a promising area for theoretical development.

On this matter, there has been no appreciable convergence of ecology and the parent discipline, despite the work of a few people such as C. Wright Mills (1951) and some of the neo-Marxists. Power seems to be generally regarded as either a personalized property or as a possession of elites. And stratification is commonly treated as simply a status scale, with little thought given to how strata operate in a system. Here, as in a number of other respects, I think the price of looking upon human events from the perspective of the individual is a failure to recognize system properties.

I come finally to the last component of the paradigm, that is, the holistic emphasis. This, more than anything else, it seems to me, identifies human ecology as a sociological concern. As a matter of fact, I am inclined to the view that human ecology had adopted a more thorough sociological position than has much of sociology. It sees the social system, as I have said, as the product of an irrevesible process and as constituting, therefore, a unit that cannot be resolved into its parts except for analytic purposes. It is anti-reductionist. It seeks to avoid the sociological fallacy, if I may return a compliment, of claiming to know the whole through knowledge of the psychological characteristics of the parts. The human ecologist looks with dismay on the reckless use of analogy by his fellow sociologists, as in the attribution of goals and other individual characteristics to groups and organizations. The announced purposes of individuals should not be regarded as synonymous with ways in which organizations function, even though there may be agreement between the two.

The use of aggregate data often obscures the holistic posture of human ecology. While it is correct that an age distribution, a vital rate, or a population size are accumulations of individual events, it is also true that they would not have accumulated to any given magnitude or pattern under any or all conditions. Thus, they may be regarded as descriptive of structural properties. Or, to put it differently, the greater the concentration of behavior on a central tendency, the less probable is an explanation in individual terms. Where there is a high degree of uniformity, the explanation must be found either in genetic factors, or, more probably, in social-structural factors. Individual factors may become important, of course, where there is little or no concentration on a mean. But in that event, there is no social system.

Now to return to the question of the future of human ecology. As I have pointed out, there has been a noticeable convergence between ecology and the parent discipline. Doubtlessly, that trend will continue. Perhaps ecology can take some credit for the macro-level thinking that has appeared in sociology, for an awareness of the relevance of population parameters in sociological studies, and for an appreciation of social system characteristics as independent variables affecting micro-level events. And I suspect that sociological considerations have led human ecologists to broaden their conceptions and their problem statements. Nevertheless, the convergence, has been piecemeal; it has occurred here and there, in some respects very markedly, in others barely perceptibly.

The point of view of human ecology is defined by the paradigm as a whole and not by one or another of its parts taken separately. And, in its wholeness, it is a robust approach to the study of human social systems. Its promise of a distinctive contribution should be apparent, given the sociological ambit in which a strong psychological orientation prevails. But, if the potentialities of human ecology are to be realized, a great deal more effort will have to be devoted to extracting the theoretical implications of its basic assumptions than has been spent on the task thus far. Without a source of logically connected hypotheses, the research carried on under the rubric of ecology will lack pertinence and will have but a slight chance of being cumulative. I regard a theoretical development as being of critical importance for the future of the subject.

My use of the term, theoretical development, means a drawing out of the implications of the paradigm and their statement in propositional form. From that, we should obtain a clear working idea of what a system consists in, how the parts operate relative to one another, and how the system unfolds in the interaction with environment. In other words, the end result should be both a theory of change and a theory of organization. We cannot, of course, be content with space as a surrogate for environment, for space is experienced as a resistance or facility in movement and that, in turn, is a function of how a system is organized. The substantive features of environment are much more important than its linear features. The model that recommends itself very persuasively is that of the ecosystem, as developed by bioecologists. In this model, adaptation is viewed as a successional development culminating in an equilibrium comprising a hierarchy of relationships presided over by a dominant species. Cyclings of matter are regularized and the maximum bio-mass supportable in an area is attained (Odum, 1969). This model includes a number of elements we would want in an ecological theory, such as the conception of adaptation as a growth process feeding on environmental inputs, a notion of structure built on a dominance scale, a suggestion of how energy is transmitted through the system and recycled, and an indication of the possible use of the equilibrium concept. The ecosystem provides us with a rough guide from which to work. But the bioecologist's ecosystem is not directly transferable to the material with which we must deal. It makes at least two assumptions, one of which is unacceptable, the other, premature, and a conclusion that is much too simple. The first is that only a proximate environment need be considered, whereas the human system is exposed to a remote as well as a proximate environment. The second assumption is that there is a conclusion to the developmental process, an assumption that is tenable perhaps where environment is completely definable and fixed in content. The conclusion, which presents the systems as just a hierarchy of strata, is much too simple for our purposes. The ecosystem concept has nothing to say about the nature of subsystems, how they are arrayed in a structure, and how they are interwoven with strata. But, all of this is merely to say that one must be guarded in his use of analogy.

These problems notwithstanding, a very promising line of theoretical development has appreared in three recently published papers dealing with what is called organizational ecology. Bidwell and Kasarda (1975) have analyzed organizational effectiveness in standardized environments using differently organized school units and measuring effectiveness by the performance of high school students on standard tests. The results confirm the main hypothesis regarding the significance of organizational structure. In a review of the literature on the interactive relations of environments and organizations, Aldrich and Pfeffer (1976) utilize the variation-selection-retention model of ecological evolutionary thought to demonstrate its greater explanatory power than the resource dependence or adaptation model commonly used in psychologically oriented approaches. And finally in a closely reasoned theoretical paper, Hannan and Freeman (1977) adapt the Lotka-Volterra model to the problem of organizational selection through a competitive process in a context of limited environmental carrying capacity.

These and other as yet unpublished papers that have come to my attention convince me that human ecology is enjoying a renaissance. I believe, however, that its continued welfare will be determined by adherence to a number of principles. Foremost among these, it seems to me, is the extent to which ecologists adhere to their holistic position. If that position is compromised out of deference to prevailing beliefs about the individual as cause, the result will be unrecognizable as ecology. Adherence to a holistic position, furthermore, sets limits to the range of phenomena to be explained. It provides no clues as to how individual aberrations are caused or what lies behind current fads and fashions. Rather is the student confined to a study of the formation and the operation of systems under varying environmental conditions. The shape assumed by ecological theory will also be affected by consistency with reference to a given level of abstraction. The ecologist's task is to arrive at general principles. He should not be diverted by historical oddities or poorly reported "contradictions" to his hypotheses. Nor is the contemporary scene a sufficient basis for generalization. A very real problem here is how to extract a dependable sample from historical data. But that can wait until a theory is at hand for the testing. Reference to adherence to a level of abstraction reminds me of the importance of parsimony. Our typologies of events are often so arbitrarily drawn that we deprive ourselves of much of the power inherent in any hypothesis. For example, it seems to me that all instances of organization, whether as system or subsystem, are governed by common principles, and that hierarchy, wherever or however manifested, arises from the exigencies of an environmental relationship. I will end this list of metatheoretical thoughts with an endorsement, heard many times in the past, of the desirability of a common dictionary. Just as a standardized universe of discourse is essential to the efficient operation of any system, so it is to the productivity of the concerted efforts of students of systems. Ecologists enjoy greater consensus than do our colleagues elsewhere in sociology, but there is progress still to be made.

In conclusion one might reasonably ask: What has sociology to gain from the harboring within its domain of an ecological perspective? I'm sure such a question would be answered differently by persons with various conceptions of sociology. From my viewpoint, I can see a number of answers to the question. For one thing, it provides an alternative paradigm in the discipline to be used for purposes of comparison and criticism. In the end, the one with the greatest explanatory power presumably will gain ascendancy. But, long before that eventuality comes to maturity, human ecology will continue to offer a way of treating a set of problems not manageable in other paradigms. It allows the researcher to get beyond oral and symbolic behavior to some of the more substantial content of collective life. A third possible benefit to sociology is that human ecology offers a bridge to other disciplines. Some are inclined to argue it is the one possibility for a synthetic social science. The fourth and most important answer to that question, in my judgment, is that the conception of social system structure developed in human ecology defines a framework in which a great many other aspects of society can be seen to be interrelated. It supplies, therefore, the independent variables needed in studies of individual behavior.

REFERENCES

Aldrich, H. E., and J. Pfeffer (1976). "Environments of organization." Annual Review of Sociology, 2:79-105.

Bidwell, C., and J. Kasarda (1975). "School district organization and student achievement." American Sociological Review, 40:55-70.

Burgess, E. W. (1925). "The growth of the city: an introduction to a research project." Pp. 47-62 in R. E. Park, E. W. Burgess, and R. D. McKenzie (eds.), The City. Chicago: University of Chicago Press .

Duncan, O. D., et al. (1960). Metropolis and Region Baltimore: Johns Hopkins University Press .

Hannan, M., and J. Freeman (1977). "The population ecology of organizations." American Journal of Sociology, 82: 929-964.

Hawley, A. H. (1944). "Ecology and human ecology." Social Forces, 22:398-405.

Kasarda, J. (1971). "Economic structure and fertility." Demography, 8:307-317.

Lenski, G. (1970). Human Societies. New York: McGraw-Hill.

Lieberson, S. (1961). "The division of labor in banking." American Journal of Sociology, 66:491-496.

McKenzie, R. D. (1927). "The concept of dominance and world organization." American Journal of Sociology, 66: 491-496.

Mills, C. W. (1951). White Collar: The American Middle Classes. New York: Oxford University Press.

Notestein, F. W. (1945). "Population: the long view." In T. W. Schultz (ed.), Food for the World. Chicago: University of Chicago Press.

Odum, E. (1969). "The strategy of ecosystem development." Science, 164:262-270

Pappenfort, D. M. (1959). "The ecological field and the metropolitan community: manufacturing and management." American Journal of Sociology, 34:959-975.

Rubinson, R. (1976). "The world-economy and the distribution of income within states: a cross-national study." American Sociological Review, 41:638-659.

Thompson, W. S. (1929). "Population." American Journal of Sociology, 34:959-975.

Turk, H. (1970). "Interorganization networks in urban society: initial perspectives and comparative research." American Sociological Review, 35:1-18.

Vance, R. B. and S. Smith (1954). "Metropolitan dominance and integration." Pp. 114-134 in R. B. Vance and N. J. Demerath (eds.), The Urban South. Chapel Hill: University of North Carolina Press.

Wallerstein, I. (1974). The Modern World System Capitalist Agriculture and the Origins of the European World-Economy in the Sixteenth Century. New York: Academic Press.

Warren, R. (1972). The Community in America, second edition. Chicago: Rand McNally.

White, L. (1949). The Science of Culture. New York: Grove Press.

# Part I

## THE FOUNDATIONS
## OF ECOLOGICAL KNOWLEDGE

# Introduction

*the Editors*

The four chapters comprising Part I examine some fundamental aspects of the ecological perspective in sociology. The first two chapters cover relationships between sociological human ecology and other disciplines, beginning with its potential connections with the "mother" science, bioecology, followed by a comparison of ecological approaches developed in several social sciences. Chapter 3 surveys and assesses ecological theory in sociology, and suggests directions for needed development. The final chapter in Part I accomplishes a similar analysis for the methodology of ecological research.

Paul Siegel's chapter, "Ecology and Human Ecology," is both ambitious and audacious. The author suggests that a true human ecology would use the theories and methods of general ecology, explicitly fitting humans, as a species, into the scheme. In this way, social scientists could discover whether humans have an ordinary or unique place in ecosystems. Siegel advises the analyst to view ecosystems containing human populations from a traditional bioecological perspective, asking, for example, what are the characteristics of the niche occupied by humans and how do human activities fit in the pattern of energy flows? The answers to such questions should highlight any distinctively "human" quality of our species.

Unlike most writers in sociological human ecology, Siegel incorporates a good deal of contemporary bioecology into his discussion and his bibliography. He uses the vocabulary and quantitative models of that field to develop his argument. The reader may infer that Siegel considers much sociological human ecological research and theory to be uninformed by the best of modern biology. Perhaps sociologists have been getting too much of their ecology from other sociologists rather than from its originators.

Michael Micklin's chapter provides an overview of uses of the ecological perspective in the social sciences. He focuses on anthropology and sociology, but also discusses the fields of geography and political science. Micklin finds a number of commonalities in the approaches taken by writers in the four disciplines who explicitly subscribe to an ecological point of view. He notes that they all deal with aggregates rather than individuals. All are concerned with problems of societal adaptation and change. All tend, more than their nonecological colleagues, to incorporate materialistic elements into their frames of reference—environment, population, and technology, in particular.

Micklin devotes considerable attention to anthropology, particularly the recent writings of John W. Bennett, Richard N. Adams, and Marvin Harris. He notes that the anthropologist expands the typical definition of sociological ecology by emphasizing the role of culture, not narrowly defined in terms of technology.

In general, Micklin draws an optimistic picture of the use of ecology in the social sciences, pointing toward common ground and the potential for the development, perhaps, of a common paradigm. "The thesis underlying this chapter," he writes, "is that during the past quarter century there has been a convergence of ideas among social scientists such that a synthetic, multidisciplinary human ecology is not only possible, but actually emerging."

Chapter 3, by Dudley Poston, Parker Frisbie, and Michael Micklin, offers an historical perspective on the development of human ecological theory in sociology. Considering the period since about 1950, the authors delineate three lines of development: the general theory elaborated by Amos Hawley; the ecological complex, as outlined by Otis Dudley Duncan and Leo F. Schnore, and the sustenance organization model, developed initially by Jack P. Gibbs and Walter T. Martin. In each case, the authors present the historical development of the theory, its central ideas, its utility for empirical research, and its viability.

The authors clearly appreciate Hawley's work, crediting him with setting forth the basic conceptual framework of contemporary sociological human ecology. They discuss the evolution of his ideas from his earlier essays, through the publication of *Human Ecology* in 1950, and into his more recent contributions. The authors note the expansion of Hawley's scope of interest from the community to the broader social system and suggest that his later writing sets forth a broad theory of social change. Their evaluation concludes that his writings represent a general theory because they have proven to be applicable to a variety of empirical problems and historical changes.

The authors then turn their attention to the ecological writings of Otis Dudley Duncan and his students. They consider his essays on the ecosystem and the ecological complex to be cornerstones of contemporary theory and research. They suggest, as well, that these ideas have proven to be fruitful as a framework for empirical research.

Finally, Poston, Frisbie and Micklin present the sustenance organization model as an emergent major theory. Like Hawley, analysts employing this theory emphasize questions of organization and adaptation. They are concerned with the conditions under which a population becomes differentiated in terms of its division of labor. They ask how a population organizes its sustenance-generating activities and what conditions lead to one form of organization rather than another. This concluding section of the chapter sets forth a carefully delineated analytical scheme which suggests how research can be conducted in accord with the sustenance organization model.

Chapter 4, by Parker Frisbie, presents an exhaustive coverage of methodological concerns in sociological human ecology. Frisbie presents different measures of the division of labor, noting the strengths and weaknesses of each. He then turns his attention to urban structure, a topic which has received considerable empirical attention. Here he covers residential distribution and differentiation, involving the analysis of the social geography of cities and metropolitan areas. The chapter summarizes recent debates on factor analysis as an ecological technique, particularly its manifestations in urban analysis (Social Area Analysis and Factorial Ecology), and segregation indexes. A particular contribution of this chapter is Frisbie's justification and defense of research at the aggregate level, obviously central to human ecology, by means of his discussion of the "ecological fallacy." This concept has long served as an impediment to human ecological research, and Frisbie explains why and how the discipline has overcome its implied constraints.

In sum, Part I contains a series of papers setting forth the scope of sociological human ecology—its major theories and methods and its relationship to bioecology and the other social sciences.

# 1
# Human Ecology and Ecology

*Paul M. Siegel*

[the concept of the division of labor]... applies
to organisms as to societies... [and] is no longer
considered only as a social institution that has
its source in the intelligence and will of men, but
is a phenomenon of general biology whose conditions
must be sought in the properties of organized
matter. The division of labor in society appears to
be no more than a particular form of this general
process, and societies, in conforming to that law,
seem to be yielding to a movement that was born
before them, and that similarly governs the entire
world (Durkheim, 1938).

Probably most of the difficulties which beset human
ecology may be traced to the isolation of the subject from the mainstream of ecological thought
(Hawley, 1944).

...adaptation is necessarily an organizational
process (Hawley, 1973).

Revised during a sabbatical year as a visiting scholar in
the Department of Sociology, University of Washington. That
institution's courtesy, and David Ragozin's typewriter, are
sincerely appreciated.

21

All the ecologies--human ecology, population ecology, community ecology, etc.--are studies of differentiation and organization in arbitrarily bounded systems of organisms and environments. This paper attempts to review some recent developments in some bio-ecologies and to suggest their relevance for several ecologies which might be called human. The domain of this inquiry will be limited largely to community and population ecology--subfields of biology. The range of the inquiry encompasses two versions of what human ecology might be.

On the one hand, human ecology might take as its domain the ecosystem--"the interacting environmental and biotic system" (Allee, et al., 1949:695)--taking the point of view that man is an integrated, natural component of ecosystems and focusing on ecosystem processes, which surely include but are not coextensive with societal processes. By now one should need no elaborate defense for the proposition that human activity is importantly shaped by the environmental and biotic system. Not only does current human behavior respond to immediate ecosystem conditions and affect them, but the structure of current organization of human activity itself has arisen through a process of ecosystem adaptation. This view denies that there is "a human ecology, as distinct from bioecology" (Hawley, 1973) save in the accident of academic organization. In this view the "system" whose structure, dynamics, and development is of interest is the ecosystem, and such problems as "pollu tion," changes in species composition and diversity, urbanization, and changes in urban function are all to be viewed from the standpoint of their impacts on or representation in variables of state for the ecosystem as a whole. This does not mean that one must enshrine the list of endangered species, but it does imply that one must rise to the bait of the Club of Rome. The most obvious need within this "new integrative discipline" (Odum, 1977) is for the development of variables of state to supplant the crudities of *Limits to Growth,* and for a rigorous model of the evolution of ecosystems in terms of these variables to replace the vague and controversial notions of a "strategy of ecosystem development" (Odum, 1969). The challenge of this view of ecology is its explicit concern with a detailed and rigorous approach to the question "what is the direction of evolution"--a question left largely untouched in both the biological and social sciences to date.

On the other hand, human ecologists claim the study of *social* organization as their domain. On this view eco-systems or biological communities may offer models of or-ganization which can prove fruitful when employed in the study of social organization (see, for instance, Winter, 1964; Hannan and Freeman, 1977). This view requires much less modification of the traditional concerns of human eco-logists: communication with "mainstream biological thought" consists in the importation of models and metaphors whose only test is their utility in the study of social organiza-tion. One need not be concerned that ecosystem models *must* apply to social organization *because* it is ecological.

Of necessity, much of this chapter will be devoted to creating abstractions under which the "obvious" differences between plants, animals, and men can be ignored and atten-tion devoted to the systemic properties which they share and which unite them. As may be appropriate in this conference directed at re-appraising the human ecological theory most notably associated with Amos Hawley, much of this paper will be concerned to salvage some of the ecology he has rejected for the study of human populations.

*Adaptation*

Perhaps the fundamental abstraction underlying and uniting the ecologies is the notion of adaptation. Among human ecologists, "adaptation" seems concerned with "... cope [ing] with concrete environmental conditions in the course of satisfying subsistence needs" (Micklin, 1973:3) and particular emphasis seems placed on "subsistence," that is, upon conditions of existence. I take this to be the sense of Hawley's (1973) "adaptation to environment is an imperative and omnipresent concern for every living thing." But by "adaptation" we also commonly mean something like "change in response to (changing) external conditions." That is, "adaptation" refers both to a state of being and a pro-cess of change. Of course human ecologists have been in-terested in both senses of adaptation, though I don't think it unfair to say they have largely been concerned with recording changes in the organization of sustenance activi-ties rather than with the characteristics of organization which determine the kinds of external conditions and varia-tions which can be responded to and the kinds of responses possible. The bio-ecologies differentially emphasize these two aspects of adaptation. Population ecology and popula-tion genetics are firmly grounded in models of some mecha-nisms which allow structure or organization to be modified in response to external conditions or changes in them. These models are employed to ask fairly abstract questions about the kinds of structures and organization that will emerge from the process of adaptation in environments with particular structure and patterns of variation. Community ecology, on the other hand, has concentrated much more closely on the state of adaptation—on the means by which the diverse populations constituting the community sustain themselves and each other. It is of some interest that while concentrating on the roles of various member populations in the cycling of materials and the regulation of community metabolism, this approach has also developed strong notions about the direction of community development—in the context of a much less well-specified model of the adaptive process.

I shall use the term "adaptation" in a way likely to irritate nearly everyone. I intend it to refer to the process by which aggregates respond to external conditions by self-modification. And I mean to include as aggregates behavioral repertoires, at one extreme, and communities, at the other. Thus the individual human actor is viewed as (merely) a collection of behaviors and a community is viewed as a set of species populations. (It may help following my abstraction to realize that I'm trying to extend the notion of a gene pool.) The units which comprise these aggregates are held to be invariant over time—that is, each may differ from the other, but each retains its individual identity. The properties of the aggregate change as its composition changes, that is, as units with different properties are differentially replaced, added, or removed. Insofar as these compositional changes are affected by external conditions, I will speak of adaptation. An adaptive mechanism is defined by specification of the structure by which external conditions effect the differential demography of units, and thus modify the composition of the aggregate, and specification of the source(s) of inter-unit variation. Thus in "natural selection" reproduction with phenotypic parent-offspring fitness correlations produced via genotypes are the mechanism by which external conditions (expressed as fitnesses) affect population composition, and recombination and mutation are the sources of variety. (See Lewontin, 1970, for an elaboration of the units—individuals, populations, species, communities—on which natural selection may operate.) In "learning," differential extinction and enhancement of behavioral responses through schedules of reinforcement change the composition of the behavioral repertoire, and varieites of response arise through random search and generalization. (See Campbell, 1965; Pringle, 1951.)

In "ecological succession," as we will see, several kinds of mechanisms work through longevity, replacement, and competition to effect changes in the species composition of communities, with outside communities serving as the source of novel species. All adaptive mechanisms share a common form --a collective entity is modified by changes wrought in its composition by external conditions. (For a sense of the novelty of treating succession and natural selection as the same, see Orians, 1973.)

If we take an organization to be an aggregate of rules and procedures, the organization may change by changing the composition of the set of rules or the population of organizations of a given kind may change as organizations with different sets of rules are differentially added to and removed from the aggregate. The fundamental (and crucial) insight of Hannan and Freeman (1977) is that there are aspects of the structure of organizations and the structure of the environment which constrain the extent to which organizations can respond to their environment by "somatic" adaptations, and make it likely that populations of organizations will adapt by changes in their "genetic" composition.

The distinction between somatic and genetic adaptation masks a continuum of adaptive mechanisms. A concrete entity responds to (changes in) its environment with a battery of adaptive mechanisms which are hierarchically ordered in that (a) the "deeper" mechanisms involve greater structural modification and take place more slowly, and (b) if a given mechanism is effective in meeting the environmental challenge, the engagement of deeper mechanisms may be averted or modified. The structure of a particular mechanism determines the range of environmental conditions or perturbations it can respond to. In turn, the character of the environment or its perturbation--its severity, duration, regularity, and period--determines what mechanism, if any, will likely be effective, and at what depth the mechanism "designed" to cope with it is likely to lie. (See Slobodkin, 1968; Bateson, 1963; Slobodkin and Rapoport, 1974.) Thus a catastrophic disturbance which recurs less than once a generation and simply eliminates individuals without regard for their characteristics will, in its effect on population composition, select for rapid replacement. A more mild and frequent perturbation may only invoke behavioral responses with neither physiological changes within individuals nor changes in the genetic composition of the population taking place.

Obviously even the most extremely somatic adaptation requires some genetic (structural) substrate, i.e., a "metastructure" which permits learning or provides some other generalized capability. It seems to me there is some advantage to be gained by thinking of all adaptive mechanisms as structures which interact with the environment to produce or modify structure. Our thinking about human intelligence, for instance, would benefit from the realization that what is "in" the genes is *not* a blueprint for structure, Hannan and Freeman (1977) notwithstanding, but a "program" which will permit the development of a particular phenotype out of the interaction of genotypes with environments or sequences of environments. (Because sociologists tend to think of gender as entirely determined by genes, the account of the development of gender in the human embryo as an interactive process is instructive. See Money and Ehrhardt, 1972.)

To understand the present organization of any entity produced by adaptation one must understand both the nature of the adaptive mechanisms involved and the sequence of environments to which they have responded in producing the present structure. (For an elaboration of this point, see Maruyama, 1963; for examples, see Hauser, 1969:8-10.) As an example of the importance of knowing the adaptational history of an entity, consider the description of the industrialized human population as occupying the decomposer trophic level in the ecosystem (Catton, this volume). It is true that our dependence upon fossil fuel puts us in the same trophic position as decomposers--our inputs are the solar energy trapped in the biomass of dead organisms--and that like them, our use of energy, if not our population, has expanded to the point where the rate of use exceeds the rate of replacement. But a complete characterization of decomposers must include not only reference to their position in the trophic flow of energy, but also a description of the adjustment of their population dynamics to the temporal pattern of the availability of energy. Decomposers have evolved an opportunistic bionomic strategy of population bloom and crash in an environment in which energy is accumulated in plant and animal biomass and periodically made available in leaf fall and the death of organisms in other trophic levels. The parallel to humans is instructive precisely because it fails on this point: the opportunistic expansion of human energy use is not the product of an adaptive mechanism which has been sensitive to the rate of accumulation, it is more like a projection of a structure with fixed parameters. So while humans are (currently) like decomposers in their trophic position, they are not at all like them in the manner by which they achieved that position. The likely human response to the excess of use over replacement of fossil fuel will be to change trophic position -- to become "herbivores" utilizing what are now called biomass energy systems, or to become producers (plants) converting solar (or nuclear) energy directly.

Since learning, planning, evolution, and succession are all adaptive processes, it seems at least premature to conclude, as Bennett (1976:35ff) does, that the ecology of humans must differ fundamentally from that of other organisms because humans behave with purpose and motive. Rather it seems prudent to recognize that any ecologically interesting system likely contains a hierarchy of adaptive mechanisms, ordered by their ability to respond and preclude the operation of higher-ordered systems. Our task as human ecologists, then, is to characterize mechanisms and environments in a way that allows us to assert with some confidence that environmental variation or fluctuation of a particular kind is likely to invoke response at a particular level of adaptation. This is particularly important for nonexperimental studies because there are levels of adaptive mechanisms which are invisible in the historical and contemporary data on human organizations.

Major developments in characterizing the joint properties of adaptive mechanisms and environments have followed from the work of Levins (1968). Temporal and spatial variation of the environment are described in relation to the life-span or life-space of the unit of selection (the individual organism) because what matters to adaptation is whether the unit experiences environmental variation as an average--the individual moves through different environments separated in space or the environment changes within the individual's lifetime--or as exclusive alternatives--the individual is in one or another environment for life. Lifespan is the measure of time because of its relation to the speed of response of the adaptive mechanism of interest here --differential replacement of genes. When the environmental period is short relative to the adaptive response time, environmental variation is experienced as an average. When the period is long, the alternating environments are responded to specifically. These aspects of its variation are referred to as the grain of the environment. The amplitude of environmental variation--how different the different environments are--is measured by the "fitness" of units of each type in each environment. In the multidimensional space with a dimension measuring fitness in each environment, the collection of points representing individuals of different types is called the fitness set, and the shape of this set depends upon how different the environments are in these terms. The shape of the fitness set and the grain of the environment interact to produce different strategies for coping with environmental variation under natural selection, that is, the model yields predictions of the composition towards which the population will move. The results--alternative strategies include producing "specialists" for only one environment, producing "generalists" who do moderately well in any, or producing a mixture of specialists--seem to offer insights for the study of populations of human organizations, though they may depend critically upon the nature of the adaptive mechanism. (Since Levins' population genetics is largely implicit, it is not clear to what extent the ecology depends upon it.) By arguing that individual organizations are the units of selection, Hannan and Freeman (1977) justify using these models of selection to represent the adaptive mechanism at work in populations of organizations facing variable environments, as they ask "what kinds of strategies will be adopted by populations of organizations," and the more fundamental question, "why are there so many kinds of organizations." This usage invites us to think of societies or social systems as communities of populations of organisms, and when useful we can move from social systems to ecosystems by recognizing that the individual members of non-human populations play the same role as human organizations in the adaptation of their respective aggregates. Thus the communities we should be dealing with are sets of interacting populations of organizations, and the insights we seek from the biological ecologists concern the ways in which these interpopulation interactions are organized.

## Species and Niches

Hawley's objection to application of the ecosystem concept to human societies rests upon his taking that concept to concern relations among *species* and their environments. And since humans are a single species, he argues, one is led to "treat man simply as a species, as an aggregate of homogeneous individuals rather than as a highly differentiated and organized population" (1973:1197). The term "species" is as problematic for ecologists as for human ecologists, as Emlen (1973:78ff) points out. (See too, MacArthur, 1972:71.) On the one hand, in the "biological concept of species" they are held to be groups of *interbreeding* populations that are reproductively isolated from other such groups (Mayr, 1969; 1957). Here interbreeding is an important component of the definition because of its role in the adaptive mechanism of the local population, and the species concept is

best thought of as a way of *distinguishing* sympatric syn-
chronic populations. On the other hand, the "principle of
competitive exclusion" (about which more below) leads to a
close identification of "species" with "niche" or "function," that is with the material inputs and outputs of a
species population in the course of individuals' getting a
living, and their spatial and temporal patterns within a
given community. In fact much of the current research on
niches deals precisely with the ways in which spatially distinct populations called by the same species name come to
occupy different niches within their respective communities
through (competitive) interaction with the other species
populations there. (The "modern" notion of niche is in
Hutchinson, 1957; the standard review is Vandermeer, 1972;
an instructive application is Schoener, 1974; and everyone
who can cites Dr. Seuss, Geisel, 1955.) The identification
of species with the niche of a population in a community
strongly resembles the view proposed here of populations of
organizations--the latter are defined by a combination of
industry-like categories with a set of distinctions among
organizational forms. An even more striking parallel is to
be found between the notion that niche differentiation is a
means of avoiding competition in "An Ecologist's View of
Species" (Colinvaux, 1973: Chapter 24) and Durkheim's account of the division of labor in society. (Don't read
Durkheim, read Schnore, 1958.) The above should not be taken
to gainsay the difficulty of identifying populations of or-
ganizations--at least to an outsider it seems relatively
easy to assign an organism to a species--but rather to
emphasize that the importance of being able to treat populations of organizations require that we solve the problem
of their identification.

On the view taken here, the human population--i.e., the
number of human organisms--is a rather strange kind of
quantity. Like the number of organisms in a field or lake,
it combines onions and alligators. But this same view allows
us to make Hawley's main point even more strongly. The analytic distinction between a community and a mere assemblage
of populations of organizations lies in the interpopulation
organization of the community. One way of characterizing
that structure, crude though it may be, is by the numbers of
organizations of each kind, which results from the nature of
interpopulation relations. The number of humans in such a
community can be obtained from the sizes of the populations
of organizations made up of humans and the number of humans
typical of each kind of organization. In this sense "population" in an old sense (the number of humans) is derived from
community organization, the structure of interpopulation
relations.

This view also allows us to overcome Hawley's objection to the ecological (Malthusian) assumption that populations grow to "the maximum carrying capacity" of the environment, arriving at "an equilibrium of numbers with resources at a subsistence level." The notion of carrying capacity is fraught with interpretive dangers, and we shall return to it in the next section. For the present it suffices to observe that while the number of humans may not be directly limited in this fashion, the size of a community's populations of a given kind surely is. The number of fast-food franchise outlets, for instance, must surely be limited in precisely that way.

Empirical work in human ecology has touched these points only remotely. Studies of the urban hierarchy (Duncan et al., 1960) and of urban function (Ullman, 1969) have established relations between the total human population of places and the total number of individuals employed in various industries, but the intervening relations of numbers of employees to numbers of organizations have not, to my knowledge, received much attention.

The fast-food example brings out an important point about the use of the models we are about to consider. Having established or accepted the nature of the adaptive mechanism by which organizational properties are arrived at, population models generally explore implications for the growth and relative and absolute size of populations of organizations whose properties are fixed, in environments whose properties are also fixed (though not necessarily stable), by an appropriate choice of time scale. Thus the model which describes the growth to carrying capacity of the population of fast-food franchise outlets implicitly assumes no structural adaptation on the part of full-service restaurants, eateries, and domestic food preparation. Instead it merely projects the stable distribution of eating over providers of various sorts achieved through competition; much as a population projection merely displays the ultimate implications of the operation of a (model) system with fixed structure. Even the models of co-evolution (e.g., Roughgarden, 1976) have this quality. Population genetics and population ecology have little or nothing to say about the direction of evolution beyond the time scale of fixing traits already present.

*Single Population Models*

The "Malthusian" model to which Hawley objects appears to be an interpretation of an extremely simple, and therefore necessarily highly abstract model—the logistic growth function of Verhulst (1838) and Pearl and Reed (1920)—in which the amount by which the population grows in an instant, dN/dt, is damped by population size (see Equation 1). But as McLauren (1971: Introduction) shows, there are many interpretations of this model, some of which entail organization of the very kind whose lack Hawley decries.

$$\frac{dN}{dt} = rN \left(\frac{K - N}{K}\right) = rN(1 - \frac{N}{K}) \qquad \text{Eq. 1)}$$

May and Oster (1976) present a catalogue of models which preserve the essential features of Equation 1—monotone growth and return to a stable equilibrium size N*=K—while more realistically representing various aspects of the growth and replacement of individuals. The model says merely that ignoring the expression in parentheses, the instantaneous growth rate of N is r (taken to be a positive non zero quantity) and the expression in parentheses lowers that growth rate (it is always less than unity) by an amount that depends on the present size of the population, N, and some number K. Once one has an interpretation for K, that of r follows, since it is the rate at which N would grow if it were so small that whatever K represents had no effect. Alternatively, one could start with an interpretation for r.)

An interpretation which seems to correspond to one version of the crowding or "behavioral sink" notion takes as important the definition of population in terms of spatial or interactional boundaries, so that as N increases, either or both of physical or social density increases. In this interpretation, K is a density at which physiological responses to density swamp patterns of behavior built into more permanent structures and interfere with reproductive behavior.

The standard interpretation of K takes it as a measure of the population which the environment can support, in terms of the number of individuals worth of some critical resource provided. This interpretation is fundamental to many further models which elaborate Equation 1 to include additional aspects of the community, for it is taken to represent the *competition* of identical individuals—each uses the environment in the same way, and the seeds, light, or sales captured by one individual cannot be utilized by another--and most of these elaborated models behave plausibly only if this intrapopulation effect is present and relatively strong.

The model of Equation 1 is, of course, equilibrium seeking or homeostatic. We note that such systems have a "characteristic return time" R, which is roughly the time it takes the system to return to equilibrium after a disturbance from it. (See May et al. 1974.) In the present model R is on the order of 1/r. As is well known, minor modification of Equation 1 in the direction of realism can give a model which, while still homeostatic, continually varies population size over time without continued perturbation. We simply allow the regulating effects to operate with a built-in time lag, say of magnitude T, so that rN(t) is depressed by (1 - N(t-T)/K). In this model, if the time delay in the regulating mechanism, T, is short compared to the characteristic response time, R, the model behaves much as Equation 1, smoothly approaching equilibrium following perturbation. If T is close to R, the model will return in an oscillatory fashion; and if T is longer than R there will be overcompensation and the population will cycle around but never reach equilibrium, though the cycle itself will be stable. Thus such a system might never be observed to be perturbed, yet never settle down to an equilibrium size.

Allowing K to vary in time seems an obvious move in the direction of realism. Not only does K vary for any species on the scale of geologic time, but fluctuations on the order of a year or several years introduce important complications to the notion of a carrying capacity and the analysis of "equilibrium population size." For K varying in time, and r constant, the equilibrium population size is a weighted average of past values of K, and how far into the past the average extends depends on R, the characteristic response time. If K varies periodically (with a regular period) the behavior of population size depends on whether R is short or long relative to the period of the environment. For long response times (short environmental period) the population "averages" out environmental variation, but it approaches an equilibrium size lower than the average value of K. For short response times (long environmental period) the population tends to track the environment, mirroring in its size the fluctuations of the environment. (For a full exploration of the implications of exogenous variation in K and r, see Lewontin and Cohen, 1969; Levins, 1969.) Thus one might observe a population temporally stable and also observe that the environment could "carry" a larger population without contradicting the applicability of a model nearly as simple as that of Equation 1.

While the preceeding interpretations of Equation 1 do not explicitly depend upon social organization, two others come closer to doing so. The parameter K might be interpreted as representing a sort of symbolic or "social" upper limit on population, implicit in the conventions or social organization which limits reproduction. Thus Wynne-Edwards (1962) argues that animal populations are normally smaller than they could be, smaller than current levels of resources might permit, and that this is no coincidence. He sees it as the product of conventional defense of territory--conventional in the sense that the defense involves symbolic displays recognized as defensive by both parties, rather than physical violence--and the limitation of reproduction to individuals "owning" territory. (Wynne-Edwards argues for other "socially" imposed limitations on reproduction in species which do not use territory, what is crucial and common to all his examples is that at certain levels of population density, individuals "voluntarily" refrain from reproducing, even though they are physiologically capable of it.) This much of the argument does not seem hotly disputed. Wynne-Edwards goes on to argue that this organization for population limitation avoids the "tragedy of the commons" (Hardin, 1968) by preventing the population from so closely tracking the environment in good times that it cannot be sustained in hard times, or from exploiting a resource past the level at which it can maintain a sustained flow. And he goes on to claim that this form of organization has arisen by natural selection of the groups which practiced it even though it has obvious reproductive disadvantages for the individuals involved. The problems of group or kin selection thus raised are not insoluble, though they are a matter of some controversy (see Williams, 1971). What is important for us is that the argument turns not on whether the pattern would be functional for the populations involved, but on whether or not there is an adaptive mechanism which could produce it. While there are obvious parallels between "territoriality" and population limitation among humans by means of inheritance and rules linking marriage and reproduction to the possession of property or livelihood, Wynne-Edwards, unlike others with whom he shares the kin-group selection problem, carefully avoids arguing that the form of organization arose in the same fashion in human and non-human societies (cf. Wilson, 1975).

Finally, one might interpret 1/K in Equation 1 as representing population regulation by predators, parasites, or diseases, i.e., by the action of other populations in the community upon the population of interest. This interpretation broaches the kind of interpopulation organization we are looking for in models of communities, but does such a poor job of representing that organization that we are led almost immediately to abandon Equation 1 for a more adequate representation. While Equation 1 does represent the effect of the other populations on N, it is perfectly silent about the effect of that interaction upon those other populations. And since those effects could in turn effect future values of N, we turn to models in which more of the interactions between populations are explicitly represented. Before doing so, however, we digress to comment on an empirical human ecological problem which appears to fit the single population model we have been considering.

The !Kung Bushmen of the Dobe area of Botswana are a very special band of people. They are one of the last populations of hunters and gatherers and perhaps one of the most thoroughly studied (see Lee, 1968; and Lee and DeVore, 1976). Because they remained hunters and gathers for so long into the modern era the situation of the !Kung is almost surely not typical of most hunting and gathering populations. And there are apparently serious questions about the empirical adequacy of the characterization of their present or recent situation. (See Godelier, 1974; Williams, 1977a, 1977b; Lee et al., 1977.) Nevertheless, the problems raised by the !Kung do not disappear merely because we may not have a good empirical example. The problems arise from the (putative) fact that, like Wynne-Edwards' birds, the size of the !Kung population seems to be stable or "balanced" with their environment at a size smaller than that environment would appear capable of supporting with the !Kung's present organization and technology. The first set of problems raised has to do with how this balance is maintained. The answers are first, that population size appears to be limited via reproduction rather than via elevated levels of mortality, and second, that this limitation on fertility is accomplished by a set of complex interactions between a nutritionally balanced and adequate diet, levels of caloric intake which permit lactation to suppress ovulation, a pattern of frequent migration and lack of soft foods suitable for infants and small children which promotes long periods of lactation (see Dumond, 1975; Howell, in Lee and DeVore, 1976). The second set of problems depends more upon infering from the situation of the !Kung to that of hunters and gatherers in other times and places. Sahlins (1968; 1972) is outraged to discover that hunting and gathering bands are not (all) mere subsistence economies, characterized by incessant quest for food and limited leisure save in exceptional circumstances. Instead the !Kung seem to spend far less time and energy in getting a living than the

typical member of urban industrialized societies. Why then
would any population move "up" in the taxonomy of technological levels of society? Clark and Haswell (1964) and
Boserup (1965; see too Spooner, 1972) have argued that,
evaluated in terms of the effort and energy expenditures
required of individuals, technological "progress" at these
levels is not attractive, rather population pressure drives
the evolution of social organization. Yet the !Kung population seems far from pressing on resources and is held to
have been in that situation for nearly a millenium! Why did
any population leave the state of nature? The easy answer is
that the !Kung are not typical, as evidenced by the fact
that they did not leave that state. A more satisfying
answer, which might add evidence to the population push
versus technological/organizational pull argument, may lie
in a more adequate characterization of the habitat of the
!Kung, which may be more severe than that faced by those
hunting and gathering populations which did evolve. More
adequate characterization of their habitat may also show the
!Kung to be limited by some other environmental factor--
water has been suggested--and it is not difficult to imagine
environmental fluctuations that have short periods relative
to the response time of a human population. While we cannot
pursue these matters here, they are too important to be left
to the anthropologists. For the same issues are raised by
Hawley's insistence (1973) that social organization induces
population growth.

## Models of the Interaction of Two Populations

There are three broad classes of models of the interaction of two populations: interpopulation competition,
predator-prey models, and models of mutualism. Competition
models are perhaps the most successful, in the sense that
they lead to important theoretical understandings in the
principle of competitive exclusion and the theory of the
niche. Predator-prey models are important because among the
three classes they alone explicitly deal with relations between widely different populations of organizational forms.
These models have also been successful in producing, and
thus "explaining" oscillations in population sizes similar
to those observed in nature. Mutualism seems the least successfully modeled phenomenon--perhaps because the kinds of
positive interactions encompassed by models of the phenomenon fall so far short of representing the diversity of
beneficial relations we would like to derive as consequences
of community interaction. Nevertheless, this last class of

models does lead naturally to consideration of models of the interaction of many populations—the closest we shall come in this chapter to models of community organization.

Models of competition between two populations ($N_1$ and $N_2$) were formulated by Lotka and Volterra as rather simple elaborations of the single-population logistic we have already examined in Equation 1. The elaboration consists of adding a term reflecting the impact of the second population on the first to the equation for the growth of the first population, and vice versa.

$$\frac{dN_1}{dt} = r_1 N_1 (1 - \frac{N_1 + a_{12} N_2}{K_1})$$   Eq. 2a)

$$\frac{dN_2}{dt} = r_2 N_2 (1 - \frac{N_2 + a_{21} N_1}{K_2})$$   Eq. 2b)

Here $r_1$ and $r_2$ are the per-individual growth rates of the two populations in the absence of both competition from the other explicitly recognized population and limitation by the rest of the environment. $K_1$ and $K_2$ represent the carrying capacity of the environment for each population in the absence of the other, and the $a_{ij}$ represent the extent to which an individual of population $j$ depresses the carrying capacity of the environment for population $i$. Investigations of this model assume the environment and organizational properties of the two populations are fixed, so that the r's, K's, and a's do not change, and asks what conditions on those properties allow one population or the other or both to persist indefinitely. The results are simple and well-known (see Slobodkin, 1961: Chapter 7; MacArthur, 1972: 33-56). If for at least one population the marginal impact of adding a member is to decrease the carrying capacity for the other population by more than the addition of that member decreases the carrying capacity for its own population (i.e., if $a_{ij}/K_i$ is greater than $1/K_j$) then competition will ultimately eliminate one of the populations. While if for both populations the marginal interpopulation effect is smaller than the intrapopulation effect (i.e., if $a_{12}/K_1$ is less than $1/K_2$ and $a_{21}$ is less than $1/K_1$) then both populations can coexist in stable competition. This condition can be reformulated algebraically as:

$$1/a_{21} > K_1/K_2 > a_{12}$$   Eq. 3)

from which it is clear that if the a's (the interspecific
effects) are both small the condition for stable competition
will be met.

A particularly interesting case arises where the K's are
taken to refer solely to limitation by resources and the two
populations use the resources in identical ways ($a_{12}$ =
$a_{21}$ = 1 and $K_1$ = $K_2$). Clearly the condition of Equation 3 is not met and the populations cannot coexist. Early
theoretical work led from this result to the "principle of
competitive exclusion," the notion that populations which
play the same role in an ecosystem, i.e., are limited in the
same way by the same resources, cannot coexist (see Hardin,
1960). This led to an identification of species populations
with niches--taken as the function of a population in an
ecosystem. Observationally, species populations appear to
coexist with at least very substantial overlap between their
niches. MacArthur (1958) observed five very similar species
populations of warblers apparently violating the principle
of competitive exclusion in a single New England spruce
forest. The conflict was resolved by the observation that
the populations fed at different times and at different
heights in the forest. These observations were taken as indicating that the niches of the warblers were in fact different, thus saving the principle. More recently attention
has shifted to how similar competing populations can be and
still persist--what are the limits of similarity? The basic
results indicate that stable coexistence requires that
interpopulation niche difference be of roughly the same size
as intrapopulation niche width (see Abrams, 1976). These
results from static models are strengthened by the outcomes
in models in which competition is allowed to direct evolutionary change in the way the species populations use the
resource spectrum. Here too, stable coexistence is achieved
through setting niche difference at about the same magnitude
as niche width (Roughgarden, 1976).

When all is said and done, competition models deal with
relations between relatively similar populations--with the
degree of similarity limited by the requirements of stability. Predator-prey models, on the other hand, allow treatment of relations between more disparate populations. On the
notion that ecosystems organize the flow of energy and the
cycling of materials through them (Duncan, 1964:37-44)
models which look explicitly at relations between populations which form stages in these flows should be particularly important. Unfortunately, as Caughley (1976) points
out, emphasis in the development of these models has been
placed on producing systems that would manifest the oscillations of predator and prey numbers observed in nature, to

the neglect of the relations between the prey and aspects of their environment other than their predators. Perhaps the worst offender in this regard is the classic Lotka-Volterra model, in which the prey population grows without limit in the absence of the predators and the predators just die in the absence of the prey. This system has "pathological dynamical properties," namely, a fragile neutrally stable oscillation which depends exquisitely upon the initial conditions and exact structure of the model. When perturbed, neutrally stable systems eventually settle down to oscillations again, but to a different pattern of oscillation depending on the perturbation. By allowing some intrapopulation effects among the prey, and competition among the predators, i.e., by making both populations "self-damped" in the sense of Equation 1, the stability of these models can be increased, so that the system returns to oscillations of the same period and amplitude after perturbation. Alternatively, by expanding loosely in the direction of providing alternative prey for the predators and refuges in the environment for the prey, the models can again attain this kind of stable limit cycle. But neither of these modifications gets at a more fundamental problem with the models. If we are modeling the short-run dynamics of predator and prey numbers, shouldn't our models also include short-run dynamics of prey and their resources?

It seems obvious that the dynamic concerns manifest in the predator-prey models need to be wed to the kind of community structure models represented statically by input/output tables (Isard, 1969; 1972). A predator-prey model, where rabbits and foxes are replaced by plants and lemmings, is suggested by studies of the arctic tundra. Here communities comprise few species, there are no large inputs of essential elements, and there are no large abiotic reserves or storage compartments for them. Thus the recycling of these essential elements is crucial to the stability of the community. Schultz (1964) showed that the oscillatory abundance of lemmings is correlated with changes in vegetation, litter, depth of permafrost melt, and fluxes of nitrogen, phosphorus, potassium, and calcium. The cycle can be experimentally obliterated by either eliminating the lemmings or fertilizing the tundra. While there is disagreement on the roles of the various species/niches/trophic levels (see Bowen, 1972) it is clear that tying up the essential elements in either the plants or the animals has a crucial effect on the temporal behavior of the system.

Assembling these input/output matrices is a Heraklean labor, and most of the work to date has been either the analysis of partial tables or the abstract analysis of tables with wholly fictitious entries (see Levin, 1960; Margalef, 1968:6-8; Odum and Pigeon, 1970; Levins, 1975). The analysis of these "community matrices" must be acknowledged to be in its infancy. We shall examine some results shortly. In the interpopulation models examined so far, the only direct beneficiary of interaction has been the predators. Every other participating population has benefitted only indirectly--through limitation of its inherent tendency to grow beyond the ability of the environment to sustain it. The situation in which neither population's growth rate is depressed and at least one's is increased by interaction is called "mutualism." The simple Lotka-Volterra models of Equation 2, when modified to express this kind of interrelation, produce silly results, in which the two populations increase without bound if the reciprocal effect is at all strong. Yet, while relatively rare in temperate lattitudes, apparently stable mutualistic relations seem common in the tropics. Recent work by Whittaker (1975:39-41) and May, (1973) provides several models which allow for saturation of the reciprocal benefits in various ways (so that there can be too much of a good thing). These models produce reasonable results, in the sense that the populations arrive at finite equilibrium sizes and each is larger than it would be in the absence of the other population, though the return time from a perturbation is longer than would be the case for the populations taken separately. In a further refinement May, (1976) allows for coevolution, so that the mutualism can become obligatory for at least one of the populations. In this case, in addition to the above results, which are preserved, an environment subject to strong perturbations is likely to eventually sweep the system into a combination of sizes for the two populations from which the only escape is extinction for the obligate. This may explain why mutualism is found where it is (see Farnsworth and Golley, 1974:29-31) though Roughgarden (1977) argues that on purely evolutionary consideration mutualistic associations should not arise in temperate or highly fluctuating environments, so the issue of their stable persistence in those lattitudes is moot. Beyond these sparse hints about the conditions under which mutualism might develop and be maintained, consideration of this form of interpopulation relation seems to also demand embedding in larger models of communities and ecosystems. In any case, models of this type seem doomed to formalize away the rich diversity of behavioral patterns that comprise the various forms of mutualism actually observed (see Trager, 1970; Henry, 1966, 1967;

Society for Experimental Biology, 1975), and it is not clear that energy flows or materials cycles are the appropriate terms in which to capture the vital dependencies of, say, plant-pollinator plant-seed disperser relations.

## Models of Community Organization

A community is an assemblage of interacting (species) populations. One of the simplest ways of describing the structure of communities is by the number of populations they contain—often, but not uniformly, called "richness." From there it is but a short step to looking at the size distribution of the constituent populations of a community, its "evenness" or "diversity." As with so many size distributions, for large and relatively heterogeneous communities the size distribution of their constituent populations is usually lognormal or almost lognormal. Community ecologists have played out several familiar scenarios around this empirical regularity (see Simon, 1955)—developing various ways of measuring the size distribution, including some with tenuous links to information theory, attempting to develop models of processes which might give useful structure to this universality, discovering that nearly everything, even trivia, is lognormally distributed (see Clark, et al., 1964), and realizing that the conjunction of a moderate number of independent processes is also likely to produce such a distribution. While some use has been made of changes in diversity as a way of measuring the degree of perturbation or pollution by man (Patrick, 1975), more interesting is the work relating the richness of communities to their stability.

In a book whose title makes clear the object of its study and thereby offers model caution to the reader of *this* paper, May (1973) examines the generally plausible proposition that communities with more species, and therefore more inter-relations between populations, have greater stability over time than less rich communities (see Elton, 1958:145-50; MacArthur, 1955). The proposition is often buttressed by the observation that tropical communities, with their rich assemblage of species, appear much more stable than the relatively species-poor temperate or boreal communities. May's investigations show that in models which describe communities (a) by a multi-species generalization of the predator-prey equations; (b) by a community matrix in which the inter-species relations are assembled at random; or (c) by only the signs of the relations between trophic levels, the greater complexity—roughly the nature and number of links in the food web—the more fragile the system, in the sense that the system will persist as constituted only for a tightly constrained set of possible values for environmental and interactional parameters. May's properly guarded conclusions are (a) that while his work demonstrates that it is not *generally* true that complexity leads to stability, it does not show that it is never true, and it is precisely the peculiar patterns of complexity that give stability that nature would have picked out; and (b) that communities *may* evolve to maximize complexity subject to the constraints imposed on complexity by local environmental harshness and unpredictability through their effects on the stability of complex structures. This hint of the possibility of a direction in community adaptation is part of a heated and not altogether profitless debate between population and community ecologists over the direction of succession, to which we will return, below.

Concern with community structure has also led some investigators to concentrate more keenly on the "ecological" or "functional" definition of populations rather than the species definition. The suggestion is that communities may have rather stable and persistent trophic skeletons even though they undergo changes in the species filling the various niches. Thus Heatwole and Levins (1972) characterized the community structure of six tiny mangrove islets by the number of species of land arthropods in each of seven "trophic levels" before and after fumigation and recolonization of the islets. (The trophic levels are herbivore, scavenger, detritus feeder, wood borer, ant, predator, parasite, and other and undetermined.) While the number of species per level before and after recolonization was quite similar, the species playing particular roles on particular islets varied radically across islets and between pre- and post-treatment censuses. The process by which the stable trophic skeleton of these communities is fleshed out with species populations is treated as a kind of succession to a dynamic balance between invasion and local extinction, more usually of animal than plant species, in the "theory of island biogeography" (MacArthur and Wilson, 1967). Islands, in this theory, can be hill tops, lakes, or forests surrounded by grasslands, as well as real islands. The direction of succession here is merely to fill out the implicit local skeleton.

Underlying the notion of a trophic structure of communities is the image of a hierarchical system in which each trophic level extracts energy from the level below it, degrades some of the energy it receives, and passes the rest to the next level, linked to a system of cycles of materials --elements--through processes and storages in the biotic and abiotic parts of the ecosystem. The relations we have been examining throughout this paper are some of the means by which these flows and cycles are organized. In a larger, evolutionary sense, the flow of energy gives rise to the organization. The development and evolution of human societies has often been characterized in terms of the quantity of energy flowing through it and the organization to which that flow gives rise (see Duncan, 1964; Odum and Odum, 1976). I cannot adequately review the energetic version of community ecology here. For present purposes let us note that it takes a somewhat different view of the kinds of relations discussed above, treating the entire local ecosystem—community and abiotic environment—as an energy processing network and assigning to each species population various roles in the transformation of energy, the recycling of essential elements, and the control of these processes. Energy flow and element recycling cannot be interpreted separately from one another, but authors differ in the relative emphasis given one or the other of these viewpoints (compare Reichele, et al., 1975 with Odum, 1970). The source of the energy in this network is, of course, the solar input and its conversion to chemical energy by plants. One important structural component of ecosystems is a large, slow turnover reservoir of energy stored in the form of nutrients, as a hedge against environmental perturbation. In various systems this role is played by soil, peat, or semi-dead woody structures of living plants, or it may be absent altogether (see Pomeroy, 1970). Given the reservoir, two further structural components are important—the mechanisms by which nutrients are released from the reservoir and the regulation of the rate at which release occurs. The level of biomass attainable in the system is set by the net influx of elements from outside the system and the rate at which elements are released from the internal reservoir. Thus the role of most of the animals with which we are familiar is to influence the rate at which decomposers remineralize nutrients, and to regulate various other aspects of this basic flow process.

The most general properties of adaptive mechanisms—that those elements which persist come to dominate the composition of the aggregate—are invoked to assert that ecosystems, constructed of hierarchies of adaptive systems, grow to maximum persistent biomass—surely as unverifiable a claim as that a population is at its carrying capacity. It is further asserted that there may be characteristics of the ecosystem itself which contribute to the persistence of the community. In this view succession is the course of ecosystem development. In the familiar definition of Odum

(1969) succession consists of an orderly process of community change that is reasonably directional and, therefore, predictable. It results from modification of the physical environment by the community. And it culminates in a stabilized ecosystem in which maximum biomass and symbiotic function between organisms are maintained per unit of available energy flow. In Odum's view succession maximizes homeostasis with or control of the physical environment, directed towards maximum protection from environmental perturbation.

These "outrageous" claims, which can be traced at least as far back as Lotka (1922, 1925) and which bear a curious resemblance to the claims about the invisible hand in classical economics, have produced a great deal of useful debate. On the one hand, Levins (1975) has demonstrated that natural selection acting on species populations within ecological communities provides no *necessary* direction to the evolution of macroscopic, community-level properties. He concludes that various properties of individual species which are interchangeable in their effect on the fitness of the species may have quite different implications at the level of the community. On the other hand, a great deal of insight has been gained by more careful examination of the changes in species composition in actual ecological communities following perturbation and the mechanisms which determine these changes, (see Horn, 1974.) Connell and Slatyer (1977) derive three broad classes of models, one of which rests on the kind of obligatory sequence of organisms to modify the physical environment which Odum seems to have in mind, one of which rests solely on differences in interspecies competitive ability, and the third of which rests on differential longevity, to provide the sequence of species compositions that constitute succession. The models differ in the kinds of environments and settings to which they are likely to apply and in the extent to which they yield any directional implications for succession, let alone those claimed by Odum. One cannot get a sense of the relative importance of successions of the various types, though Connell and Slatyer's discussion of Odum's model clearly separates its empirical features from the claims which are derived from a priori characterization of the climax.

In the issues of succession, as in the other matters we have addressed, what human ecologists have to gain from a review of biological ecology is primarily the clarification and elaboration of ideas which we have long-since borrowed. Whether there is any payoff to continuing the periodic contact between disciplines depends upon our ability to make intelligent use of fundamental ecological concepts and our willingness to redefine the scope and purpose of human ecology.

REFERENCES

Abrams, P. (1976). "Limiting similarity and the forms of the competition coefficient." Theoretical Population Biology 8:356-375.

Allee, W. C., et al. (1949). Principles of Animal Ecology. Philadelphia: Saunders.

Bateson, G. (1963). "The role of somatic change in evolution." Evolution 17:529-539.

Bennett, J. W. (1976). The Ecological Transition. New York: Pergamon.

Boserup, E. (1965). The Conditions of Agricultural Growth. Chicago: Aldine.

Bowen, S. (ed.) (1972). Proceedings of the 1972 Tundra Biome Symposium. Hanover, NH.: CRREL.

Buckley, W. (1968a). "Society as a complex adaptive system." In W. Buckley (ed.), Modern Systems Research for the Behavioral Scientist. Chicago: Aldine.

Buckley, W. (Ed.) (1968b). Modern Systems Research for the Behavioral Scientist. Chicago: Aldine.

Campbell, D. T. (1965). "Variation and selective retention in socio-cultural evolution." In H. R. Barringer, G. Blanksten, and R. Mack (eds.), Social Change in Developing Areas. Cambridge, MA.: Schenkman.

Caughley, G. (1976). "Plant-herbivore systems." In R. M. May (ed.), Theoretical Ecology. Philadelphia: Saunders.

Clark, C., and M. R. Haswell (1964). The Economics of Subsistence Agriculture. London: Macmillan.

Clark, P. J., P. T. Eckstrom, and L. C. Linden (1964). "On the number of individuals per occupation in a human society." Ecology 45 (2):367-372.

Colinvaux, P. (1973). Introduction to Ecology. New York: Wiley.

Connell, J. H., and R. O. Slatyer (1977). "Mechanisms of succession in natural communities and their role in community stability and organization." American Naturalist, III (982):1119-1144.

Dumond, D. E. (1975). "The limitation of human population: a natural history." Science 187 (28 February):713-721.

Duncan, O. D. (1964). "Social organization and the ecosystem." In R.E.L. Faris (ed.), Handbook of Modern Sociology. Chicago: Rand McNally.

Duncan, O. D., et al. (1960). Metropolis and Region. Baltimore: John Hopkins University Press.

Durkheim, E. (1938). The Rules of the Sociological Method. Chicago: University of Chicago Press.

Elton, C. S. (1958). The Ecology of Invasions by Animals and Plants. London: Methuen.

Emlen, J. M. (1973). Ecology: An Evolutionary Approach. Reading, MA.: Addison Wesley.

Farnsworth, E. G., and F. B. Golley, (eds.) (1974). Fragile Ecosystems: Evaluation of Research and Applications in the Neotropics. New York: Springer Verlag.

Geisel, T. S. (Dr. Seuss). (1955). On Beyond Zebra. New York: Random House.

Godelier, M. (1974). "Anthropology and biology: towards a new form of cooperation." International Social Science Journal 26:611-635.

Hannan, M. T., and J. Freeman (1977). "The population ecology of organizations." American Journal of Sociology 82 (March):929-964.

Hardin, G. (1960). "The competitive exclusion principle." Science 131 (April):1292-1297.

Hardin, G. (1968). "The tragedy of the commons." Science 162 (December):1243-1248.

Hauser, P. M. (1969). "The chaotic society: product of the social morphological revolution." American Sociological Review 34 (February):1-19.

Hawley, A. (1944). "Ecology and human ecology." Social Forces 22 (May):398-405.

Hawley, A. (1973). "Ecology and population." Science 179 (March):1196-1201.

Heatwole, H., and R. Levins. (1972). "Trophic structure stability and faunal change during recolonization." Ecology 53:531-534.

Henry, S. M., (ed.) (1966). Symbiosis (Vol.1). New York: Academic Press.

Henry, S. M., (ed.) (1967). Symbiosis (Vol.2). New York: Academic Press.

Horn, H. S. (1974). "The ecology of secondary succession." Annual Review of Ecology and Systematics 5:25-37.

Hutchinson, G. E. (1957). Concluding remarks. Cold Springs Harbor Symposium in Quantitative Biology 22:415-427.

Isard, W. (1969). Some notes on the linkage of the ecologic and economic systems. Papers of the Regional Science Association 22:85-96.

Isard, W. (1972). Ecologic-Economic Analysis for Regional Development. New York: Free Press.

Keyfitz, N. (1975). "How do we know the facts of demography?" Population and Development Review (December)1:2.

Lee, R. B. (1968). "What hunters do for a living, or, how to make-out on scarce resources." In R. B. Lee and I. DeVore (eds.), Man the Hunter. Chicago: Aldine

Lee, R. B., and I. DeVore, (eds.). (1976). Kalahari Hunter-Gatherers. Cambridge, MA.: Harvard University Press.

Lee, R. B., N. Howell, and H. Harpending (1977). "Letter." Science, 197:1234.

Levin, S. A. (1970). "Community equilibria and stability, and an extension of the competitive exclusion principle." American Naturalist 104 (938):413-423.

Levins, R. (1968). Evolution in Changing Environments. Princeton: Princeton University Press.

Levins, R. (1969). The effect of random variations of different types on population growth. Proceedings of the National Academy of Science (USA) 62:1061-1065.

Levins, R. (1975). "Evolution in communities near equilibrium." In M. L. Cody and J. M. Diamond, (eds.), Ecology and Evolution of Communities. Cambridge, MA.: Belknap.

Lewontin, R. C. (1970). "The units of selection." Annual Review of Ecology and Systematics 1:1-18.

Lewontin, R. C., and D. Cohen (1969). On population growth in a randomly varying environment. Proceedings of the National Academy of Science (USA) 62:1056-1060.

Lotka, A. J. (1922). Contribution to the energetics of evolution. Proceedings of the National Academy of Science (USA) 8:147-151.

Lotka, A. J. (1925). Elements of Physical Biology. Baltimore: Williams and Wilkins.

MacArthur, R. H. (1955). "Fluctuations of animal populations, and a measure of community stability." Ecology 36: 533-536.

MacArthur, R. H. (1958). "Population ecology of warblers of northeastern coniferous forests." Ecology 39 (4):599-619.

MacArthur, R. H. (1972). Geographical Ecology: Patterns in the Distribution of Species. New York: Harper and Row.

MacArthur, R. H., and R. Levins (1964). "Competition, habitat selection, and character displacement in a patchy environment." Proceedings of the National Academy of Science (USA) 51:1207-1210.

MacArthur, R. H., and E. O. Wilson (1967). The Theory of Island Biogeography. Princeton: Princeton University Press.

McLauren, I. A. (1971). Natural Regulation of Animal Populations. New York: Atherton.

Margalef, R. (1968). Perspectives in Ecological Theory. Chicago: University of Chicago Press.

Maruyama, M. (1963). "The second cybernetics: deviation-amplifying mutual causal processes." American Scientist 51: 164-179. Reprinted in Buckley 1968b.

May, R. M. (1973). "Qualitative stability in model ecosystems." Ecology 54:638-641.

May, R. M. (1973). Stability and Complexity in Model Ecosystems. Princeton, NJ.: Princeton University Press.

May, R. M. (1976). "Mathematical aspects of the dynamics of annual populations." In S. A. Levin (ed.), Studies in Mathematical Biology. Providence, RI.: American Mathematical Society.

May, R. M., G. R. Conway, M. P. Hassell, and T. R. E. Southwood (1974). "Time delay, density dependence, and single species oscillations." Journal of Animal Ecology 43 (3):747- 770.

May, R. M., and G. F. Oster (1976). "Bifurcations and dynamic complexity in simple ecological models." American Naturalist 110.

Mayr, E. (1957). "Species concepts and definitions." In E. Mayr (ed.), The Species Problem. Washington: American Association for the Advancement of Science.

Mayr, E. (1969). "The biological meaning of species." Biological Journal of the Linnean Society 1:311-320.

Micklin, M. (1973). Population, Environment, and Social Organization. Hinsdale, IL.: Dryden.

Money, J., and A. A. Ehrhardt (1972). Man and Woman, Boy and Girl. Baltimore: Johns Hopkins University Press.

Odum, E. P. (1969). "The strategy of ecosystem development." Science 164:262-270.

Odum, E. P. (1977). "The emergence of ecology as a new integrative discipline." Science 195 (25 March):1289-1293.

Odum, H. T. (1970). "Summary." In H. T. Odum and R. F. Pigeon, A Tropical Rainforest. U.S. Atomic Energy Commission, Division of Technical Information.

Odum, H. T., and E. C. Odum (1976). Energy Basis for Man and Nature. New York: McGraw Hill.

Odum, H. T., and R. F. Pigeon (1970). A Tropical Rainforest. U.S. Atomic Energy Commission, Division of Technical Information.

Orians, G. H. (1973). "Review of six ecology textbooks." Science 181 (28 September):1238-1239.

Patrick, R. (1975). "Structure of stream communities." In M. L. Cody and J. M. Diamond (eds.), Ecology and Evolution of Communities. Cambridge, MA.: Harvard University Press.

Pearl, R., and L. J. Reed (1920). On the rate of growth of the population of the United States since 1790 and its mathematical representation. Proceedings of the National Academy of Sciences (USA.) 6:275-288.

Pomeroy, L. R. (1970). "The strategy of mineral cycling." Annual Review of Ecology and Systematics 1:171-190.

Pringle, J. W. S. (1951). "On the parallel between learning and evolution." Behaviour 3:174-215. Reprinted in Buckley, 1968b.

Reichle, D. E., R. V. O'Neill, and W. F. Harris (1975). "Principles of energy and material exchange in ecosystems." In W. H. van Dobben and R. D. Lowe-McConnell (eds.), Unifying Concepts in Ecology. The Hague: Dr. W. Junk BV Publishers.

Roughgarden, J. (1976). "Resource partitioning among competing species--a coevolutionary approach." Theoretical Population Biology 9 (June):388-424.

Roughgarden, J. (1977). "Review of May, Theoretical Ecology." Science 196 (1 April):51.

Sahlins, M. (1968). "Notes on the original affluent society." In R. B. Lee and I. DeVore (eds.), Man the Hunter. Chicago: Aldine.

Sahlins, M. (1972). Stone Age Economics. Chicago: Aldine.

Schnore, L. F. (1958). "Social morphology and human ecology." American Journal of Sociology 63 (May):6.

Schoener, T. W. (1974). "Resource partitioning in ecological communities." Science 185 (5 July):27-39.

Schultz, A. M. (1964). "The nutrient recovery hypothesis for arctic microtine cycles, part 2." In D. J. Crisp, (ed.), Grazing in Terrestrial and Marine Environments. Cambridge, MA.: Blackwell.

Simon, H. A. (1955). "On a class of skew distribution functions." Biometrika 42 (December).

Slobodkin, L. B. (1961). Growth and Regulation of Animal Populations. New York: Holt, Rinehart, and Winston.

Slobodkin, L. B. (1964). "The strategy of evolution." American Scientist 52:342-357.

Slobodkin, L. B. (1968). "Towards a predictive theory of evolution." In R. C. Lewontin, (ed.), Population Biology and Evolution. Syracuse, NY.: Syracuse University Press.

Slobodkin, L. B., and A. Rapoport (1974). "An optimal strategy of evolution." Quarterly Review of Biology 49 (3): 181-200.

Society for Experimental Biology (1975). Symposium 24: Symbiosis. Cambridge, MA.: Cambridge University Press.

Spooner, B. (1972). "Introduction." In B. Spooner (ed.), Population Growth: Anthropological Implications. Cambridge, MA.: MIT Press.

Trager, W. (1970). Symbiosis. New York: Van Nostrand.

Ullman, E. L. (1969). The Economic Base of American Cities. Seattle: University of Washington Press.

Vandermeer, J. H. (1972). "Niche theory." Annual Review of Ecology and Systematics 3:107-132.

Verhulst, P. F. (1838). "Notice sur la loi que la population suit dans son accroissment." Correspondances Mathematiques et Physiquis 10:113-121.

Whittaker, R. H. (1975). Communities and Ecosystems, 2nd ed. New York: Macmillan.

Williams B. J. (1977a). "Review of Lee and DeVore, 1976." Science 196:761-762.

Williams B. J. (1977b). "Letter." Science 198:782.

Williams, G. C. (1971) Group Selection. Chicago: Aldine.

Wilson, E. O. (1975). Sociobiology. Cambridge, MA.: Belknap.

Winter, S. G., Jr. (1964). "Economic 'natural selection' and the theory of the firm." Yale Economic Essays 4:224-272.

Wynne-Edwards, V. C. (1962). Animal Dispersion in Relation to Social Behaviour. New York: Hafner.

# 2
# The Ecological Perspective in the Social Sciences: A Comparative Overview

*Michael Micklin*

This chapter describes and compares approaches to human ecology in a number of social science disciplines. The ecological perspective originated in the natural sciences--plant and animal ecology--beginning in the latter third of the nineteenth century. Nonetheless, social scientists soon recognized that ecological principles can contribute to understanding and explanation of human social organization (e.g., Hettner, 1895; Schluter, 1899, Park, 1916; Barrows, 1923; Kroeber, 1939). Social scientists' use of ecological concepts, theories, and hypotheses varies considerably over time and among disciplines. Nevertheless, the thesis underlying this chapter is that during the past quarter century there has been a convergence of ideas among social scientists such that a synthetic, multidisciplinary human ecology is not only possible, but actually emerging. Moreover, the new version of human ecology is closely linked to the natural science approach. Finally, it will be argued that adequate description and explanation of the structure and dynamics of human ecosystems requires a multidisciplinary perspective.

The first section outlines the key concepts and principles that underlie the ecological perspective. Attention is focused on those elements of general ecology that are most relevant for the substantive concerns of human ecologists.

In the second section problems of adapting general ecological concepts and principles for the subject matter of
the social sciences are considered. Three paramount concerns are highlighted. First, how adequately do basic ecological assumptions and concepts characterize the situation
of human populations? Second, what additional concepts are
necessary as a result of differences between humankind and
other forms of life? Third, what are the operational
problems in analyzing the ecology of human populations?

Following these preliminary considerations, formulations
of the ecological perspective in a number of social science
disciplines are compared. This analysis is guided by a set
of analytic questions designed to uncover similarities and
differences among these approaches to the field. It will be
apparent that some disciplines (e.g., sociology and anthropology) have developed relatively elaborate ecological
approaches to their substantive domains, while others (e.g.,
political science and geography) have only begun to explore
the utility of the ecological perspective.

The concluding section of the chapter presents a preliminary synthesis of the ecological approaches developed in
the various social science disciplines. Common themes are
identified, and problems inherent in the limited scope of
each approach are discussed. Finally, an agenda for further
conceptual and theoretical elaboration is outlined.

The scope of this chapter is necessarily limited. First,
the emphasis is on general paradigmatic issues, with little
attention given to specific theoretical or methodological
issues which are treated in Chapters 3 and 4, respectively.
The aim of this discussion is to examine the ecological
perspective in terms of its utility for organizing and
focusing empirical inquiry in diverse social science disciplines. The degree to which empirical questions have been
resolved through ecological investigations is another matter.

Second, no attempt is made to discuss comprehensively
the variety of ways social scientists have employed ecological concepts. Emphasis is placed on writings that best
illustrate particular disciplinary uses of the ecological
perspective and, even then, this discussion cannot do justice to the complexities of each argument.

## THE ECOLOGICAL PERSPECTIVE

The commonly recognized definition of ecology, "...the
study of the relation of organisms or groups of organisms to
their environment" (Odum, 1971:3) is too general to be of
much use. Perhaps owing to this lack of rigor in the definition of the field, even among natural scientists, a wide

variety of studies having little in common have been called ecological by their authors. In order to compare disciplinary approaches to human ecological investigation it is necessary to develop a generic definition of the ecological perspective. Several general treatises on ecology are available from which such a definition can be derived (e.g., Dice, 1952; Reid, 1962; Odum, 1971; Emmel, 1973). The elementary definition cited earlier can provide a point of departure, but its components—organism/population, environment and, particularly, relations between the two—require considerable elaboration.

A *population* is a collectivity, usually territorially and/or temporally defined, of individuals conforming to a given definition (Ryder, 1964). Although members of the population share at least some basic attributes, they may be differentiated in terms of a wide range of additional features, e.g., size, color, physical abilities, age, and sex. These characteristics are important because they influence the probability of survival of individual organisms as well as the population as a whole. Likewise, the population can be characterized by its collective attributes, e.g., size, rates of reproduction, mortality, migration, and growth, sex ratio, age distribution, and density.

*Environment* refers to all conditions and events external to the unit being observed (organism or population) that "...directly impinge upon it to affect its mode of life at any time throughout its life cycle as ordered by the demands of the ontogeny of the organism [population] or as ordered by another condition of the organism [population] that alters its environmental demands" (Mason and Langenheim, 1959:332). The environment can be divided conveniently into four categories: natural, man-made, social, and symbolic. (The symbolic environment is of importance primarily for ecological studies of the human species.)

It is important to note that as defined here this "effective environment" includes only those external conditions that impinge directly on the behavior of the unit in question rather than all possible external conditions. This limited conception of the environment has sometimes been referred to as the "habitat" of the organism or population (Dice, 1952; Reid, 1962).

Nearly any habitat includes a variety of populations, the totality of which make up a *community*. This community of organisms along with their associated environments constitute an *ecosystem*: "Any unit that includes all the organisms in a given area interacting with the physical environment so that a flow of energy leads to clearly defined trophic structure, biotic diversity, and material cycles (i.e., exchange of materials between living and nonliving parts) ..." (Odum, 1971:8).

The ecosystem concept represents the most inclusive unit of analysis in modern ecology. Ecosystems can range in scope from a laboratory culture to a pond, lake, or forest to a watershed, region, or continent. At the most inclusive level, the entire planet can be viewed as a single ecosystem. Any ecosystem is organized in terms of a complex set of relationships. In simplified form, however, ecosystems can be characterized in terms of a continuous flow of materials, energy, and information (Duncan, 1964). Materials follow circular paths, while the flow of energy and information is noncircular. In other words,

"Materials are used over and over again...extracted from the environment by some organisms, passed along to other organisms, and returned finally to the environment to become available for a repetition of the cycle... The flow of materials...is accomplished only if work, an expenditure of energy, is done... The ecosystem continually loses potential energy as work is done, with the supply being replenished from the outside..." Energy inputs, in even the simplest living creatures, are dependent upon "...information or 'instructions' on how the energy is to be expended.... Information is increasingly recognized as a fundamental economic and technological 'stuff' comparable to energy" (Duncan, 1964:37-40).

These flows of materials, energy, and information are the fundamental processes necessary to maintain an ecosystem. They are resources without which no population can survive, and their relative abundance ultimately determines the "carrying capacity" of any environment for a given species (see Catton, 1978).

The third element in the standard definition of ecology is *relations* among (1) organisms of the same species, (2) populations of different species, and (3) organisms, populations, and the environment. The most fundamental relationship characterizing ecosystems is interdependence (Reid, 1962:53-60; Duncan, 1964:37; Odum, 1971:10). Plants and animals depend upon one another, and both owe their existence to the availability of resources in the physical habitat.

Relationships between species in an ecological system can be further specified as to whether the resulting interaction is "positive," "negative," or "neutral" (Odum, 1971: 211-233). Positive interactions include "commensalism," in which one population is benefited but the other is not affected; "protocooperation," in which both populations benefit but relations are not obligatory; and "mutualism," in which growth and survival of both populations is benefited and neither can survive under natural conditions without the other. Negative interactions are indicated by "mutual inhibition competition," in which both populations actively inhibit one another; "competition resource use," in which each population adversely affects the other in the struggle for resources in short supply; and "amenalism," in which one population is inhibited and the other not affected. Interaction types having both positive and negative consequences include "parasitism" and "predation," in which one population adversely affects the other by direct attack but is nevertheless dependent on the other. Finally, "neutralism" implies a relation in which neither population is affected by association with the other. Obviously, the greater the number of species an environment contains, the greater the potential for multiple types of interspecies relationships.

Another important concept for describing ecological relations is the principle of "dominance," whereby "...one or more species, frequently only one, exercises primacy over the others" (Reid, 1962:50). Dominance is achieved through control over the flow of materials, energy, and/or information, and in this way dominants are able to exert a strong influence over the environment—and, ultimately, the survival potential—of all other species in the community.

The emphasis thus far has been on describing the structure of ecological systems. However, it should be recognized that ecologists are equally, if not more, concerned with analyzing the causes and consequences of ecosystem development (ecological change). Ecosystem change can be defined in terms of three parameters (Odum, 1971:251):

(1) "It is an orderly process of community development that involves changes in species structure and community processes with time; it is reasonably directional and, therefore, predictable."

(2) "It results from modification of the physical environment by the community; that is, succession is community controlled even though the physical environment determines the pattern, the rate of change, and often sets limits as to how far development can go."

(3) "It culminates in a stabilized ecosystem in which maximum biomass (or high information content) and symbiotic function between organisms are maintained per unit of available energy flow."

Stated otherwise, the essential features of ecological change include (predominantly) unidirectional alterations in species characteristics and community relationships resulting from restricted modifications of the physical environment and culminating in a relatively stable "climax community." Depending upon the ecosystem in question, the process of change may last from decades to much longer periods.

Presumably, the climax community is "...self-perpetuating and in equilibrium with the physical habitat" (Odum, 1971:264). However, ecologists vary as to whether they accept the idea of an ultimate equilibrium or, alternatively, recognize the possibility of further change following a period of apparent equilibrium. Furthermore, it is widely accepted that some species, particularly *Homo sapiens*, can interfere drastically with what would otherwise be an orderly progression toward a climax community.

Concepts useful for describing the structure of ecological systems and the process of ecological change are essential components of the ecological perspective. Yet, they alone do not define the central problems addressed in ecological analysis. Rather, these problems must be sought in the relationships between system structure and behavioral processes.

It has been suggested that "adaptation" is the central problem in ecology (e.g., Dice, 1952:5). Although this concept has been defined in a variety of ways (Williams, 1966) and poses some difficult measurement problems (Alland and McCay, 1973), its intuitive meaning is readily apparent. Ecological units at all levels of organization—individuals, populations, and communities—in order to live effectively, must be able to contend with a restrictive and constantly changing environment. Adaptation involves the development and maintenance of an "ecological niche," which depends "...not only on where the unit lives [the habitat] but also what it does (how it transforms energy, behaves, responds to and modifies its physical and biotic environment), and how it is constrained by other species" (Odum, 1971:234). In short, "...when we say a population is adapting we mean that it is altering its relationship to its habitat in order to make that habitat a more fit place in which to live, or to make itself more fit to live in that milieu" (Cohen, 1968b: 3).

A major analytic problem for ecological analysis is to explain variations in adaptation. Examples of questions bearing upon this issue include: What are the conditions that give rise to the need for adaptive response? Why do some ecological units adapt more readily and with greater success than others? Which of the various adaptive capabilities or strategies available to an ecological unit are employed most frequently and with what consequences? In summary, the ecological perspective is designed to address questions about the behavior of organisms in an environmental context. The unit of analysis can range from a specific population and its habitat to an entire ecosystem. An underlying assumption is that the unit of analysis constitutes a system of interdependent relationships, such that changes in one component of the system will necessitate change or adjustments in others. Attention is focused on the causes, mechanisms, and consequences of adaptive response to environmental constraints and changes.

## ECOLOGY AND THE SOCIAL SCIENCES

All sciences operate in terms of fundamental "paradigms" which include definitions of the subject matter, assumptions about logical-theoretical constructs, identification of key concepts and explanatory variables, and procedural rules for empirical inquiry (see Sjoberg and Nett, 1967:58-66; Kuhn, 1970; Masterman, 1970). Frequently a paradigm characteristic of one science is adopted by other sciences in the hope that its organizing principles can be utilized to improve understanding and explanation within the domain of interest. Such has been the case with the ecological perspective, which has been incorporated increasingly into a variety of social science disciplines.

Interdisciplinary applications of scientific paradigms must be approached cautiously and, at least initially, with more than a little skepticism. Although use of a different paradigm may provide a new way of looking at some substantive phenomenon, there is no guarantee that the result will be an increase in predictive or explanatory power. All too frequently paradigm adoptions have been based on analogies between two classes of phenomena rather than a demonstration that cause-effect relationships in the two domains operate by the same principles. For example, in the social sciences there continues to be considerable debate over the applicability of the organismic and physical models drawn from biology and physics, respectively.

In order to judge the appropriateness of the ecological perspective for the subject matter of the social sciences several preliminary issues must be addressed. First, how well do ecological assumptions and concepts fit substantive domains of the disciplines in question? It should be remembered, however, that the scope of most disciplines is broadly defined, so that some constituent phenomena may be appropriate for ecological inquiry while others may not. Second, although studies of human behavior may benefit from the incorporation of paradigms developed for investigations of other forms of life, the unique characteristics of humankind cannot be ignored. Necessarily, then, an ecological approach to human behavior and social organization will not correspond completely to one appropriate for plant and animal communities. Finally, the adequacy of operational definitions of key concepts and variables may be problematic when paradigms are adopted from another discipline (see Lachenmeyer, 1971). (A good example is the concept of "stress," which has a well-defined meaning in engineering that is approximated only vaguely in the writings of behavioral scientists.)

The primary assumption of the ecological perspective, that of interdependence, is not problematic for the social sciences. Indeed, the systems perspective, which takes for granted the interconnectedness of human activities and institutions, is a dominant paradigm in modern social science (Buckley, 1968). More complex, yet still compatible with social science perspectives, is the assumption that survival of ecological units depends on successful adaptation to the constraints of the environment. With few exceptions, individual human beings and the various aggregates into which they are organized must deal with problems involving the flow of materials, energy, and information. In doing so, they transform themselves and/or the environment in ways that are designed to maximize the likelihood of survival. Such responses are seen in many spheres of human activity, e.g., the minority political party that forms a coalition with other minority parties so as to gain a broader base of support, the couple that consciously limits its fertility in the context of a stagnant economy, and the nation that builds a highway system to link its population centers. What *is* problematic is the identification of a generic set of adaptive mechanisms potentially available to a wide range of human collectivities.

Another assumption inherent in the ecological perspective states that ecosystems tend toward equilibrium or "homeostasis." The underlying idea is really quite simple, i.e., the environment's carrying capacity sets limits on how large a population or community can grow and, after a period of adjustment to a new environment, an ecological unit will approach and ultimately remain at the upper limit. This ecological balance can be upset by changes in the population or the environment, but in natural systems it is assumed that self-correction occurs through "feedback" processes (Odum,

1971:33-36). The equilibrium concept has also been used extensively to characterize human social systems, but there is considerable disagreement over its utility in that realm (Easton, 1956; Hagen, 1961). This argument can be abated somewhat if it is recognized that while social systems do show a great deal of stability and order, there are nevertheless constant pressures or disturbances, eminating from both within and without, that necessitate constant changes in structure and function, i.e., adaptation.

The question of change in ecosystems brings up what is probably the most questionable assumption in the ecological perspective when it is applied to human ecosystems. The idea that ecosystems follow a unilinear path of development, culminating in a "climax community" characterized by stable interdependence, was mentioned earlier. While models of social change based on evolutionary concepts have once again become popular with social scientists (e.g., Sahlins and Service, 1960; Parsons, 1966; Adams, 1975; Lenski, 1979; Lenski and Lenski, 1978) they do not posit specific stages of development and leave as an open question the end-point of the evolutionary process. Indeed, twentieth century trends in relationships between humankind and its environment suggest anything but progression toward a balanced, climax relationship (Catton, 1978).

The applicability of ecological concepts for the social sciences is the next issue to be considered. As pointed out earlier, the ecological perspective focuses primarily on populations, environments, and their interrelationships. The concept of a population refers to any aggregate defined in terms of at least one common characteristic, but those of concern to ecologists also involve two additional features: territoriality and interaction. Social scientists study a great diversity of populations, although the most common are groups, organizations, communities, and societies.

In contrast, the environment concept is much less developed in the social sciences. A distinction between physical and social environments is common, though much greater attention has been given to the latter. Only in recent years have social scientists given serious attention to the nonsocial environment, but there are exceptions to be found among some disciplinary specialties, e.g., resource economics, physical geography and, not surprisingly, human ecology. Nevertheless, there has been a long-standing recognition that the organization of human populations is, to some extent, a response to environmental constraints and possibilities.

Relationships between populations and their environments have been given limited attention by the social sciences. No system for classifying these relationships, comparable to that developed by general ecologists, is to be found among social scientists' conceptual repertoires. Some terms have been borrowed directly, e.g., competition, commensalism, symbiosis (mutualism), invasion and succession but, as will be argued later, their operational definitions are not as commonly agreed upon as they are in general ecology. Part of the problem is that human populations have open to them a much greater variety of potential responses to environmental conditions, although it may be possible to formulate an analytically useful and limited set of generic categories.

Differences between the human species and other life forms require at least one additional concept before the ecological perspective can be applied to human ecosystems. Human beings have developed technologies that permit them to control, exploit, manipulate and, unfortunately, destroy the physical habitat as well as other populations. Technological developments are also responsible for humankind's much greater capability of physical mobility, thus freeing people from constraints imposed by the geographic limits of a given habitat. Moreover, through language the human species has an infinitely greater capacity to organize efforts to collectively overcome environmental limitations and to exploit environmental resources. These capabilities give human beings the dominant role in the world ecosystem. They can be traced to a feature of human society that sets it apart from all other communities of life forms, i.e., human culture. The capacity to symbolize things and events, and to conceptualize and communicate abstract meanings, makes culture possible. And culture provides us with a variety of possibilities for dealing with our environment (Cohen, 1968a). In short, the concept of culture is a necessary and useful element of the ecological perspective when it is applied to human ecosystems.

To be empirically useful a conceptual framework must contain terms that can be operationally defined. One of the reasons that physics has produced a large body of cumulative knowledge is that its basic concepts, e.g., force, mass, and velocity, have been defined in ways that permit valid and reliable measurement. In the social sciences commonly agreed upon conceptual definitions are generally lacking, and this is no less true of ecological concepts.

Several key ecological concepts pose difficult operational problems for social scientists. Perhaps the most difficult is adaptation. A comprehensive examination of this concept is found in the work of Alexander Alland (1972,

1975; also see Alland and McCay, 1973) who points to some
fundamental differences between biological and sociocultural
adaptation and cautions against tautological definitions of
the term (which are frequently encountered in the writings
of social scientists). According to Alland (1975:60):

"A processual theory of adaptation must account for
continuity and change of evolutionary systems rather
than the specific characteristics of the systems themselves. It must begin with some understanding of the
human potential for adaptation in the biological sense,
uncover those mechanisms which maintain continuity or
produce change, and generate transformational rules
which can be used to explain and predict changes in
behavioral systems with specific characteristics under
stated sets of conditions."

While the literature Alland reviews is almost wholly anthropological, examination of the uses of adaptation in the ecological writings of sociologists, geographers and other
social scientists would not alter his principal conclusion:
greater attention needs to be given to developing a useful
operational definition of the concept.

Three fundamental issues surround the measurement of
adaptation. First, there is a need to specify the mechanisms
through which adaptation is accomplished, i.e., the determinants of continuity and change in population-environment
relationships. For most social scientists these are to be
found in social and cultural organization, but attempts to
identify the mechanisms involved remain at a rudimentary
level (see Micklin, 1973, 1977). Second, the ultimate goal
of adaptive processes is frequently stated in terms of
"survival," but more often than not this relationship turns
out to be tautological. Survival is measured in terms of
adaptation, and vice versa. One proposed solution (Micklin,
1973) suggests a variety of qualitative and quantitative
indicators of collective survival, while another (Bennett,
1976a, 1976b) suggests that survival be defined in terms of
the production of "sustained yields." In any case, the
matter merits further attention. Third, one of the factors
assumed to influence adaptation is the "carrying capacity"
of the environment, but this concept also requires more
adequate operational definition (Masering, 1976), especially
when applied to environmental settings of varying scope.

As mentioned earlier, the concept of "environment" has
been used quite imprecisely by social scientists. At the
very least, physical and social components of an ecological
unit's environment should be distinguished. The former can

be further broken down into natural (soil, water, minerals, etc.) and man-made (buildings, transportation routes, etc.) features. Social components would include other populations and their organizational characteristics, as well as symbolic features, i.e., culturally constructed and transmitted meanings. The point is that finer differentiation of the environment is necessary before it becomes possible to identify the "effective environment," i.e., those components that are taken into account by ecological units in the development of adaptive strategies.

The argument presented in this section can be summarized as follows. The ecological perspective provides a useful approach to the understanding and explanation of problems of collective life. Assumptions regarding interdependence and continual pressures to adapt to restrictive and changing environmental conditions are as relevant for human populations as they are for other species. However, assumptions regarding equilibrium and unidirectional development of ecological systems must be modified. The concepts of population, environment, and population-environment (ecological) relationships require detailed specification, perhaps more so than in general ecology. A major difference between ecological systems of humans and other species is the role of culture in guiding adaptive responses in the former. Finally, a number of problems regarding the operational definition of some key concepts have yet to be resolved.

The preceding sections of this chapter have outlined the ecological perspective and examined some issues relevant to its application in the social sciences. In the following section attention is focused on ways in which this paradigm has been employed to address substantive issues in selected social science disciplines. Emphasis is placed on a limited number of questions designed to bring out similarities and differences among these disciplines in their conceptualization and operationalization of the ecological perspective.

## APPROACHES TO HUMAN ECOLOGY

This discussion will be concentrated on approaches to human ecology developed in four disciplines: sociology, anthropology, geography and political science.[1] Within each discipline one or more orientations labeled as "ecological" have emerged, though there is considerable variation among these perspectives with regard to conceptual, theoretical, and methodological details. Attention will be focused on recent statements reflecting each discipline's attempt to adapt the ecological perspective to fit its substantive concerns. No attempt will be made to review the historical development of these approaches to human ecology. For some disciplines such accounts are already available (e.g., Quinn, 1940; Wagner, 1960; Helm, 1962).

---

[1]The term "ecology" has been used in a variety of social science contexts, leading Duncan (1959:680) to charge that it "... is sometimes applied rather casually--even irresponsibly." The disciplines represented include several that will not be discussed here: city planning (Simmie, 1967), economics (Boulding, 1966; Daly, 1973, 1977), psychology (Barker, 1963, 1965, 1968; Emery and Trist, 1973; Moos and Insel, 1974) and public health (Rogers, 1960).

Demography is not given separate attention because it is so closely related to human ecology. Populations form one component of an ecological system, and demography focuses on the internal structure and dynamics of a population as a closed system, i.e., not subject to external influence (Micklin, 1977). On the one hand, a better understanding of population dynamics can be achieved if the environmental context is specified (Duncan, 1959; Hawley, 1973). On the other hand, population variables can clearly influence the environment through other variables (e.g., organization). According to Hawley (1973:1200), the major contribution of ecology to population study is "...the formulation of the population-environment problem in organization terms..."

The questions guiding this overview are the following.

1. What is the range of substantive problems addressed?

2. What units of analysis are typically employed?

3. How is the environment defined and what significance is attributed to it as a determinant of adaptive behavior?

4. What are the major independent and dependent variables?

5. How are ecological processes and ecological change dealt with?

6. How is adaptation defined and what role does it play in the ecological system?

Not all of these questions will be salient, especially for those disciplines within which an ecological approach has emerged only recently. Nevertheless, this analysis should lead to an improved understanding of the similarities and differences, strengths and weaknesses, in these attempts to apply ecological principles to the analysis of relationships between human populations and their environments.

*Sociology*

The ecological approach in sociology has a long history, dating from the early writings of Robert E. Park, Ernest W. Burgess, Roderick D. McKenzie, and their students (see Theodorson, 1961). During the past three decades developments in sociological ecology have involved a marked shift away from the early emphasis on describing "natural areas" of the city and the spatial distribution of social institutions and activities. Modern versions are concerned with explaining functional interrelationships among variously defined components of ecological systems.

The major stimulus to contemporary human ecology in sociology was Amos Hawley's *Human Ecology: A Theory of Community Structure* (1950). These ideas have been elaborated in Hawley's more recent work (1968, 1971, 1979) and in the writings of some of his students (e.g., Kasarda, 1972, 1974; also see Berry and Kasarda, 1977). According to Hawley (1950:68), human ecology is "...the study of the form and development of the community in human populations." Attention is concentrated on variations in ecological organization, i.e., "..the complex of functional interrelationships by which men live" (Hawley, 1950:178). Organization is hypothesized to arise from the interaction of population and environment (Hawley, 1968:329). The unit of analysis in Hawley's view is organization, which is "...exclusively a property of the population as a whole" (1968). Originally the principal unit of organization was denoted as the community (Hawley, 1950), but more recently (1968) the term "social system" has been suggested as being more appropriate. The social systems of interest to the sociological human ecologist can range from a formal organization to the world system of nations, although empirical studies remain concentrated on cities and geographic regions.

The environment is defined as "...whatever is external to and potentially or actually influential on a phenomenon under investigation" (Hawley, 1968). Beyond that it's content is not specified. Nevertheless, it is clear that the environment is not seen as a fixed entity; rather, it is subject to fluctuation in terms of both content and the degree of influence or constraint.

Population and environment may be viewed as either independent and dependent variables, but the relationship between the two is mediated through organization. Five "principles of ecological organization" are held to be particularly salient (Hawley, 1968:331-334):

1. *Interdependence:* Organizational units, such as localities and industries, are linked together through two types of relationships--*symbiotic* based on complementary differences, and *commensal* based on supplementary similarities--that influence their temporal and spatial dimensions.

2. *The key function:* Relationships between the environment and the population are mediated by a small number of activities that sustain the population, for example, exploitation, distribution, and exchange.

3. *Differentiation:* The degree of functional differentiation (specialization) varies directly with the productivity of the key functions and constitutes the principal limiting condition on system diversification, the population size that can be supported, and the area that can be occupied.

4. *Dominance:* Units that perform the key functions determine or regulate the conditions essential to the functions of other units in the system.

5. *Insomorphism:* Units subject to the same environmental conditions, or to environmental conditions as mediated through a given key unit, acquire a similar form of organization.

Hawley's view of ecological change emphasizes the influence of external conditions. Changes that result in an increase in productivity of key functions stimulate system growth, or cumulative change, which is generalized in the principle of "expansion" (Hawley, 1950:322, 1968, 1979; also see Kasarda, 1972). Expansion involves growth of a dominant center of activity as well as enlargement of its scope of influence. This process is limited primarily by the boundaries, physical as well as social, of other systems. When the limits to expansion are reached, equilibrium conditions tend to be reestablished.

Adaptation is viewed as a collective accomplishment." As a population develops an organization, it increases the chances of survival in its environment" (Hawley, 1971:11). For example, the division of labor is directly related to specialization which results in greater productivity of the key functions, expansion, and other changes in ecological organization.

Hawley's influence is evident in several alternative approaches to human ecology developed by other sociologists. Curiously, the most widely cited conceptual framework is the so-called "ecological complex" formulated by O. D. Duncan and Leo Schnore (Duncan, 1959, 1961, 1964; Duncan and Schnore, 1959; Schnore, 1958), though it is much more rudimentary than Hawley's scheme. The ecological complex consists of four interdependent categories of variables: population, organization, environment, and technology (typically represented by the acronym POET). The unit of analysis is a human population, more or less territorially defined (Duncan, 1959:681), viewed in the context of the entire ecosystem (Duncan, 1964). The environment, which may include other populations as well as physical, biotic, and chemical features, offers resources that can be exploited for the maintenance of life but also poses restrictive conditions that must be adjusted to. Any of the four rubrics—population, organization, environment, technology—can serve as independent or dependent variables, although the majority of studies using this approach have concentrated on some aspect of organization as the phenomenon to be explained. An example of the analytic potential of the ecological complex is seen in Duncan's (1961) examination of an urban ecosystem. Although ecological change is considered explicitly in only one of Duncan's works (1964), it is clear that Hawley's concepts of "expansion" and "accumulation" are central. Finally, consistent with Hawley's position, Duncan and Schnore view organization as the means by which adaptation is achieved:

> "For the ecologist, the significant assumptions about organization are that it arises from sustenance-producing activities, is a property of the population aggregate, is indispensible to the maintenance of collective life, and must be adapted to the conditions confronting a population—including the character of the environment, the size and composition of the population itself, and the repertory of techniques at its command" (Duncan, 1959:683).

A related approach appeared about the same time as the initial statement of the ecological complex (Gibbs and Martin, 1959). Gibbs and Martin take issue with Hawley's (1950) conception of human ecology, though they acknowledge a number of parallel features. Beginning with the question "How does the human species survive?", Gibbs and Martin argue that the proper subject matter of human ecology is "sustenance organization": Man survives by collective organization in the exploitation of natural resources" (1959:31). From this perspective, the goals of human ecology are (1) to explain the presence and absence of particular characteristics of sustenance organization among human populations and (2) to establish the consequences of the presence or absence of particular characteristics of sustenance organization. Thus, this approach suggests a more restricted focus than that of Hawley or Duncan and Schnore. In further contradistinction to Hawley's early position, Gibbs and Martin argue that any level of collective organization, not simply the community, is a proper unit of analysis for human ecological inquiry. The environment is not given detailed consideration in this conception of the field, although it is apparent that the presence (absence) of particular environmental resources facilitates (constrains) possible modes of sustenance organization in a population. Gibbs and Martin are precise in their specification of the dependent variable in human ecology, i.e., sustenance organization, but they admit a wide range of

potentially relevant independent variables—"purely demographic characteristics of populations, geographical variables, the purely technological aspects of man's culture,
and the different forms of sustenance organization." Ecological change is not dealt with, although it can be assumed
that changes in sustenance organization result from changes
in the independent variables. Finally, adaptation is equated
with changes in sustenance organization that arise from the
mechanism of "selective survival." Changes in external conditions that affect the viability of one or another mode of
sustenance organization tend to select those populations
that are able to adapt (whether by altering the existing
mode of sustenance organization or changing the external
conditions) and to eliminate those that cannot.

The three approaches reviewed here provide a sense of
the conceptual orientation guiding human ecological inquiry
in sociology over the past quarter century. All are macro-
sociological (in that they focus on the organization of
populations) and all eschew a concern with subjective
factors (e.g., values, motives, sentiments). Although each
of these conceptualizations gives lip service to the influence of culture on ecological organization, this is primarily with regard to technology as a reflection of material
culture. Alternative approaches that incorporate subjective
orientations have appeared in recent years (e.g., Firey,
1960; Burch, 1971; Klausner, 1971; Micklin, 1973), but as
yet they have not had much impact on work in the field.

*Anthropology*

Several versions of human ecology have been developed by
anthropologists, generally under the rubric of "cultural
ecology" (Steward, 1968). Only recently has a fully
developed conceptual scheme comparable to that introduced by
Hawley appeared (Bennett, 1976b), and it remains to be seen
whether this framework will have a similar integrating influence within the discipline. Anderson (1973) divides ecological perspectives in anthropology into three categories:
cultural ecology, ethnoecology, and quasi-population or
systemic ecology.

Generally, cultural ecology (Steward, 1955, 1968:337) is
concerned with "the processes by which a society adapts to
its environment." It differs from sociological ecology in
that it attempts to identify origins of the particular
cultural features of different areas rather than derive
general principles applicable to any environment. Cultural
ecology emphasizes subsistence activities and economic

arrangements characteristic of particular types of environment (Steward, 1955:39). The units of analysis are "...the
equilibrium plateaus of sociocultural-environmental systems"
(Anderson, 1973:187). The environmental component is defined
as "...the total web of life wherein all plant and animal
species interact with one another and with physical features
in a particular unit of territory" (Steward, 1955:30). Culture traits or complexes of traits are the principal dependent variables for cultural ecology, while the independent
variables are drawn from relevant environmental conditions
(e.g., topography, animal and plant resources) and, to a
lesser extent, the presence of other populations in the
area. Ecological changes are alterations in cultural practices related to the environment. Change is viewed in an
evolutionary framework, based on stages of cultural development defined in terms of increasing complexity. Such changes
may be due to diffusion or developments internal to a given
culture (Steward, 1955). Finally, adaptation is defined by
the acquisition of culture traits that equip a population to
survive within the constraints of its environment. For
Steward (1955:39), "...the concept of environmental adaptation underlies all cultural ecology..."[2]

Ethnoecology focuses on the description and elaboration
of culturally-based cognitions or perceptions of the natural
environment (see Frake, 1962). It seeks "...adequate emic
descriptions of cultural domains, including the perceptual
environment, principally by means of formal semantic
analysis" (Anderson, 1973:189). The unit of analysis is a
cultural vocabulary for classifying the natural environment,
with little attention given to functional interrelationships
with the wider ecosystem. Cause and effect relationships are
generally ignored, as are considerations of ecological
change. Adaptation is addressed in a limited sense: the
benefits to the organism or culture of a particular system
for classifying the natural environment. As such, ethnoecology remains on the periphery of the broader field of
human ecology.

Systems ecology (within anthropology) is closely related
to its intellectual cousin in sociology. However, several
key differences distinguish the two disciplinary approaches,
the principal one being the deterministic role given to

---

[2]For an interesting application of cultural ecology see
Geertz's (1963) study of agricultural systems in Indonesia.

culture by most anthropological ecologists. The most comprehensive treatment of the ecological approach in anthropology is seen in John Bennett's recent book *The Ecological
Transition* (1976b). For Bennett the domain of human ecology
includes relationships among the physical environment
(earth, climate, other species), natural resources, energy
and goods, social organization (population, differentiation,
interaction, power, ritual), "formal controls" (law, regulations), "presses" (values, needs, goals), technology (tools,
machines) and human biology (population, physiology, genes).
Ecological processes are represented by a number of functional relationships among these components. For example,
the physical environment is transformed into natural resources and used to produce energy and goods. Energy and
goods affect human biology as well as social organization,
formal controls, and "presses." Cultural ecology can be
narrowed down to "...the relationships between energy output
and social and psychological components...", although
"....human ecology...for scientific purposes is virtually
identical with cultural ecology" (Bennett, 1976b:39).

The units of analysis in Bennett's paradigm may be
particular subsystems or the larger ecosystem. Regardless of
the level of analysis employed, the focus is on "adaptive
systems" that are involved in energy exchanges with the environment and are capable of internal innovation (Bennett,
1976b:94). Bennett argues that the natural scientist's ecosystem concept has limited utility for human ecology to the
extent that it is difficult to incorporate social-behavioral
and valuational factors.

The relevant environment, in Bennett's framework, depends on the system or subsystem being observed. Greatest
emphasis is placed on the physical environment from which
humans "...extract substances...that are transformed sym-
bolically into 'natural resources' which are then used to
produce or transform energy" (1976b:43). The environment is
not viewed as a "determinant" of ecological conditions or
processes. Rather, " it can be a resource, a stimulus, a
constraint, an information 'bit', a source of uncertainty
--and so on--depending upon the other circumstances influencing and participating in the system" (1976b:258). In
short, the physical environment serves as a variable rather
than a constant in human ecological systems. Bennett leaves
open the question of whether society itself is a component
of the environment. However, the implied answer is in the
affirmative (1976b:18-19).

Bennett's ecological paradigm is composed of a number of
relationships that can be topics for empirical inquiry. For
cultural ecology the central concern is the influence of

energy output on various aspects of human behavior: value and need presses, social organization, and technology and other cultural factors (1976b:74). Nevertheless, it should be recognized that this model reflects a complex system from which a variety of partial relationships can be isolated. For example, production of energy and material goods feeds directly back to the physical environment, and indirectly influences this environment through social organization, technology, formal controls, and symbolic culture ("presses"). Additionally, reciprocal relationships exist among technology, social organization, and the "press" factors. Perhaps the most distinctive feature of this paradigm is the central causal role given to culture. Bennett (1976b:40) states that "...cultural considerations--symbolic values, tradition, socially stimulated wants--underlie every human relationship with Nature, directly or indirectly; in the long run, all human ecological study must deal with this."

Considerable attention is given to ecological change. Historically, the "ecological transition," roughly equivalent to what some anthropologists (e.g., Sahlins and Service, 1960) have called cultural evolution, is concerned with the changing balance between resources and population. The central question is "...how human societies do manage to maintain a sustained-yield balance with resources and control over population increase for reasonable periods of time; and how these same societies move away from such balance toward demographic and economic-technological growth with its more intensive use of resources" (Bennett, 1976b: 124). Bennett examines this transition from two perspectives: first, material progress, involving increased exploitation of natural resources and resulting in population increase; and, second, the process through which a disequilibrium between resources and population arises.

The second of these perspectives is much more critical for an understanding of contemporary ecological systems. Equilibrated systems (or societies) are those that have "adapted" in the sense of stabilizing their social organization and technology such that resource use is managed and significant environmental deterioration avoided. In contrast, the disequilibrated society seeks and exploits resources wherever they can be found, and is characterized by a philosophy of growth, requiring increasing amounts of energy (Bennett, 1976b:137-138). The trend toward disequilibrium is established when a society discovers "...new sources of energy in...economic organization, technology, and fossil fuels" (Bennett, 1976b:138). The transition from low-to-high energy technology is not simply a result of technological innovation, but is also due to social organizational and ideological (cultural) transformations. As a society becomes larger, more differentiated and stratified, as communication networks grow, and culturally-based "wants" become more diversified, Nature comes to be viewed as something to be mastered for the service of man. Nowhere is this more evident than in the exponential increase in energy consumption and the production of material goods so characteristic of industrial society.

Finally, adaptation plays a central role in Bennett's ecological paradigm (1976b:243-305; 1976a). Adaptation (coping, adjustment, etc.) refers to "The patterns and rules of social adjustment and change in behavior by individuals and groups in the course of realizing goals or simply maintaining the *status quo*..." (1976b:269). An understanding of adaptive processes is viewed as essential for cultural (and human) ecology. Adaptive strategies consist of behavior aimed at maintaining, modifying, changing—in short, doing something about—external circumstances in order to achieve some goal. The task for human and cultural ecology is to determine what people, individually and collectively, *do* in terms of extracting resources from the environment (social as well as physical) and regulating their use. Adaptive processes need to be studied both synchronically and diachronically.

Bennett (1976b:283-288) describes a number of specific adaptive processes, but their underlying dimensions cannot be categorized easily. With some the relevant dimension is temporal (e.g., strategies with immediate, delayed, or sustained effects), while others seem to be defined by their relational qualities (e.g., resource competition, specialization of resource potential). Still others appear to be premised on their anticipated outcome (e.g., rationalized approval, action constraint). Nevertheless, all of these "adaptive processes" reflect modes of behavior designed to achieve some end with regard to resource use and the satisfaction of needs and wants.

Adaptive strategies are highly variable both within and among societies and cultures. It is therefore most difficult to judge the relative effectiveness of alternative strategies. Bennett does, however, offer a guiding criterion for assessing normative adaptation: sustained yield of resources, which refers to "...a condition that permits both human and environmental survival..." (1976b:298). In other words, adaptation reflects a homeostatic balance between the demands a population places on Nature and the

ability of Nature to meet those demands without serious
disruption. More specific criteria are offered for distinguishing adaptive from maladaptive actions in the human
ecological system (1976b:298-299). These include:

1. The conditions of the natural (and social) environment, including biological species as well as inanimate
species, before and subsequent to human actions;

2. The biological conditions of the human population
(size, distribution, state of health); and

3. States of being as defined by the human group as
necessary to social continuity and peace of mind.

It is recognized that these criteria may conflict in that
adaptive response in terms of one may be maladaptive in
terms of another. That is why adaptive strategies need to
be carefully considered in terms of their overall, system-
wide effects.

Detailed consideration has been given to Bennett's ecological paradigm for two reasons: it is the first comprehensive statement of a systems approach to ecological anthropology, and it contains ideas and concepts relevant to ecological paradigms developed in several other disciplines.
As such, it could rank with Hawley's *Human Ecology* as a
fundamental guide for future development of the ecological
perspective in the social sciences.

Several other applications of the ecological perspective
by anthropologists deserve brief mention. Erik Cohen (1976)
has suggested a framework for examining "environmental
orientations" (cf. Vayda and McCay, 1975). Its purpose is to
understand how "...differential perspectives on the environment...lead man to *act* upon it in different ways; and by
such action the relationship between man and his environment
and eventually the ecological system itself are differentially shaped and modified (Cohen, 1976:49). This approach,
Cohen claims, will help the anthropologist grasp the ecological complexities of urban and other complex settings.
The orientations may be characteristic of individuals or
communities.

Environmental content is not defined, but it is apparent
that the major referent is the physical habitat. Totally
absent from this perspective is any recognition that the
nature of the environment may condition or restrict orientations toward it.

Environmental orientations are discussed in terms of their purpose, modes, regulative mechanisms and processes, types of environmental organization, institutions, and functional sphere. The result is four categories of environmental orientation, each of which is further differentiated. The "instrumental" orientation views the environment as a resource base. The "territorial" orientation refers to the control of space. The "Sentimental" orientation is concerned with the sense of attachment to space and, finally, the "symbolic" orientation relates to the environment in terms of its symbolic significance. Whether these four dimensions are truly independent of one another is questionable. Cohen (1976:57) attaches theoretical significance to this complex typology by way of its treatment of three major problems in ecological theory. They are:

1. Ecological institutionalization: "the problem of conflict between various environmental orientations (and their respective regulative mechanisms) over the allocation of space, or of different environmental features, to alternative uses;"

2. Ecological consequences: "the problem of the differential impact of the various orientations on the ecosystem;"

3. Ecological transformation: "the problem of the differential dynamics of ecosystems dominated by different orientations or 'mixes' or orientations."

Ecological change (or "transformation") is hypothesized to result from shifts in dominant ecological orientations. How these shifts originate is not addressed, however, which greatly reduces the explanatory value of the model.

Adaptation occupies a peripheral role in this approach. However, Cohen does suggest that while these orientations reflect means by which a population adapts to its environment, conflicts among them may actually impede adaptation due to a reduced ability to cope with existential problems. This approach offers an interesting and potentially useful way of classifying population-environment relationships. But until the paradigm is revised to incorporate ecological processes, it is unlikely to be useful for empirical analysis.

Roy Rappaport (1968), in the context of studying a group of slash-and-burn farmers in the central highlands of New Guinea, has emphasized the role of culture in mediating population-environment relationships. Specifically, he shows how ritual "operates as a regulating mechanism in a system, or set of interlocking systems, in which such variables as the area of available land, necessary lengths of fallow periods, size and composition of both human and pig populations, trophic requirements of pigs and people, energy expended in various activities and the frequency of misfortunes are included" (Rappaport, 1968:4).

The unit of analysis employed is a single human group considered in the context of its ecosystem. Contrary to most comparable studies, Rappaport incorporates in his analysis the entire relevant ecosystem, including animal and plant life, other human populations (the "regional system"), and flows of energy, materials, and information within the system. The detail achieved by this investigator is partly a function of working with a relatively small and isolated population but, at the same time, it represents the type of ecosystem analysis that is the goal of a truly holistic ecological perspective.

The focus of Rappaport's research was, consistent with Bennett's (1976b) concept of adaptive strategies, what people *do* to maintain and regulate environmental conditions. Thus, the size of the pig population, the amount of land under cultivation, the deterioration of plant life, the amount of labor expended, and the frequency of warfare were explained through the organization and meaning of ritualized activities. Drastic ecological change is thus avoided, and the ecosystem takes on a homeostatic quality.

Richard Adams' (1975) attempt to derive a theory of the evolution of social structure provides another example of the use of ecological principles by an anthropologist. Although he is concerned ultimately with explaining the causes and consequences of the growth and differentiation of social power relationships in human society, Adams analyzes these phenomena in the context of the ecosystem, in general, and the conversion of energy resources, in particular.

Adams (1975:131-137) distinguishes four hierarchically arranged units of analysis. The "operating unit" consists of an arbitrarily chosen population characterized by a "common adaptive stance" to its environment. The "power system" includes "...all the human population with which the focal operating unit experiences exchange...of energetic forms and processes...". These exchange relations are interpreted to encompass any vehicle—social, economic, genetic, etc.—through which one population influences another. At still more inclusive levels are the "ecosystem" and the "universe." In Adams' model, these four systems and their interrelationships are the settings in which energy flows and conversions occur.

The environment, defined as "...the material, physical, or energy-form-and-flow aspect of man's social and physical habitat," (Adams, 1975:13) plays a critical role in this conceptualization. Control over environmental resources is the basis of social power; in particular, it is control over the forms and flow of energy that is crucial.

In Adams' scheme, energy is the principal independent variable. The success of a given operating unit in capturing, converting, and utilizing energy resources determines its pattern of social organization, "...most specifically the pattern of evolution of the power structure" (Adams, 1975:137).

Ecological change is discussed in the context of societal evolution, the principal feature of which is expansion, or growth, of population and of the cultural stock of materials and symbols. Expansion is seen as both cause and effect of increased control over the environment which results in an improved capacity to convert energy resources for human purposes. Expansion alters the nature of both the operating unit and its environment, as well as the relationship between them. Adams suggests that the growth of energy systems characteristic of most of the modern era may ultimately seal the fate of human society: "The core of the energetic problem confronting humanity today is expansion, both cultural and biological... A good case may be made that every major problem facing mankind today is either directly or indirectly a consequence of this expansion" (1975:143).

Adaptation, in Adams' scheme, involves an operating unit's ability to change its controls over its environment and the power it derives from other sources. However, this "capacity to respond" is limited by "the mental structures of man," i.e., the symbolic distinctions through which individuals and groups create order out of the external world (Adams, 1975:153-196). Adaptation consists of selecting those responses that result in the survival of the operating unit given specific environmental constraints and resources.

The final approach to be discussed in this section is Marvin Harris' (1979) "cultural materialism". Harris presents cultural materialism as scientific research strategy that offers an integrated set of theories of sociocultural organization that have ...broad scope and wide applicability" (1979:75). As such, this perspective is seen as superior to alternative anthropological paradigms.

Cultural materialism is based on what Harris (1979: 55-56) calls the "principle of infrastructural determinism." All human societies are viewed as divisible into three categories of related variables: infrastructure, structure, and superstructure. *Infrastructure* is composed of "modes of production" (technology of subsistance, techno-environmental relationships, ecosystems, and work patterns) and "modes of reproduction" (demography, mating patterns, vital processes, infant care, means of controlling demographic patterns). *Structure* includes the "domestic economy" (family structure, domestic division of labor, domestic socialization, age-sex roles, and domestic stratification) and the "political economy" (political organization, division of labor, political socialization, community and national stratification, mechanisms of social control, and warfare). *Superstructure* consists of behavioral phenomena such as art, literature, rituals, leisure activities, and science. These variables are all behavioral and "etic," i.e., they are defined in terms of material things, events, and relationships which exist independently of the constituent actors' mental constructs. Associated with each level of behavior are "mental and emic" components—"the conscious and unconscious cognitive goals, categories, rules, plans, values, philosophies, and beliefs about behavior elicited from the participants or inferred by the observer" (Harris, 1979:54).

The principle of cultural materialism asserts the strategic causal priority of infrastructural variables over structural and superstructural conditions and processes, and of etic over emic phenomena. However, Harris does not deny the possibility of exceptions to this hypothesized ordering of relationships.

Although in an earlier work Harris (1968:654-687) virtually equated cultural materialism with cultural ecology, his intent in this recent book is clearly more ambitious than other ecologically-oriented arguments. Harris (1979:77-114) proposes theoretical explanations of a vast array of substantive aspects of societal organization, covering behavioral and mental phenomena viewed etically as well as emically. Practically every feature of human societies falls within reach of the theoretical net of cultural materialism. Moreover, Harris analyzes societies at all levels of complexity, ranging from hunters and gatherers to modern industrial states.

While the environment is not defined by Harris with any precision, he clearly views it in terms of lawful regularities occurring in nature. All societies confront physical, biological, chemical, and ecological conditions that set limits on the development of patterns of sociocultural organization. Infrastructure serves as the "...principal interface between culture and nature, the boundary across which the ecological, chemical, and physical restraints to which human action is subject interact with the principal sociocultural practices aimed at overcoming or modifying those restraints" (Harris, 1979:57).

As suggested above, modes of production and reproduction are the principal independent variables of cultural materialism. They determine, in a probabilistic sense, structural and superstructural variables. Similarly, emic phenomena are generally to be explained in terms of etic phenomena.

Consistent with the ecological perspective, cultural materialism views human society as a system of interdependent relationships. Ecological processes are defined primarily in terms of relationships between the infrastructure and the environment, i.e., those activities that "...affect the balance between the size of each human population, the amount of energy devoted to production, and the supply of life-sustaining resources" (Harris, 1979:58). Accordingly, changes in this system of relationships are most likely to be brought about by infrastructural innovations. Historically, the principal changes in societal organization have resulted from escalating energy budgets, increased productivity, and accelerating population growth (Harris, 1979:67). In contrast, the principal function of structural and superstructural variables is to maintain the societal system.

The concept of adaptation does not play a central role in Harris' framework. Nonetheless, he recognizes very clearly that in order to survive all societies must come to terms with the possibilities and constraints set by the natural environment. Sociocultural systems "...survive or not as a consequence of the adaptive changes in the thought and activities of individual men and women who respond opportunistically to cost-benefit options" (Harris, 1979:61). Of central importance are the etics and emics of the societal infrastructure, and their effects on structure and superstructure.

The anthropological paradigms reviewed here reveal considerable diversity in employment of the ecological perspective. They range from the limited classificatory scheme proposed by Cohen to the more ambitious and complex explanatory models developed by Bennett and by Harris. These approaches share one obvious feature: their contention that the ecology of human social systems cannot be understood without explicit consideration of the role of culture.

## Geography

Geographers were urged to adopt an ecological perspective over half a century ago (Barrows, 1923), but only recently has this suggestion gained wide acceptance. Leo Schnore, writing in 1961, suggested that the ecological viewpoint was not appreciated in geography. Since that time it has become increasingly apparent that geographers are thinking ecologically (e.g., Stoddart, 1965, Berry, 1973; Chorley, 1973; Berry and Kasarda, 1977).

Geography is concerned primarily with the uses of space and the environment (Hagerstrand, 1973). Its substantive domain is, generally, the location and distribution of "things"--resources, activities, people, etc. But, like other disciplines, geography can be divided into a number of specialities, e.g., physical geography, resource geography, social geography, cultural geography and human geography. Recent discussions of some of these specialty areas, principally human, social, and cultural geography, reflect a concern with systems of relationships between man and the physical environment (e.g., Pahl, 1965; Hobson, 1969; Berry, 1973; Hagerstrand, 1973). Thus, within this discipline there is an emerging recognition of a close connection to human ecology.

Older conceptions of human geography viewed the unit of analysis as the "natural geographic region" (McKenzie, 1934), while more recent approaches reflect an emphasis on areas defined in terms of systems of human activities (e.g., Pahl, 1965; Hobson, 1969; Berry, 1973). It has even been suggested that "Nowadays virtually every suggestion having to do with the restructuring of geography and with its need to increase its relevance with respect to current environmental problems involves, explicitly or implicitly, the application of some measure of systems analysis" (Chorley, 1973:165).

Early geographic approaches to human activities were variations on the "environmental determinism" theme (Clarkson, 1970). Increasingly, though, it is recognized that this relationship should be reversed. It is the human presence, defined in terms of population size and distribution, patterns of movement, activities and the decisions that guide them, cultural orientations to the environment, and so on that influence environmental variables. Brian Berry (1973:14), one of the most ecologically-oriented of present-day geographers, explicitly proposes use of the ecosystem concept. He presents a "behavioral model of spatial process" which views the ecosystem as a product of interacting natural and cultural processes (also see Stoddart, 1965).

Consistent with the current emphasis on man's intrusion into and control of the natural environment, geographers are increasingly likely to explain patterns of resource use and availability in terms of social organization and "beliefs and perceptions" (Berry, 1973:14; also see Berry and

Kasarda, 1977:417-429). Accordingly, changes in ecological systems are now seen as the result of changes in social and cultural institutions related to the environment (Stoddart, 1965; Berry, 1973). Adaptation, as a mechanism of change, is not yet a key concept in the vocabulary of the geographers.

One geographer who has written on problems of ecological change (broadly conceived) is Wilbur Zelinsky (1970). He argues that the geographic approach is one of several needed to understand the imbalance between population growth and economic development in the less affluent nations, and between population and consumption in the industrialized nations. The geographic aspects of this problem center on "...the degree to which human beings have been poorly assigned in space, in terms of number, distributional pattern, and territorial ranges of activity and investigation of the consequences thereof" (Zelinsky, 1970:503). Ecological change is interpreted in terms of a "Growth Syndrome" (expansion, in Hawley's framework). Continued growth is examined with regard to its problematic consequences for the viability of the world ecosystem.

*Political Science*

The ecological perspective in political science is a relatively recent development. The most systematic formulation has been presented by Harold and Margaret Sprout (1965, 1968, 1971). They define the perspective in terms of the "ecological triad": environed organisms (population), milieu (environment, including social relationships), and interrelationships between the two. These three elements constitute an ecosystem. The unit of analysis is, typically, the world system of nations, interacting with one another, in an environmental context. Recognition is given to the importance of structural as well as cultural "entity attributes" in determining how national populations adjust to their physical and social environments.

The Sprouts (1971:31) employ the ecological approach to understand the dynamics of foreign policy and international politics: "How to cope with the diverse, cumulatively enormous, and still proliferating capabilities to alter the conditions of subsistence on this planet is becoming the central problem of international politics, just as these same changes and transformations are moving to the center of the state in nations, provinces, and cities all over the world."

Adaptation is seen as a problem of obtaining and allocating resources (materials, energy, wealth) internally as well as externally. Pressure is increasing for governments to give greater attention to intrasocietal resource demands but, at the same time, the world's nations grow more inter-dependent each year. The problems are truly transnational, beyond the capability of any single government to resolve by itself. Moreover, many of the key resources upon which nations depend for their survival are becoming increasingly scarce. This increases the likelihood of competition among nations for these resources and also points to the need for governments, the major actors in the international ecological system, to find ways to cooperate in the quest for a more equitable resource distribution (also see Russett, 1967). One consequence of any redistributive scheme would be change (exactly how much cannot be specified) in prevailing lifestyles in many nations, both rich and poor.

A quite different version of the ecological perspective is seen in the writings of some quantitatively oriented political scientists (Dogan and Rokkan, 1969). This approach addresses the spatial distribution of electoral phenomena and offers statistical and mathematical techniques for their analysis. As such, it is peripheral to the analysis of ecological systems and need not be considered further.

Another position on political ecology is seen in the writings of environmentalists who examine the politics of environmental policy (e.g., Caldwell, 1970). They focus on governmental issues related to management of the natural habitat, including resource use and environmental protection. The ecosystem perspective is important, as one of the underlying arguments put forth is that through excessive population growth and resource extraction/destruction the ecological basis of life is in danger of being destroyed. Emphasis is placed on public policy formation and enforcement as the means by which governments respond to human disruptions of the ecosystem. In addition, nongovernmental modes of response--e.g., cultural orientations toward growth and consumption--are seen as important conditions influencing the human relationship with Nature. "When the fit between man and milieu is loose, voluntary individual adaptations are possible. When social pressures on the environment are severe and the man/milieu relationship is tight, politics replaces individual choice, and priority rationing, or some other form of social decision overrides voluntary behavior" (Caldwell, 1970:132).

Finally, Victor Ferkiss (1974) has suggested an ecological perspective for the politics of advanced industrial society. His frame of reference is essentially that of the ecosystem, and he suggests that "the relationship of man to nature is the central political issue of our time" (1974: 102). Politics is viewed as that aspect of culture which keeps social systems in equilibrium. The world ecosystem is now characterized by an imbalance between natural and social processes, and to overcome this imbalance mankind needs to develop a philosophy of "ecological humanism." Although his assumptions relfect man-nature relationships, Ferkiss goes little further toward developing a framework for political ecology.

This section has examined the ecological perspective in the context of four social science disciplines. The task of the section that follows is to determine whether there is sufficient common ground among the various social science interpretations of the ecological approach to suggest a general model that can address a wide range of substantive problems. In addition, the strengths and weaknesses of existing disciplinary ecological models will be amplified briefly.

## HUMAN ECOLOGIES OR HUMAN ECOLOGY?

The preceding review of approaches to human ecology in various social science disciplines shows them to vary on a number of specific details. This is true to some extent even among alternative conceptual frameworks within the same discipline. Nevertheless, in the interest of parsimony, it is useful to ask whether there is sufficient agreement across disciplines regarding fundamental ecological concepts and issues to justify one rather than many basic paradigms. If it can be shown that the differences observed are complementary, then perhaps it will be possible to develop a unified approach, with potential contributions from a number of the social sciences, such that knowledge of human ecological systems can grow cumulatively. The analytic questions posed earlier will again be employed to guide the discussion.

The substantive problems addressed through the ecological perspective differ considerably among disciplines. *Sociologists* are generally concerned with a population's organizational response to environmental conditions. By "organization" the sociologist means persisting or institutionalized patterns of social relationships, e.g., structural differentiation, functional integration, sustenance activities, and dominance. *Anthropologists,* on the other hand, tend to include a wider range of substantive phenomena within their purview. For example, a comprehensive paradigm such as that proposed by Bennett (1976b) includes many organizational factors, but gives greater emphasis to cultural meanings, especially as they affect and are affected by the transformation of environmental substances into energy and goods. *Geographers* tend to focus on territorial or spatial variations in human activities. What the natural environment offers to man in the way of resources as well as barriers to social organization is given major attention. The *political scientist* concentrates his efforts on one specific form of organizational response to the environment, i.e., government and its primary functions of societal regulation, policy formation and implementation. It should be remembered that these are the principal substantive domains characteristic of these disciplines. In actuality, the issues addressed are elaborated considerably, frequently crossing disciplinary boundaries.

Units of analysis are typically some form of collectivity, although some anthropologists and geographers advocate concentration on individuals. In fact, the prevailing concern with various forms of organizational response dictates that emphasis will be placed on populations. In general, there is little dispute over this attribute of the ecological perspective.

The nature of the environment to which populations respond has been given insufficient attention by all but a few human ecologists regardless of their disciplinary affiliation. (An exception is Michelson, 1970.) At most, the typical distinction is between the physical environment and other populations as an environmental component. Geographers typically distinguish between natural and man-made features, and anthropologists (along with some psychologists, who have been omitted from this discussion) emphasize the significance of the symbolic or cultural environment. As yet, human ecologists have not paid sufficient attention to the complexity of the environment to which populations respond. On the other hand, the environmental component is a universal feature of paradigms or models based upon the ecological perspective. In this regard, it should be remembered that the ecosystem concept, with its biotic, physical, and chemical components, is rarely employed in human ecological studies, though exceptions are found in the anthropological literature (e.g., Rappaport, 1968 and Harris, 1979).

The selection of independent variables differs, as one would expect, among the various disciplines. As the substantive domains vary, so do the relationships analyzed. To the extent that dominant classes of independent variables can be identified, they are social structure (sociology), culture (anthropology), physical environment (geography), and legal and administrative institutions (political science).

Ecological processes--the transactions and interactions among units of an ecological system--are not well-defined in any social science discipline. Human ecologists typically pay lip service to the premise derived from general ecology that the fundamental ecological processes involve flows and transfers of energy, materials, and information. Of the three, greatest attention has been given to flows of materials, as in the division of labor and sustenance organization. Little systematic concern has been devoted to transfers of energy and information, though a few exceptions are available, mainly in the work of anthropologists (e.g., Rappaport, 1968; Adams, 1975; Bennett, 1976). Ecological change has generally been viewed as an evolutionary process characterized by expansion and accumulation (e.g., Zelinsky, 1970; Hawley, 1971; Adams, 1975; Bennett, 1976).

Finally, threre is general agreement across the social sciences that human ecology is fundamentally concerned with the process of adaptation. Care must be taken, however, to use this concept in a scientifically sound way. That is, the term must be subject to operational definition and must refer to identifiable adaptive strategies or practices. To paraphrase Bennett (1976), adaptation involves *doing something organizationally* with the aim of improving the unit's niche in the ecological system. Adaptation may involve altering the flow of materials, energy, or information, or it may be aimed at improving the population-environment balance through an alteration of one or the other of these components. To date social scientists have not done a satisfactory job of defining, categorizing, and operationalizing the components of adaptive processes.

This comparison of ecological approaches suggests a relatively high level of consensus on the nature and goals of human ecology among different disciplines. Generally there is little disagreement that collectivities should be the unit of analysis, that the environment, though poorly conceptualized, is a fundamental consideration, that ecological processes involve flows of the key resources of energy, materials, and information, that ecological change has involved a trend toward expansion such that equilibrium is an atypical condition and, finally, that the essential problem is to determine how and under what conditions populations adapt to changes and constraints of their effective environment. Differences among the disciplines are seen in terms of substantive domains and explanatory variables. Given these considerable areas of agreement, is it not likely that the differences observed can form the basis of complementary contributions to a unified multidisciplinary human ecology (cf. Cain, 1967 and Bruhn, 1974)?

## REFERENCES

Adams, R. N. (1975). Energy and Structure: A Theory of Social Power. Austin: University of Texas Press.

Alland, A., Jr. (1972). "Cultural evolution: the Darwinian model." Social Biology 19:227-239.

Alland, A., Jr. (1975). "Adaptation." Annual Review of Anthropology 4:59-73.

Alland, A., Jr. and B. McCay (1973). "The concept of adaptation in biological and cultural evolution." In J. J. Honigman (ed.), Handbook of Social and Cultural Anthropology. Chicago: Rand McNally.

Anderson, J. N. (1973). "Ecological anthropology and anthropological ecology." in J. J. Honigman (ed.), Handbook of Social and Cultural Anthropology. Chicago: Rand McNally.

Barker, R. G. (1963). "On the nature of the environment." Journal of Social Issues 19 (October):17-38.

Barker, R. G. (1965). "Explorations in ecological psychology." American Psychologist 20, 1(January):1-20.

Barker, R. G. (1968). Ecological Psychology: Concepts and Methods for Studying the Environment of Human Behavior. Stanford: Stanford University Press.

Barrows, H. H. (1923). "Geography as human ecology." Annals of the American Association of Geography 13:1-14.

Bennett, J. W. (1976a). "Anticipation, adaptation, and the concept of culture in anthropology." Science 192 (28 May):847-853.

Bennett, J. W. (1976b). The Ecological Transition: Cultural Anthropology and Human Adaptation. New York: Pergamon Press.

Berry, B. J. L. (1973). "A paradigm for modern geography." In R. J. Chorley (ed.), Directions in Geography. London: Methuen.

Berry, B. J. L. and J. D. Kasarda (1977). Contemporary Urban Ecology. New York: The MacMillan Co.

Boulding, K. E. (1966). "Economics and ecology." In F. Darling and P. Milton (eds.), Future Environments of North America. New York: The Natural History Press.

Bruhn, J. G. (1974). "Human ecology: a unifying science?" Human Ecology 2:105-125.

Buckley, W. (ed.) (1968). Modern Systems Theory for the Behavioral Scientist. Chicago: Aldine Publishing Co.

Burch, W. R., Jr. (1971). Daydreams and Nightmares: A Sociological Essay on the American Environment. New York: Harper and Row.

Cain, S. A. (1967). "Can ecology provide the basis for synthesis among the social sciences?" In M. E. Gainsey and J. R. Hibbs (eds.), Social Science and the Environment. Boulder: University of Colorado Press.

Caldwell, L. K. (1970). Environment: A Challenge to Modern Society. New York: Natural History Press.

Catton, W. R., Jr. (1978). "Carrying capacity, over-shoot, and the quality of life." In J. M. Yinger and S. J. Cutler (eds.), Major Social Issues: A Multidisciplinary View. New York: The Free Press.

Chorley, R. J. (1973). "Geography as human ecology." In R. J. Chorley (ed.), Directions in Geography. London: Methuen.

Clarkson, J. D. (1970). "Ecology and spatial analysis." Anals of the American Association of Geographers 60 (December):700-716.

Cohen, E. (1976). "Environmental orientations: a multi-dimensional approach to social ecology." Current Anthropology 17 (March):49-70.

Cohen, Y. A. (1968a). "Culture as adaptation." In Y. A. Cohen (ed.), Man in Adaptation: The Cultural Present. Chicago: Aldine Publishing Co.

Cohen, Y. A. (ed.) (1968b). Man in Adaptation: The Cultural Present. Chicago: Aldine Publishing Co.

Daly, H. E. (ed.) (1973). Toward a Steady-State Economy. San Francisco: Freeman.

Daly, H. E. (1977). Steady-State Economics. San Francisco: Freeman.

Dice, L. R. (1952). Natural Communities. Ann Arbor: University of Michigan Press.

Dogan, M. and S. Rokkan (eds.) (1969). Quantitative Ecological Analysis in the Social Sciences. Cambridge, MA.: The M.I.T. Press.

Duncan, O. D. (1959). "Human ecology and population studies." In P. M. Hauser and O. D. Duncan (eds.), The Study of Population. Chicago: University of Chicago Press.

Duncan, O. D. (1961). "From social system to ecosystem." Sociological Inquiry 31(2):140-149.

Duncan, O. D. (1964). "Social organization and the eco-system." In R. E. L. Farris (ed.), Handbook of Modern Sociology. Chicago: Rand-McNally.

Duncan, O. D. and L. F. Schnore (1959). "Cultural, behavioral, and ecological perspectives in the study of social organization." American Journal of Sociology 65: 132-146.

Easton, D. (1956). "Limits of the equilibrium model in social research." Behavioral Science 1:96-104.

Emery, F. E. and E. L. Trist (eds.) (1973). Towards a Social Ecology: Contextual Appreciation of the Future in the Present. New York: Plenum Press.

Emmel, T. C. (1973). An Introduction to Ecology and Population Biology. New York: W. W. Norton.

Ferkiss, V. (1974). The Future of Technological Civilization. New York: George Brasiller.

Firey, W. (1960). Man, Mind, and Land: A Theory of Resource Use. Glencoe, IL.: The Free Press.

Frake, C. O. (1962). "Cultural ecology and ethnography." American Anthropologist 64 (February):53-59.

Geertz, C. (1963). Agricultural Involution: The Process of Ecological Change in Indonesia. Berkeley: University of California Press.

Gibbs, J. P. and W. T. Martin (1959). "Toward a theoretical system of human ecology." Pacific Sociological Review 2 (Spring):29-36.

Hagen, E. (1961). "Analytical models in the social sciences." American Journal of Sociology 67 (September): 144-151.

Hagerstrand, T. (1973). "The domain of human geography." In R. J. Chorley (ed.), Directions in Geography. London: Methuen.

Harris, M. (1968). The Rise of Anthropological Theory: A History of Theories of Culture. New York: Crowell.

Harris, M. (1979). Cultural Materialism: The Struggle for a Science of Culture. New York: Random House.

Hawley, A. H. (1950). Human Ecology: A Theory of Community Structure. New York: The Ronald Press.

Hawley, A. H. (1968). "Human ecology." In D. L. Sills (ed.), International Encyclopedia of the Social Sciences. New York: Crowell-Collier-MacMillan.

Hawley, A. H. (1971). Urban Society: An Ecological Approach. New York: The Ronald Press.

Hawley, A. H. (1973). "Ecology and population." Science 179 (23 March):1196-1201.

Hawley, A. H. (1979). "Cumulative change in theory and in history." In A. H. Hawley (ed.), Societal Growth: Processes and Implications. New York: The Free Press.

Helm, J. (1962). "The ecological approach in anthropology." American Journal of Sociology 17 (6 May):630-639.

Hettner, A. (1895). "Die Lage der Menslichen Ansiedlungen." Geographische Zeitschrift 1:361-375.

Hobson, B. T. (1969). "Human ecology and the geography of towns." In Urban Analysis: A Study of City Structure with Special Reference to Sonderland. Cambridge: Cambridge University Press.

Kasarda, J. D. (1972). "The theory of ecological expansion: an empirical test." Social Forces 51 (December):165-175.

Kasarda, J. D. (1974). "The structural implications of social system size: a three-level analysis." American Sociological Review 39 (February):19-28.

Klausner, S. Z. (1971). On Man in His Environment. San Francisco: Jossey-Bass.

Kroeber, A. L. (1939). Cultural and Natural Areas of Native North America. University of California Publications in American Archeology and Ethnology, No. 38. Berkeley: University of California Press.

Kuhn, S. (1970). The Structure of Scientific Revolutions, 2nd ed. Chicago: University of Chicago Press.

Lachenmeyer, C. (1971). The Language of Sociology. New York: Columbia University Press.

Lenski, G. (1979). "Directions and continuities in societal growth." In A. H. Hawley (ed.), Societal Growth: Processes and Implications. New York: The Free Press.

Lenski, G. and J. Lenski (1978). Human Societies: A Macrolevel Introduction to Sociology, 3rd ed. New York: McGraw-Hill.

Masering, C. H. (1976). "Factors affecting the carrying capacity of nation-states." Journal of Anthropological Research 32 (Winter):255-275.

Mason, L. H. and J. H. Langenheim (1959). "Language analysis and the concept of environment." Ecology 38:325-340.

Masterman, M. (1970). "The nature of a paradigm." In I. Lakatos and A. Musgrove (eds.), Criticism and the Growth of Knowledge. London: Cambridge University Press.

McKenzie, R. D. (1934). "Demography, human geography and human ecology." In L. L. Bernard (ed.), The Fields and Methods of Sociology. New York: Farrar and Rinehart.

Michelson, W. H. (1970). Man and His Urban Environment. Reading, MA.: Addison-Wesley.

Micklin, M. (1973). "A framework for the study of human ecology." M. Micklin (ed.), Population, Environment, and Social Organization: Current Issues in Human Ecology. Hinsdale, IL.: The Dryden Press.

Micklin, M. (1977). "Population, ecology, scarcity." In R. Perrucci, D. D. Knudsen, and R. R. Hamby, Sociology: Basic Structures and Processes. Dubuque, IA.: William C. Brown.

Moos, R. H. and M. Insel (eds.) (1974). Issues in Social Ecology. Palo Alto, CA.: National Press Books.

Odum, H. P. (1971). Fundamentals of Ecology, 3rd ed. Philadelphia: W. B. Saunders Co.

Pahl, R. E. (1965). "Trends in social geography." In R. J. Chorley and P. Haggett (eds.), Frontiers in Geographical Teaching. London: Methuen.

Park, R. E. (1915). "The city: suggestions for the investigation of human behavior in the urban environment." American Journal of Sociology 20 (March):577-612.

Parsons, T. (1966). Societies: Evolutionary and Comparative Perspectives. Englewood Cliffs, NJ.: Prentice-Hall.

Quinn, J. A. (1940). "The development of human ecology in sociology." In H. A. Barnes and H. S. Becker, Contemporary Sociological Theory. New York: Appleton-Century-Crofts.

Rappaport, R. A. (1968). Pigs for the Ancestors: Ritual in the Ecology of a New Guinea People. New Haven, CT.: Yale University Press.

Reid, L. (1962). The Sociology of Nature. Baltimore: Penguin Books.

Rogers, E. S. (1960). Human Ecology and Health. New York: MacMillan.

Russett, B. M. (1967). "The ecology of future international politics." International Studies Quarterly 11 (March):12-31.

Ryder, N. B. (1964). "Notes on the concept of a population." American Journal of Sociology 69 (March):447-463.

Sahlins, M. D. and E. R. Service (eds.) (1960). Evolution and Culture. Ann Arbor: University of Michigan Press.

Schluter, O. (1899). "Bemerkungen zur Siedelungsgeographie." Geographische Zeitschrift 5:65-84.

Schnore, L. F. (1958). "Social morphology and human ecology." American Journal of Sociology 63 (May):620-634.

Schnore, L. F. (1961). "Geography and human ecology." Economic Geography 37 (July):208-217.

Simmie, J. M. (1967). "Urban ecology and social models." Journal of the Town Planning Institute 53:452-454.

Sjoberg, G. and R. Nett (1967). A Methodology for Social Research. New York: Harper and Row.

Sprout, H. and M. Sprout (1965). The Ecological Perspective on Human Affairs. Princeton, NJ.: Princeton University Press.

Sprout, H. and M. Sprout (1968). An Ecological Paradigm for the Study of International Politics. Research Monograph No. 30, Center for International Studies, Woodrow Wilson School of Public and International Affairs, Princeton University.

Sprout, M. and H. Sprout. (1971). Toward a Politics of the Planet Earth. New York: D. Van Nostrand.

Steward, J. (1955). Theory of Culture Change. Urbana: University of Illinois Press.

Steward, J. (1968). "Cultural ecology." In D. L. Sills (ed.), International Encyclopedia of the Social Science, Vol. 4. New York: Crowell-Collier-MacMillan.

Stoddart, D. R. (1965). "Geography and the ecology approach: the ecosystem as a geographic principle and method." Geography 50 (July): 242-251.

Theodorson, G. A. (ed.) (1961). Studies in Human Ecology. New York: Harper and Row.

Vayda, A. and B. J. McCay (1975). "New Directions in Ecology and Ecological Anthropology." Annual Review of Anthropology, 4: 293-306.

Wagner, L. (1960). The Human Use of the Earth. Glencoe, IL.: The Free Press.

Williams, G. C. (1966). Adaptation and Natural Selection: A Critique of Some Current Evolutionary Thought. Princeton, NJ.: Princeton University Press.

Zelinsky, W. (1970). "Beyond the great transition: the role of geography in the great transition." Economic Geography 46: 498-535.

# 3
# Sociological Human Ecology: Theoretical and Conceptual Perspectives

*Dudley L. Poston, Jr.*
*W. Parker Frisbie*
*Michael Micklin*

The growth of knowledge in every field of science depends on the adequacy of its theoretical base. Theory performs several functions vital to scientific progress. First, it circumscribes the domain of inquiry, defining the range of phenomena to be studied. Second, it provides the conceptual vocabulary from which common understandings are developed and without which constructive debate of principles and findings is impossible. Third, it gives the scientist a rationale for generating predictions and constructing explanations. Fourth, the theory underlying a field offers a framework for linking ideas and findings relevant to diverse substantive topics. Finally, theory is the vehicle through which research findings are synthesized and scientific knowledge is accumulated.

The history of science demonstrates that, within most fields, knowledge does not typically grow by leaps and bounds. Rather, it accumulates slowly, in small increments, and only rarely are significant advances observed (Kuhn, 1962). In sociological human ecology, however, unlike most other disciplines, especially the other social sciences, a single theoretical focus emerged at one particular point in time. The bulk of ecology's theoretical and empirical work thereafter has been linked in one way or another with this single focus. We are referring to Amos Hawley's *Human Ecology,* published in 1950, which stands today as the major theoretical treatment of the field.

In the first section of this chapter we will trace out the development of Hawley's theoretical perspective on sociological human ecology, focusing principally on his 1950 book, although some of his other work will also be identified and discussed in order to place his ideas within the proper perspective. We will then turn to the two major theoretical models or paradigms which are pre-eminent in contemporary sociological human ecology: the ecological complex model and the sustenance organization model. Each of these will be presented and attention will be directed to their substance and components; subsequently, a brief assessment of these two approaches will be presented.

## AMOS HAWLEY AND THE DEVELOPMENT OF SOCIOLOGICAL HUMAN ECOLOGY

During the early part of this century human ecology was the dominant perspective within sociology. Expressed primarily through the writing of Robert E. Park, Ernest W. Burgess, Roderick D. McKenzie, and their students, the ecological perspective served as a guiding orientation for sociological research on such diverse topics as the urban community, deviant life styles, and personality disorders. During the 1940s the influence of human ecology declined to the point that some sociologists wrote its epitaph, while others sought to revitalize it through a reconsideration of its fundamental links with general ecology and general sociology. Although several sociologists presented new approaches to human ecology during this decade, none has been as influential as the perspective developed by Amos H. Hawley.

Hawley's graduate work was guided by McKenzie, who some have argued was the most imaginative of the architects of "classical" human ecology. In fact, Hawley became established as a leader in the field through an early theoretical essay (1944) and a comprehensive text (1950), both of which recognize explicitly the influence of McKenzie's ideas. Through the years Hawley has expanded and modified his ideas on human ecology in a series of papers (1968, 1972, 1973, 1978) and another book (1971; revised edition appeared in 1981). There can be little doubt that through his writings and his teaching Amos Hawley has determined and shaped the theoretical and conceptual foundations of contemporary human ecology.

The conceptual framework underlying *Human Ecology: A Theory of Community Structure* (1950) was first presented in his 1944 article. Hawley argued there that human ecology deals with the same central issue as general ecology—"how growing, multiplying beings maintain themselves in a constantly changing but ever restricted environment." In human populations the solution to this problem is seen in the ways in which individuals act collectively in order to achieve a more effective use of their habitat. Collective actions fall into two principal categories, symbiotic and commensalistic. *Symbiotic* relations are those which involve interdependence among unlike organisms, while *commensalistic* relations reflect competitive interactions among similar organisms. The resulting pattern of collective relationships Hawley labelled the *community*. From this perspective, human ecology was seen as the study of development and change in the morphology of human communities.

Hawley's conceptualization of the field differed from earlier views in at least four important ways: (1) the assumption that general and human ecology address the same central problem, (2) the recognition that ecological relationships reflect both competition and interdependence, (3) the view that survival of human populations is essentially a collective accomplishment, thus directing the ecologist's attention to populations rather than individuals, and (4) the identification of sustenance activities as the principal component of ecological organization.

Although the data contained in *Human Ecology* are no longer current, the ideas presented continue to constitute the conceptual bases for contemporary sociological human ecology. This is particularly true of Parts III and IV which deal with "Ecological Organization" and "Change and Development," respectively. Ecological organization refers to the pattern of functional interdependencies among differentiated groups and institutions in a population. Variations in these patterns are evident temporally as well as spatially. Unlike previous conceptions of human ecology, Hawley's concern with spatial patterns was a means to better understanding social organization rather than a primary objective. While the community was viewed as the basic unit of ecological investigation, he recognized that ecological organization in modern societies often extends beyond local settlements to encompass regional relationships among a number of differentiated communities. In short, ecological organization reflects a population's adaptation to the possibilities and limitations of its environment.

Recognizing that most human populations are constantly undergoing organizational change, Hawley concluded this book with a discussion of ecological change and development. He argued that population movements, whether recurrent or non-recurrent, affect the equilibrium of organizational arrangements in a community and are thus an important consideration in ecological analysis. However, the most lasting contribution to contemporary human ecology stems from the discussion of the process of ecological expansion, i.e., the cumulative incorporation of more or less unrelated populations and land areas into a single organization. Expansion is seen at all levels of organization—the region, the city, and the local community. The process of cumulative change has been a central component of contemporary ecological analysis and has provided the conceptual basis for Hawley's elaboration of his theoretical perspective.

In spite of continuing influence of his original conceptualization of human ecology, Hawley has developed and modified his views. One significant change is his shift of emphasis from the community to the "social system" as the basic unit for ecological analysis, first evident in his summary of the field in the *International Encyclopedia of the Social Sciences* (1968). The recognition that ecological organization goes beyond the traditional view of community to encompass societal and even global relationships expanded considerably the range of problems that could be addressed from the ecological perspective. In addition, the 1968 essay contains a specification of the concept of ecological organization, defining it in terms of five principles: interdependence, key functions, differentiation, dominance, and isomorphism. Identification of these principles has resulted in a better understanding of variations in the ecological organization of social systems. Finally, Hawley reiterated in this article his view that cumulative change (the principle of social system expansion) is the key to understanding societal growth.

In *Urban Society: An Ecological Approach* (1971; 1981), Hawley applied his ecological perspective to urban social systems and the process of urban growth (also see Hawley, 1972). Urbanization is viewed as an expansion process and cities are examined in terms of their role as functional units in an expanding system of ecological relationships. Much of this book is devoted to an historical analysis of the rise of the urban community and the conditions underlying the structural and functional differentiation of urban ecological systems. Emphasis is placed on the cumulative elaboration of social organization as a means of making the urban community responsive to changing environmental conditions and requirements for system survival. These changes in social organization are evident in cultural patterns, social institutions, communication and transportation technology, the functions of government, and the spatial and temporal organization of functional activity complexes. In short, *Urban Society* provides a reasoned and well-documented ecological theory of social change.

Hawley's presidential address to the American Sociological Association in 1978 was an elaboration and generalization of this approach to social change. He argued that growth of social systems is best explained by the expansion model rather than the more frequently employed evolutionary perspective. Whereas evolution assumes independence of differentiated units, expansion posits "a tightening web of interdependencies." Expansion involves an initial increase in population and territory which is achieved through colonization. Linkages among the units of this "social field" are tightened through increased efficiency of techniques for the movement of people, materials and information, which depends on development of technology (tools and information) as well as organizational arrangements essential to the application of this technology. Cumulative change thus involves increasing the scale and complexity of social systems through expansion and increasing interdependence among system components.

A theorist's influence on his discipline depends in large part on the continuity of his ideas. This is one reason why, in the social sciences, the writings of Durkheim, Weber, and Marx still command our attention. Another requirement for lasting influence is that the scholar's ideas be relevant to problems that transcend particular cultures and historical periods. Amos Hawley's writings on human ecology satisfy both conditions. He began with an ecological perspective linking general ecology and the central problem of sociology--social organization--and developed an encompassing theory of one of the key problems faced by the human species: the growth and survival of social systems. For these reasons, Hawley's writings are truly classic contributions to the literature of human ecology.

Having outlined and discussed the major contributions of Amos Hawley and the resulting development of sociological human ecology, we turn next to a treatment of the two main theoretical perspectives in existence today: the ecological complex approach and the sustenance organization approach. Both of these perspectives can be seen as direct descendents of Hawley's pioneering ideas.

## THE ECOSYSTEM AND THE ECOLOGICAL COMPLEX

Human ecological theory begins with the issue of how human populations survive (Frisbie and Clarke, 1979). The ecological answer to this basic question is that populations survive by virtue of collective organization (Gibbs and Martin, 1959:30). In the most fundamental sense,

> Organization represents an adaptation to the un- avoidable circumstance that individuals are interdepen- dent and that the collectivity of individuals must cope with concrete environmental conditions--including, per- haps, competition and resistance afforded by other col- lectivities--with whatever technological means may be at its disposal (Duncan, 1959:683).

The foregoing will be recognized immediately as part of Duncan's classic synopsis delineating the four categories of variables--population, organization, environment, and tech- nology--that have constituted the primary concern of human ecologists at least since the publication of Hawley's *Human Ecology*. Unfortunately, the tendency in the field has been to concentrate unduly on this heuristically useful typology, and to neglect the broad conceptual sweep of the ecosystem framework which the typology represents. Initially, this misplaced emphasis on format rather than content may have stemmed partially from Duncan's reluctance to assign pre- maturely systemic properties to the interrelationships among the four dimensions of the complex (1959:684). It is also probably fair to say that the complexity of the ecosystem concept deterred even those most convinced of its analytic potential from attempting full-scale empirical tests. Never- theless, there is no substance to the frequent suggestion that the ecological complex is nothing more than a guide to the types of variables that ought to interest the human ecologist. The foundation for the analysis of social rela- tionships as ecosystem was firmly laid by Hawley (1944; 1950), who oriented the field to the insights of bioecology, and Duncan (1964), who described the systemic flows of energy, materials, and information. More recently, Kasarda and Bidwell (Chapter 5 of this volume) have provided a valu- able explication and extension of the ecological complex model with regard to formal organizations.

## COMPONENTS OF THE THEORY

Before engaging in an assessment of the place of the ecological complex/ecosystem model and the efficiency of its application, it will be useful to specify some of the objectives, assumptions and definitions on which the theory is based. Let us be clear about our terminology. The four dimensions--population, organization, environment, and technology--are not themselves the ecological complex. Rather, "the full set of relationships among these (categories of) variables is known as the ecological complex"... Since each component is assumed to be interdependent with the other, "it is possible to regard the ecological complex as a system—Duncan's (1959) 'ecosystem'" (Kasarda and Bidwell, Chapter 5 of this volume).

The theoretical objectives of the model are readily apparent. Ecosystem theory is first of all an effort to provide a framework for describing the morphology of ecological relationships. More importantly, it represents an attempt to *explain* the emergence and nature of organizational structure.

### *Dimensions of the Ecological Complex*

The four elements of the Duncan typology suggest "the scope of the ecological frame of reference" (Duncan, 1959: 683). Meanings assigned to these dimensions by human ecologists show clearly the assumed interdependence among them as well as some degree of overlap with the sustenance organization model to be discussed later in this chapter.

In some ways, the concept of *environment,* defined as "whatever is external to and potentially, or actually, influential on a phenomenon under investigation" (Hawley, 1968:330), is the most basic of the four dimensions. This concept occupies a central position in the general theoretical framework of human ecology inasmuch as it is assumed that the environment is the ultimate source of sustenance for a population (Hawley, 1968:330). However, very little empirical research in sociological human ecology has taken the environment directly into account, perhaps because of the breadth of its definition. That is, based on the definition, the environment "has no fixed content and must be defined anew for each different object of investigation" (Hawley, 1968:330). In fact, there seems to be little doubt that environment is the "least well conceptualized for the variables constituting the ecological complex" (Berry and Kasarda 1977:14).

However, a close scrutiny of the ecological treatment of the environment reveals an implicit specificity not apparent in the general definition alone. Not everything external to the phenomenon of interest is part of the environment, but only those externalities that, by virtue of setting limits on acquisition of sustenance, affect the life chances of an organized population with a given technological repertoire. In other words, "the environment is viewed as a set of limiting conditions, which may be narrow or broad, depending upon the technological devices and modes of organization that prevail in a given population" (Schnore, 1958:628; Michelson, 1976:24-25). Thus, an ecologist may, indeed must, logically narrow the arena of inquiry into environmental influences to those factors which, in light of existing technology, serve as limiting resources for the adaptation and/or growth of populations.

In an attempt to sharpen the concept's focus, it is useful to describe the kinds of factors that should not be included under the environmental rubric. The outcomes of a population's organizational and technological operations on the environment, and the adaptations (or maladaptations) thereby achieved, have often been mistaken for the environment itself. Thus, indicators of the state of a population's life chances, or quality of life, have sometimes been loosely categorized as "environmental." Interpreting the definition of environment in this most amorphous sense, one might include within the scope of the concept such factors as prevalence of crime and other deviant activities, mortality and morbidity rates, unemployment rates, industrial structures, levels of education and income and so on. For example, one often hears that some environments are more violent or criminal than others. In the same way, one might speak of a political or economic or cultural environment (or "climate"). Whatever the stylistic elegance of such phrases, this indulgence in metaphor quickly and easily destroys the precision required in empirical analysis. Put differently, the issue is much more than merely semantic, since the logical result would be to conclude that everything is environment, except the population under study.

Thus, it is not useful to consider social and economic activities (or aberrations) of local populations to be part of the environment of populations. Certain of these activities, for example, employment in given industries, must, of course, be viewed as aspects of ecological *organization*. Others, such as crime and deviance, rates of mortality and morbidity, unemployment and education and income levels, are best conceived as indicators of different aspects of life chances that emerge from a population's organized efforts to *adapt to the environment*. In a very real sense, the latter variables indicate the degree of success or failure of the adaptive process. In short, they may reveal a disequilibrium between population and life chances. But they should not be treated as aspects of the environment per se, in an ecological sense.

Inevitably, efforts to circumscribe a concept involve decisions of both exclusion and inclusion. To this point, emphasis has been on indicating the types of factors that should be excluded from the environmental rubric. We turn attention now to those types of actors which should be included.

Despite the difficulties that arise in attempts to give conceptual and operational substance to the rubric, it is clear that the ecological environment has two broad and distinct dimensions: the physical and the social. As Hawley (1981:9) puts it,

> Environment...includes not only the physical and biotic elements of an occupied area but also the influences that emanate from other organized populations in the same and in other areas. In certain circumstances the latter acquire a more critical importance than the former.

The physical environment, of course, refers to such things as climate, natural resources, and topography. In addition, one may distinguish aspects of the *man-made* physical environment (Michelson, 1970; 1976), such as type of buildings and other physical structures. The social environment refers to other populations and organizations which have an influence on the populations being investigated.

The next rubric, *population,* may be defined substantively as "any internally structured collectivity of human being that routinely functions as a coherent entity" (Berry and Kasarda, 1977:14). It goes without saying that of all the ecological rubrics, this one is the most advanced in terms of conceptual and operational detail. Indeed an entire specialization, demography, is devoted to the study of population. However, in most ecological inquiries, population enters the model mainly from the standpoint of the unit of analysis. That is, ecologists will inquire about the organizational, technological and environmental attributes of human populations, but will only seldom be concerned with their population (i.e., demographic) characteristics. (See Poston and White, 1978, for an exception.) In the 1970s some

ecologists examined the degree to which a demographic phenomenon such as migration could be conceived as a response
to changes in organization (Frisbie and Poston, 1978b) and
to changes in technology and the environment (Sly, 1972; Sly
and Tayman, 1977). But even in these contexts, the investigators failed to include population characteristics themselves as endogenous influences. Yet we know from demographic research (Price and Sikes, 1975) that population
variables such as age, race and sex compositon, *inter
alia*, have predictable effects on the organizational adaptations of populations. Indeed Hawley himself has observed
that "demographic structure contains the possibilities and
sets the limits of organized group life" (Hawley, 1950:78).

The ecological rubric of *organization* may be conceived
as "the entire network of symbiotic and commensalistic relationships that enable a population to sustain itself in its
environment" (Berry and Kasarda, 1977:14; see also Hawley,
1968). And it is not an overstatement to note that organization is the fundamental element of the subject matter of
human ecology. Indeed, some have claimed that human ecology
is mainly concerned with the organizational aspects of human
populations arising from their sustenance-producing activities (Frisbie and Poston, 1978b:14). Considerable theoretical and empirical attention has been directed to the organizational rubric, so much so that the sustenance organization
model of human ecology is one of its principal theoretical
paradigms. As such, the organizational model will be examined intensively in the next section of this chapter.

Of the four rubrics comprising the ecological complex,
*technology* is perhaps the most critical for the adaptation
of human populations. Lenski (1970:102-103) has suggested
that it is the "prime mover" in the process of social change
and adaptation.[1] Moreover, the concept is clearly prominent in ecological and other macro-level theories, and there
is a certain consensus in definitions of technology. Frisbie
and Clarke (1979:593) have summarized the situation as
follows:

---

[1]*The fact that technological advance may sometimes have
deleterious effects is beside the point here. The point is
that technological advance may be viewed as adaptive since
it allows human populations greater control over their environment and thereby facilitates the maintenance of the
ecosystem "commodity flows" (energy, materials, and information) described by Duncan (1964) as basic to survival (see
also Frisbie and Clarke, 1979; 1980).*

A fair degree of convergence is evident in efforts to theoretically circumscribe the concept. Lenski (1970: 37) defines technology as "the information, techniques, and tools by means of which men utilize the material resources of their environment." Similarly, Sjoberg (1965:214) describes technology as "the tools, the sources of energy and the knowledge connected with the use of both tools and energy that a social system employs." On a slightly less abstract level and using somewhat different terminology, Ogburn (1955:383) conceives of technology as the "kinds of capital equipment, quantity of capital goods, manner and use of nonhuman resources, scientific discovery, invention (and) machines." Finally, Duncan notes that the "concept of 'technology' in human ecology refers not merely to a complex of art and artifact...but to a set of techniques employed by a population to gain sustenance from its environment and to facilitate the organization of sustenance-producing activity" (1959:682).

Three dimensions figure prominently in the above definitions: *material features* (tools, capital equipment machines); *information* (knowledge, techniques, scientific discovery); and *energy*. And these are the same three ecosystem "commodity" flows described by Duncan (1964) as basic to the survival of populations.

## Substantive Domain

In a very real sense, the substantive domain of the ecological complex is coterminous with that of human ecology in general. As suggested above, the major question of substantive interest is the way in which populations structure their organizational response to their environment with the technological resources at their disposal (Duncan, 1959: 683). In this context, the unit of analysis is an organized aggregate, i.e., a population. As Kasarda and Bidwell (Chapter 5 of this volume) put it, "Organization is exclusively a property of the population taken as a whole and exhibits structural characteristics that can be examined apart from the personal characteristics of its individual actors." The ecological complex is "materialistic" in that ideas and ideology are essentially excluded from its purview. It adopts a "social realist" perspective, giving emphasis to the emergent properties of populations, and thus makes no recourse to individual attitudes, motivations or opinions as explanatory factors (Schnore, 1961).

It must be assumed, then, that populations can be delimited which evidence unit character (Duncan, 1959:68; Hawley, 1968). By "unit character," it is meant only that the organized aggregate has recognizable characteristics which distinguish it from others and that this aggregate has acquired the ability to retain a recognizable form through time (Hawley, 1968:331). There is no requirement here that the unit have rigid spatial boundaries. Thus, a major advantage of the ecosystem framework has to do with the assumptions it does *not* require. Specifically, the ecological complex is an open systems model which abandons "the mechanistic assumptions that boundary maintenance and internal stability are necessary conditions for effective system performance" (Kasarda and Bidwell, Chapter 5 of this volume). This view of permeability and variability of boundaries follows logically from the theory of reciprocal relationships that comprise the ecological complex (Duncan, 1959) and from the ecological understanding of how change occurs (Hawley, 1968:335-6).

## ASSESSMENT

To give substance to an assessment of the contribution of the ecological complex model in sociological research, it is necessary first to provide illustrations of its application. Numerous studies have made excellent use of certain of the ideas explicit in, or derived from, the ecological complex. Not surprisingly, among the most enlightening of these is the work by Duncan et al. (1960) which explores the hierarchy of interdependence that is the essence of urban social organization. Since systemic interdependence implies both division of labor and coordination, Duncan et al. (1960) analyzed both horizontal differentiation (i.e, functional specialization), as reflected by location quotients,[2] and vertical differentiation, measured in terms of city population size and the performance of key economic functions. Both prior and subsequent to this seminal work, other analyses of the horizontal and vertical axes appeared. (Typical of the work focusing primarily on functional specialization is research by Nelson [1955] Duncan and Reiss [1956], Hadden

---

[2]*A location quotient is the ratio of the proportion of a city's labor force in a given industry to the proportion employed nationwide in the same industry (Duncan, et al., 1960).*

and Borgatta [1965], and Kass [1973, 1977]. Research giving more emphasis to coordinative functions includes that by Vance and Sutker [1954] and Bean et al. [1972]. Wanner's [1977] analysis returns to the dual emphasis found in Duncan et al. [1960].)

However, as noted by Frisbie and Eberstein (1980:34-35), little research has gone beyond the question of the functional *bases* of the system to consider the equally (or more) crucial issue of interdependence, as evidenced by exchange flows, although the latter clearly lie at the core of Duncan's (1964) treatise on the ecosystem. A few analyses have dealt with information flows, measured in terms of newspaper circulation (Winsborough et al., 1966; Preston, 1971), and monetary flows (Lieberson, 1961; Lieberson and Schwirian, 1962, Duncan and Lieberson, 1970).[3] Finally, a recent study has examined the relationship between hierarchical differentiation and commodity exchange according to the volume and heterogeneity of trade flows as well as the number of trade linkages with the environment (Eberstein and Frisbie, 1982). But none of the work cited has taken into account all four dimensions of the ecological complex, much less attempted to specify fully the mechanisms binding them into a coherent system.

A number of additional investigations might be mentioned which concentrate primarily on one dimension of the ecological complex, such as Michelson's (1970) work on the environment or Frisbie and Clarke's (1979) research on the measurement of technology. All of these are incomplete in the sense specified above.

There are, however, studies of relationships involving all four dimensions, though a few of these allow for reciprocal effects and none come to terms with the ecosystem model in its full complexity. Duncan (1961) provided an early illustration of reciprocal relationships as they relate to "smog" in Los Angeles. Beyond this, the most prominent empirical investigations relying on the ecological complex have related a single population variable, e.g., migration, to the other three dimensions via a simple recursive model. For example, Sly (1972:619) proposed a test of the following propositions: (1) "The cause of organization

---

[3]*Duncan (1964:65) concludes that "(o)f all the devices to facilitate movement of information, money may be second only to writing itself in its significance for the operation of a system of interdependent differentiated parts."*

change (O) can be found in a population's environmental (E) and technological (T) conditions." (2) "Migration (P) is a response to changes in population organization (O)". Attention is confined to black male net migration for 253 Cotton Belt counties and operationalization of the variables was limited accordingly. Nevertheless, Sly was able to adduce a fair amount of support for the hypotheses advanced, and for the analytic utility of the ecological complex. Frisbie and Poston's (1975; 1978b) studies of nonmetropolitan growth employed much the same orientation as Sly, but their analyses were couched in a "sustenance organization" framework in which little explicit use was made of the ecosystem concept.

Sly and Tayman (1977) also explored an "environmental model" of migration based on a sample of manufacturing-oriented metropolitan areas. In this case, environment, rather than organization, emerged as the key intervening variable directly affecting migration. Organizational and technological factors were assumed to affect the dependent variable indirectly through the environment. These results suggest that a different causal ordering of the ecosystem dimensions may obtain, depending on the nature of the analytical unit under investigation.

A few scholars have endeavored to extend and/or modify the conceptual underpinnings of the ecological complex. One such effort, already mentioned, is that by Kasarda and Bidwell who draw out additional implications of ecosystem theory, and derive specific, directional propositions concerning the emergence of organizational structure in response to precisely defined environmental and technological properties. Since the extension by Kasarda and Bidwell is found in a later chapter of this volume, it will not be discussed further here.

Micklin (1973:3-19; 1977) suggested a revision of the ecological complex which differs from the conventional conceptualization in at least two ways. First, he reduced the number of interdependent dimensions in the complex to three: population, environment, and organization. Five mechanisms of organizational adaptation were identified: engineering, symbolic, regulatory, coordinating, and distributive (Micklin, 1977). However, with the exception of the symbolic component, each of the mechanisms can either be subsumed under one or another of the four original ecological complex rubrics or be viewed as one among many other *functions* of ecological organization. Second, the introduction of symbolic factors sharply distinguishes the Micklin scheme from earlier work. By incorporating "social values, ideologies, customs (and) traditions" (1973:10) into the model, Micklin explicitly abandons the purely materialistic orientation of the ecosystem framework. Thus, Micklin calls into question a key ecological principle which states that populations subject to similar environmental conditions will acquire isomorphic organizational structure, irrespective of prevailing ideologies and social values (Hawley, 1968:334). In addition, this revision (clearly adumbrated in Firey's writings [1945;1947]) leads logically to the introduction of a qualitative (and evaluative) dimension of the ecological complex. Whether this expansion of the theory is to be viewed as a welcome broadening of perspective, or as an unnecessary complication, would seem to depend on one's position regarding the place of normative and subjective judgments in social science. Micklin himself is quick to point out a lack of resolution with respect to the latter issue.

Finally, it must be acknowledged that the ecological complex is not a theory in the sense of comprising a set of middle-range hypotheses, deduced from a general theory and given operational substance via successive steps down the ladder of abstractions. But if by theory one means "two or more logically interrelated assertions about the empirical relations among stipulated variables in an infinite universe" (Gibbs, 1972a:825), the ecological complex easily qualifies. But since there is no agreement (in sociology, at least) regarding just what constitutes "theory" (Gibbs, 1972a; 1972b; Costner and Blalock, 1972), arguments along this line are probably pointless.

Perhaps the most appropriate criterion for assessing the contribution of a theoretical model is the extent to which it has influenced or directed subsequent work in the field. According to this standard, the ecological complex fares either exceptionally well or extremely poorly, depending on what one means by "influenced" or "directed." On the one hand, a very large proportion of ecological research over the past 20 years has made use of one or more of the concepts embodied in the ecological complex. On the other hand, the number of empirical investigations based specifically and directly on this theoretical perspective is limited indeed. The distinction being made is this: It is one thing for research to acknowledge the conceptual influence of the ecological complex and/or to focus on one or two of its dimensions. It is quite another to conduct research designed to test the ecosystem framework in anything like its full complexity. The first undertaking is much the simpler of the two and is quite common. The latter is obviously much more difficult to achieve and has been but rarely attempted.

THE SUSTENANCE ORGANIZATION MODEL

The sustenance organization model of contemporary human ecology is characterized by a concern with the organizational aspects of human populations arising from their sustenance-producing activities. These activities are necessary for the collective existence of populations and must be adapted to the changing conditions which confront them. Included here are an everchanging and mediating environment, the technological repertoire at their disposal, and the size, composition and distribution of the populations themselves (Duncan, 1959:678-684, Frisbie and Poston, 1978b:13-14). The sustenance organization model can be distinguished from the ecological complex model by its principal focus on the analysis of sustenance organization, with somewhat less attention given to the other ecological complex dimensions of population, environment and technology. In this light, the sustenance organization model may be viewed as a subset of the ecological complex approach.

The major focus of the sustenance organization model then is the human population and its organizational structures and attributes deriving from its sustenance-producing activities. This approach seeks to answer questions such as the following: What are the structural arrangements that characterize a population's sustenance-related endeavors? Under what conditions does one form of sustenance structure appear rather than another? What are the consequences for populations of varying configurations of sustenance-producing activities?

Although it is true that the specific emphasis on sustenance organization stems from Gibbs and Martin's (1959) insistence that ecological inquiries should investigate specifically the causes and consequences of the presence or absence of certain characteristics of sustenance organization among human populations, there is considerable agreement among other major architects of contemporary human ecology that the central focus of ecology is sustenance organization.

For instance, Hawley has observed that the basic concern of human ecology is "with the general problem of organization as an attribute of population" (1968:329). Duncan (1959:683) has written that "human ecology seeks one part of the answer to the persistent questions...on the predicament of man (such as) How is human social life possible? What is the nature of the bond that holds men together?...(Among) the general answers offered by human ecology...(is that) society exists by virtue of the organization of populations of organisms, each of which is individually unequipped to survive in isolation." Schnore (1961a:139) has stated that "not only do human ecologists focus their attention on organization, but this central role given to organization...places ecology clearly within the sphere of activities in which sociologists claim distinctive competence." Despite this agreement, there has been surprisingly little attention devoted to elaborating and specifying this central concept. In this section of the chapter our principal aim is to consider jointly the various ecological analyses of sustenance organization and thereby specify its elements and dimensions. This conceptual effort will be followed by a brief assessment of the sustenance organization model in contemporary ecological research.

## A CONCEPTUAL SPECIFICATION OF SUSTENANCE ORGANIZATION

Hawley (1950:178) has observed that ecological organization "is the broad and general term used to refer to the complex of interrelationships by which men live." An organization is defined as "an arrangement of differentiated parts suited to the performance of a given function or set of functions."

Gibbs and Martin (1959:30) have written that "a brief consideration of what is entailed in sustenance organization can best begin with the conception of a population as an aggregate of individuals engaged in activities that provide them with a livelihood." The ultimate goal of human ecology is, therefore, a description of the "characteristics of sustenance organization for the population as a whole, that is, the patterning of social relationships within the population that are manifested in sustenance activities" (1959:30).

The first dimension, thus, should concern these arrangements of differentiated parts, this patterning of social relationships; that is, the degree to which the population is differentiated in its sustenance activities, viz., *sustenance differentiation*.

It is convenient to think of sustenance differentiation as consisting of two elements: the number of sustenance activities in a population (i.e., structural differentiation), and the degree of uniformity in the distribution of population members across the sustenance activities (i.e., distributive differentiation) (see Poston, Chapter 8 of this volume). A high degree of sustenance differentiation will obtain when there is a relatively large number of sustenance activities characterizing the population, and when the population members are evenly distributed across these sustenance activities.

The second dimension of sustenance organization is suggested by the "complex of interrelationships" referred to by Hawley (1950:178), and by Durkheim's insistence that there is more to the division of labor than sustenance differentiation (1949 [1893]:265). In particular, it is also necessary to focus on the degree to which goods and services are exchanged among population members in their sustenance activities, i.e., *functional interdependence* between sustenance activities. Substantial, or even modest, amounts of exchange should equire a like amount of differentiation since population members can hardly produce a surplus sufficient to exchange with others without specializing in some type of sustenance activity. To this point, the first two dimensions of sustenance organization specified are the two main features of the division of labor (cf. Gibbs and Poston, 1975).

Another structural characteristic or dimension of sustenance organization deals with the degree of *use of population members in sustenance-related pursuits*. What patterns of utilization of population members typify one population versus another, especially with regard to ascribed statuses? How fully are population members used? To what extent do inequalities exist in the population by ascribed statuses? The way populations employ their members in sustenance activities should be a particularly crucial dimension for consideration, especially if the analyst is interested in sustenance productivity and other output-related items. The degree to which populations differentiate by ascribed statuses in allocating sustenance roles to their members is therefore another characteristic of sustenance organization.

A fourth dimension of sustenance organization is its degree of *bureaucratization*. Ecologists seldom think in terms of bureaucratization when conceptualizing sustenance organization, but the concept obviously deals with aspects or features of population organization. As Frisbie (1975: 563) has observed, "an organization is bureaucratic to the extent that it has systematic, continuous administration and principles of organization characterized by specialization of function, rationality of decision-making, hierarchy of authority, and routinization of tasks...[A population] is viewed as bureaucratized to the extent that the aggregate of all organizations comprising that society reflects these attributes." Although there is some conceptual overlap between aspects of bureaucratization and sustenance differentiation,

there are also unique features in the bureaucratization
concept. It is most appropriate therefore to consider the
degree of bureaucratization as a dimension of sustenance
organization.

A fifth dimension of sustenance organization concerns
the *volume of sustenance produced* by the population. Here
we are concerned with the productivity of the particular
sustenance configuration. Certainly, some forms or configurations are more productive of sustenance than others. A
dimension measuring per capita productivity would signify
another crucial element of sustenance organization.

Related to, yet not a function of, the preceding is the
degree of *efficiency of the sustenance organization,* the
sixth dimension. It has been suggested elsewhere that a
reasonable working definition of sustenance activity is an
expenditure of energy "in the production of some good or
service, including but not limited to the pursuit of food,
water, and shelter" (Gibbs and Poston, 1975:468). A particularly appropriate operationalization of sustenance organization efficiency, perhaps, would involve examining a population's level of productivity in light of the amount of
energy consumed in the process.

A seventh dimension is concerned with the position of
the population, vis-a-vis the other ecological units *in the
hierarchy,* and reflects the degree to which the population
has influence or dominance over other populations in the
larger ecological system. This dimension of sustenance organization follows previous ecological work on nodal populations and their locations in the larger system or hierarchy.
(See the latter parts of Poston's Chapter 8 in this volume.)
The position of a particular population in the hierarchy
will depend *(inter alia)* not only on the degree to which
it generates sustenance for other populations, but also on
the degree to which it mediates the flow of sustenance
(Eberstein and Frisbie, 1982). A major issue for future ecological research thus involves the development of operational measures of hierarchical position. (The work of
Wanner 1977 is particularly instructive.)

Finally, it is necessary to consider another feature of
sustenance organization which is not a dimension in the
sense of the preceding seven. To this point, there has been
no substantive reference to sustenance organization and the
"patterning of social relationships within the population
that are manifested in sustenance activities" (Gibbs and
Martin, 1959:30). That is, the *constellation or configuration of sustenance activities* about which a population has

organized itself for survival has only been dealt with abstractly. We can now address the specific strategies whereby populations obtain sustenance.

A major product of the ecological work of Duncan and his colleagues (Duncan, et al., 1960; Galle, 1963; Duncan and Lieberson, 1970) is identification of the dominant sustenance functions in the principal metropolitan areas of the United States, allowing them to link these key functions to others in the social system. While specification of these linkages is of central importance for the study of metropolitan regions, the identification of sustenance functions is in itself of equal import to ecologists.

Most of the earlier ecological research on the sustenance differentiation dimension of the division of labor (principally the work of Gibbs and his colleagues) investigated the substance and correlates of differentiation, nationally and internationally. The major interests were in the distribution of population members in sustenance activities and the number of activities characterizing the population. In an impressive series of inquiries, these questions and interests were addressed and, as a result of this research, our knowledge of differentiation and the division of labor has been enhanced. Seldom in this tradition, however, were the specific components or major activities making up sustenance organization identified and discussed.

In research published in the 1970s, Frisbie and Poston (1975; 1976; 1978b) have attempted to integrate these two research traditions in human ecology by concerning themselves with the number, types, and principal effects of different constellations of sustenance activities that are dissimilar enough to warrant substantive specification. And they have demonstrated that the effects on demographic change vary depending upon the sustenance component or components examined.

Accordingly, in considering the seven dimensions of sustenance organization discussed above, it is also useful to identify the principal activities around which the population's pursuits for sustenance are organized. Thus, in obtaining a comprehensive representation of a population's sustenance organization, the ecologist would want to identify the major sustenance functions that characterize the organization, as well as its levels of sustenance differentiation, functional interdependence, differentiation by ascription, sustenance productivity, sustenance efficiency, and its position in the larger hierarchy of populations. The result is a more complete and definitive elaboration of the pattern of sustenance organization.

In Figure 1, the seven dimensions are listed vertically; a suggested list of seven sustenance functions or activities is presented on the horizontal axis. The actual specification of sustenance functions must be determined empirically but the seven components identified (manufacturing, retailing, wholesaling, transportation/communication, construction, education, finance/commerce) suggest the kinds of sustenance components typical of many of the populations studied by hguman ecologists. These are meant as examples and, thus, some components are omitted. For example, many populations are characterized by one or more agricultural functions (Frisbie and Poston, 1975; 1978b) as well as by additional service functions.

Referring to Figure 1, a population's sustenance organization may be characterized by two elements of sustenance differentiation when this dimension is measured over all the sustenance components: structural differentiation $(A_{1a})$ and distributive differentiation $(A_{1b})$. The ecologist may also determine the level of exchange across all the sustenance components, i.e., functional interdependence $(A_2)$. Moreover, there should be an interest in the degree to which the population is differentiated in the assignment of sustenance activities by sex, age, ethnic status, and so on, across all the sustenance functions $(A_3)$. The degree of bureaucratization $(A_4)$ and the amount of productivity $(A_5)$ of the populations sustenance organization may also be ascertained. Also of interest is the degree of efficiency in the productivity of the population's sustenance organization $(A_6)$. Finally, one could determine the location of this particular population's sustenance organization in the larger hierarchy of sustenance organizations $(A_7)$.

In addition to involvement in one or more of these seven dimensions of sustenance organization, the population will also participate in a number of sustenance functions at particular levels of involvement, and it is possible to develop indexes reflecting these participation levels. Considered in Figure 1, as the eighth dimension, is the population's level of sustenance involvement. Since the population will likely be involved in each of the sustenance functions, albeit in varying degrees, these overall levels of involvement in each function are represented on the bottom row of Figure 1. There is a level of involvement for each sustenance function $(M_8, R_8, W_8, T_8, C_8, E_8, F_8)$.

Having specified a population's standing on each of seven dimensions, and having ascertained the level of participation of the population in each of the sustenance functions, the human ecologist is now in a position to examine

112

Figure 1.

A TAXONOMY OF SUSTENANCE ORGANIZATION: DIMENSION BY COMPONENTS

| DIMENSIONS | All Components Combined (Total) | COMPONENTS (functions) | | | | | | |
|---|---|---|---|---|---|---|---|---|
| | | Manufacturing | Retailing | Wholesaling | Transportation/ Communication | Construction | Education | Finance/ Commerce |
| 1. Sustenance Differentiation | | | | | | | | |
| 1.a. Structural Differentiation | $A_{1a}$ | $M_{1a}$ | $R_{1a}$ | $W_{1a}$ | $T_{1a}$ | $C_{1a}$ | $E_{1a}$ | $F_{1a}$ |
| 1.b. Distributive Differentiation | $A_{1b}$ | $M_{1b}$ | $R_{1b}$ | $W_{1b}$ | $T_{1b}$ | $C_{1b}$ | $E_{1b}$ | $F_{1b}$ |
| 2. Functional Interdependence | $A_2$ | $M_2$ | $R_2$ | $W_2$ | $T_2$ | $C_2$ | $E_2$ | $F_2$ |
| 3. Differentiation by Ascription | $A_3$ | $M_3$ | $R_3$ | $W_3$ | $T_3$ | $C_3$ | $E_3$ | $F_3$ |
| 4. Bureaucratization | $A_4$ | $M_4$ | $R_4$ | $W_4$ | $T_4$ | $C_4$ | $E_4$ | $F_4$ |
| 5. Sustenance Productivity | $A_5$ | $M_5$ | $R_5$ | $W_5$ | $T_5$ | $C_5$ | $E_5$ | $F_5$ |
| 6. Efficiency of Productivity | $A_6$ | $M_6$ | $R_6$ | $W_6$ | $T_6$ | $C_6$ | $E_6$ | $F_6$ |
| 7. Hierarchical Location | $A_7$ | $M_7$ | $R_7$ | $W_7$ | $T_7$ | $C_7$ | $E_7$ | $F_7$ |
| 8. Level of Sustenance Involvement | $A_8$ | $M_8$ | $R_8$ | $W_8$ | $T_8$ | $C_8$ | $E_8$ | $F_8$ |

again each of the seven sustenance dimensions, but this time *within* each of the sustenance components or functions. Put another way, the investigator may take each of the seven sustenance functions, one at a time, and examine the population's standing on each of the seven sustenance dimensions in light of the particular sustenance component.

For example, under the manufacturing function (M), one could identify the population's degree of sustenance differentiation in manufacturing. How many manufacturing activities comprise the manufacturing function, structural differentiation ($M_{1a}$), and how evenly are the population members distributed in these manufacturing activities, i.e., distributive differentiation ($M_{1b}$)? One could also examine the degree of functional interdependence across the specific manufacturing activities ($M_2$) and how much exchange of product occurs from one manufacturing activity to the other. One could then ascertain the extent to which the population differentiates among its members, according to sex, race and age, in allocating manufacturing sustenance roles to its members ($M_3$). Also of interest would be the level of bureaucratization of the manufacturing portion of the population's sustenance organization ($M_4$). The next questions entertained would have to do with the amount of manufacturing sustenance produced by the population ($M_5$), the extent to which the manufacturing productivity was efficient ($M_6$) and a determination of where the population was located in the larger ecological system of manufacturing units ($M_7$).

Thus, instead of referring to overall sustenance productivity ($A_5$), for example, one could speak of manufacturing productivity ($M_5$), retailing productivity ($R_5$), construction productivity ($C_5$). Instead of speaking gnerally of the extent to which the population differentially allocates all sustenance roles by ascription ($A_3$), one could refer to differentiation by ascription in manufacturing ($M_3$), in retailing ($R_3$), in wholesaling ($W_3$), in construction ($C_3$), etc. And one could continue through the remaining four dimensions of sustenance organization, suggesting how each component could be represented in terms of the respective dimensions.

In earlier research, Frisbie and Poston (1975; 1978b) found no reason to assume that the populations they were studying should array themselves in the same manner on each of a number of components of sustenance organization; they neither hypothesized nor found that the effects of each of the sustenance components on population change would be identical. Similarly, one should not necessarily anticipate a *priori* that populations will display the same patterns of variability on, say, all forms of sustenance productivity, irrespective of the particular sustenance component examined, or that populations will differentiate by ascription at the same levels in the assignment of sustenance roles irrespective of the sustenance components, and so on.

The taxonomy of sustenance organization presented in Figure 1 appears to be logically consistent and amenable to empirical inquiry. In an attempt to develop a better understanding of the structure and form of sustenance organization, ecologists need now to examine the matrix empirically: How do the component-specific dimensions of sustenance organization vary with one another? Although it appears that the seven sustenance dimensions are conceptually distinct from one another, it is possible that empirically one (or more) of them is highly related with others. Such a result could well be obtained when the seven dimensions are examined empirically in their component-specific forms. At this date there simply has not been sufficient empirical attention directed to this question. However, ecologists have engaged in empirical investigations of many of the sustenance dimenions per se (that is, with regard to the component-specific features of them), and we turn now to a brief assessment of these activities.

## ASSESSMENT

This section would normally involve an examination of each of the dimensions of sustenance organization in light of the extent to which they have contributed to the advancement of empirical inquiry in human ecology. However, since Chapter 8 in this volume reviews in detail the theoretical and empirical literature of human ecology dealing specifically with the dimensions of sustenance organization, it is not necessary to detail these same studies here. Instead, we will subject each of the sustenance dimensions to a rather brief empirical review, leaving the more intensive discussions of the principal dimensions of sustenance organization to the later chapter.

Of all the dimensions of sustenance organization, those receiving the most attention from a theoretical point of view are the first two listed in Figure 1: sustenance differentiation and functional interdependence. These two dimensions are the major features of the division of labor as defined by Durkheim (1893) and others (e.g., Lampard, 1955; Gibbs and Martin, 1962; Gibbs and Poston, 1975). Indeed, Poston (Chapter 8 of this volume) notes that most ecological inquiries conducted through the 1960s dealing with sustenance organization focused conceptually on the

division of labor, while operationalizing it with the
sustenance differentiation dimension alone (Gibbs and
Martin, 1962; Labovitz and Gibbs, 1964; Gibbs and Browning,
1966; among others). Ecologists have largely restricted
their investigations of the division of labor to the sustenance differentiation dimension both in their empirical
inquiries (cf. those studies just mentioned), and in their
conceptual and methodological work (Gibbs and Poston, 1975).
The functional interdependence dimension has received
virtually no empirical attention (see Eberstein, 1979, and
Eberstein and Frisbie, 1980, 1982 for important exceptions).
Some have operationalized only the differentiation dimension
assuming that it varies with the interdependence dimension
(Browning and Gibbs, 1971:234).

Despite these emphases, the sustenance differentiation
dimension of the division of labor has been the subject of
numerous ecological inquiries. Some have investigated the
determinants of differentiation in human populations (Gibbs
and Martin, 1962; Clemente and Sturgis, 1972) while others
have addressed the consequences of varying patterns of
sustenance differentiation on such dependent variables as
population change (Sly, 1972; Frisbie and Poston, 1978a,
1978b:54-65; Sly and Tayman, 1977), crime (Webb, 1972) and
suicide (Miley and Micklin, 1972).

The dimension of sustenance organization dealing with
differentiation by ascription has also been the subject of
ecological investigations. Hawley (1950), of course, discusses this dimension at length from a theoretical standpoint, and the literature is replete with descriptive
investigations of the phenomenon (Gibbs, 1965; Johansen,
1970; Johnson, 1972; Martin and Poston, 1972). There has
been limited attention directed to the determinants of
differentiation by ascription from an ecological vantage
point (see Poston and Johnson, 1971; Martin and Poston,
1976; and Johnson, 1977; as examples). These studies have
sought to demonstrate the viability of an ecological approach for furthering the understanding of variations among
human populations in the extent of differential allocation
of population members (especially by race and by sex) in
sustenance activities.

The major ecological analysis of bureaucratization is
Frisbie's (1975) study which is discussed at length by
Poston (Chapter 8 in this volume). South (1979) has recently
examined the ecological determinants and consequences of
variability in bureaucratization among metropolitan areas of
the United States. He shows that bureaucratization plays an

important role in understanding metropolitan community structure and process and thus deserves more theoretical and empirical attention in ecological studies than it has received to date (1979:84).

The two dimensions of sustenance productivity and efficiency of productivity have received only minimal conceptual and empirical attention by ecologists. In two companion studies of ecological determinants of migration in the first half of the 1970s, Poston (1980, 1981) has shown that both of these dimensions have influential effects. Labovitz and Gibbs (1964) and Gibbs and Browning (1966), developed an efficiency index in their ecological studies, but applied the measure as a representation of technological rather than organizational efficiency. Ecologists have not yet studied the determinants of sustenance productivity and efficiency.

The seventh dimension of sustenance organization is hierarchical location. Next to the sustenance differentiation dimension, it has perhaps received the most attention from ecologists since 1950. The phenomenon has been addressed descriptively and methodologically, and it has been studied from the standpoints of both its determinants and its consequences (Duncan et al., 1960; Wanner, 1977). The latter half of Chapter 8 (below) examines in detail the considerable literature directed to the analysis of this dimension.

Finally, the last dimension to be addressed is sustenance involvement. We have noted earlier in this section of the chapter that studies examining a population's involvement in sustenance activities, i.e., the components of sustenance organization, have merited the attention of human ecologists in only the last few years. Indeed, the work of Frisbie and Poston (1975; 1978a; 1978b) dealing with the effects of sustenance components on population change stemmed from their interest in linking two influential research traditions in human ecology, those of Duncan and his colleagues, and of Gibbs, Martin and their colleagues. A discussion of these foci, and their culmination in investigations of sustenance components, receives considerable attention elsewhere, both in this chapter, and in Chapter 8, below.

We concluded the preceding section by asking to what extent the ecological complex model has influenced or directed subsequent research in human ecology. We might now seek to answer the same questionfor the sustenance organization model. Gibbs and Martin have written that ecological inquiries should investigate the causes and consequences of the presence or absence of certain characteristics of sustenance organization. If this mandate is taken to represent the objectives of research within the framework of sustenance organization, then one must conclude that extensive research has been conducted over the past decades, particularly since 1970, following this approach. The number of empirical investigations is impressive, and the body of research addresses both the determinants and consequences of dimensions of sustenance organization. On the other hand, the sustenance organization model has not been the subject of investigations utilizing its full potential and complexity, as tentatively outlined in Figure 1. Hopefully ecologists in the years ahead will examine more complex models of sustenance organization and attempt to identify their causes and consequences. More detailed and systematic research endeavors are necessary before we will possess more than an elementary understanding of the structure and form of sustenance organization.

## CONCLUDING COMMENT

In this chapter we have reviewed three related lines of development in the theoretical foundation of sociological human ecology. The early work of Amos Hawley--particularly his *Human Ecology* (1950)--provided the basic structure and direction for the subsequent development of the ecological complex and sustenance organization approaches. Although these latter two models differ somewhat in conceptual organization, they share a common set of underlying assumptions and circumscribe a more or less common domain of inquiry. In short, the major theoretical developments in sociological human ecology over the past three decades show a remarkable degree of continuity and consistency.

As concluded earlier in this chapter, the ecological complex and sustenance organization models have generated and guided a substantial number of empirical studies. This fact alone is indicative of the vitality and productivity of these theoretical orientations. Nonetheless, further theoretical advancements are needed. One direction for future work would involve a comprehensive and critical synthesis of the findings from the empirical research mentioned above. This would serve to identify those components of ecological theory that are most useful for explaining empirical variations and would begin to build a body of cumulative knowledge. Another task for sociological ecologists is to formalize the core of their theoretical system into a set of specific assumptions, postulates, and hypotheses that reflect the underlying integrity of the field. Finally, though this recommendation may generate considerable resistance from within, it may be both useful and interesting to begin to bridge the gap between the theoretical foundation of sociological human ecology and that which characterizes the ecological approach in other disciplines. Parsimony is one of the principal goals of scientific inquiry, and this is no less true of work in human ecology.

REFERENCES

Bean, F. D., D. L. Poston, Jr., and H. H. Winsborough (1972). "Size, functional specialization and the classification of cities." Social Science Quarterly 53 (June):20-32.

Berry, B. J. L. and J. D. Kasarda (1977). Contemporary Urban Ecology. New York: Macmillan.

Browning, H. L. and J. P. Gibbs (1971). "Intra-industry division of labor: the states of Mexico." Demography 8 (May):233-245.

Clemente, F. and R. Sturgis (1972). "The division of labor in America: an ecological analysis." Social Forces 51 (December):176-182.

Costner, H. L. and H. M. Blalock, Jr. (1972). "Scientific fundamentalism and scientific utility: a reply to Gibbs." Social Science Quarterly 52 (March):827-844.

Duncan, B. and S. Lieberson (1970). Metropolis and Region in Transition. Beverly Hills: Sage.

Duncan, O. D. (1959). "Human ecology and population studies." Pp. 678-716 in P. M. Hauser and O. D. Duncan (eds.), The Study of Population. Chicago: University of Chicago Press.

Duncan, O. D. (1961). "From social system to ecosystem." Sociological Inquiry 31 (Spring):140-149.

Duncan, O. D. (1964). "Social organization and the ecosystem." Pp. 36-82 in R. E. L. Faris (ed.), Handbook of Modern Sociology. Chicago: Rand McNally.

Duncan, O. D. and A. J. Reiss, Jr. (1956). Social Characteristics of Urban and Rural Communities, 1950. New York: Wiley.

Duncan, O. D., W. R. Scott, S. Lieberson, B. Duncan and H. H. Winsborough (1960). Metropolis and Region. Baltimore: Johns Hopkins University Press.

Durkheim, E. (1893). The Division of Labor in Society. New York: Free Press, 1949.

Eberstein, I. W. (1979). Intercommunity Sustenance Flow and the Metropolitan Hierarchy. Austin: The University of Texas at Austin, Department of Sociology. Unpublished doctoral dissertation.

Eberstein, I. W. and W. P. Frisbie (1980). Metropolitan Function and Intercommunity Exchange in the U.S. Urban System. Austin: University of Texas Population Research Center Papers. Series 2: No. 2.007.

Eberstein, W. W. and W. P. Frisbie (1982). "Metropolitan function and interdependence in the U.S. urban system." Social Forces 60 (June): forthcoming.

Firey, W. (1945). "Sentiment and symbolism as ecological variables." American Sociological Review 10(2):140-148.

Firey, W. (1947). Land Use in Central Boston. Cambridge, MA.: Harvard University Press.

Frisbie. W. P. (1975). "Measuring the degree of bureaucratization at the societal level." Social Forces 53 (June): 563-573.

Frisbie, W. P. and C. J. Clarke (1979). "Technology in evolutionary and ecological perspective: theory and measurement at the societal level." Social Forces 58 (December): 591-613.

Frisbie, W. P. and C. J. Clarke (1980). "Further notes on the conceptualization of technology." 59 (December): 529-534.

Frisbie, W. P. and D. L. Poston, Jr. (1975). "Components of sustenance organization and nonmetropolitan population change: a human ecological investigation." American Sociological Review 40 (December):773-784.

Frisbie, W. P. and D. L. Poston, Jr. (1976). "The structure os sustenance organization and population change in nonmetropolitan America." Rural Sociology 41 (Fall):354-370.

Frisbie, W. P. and D. L. Poston, Jr. (1978a). "Sustenance differentiation and population redistribution." Social Forces 57 (September):42-56.

Frisbie, W. P. and D. L. Poston, Jr. (1978b). Sustenance Organization and Migration in Nonmetropolitan America. Iowa City: Iowa Urban Community Research Center, University of Iowa Press.

Galle, O. (1963). "Occupational composition and metropolitan hierarchy: the inter- and intra-metropolitan division of labor." American Journal of Sociology 69 (November): 260-269.

Gibbs, J. P. (1972a). "Causation and theory construction." Social Science Quarterly 52 (March):813-826.

Gibbs, J. P. (1972b). "A fundamentalistic rejoinder." Social Science Quarterly 52 (March):845-851.

Gibbs, J. P. (1965). "Occupational differentiation of Negroes and white in the United States." Social Forces 44 (December):159-165.

Gibbs, J. P. and H. L. Browning (1966). "The division of labor, technology and the organization of production in twelve countries." American Sociological Review 31 (February):81-92.

Gibbs, J. P. and W. T. Martin (1959). "Toward a theoretical system of human ecology." Pacific Sociological Review 2 (Spring):29-36.

Gibbs, J. P. and W. T. Martin (1962). "Urbanization, technology and the division of labor: international patterns." American Sociological Review 27 (October):667-677.

Gibbs, J. P. and D. L. Poston, Jr. (1975). "The division of labor: conceptualization and related measures." Social Forces 53 (March):468-476.

Hadden, J. K. and E. F. Borgatta (1965). American Cities: Their Social Characteristics. Chicago: Rand McNally.

Hawley, A. H. (1944). "Ecology and human ecology." Social Forces 22:398-405.

Hawley, A. H. (1950). Human Ecology: A Theory of Community Structure. New York: Ronald Press.

Hawley, A. H. (1968). "Human ecology." In D. L. Sills (ed.), International Encyclopedia of the Social Sciences, Vol. 4. New York: Crowell, Collier and MacMillan, pp. 328-337.

Hawley, A. H. (1971; revised 1981). Urban Society: An Ecological Approach. New York: Ronald Press.

Hawley, A. H. (1972). "Population density and the city." Demography 9:521-529.

Hawley, A. H. (1973). "Ecology and population." Science 179:1196-1201.

Hawley, A. H. (1978). "Cumulative change in theory and in history." American Sociological Review 43:787-796.

Johansen, E. J. (1970). The Sexual Basis of the Division of Labor: Interstate Variation in Labor Force Participation Rates by Sex in the United States. Austin: The University of Texas at Austin, Department of Sociology. Unpublished Ph.D. dissertation.

Johnson, G. C. (1972). Professional Differentiation by Sex in the Metropolitan United States: A Descriptive and Methodological Study. Austin: The University of Texas at Austin, Department of Sociology. Unpublished M.A. thesis.

Johnson, G. C. (1977). Metropolitan Sustenance Organization and Professional Sexual Differentiation: An Ecological Study. Austin: The University of Texas at Austin, Department of Sociology. Unpublished Ph.D. dissertation.

Kass, R. (1973). "A functional classification of metropolitan communities." Demography 10:427-445.

Kuhn, T. (1962). The Structure of Scientific Revolutions. Chicago: University of Chicago Press.

Labovitz, S. and J. P. Gibbs (1964). "Urbanization, technology, and the division of labor: further evidence." Pacific Sociological Review 7 (Spring):3-9.

Lampard, E. E. (1955). "The history of cities in the economically advanced areas." Economic Development and Cultural Change 3 (January):81-136.

Lenski, G. E. (1970). Human Societies. New York: McGraw-Hill.

Lieberson, S. (1961). "The division of labor in banking." American Journal of Sociology 66 (March):491-496.

Lieberson, S. and K. P. Schwirian (1962). "Banking functions as an index of inter-city relations." Journal of Regional Science 4:69-81.

Martin, W. T. and D. L. Poston, Jr. (1972). "The occupational composition of white females: sexism, racism and occupational differentiation." Social Forces 50 (March): 349-355.

Martin, W. T. and D. L. Poston, Jr. (1976). "Industrialization and occupational differentiation: an ecological analysis." Pacific Sociological Review 19 (January):82-97.

Michelson, W. (1970; revised 1976). Man and His Urban Environment: A Sociological Approach. Reading, MA.: Addison-Wesley.

Micklin, M. (1973). "Introduction: a framework for the study of human ecology." Pp. 2-19 in M. Micklin (ed.) Population, Environment, and Social Organization: Current Issues in Human Ecology. Hinsdale, IL.: Dryden.

Micklin, M. (1977). "Population, ecology, scarcity." In R. Perrucci et al., Sociology: Basic Structures and Processes. Dubuque: W. G. Brown, pp. 507-551.

Miley, J. D. and M. Micklin (1972). "Structural change and the Durkheimian legacy: a macrosocial analysis of suicide rates." American Journal of Sociology 89 (November):657-673.

Nelson, H. J. (1955). "A service classification of cities." Economic Geography 31:189-210.

Ogburn, W. F. (1955). "Technology and the standard of living in the United States." American Journal of Sociology 60:380-386.

Poston, D. L., Jr. and G. C. Johnson (1971). "Industrialization and professional differentiation by sex in the metropolitan Southwest." Social Science Quarterly 52 (September):331-348.

Poston, D. L., Jr. and R. White (1978). "Indigenous labor supply, sustenance organization, and population redistribution in nonmetropolitan America: an extension of the ecological theory of migration." Demography 15 (November): 637-641.

Poston, D. L., Jr. (1980). "An ecological analysis of migration in metropolitan America, 1970-75." Social Science Quarterly 61 (December):418-433.

Poston, D. L., Jr. (1981). "An ecological examination of southern population redistribution, 1970-1975." Chapter 5 in The Population of the South: Structure and Change in Social Demographic Perspective, D. L. Poston, Jr. and R. H. Weller (eds.). Austin: The University of Texas Press.

Preston, R. E. (1971). "The structure of central place systems." Economic Geography 47:136-155.

Price, D. O. and M. M. Sykes (1975). Rural-Urban Migration Research in the United States. Washington, D.C.: U.S. Government Printing Office.

Schnore, L. F. (1958). "Social morphology and human ecology." American Journal of Sociology 63 (May):620-634.

Schnore, L. F. (1961). "The myth of human ecology." Sociological Inquiry 31 (Spring):128-139.

Sjoberg, G. (1965). "Cities in developing and in industrial societies: a cross-cultural analysis." Pp. 213-263 in P. M. Hauser and L. F. Schnore (eds.), The Study of Urbanization. New York: Wiley.

Sly, D. F. (1972). "Migration and the ecological complex." American Sociological Review 37 (October):615-628.

Sly, D. F. and D. Tayman (1977). "The ecological approach to migration re-examined." American Sociological Review 42 (October):783-795.

South, S. J. (1979). An Ecological Approach to Bureaucratization. Austin: The University of Texas at Austin, Department of Sociology. Unpublished M.A. thesis.

Vance, R. B. and S. S. Sutker (1954). "Metropolitan dominance and integration." Chapter 6 in R. B. Vance and N. J. Demerath (eds.), The Urban South. Chapel Hill: University of North Carolina Press.

Wanner, R. A. (1977). "The dimensionality of the urban functional system." Demography 14 (November):519-537.

Webb, S. D. (1972). "Crime and the division of labor: testing a Durkheimian model." American Journal of Sociology 78 (November):643-656.

# 4
# Data and Methods
# in Human Ecology

*W. Parker Frisbie*

> There is such a surfeit of methodological litera-
> ture in the social sciences that one who proposes
> to contribute an increment thereto is well advised
> to make his apologies in advance.
>
> —Duncan, Cuzzort and Duncan (1961:3)

So spoke three wise social scientists in a preliminary
statement to a methodological volume for which little in the
way of apology is necessary. However, the general point no
doubt remains applicable. Perhaps the most relevant apologetic to be made for this essay on recent trends in data
manipulation and methodology in human ecology—one set in
the midst of a number of theoretical and/or policy oriented
statements—is to point out the necessary, but not sufficient, nature of the relationship between methods and substantive analysis. That is, good methodology does not
guarantee a substantive contribution, but certainly no contribution will emanate from poor methodology. Thus a volume

125

surveying trends in ecological theory and research would be incomplete without recognition of some of the issues involved in the actual measurement and manipulation of variables. Obviously this task cannot be accomplished in a single essay of moderate length, nor, for that matter, in an entire volume. Nonetheless, it should prove useful to review selectively the progress made by ecologists over the past three decades in resolving salient methodological problems.

As is well known, the substantive thrust of human ecology has shifted away from a narrow focus on spatial arrangements. In fact, while much of the work of early ecologists was descriptive rather than analytical in nature, the perception that classical ecology was typified by a unidimensional obsession with spatial patterns is erroneous. The constricted emphasis on mapping of characteristics of urban areas itself represented an unfortunate diversion from an earlier and more comprehensive interest in community structure—i.e., an overreaction to trenchant critiques such as those by Davie (1937), Alihan (1938), and Firey (1945). (See Berry and Kasarda [1977] for elaboration.) For a brief period, the view of human ecology "as little more than a collection of techniques for the study of spatial distributions" (see Duncan, 1959:678 for corrective comments) may have been partially appropriate. Rather soon, however, as a result of the landmark contributions by "neo-ecological" theorists (Hawley, 1944b, 1950; Schnore, 1958, 1961; Gibbs and Martin, 1959; Duncan, 1959, 1961, 1964), the central interest of human ecology came to reside in macro-level analysis of the organizational structures and processes through which human populations adapt to and compete within their environment both natural and social. (For a more complete statement see Duncan, 1959:681-684). Since human populations constitute the analytical frame of reference of human ecology (Hawley, 1950), a crucial assumption is that it is possible to identify "spatially delimited population aggregates (that) have unit character"[1] (Duncan, 1959: 681). Therefore the methodology of human ecology has come to have at least two general characteristics:

---

[1] *An organized population is possessed of unit character to the extent that it "tends to be a self-maintaining whole," not in the sense of independence from the environment, but in the sense that it has acquired "the instrumentalities for continuing its existence indefinitely" (Hawley, 1971b:8).*

(1) a focus on measurement of organizational structural and processual variables, and (2) a necessary concentration on macro-level analytic techniques.

Although the methodological and statistical issues (the two are always linked either directly or indirectly) treated in this paper are by no means exclusively ecological, they are certainly closely related to the emphases that are unique to the ecological perspective. Inevitably, of course, certain significant issues are treated superficially or not at all. But, wherever possible, those selected for comment are accompanied by concrete illustrations drawn from the literature and, in a few instances, from examples developed by this author. In general, the argument is made that the predictive power of ecological theory can be most forcefully established by broadening its application through methods designed to take advantage of cross-temporal, cross-level, and cross-national analyses.

The general conceptual model underlying this discussion derives from Hawley's neoclassical perspective (1944b, 1950, 1968, 1971a) in which the "central problem...is understanding how *a population organizes itself* in adapting to a constantly changing yet restricting environment" (Berry and Kasarda, 1977:12; (emphasis added). Duncan (1959) of course has identified four variables central to ecological analysis: population, organization, environment, and technology. However, the emphasis throughout is primarily on the organizational dimension since it is apparent that it is this component that, since 1950, has been the focus of the overwhelming majority of ecological analyses carried out by sociologists.

## MEASUREMENT OF ECOLOGICAL CONCEPTS:
## ORGANIZATIONAL STRUCTURE AND PROCESS

An illuminating and representative statement of the general analytical focus of contemporary human ecology is given by Duncan who notes that "the framework for its elaboration of theory and an outline of its research tasks" emerges from human ecology's answers to the fundamental question of how collective life is possible:

> Society exists by virtue of the organization of a population of organisms, each of which is individually unequipped to survive in isolation. Organization represents an adaptation to the unavoidable circumstance that individuals are interdependent and that the collectivity of individuals must cope with concrete environmental

conditions—including, perhaps, competition and resistance afforded by other collectivities—with whatever technological means may be at its disposal. The "social bond," in its more basic aspect, is precisely this interdependence of units in a more or less elaborated division of labor, aptly described as "functional integration" (1959:683).

In the following sections, the progress made in giving operational substance to several prominent ecological concepts, either explicit or implicit in Duncan's concise statement, is reviewed.

## SUSTENANCE ORGANIZATION

The central role of the concept of sustenance organization in ecology is seen in the statements of major contemporary theorists. Hawley defines organization as the "entire system of interdependences among the members of a population which enables the latter to *sustain itself as a unit* (1971a:12, emphasis added). Earlier Hawley (1948:155) suggested that

> The ecological problem is: How does a population organize to maintain itself in a given area? This places an emphasis on sustenance relations, yet sustenance relations are regarded as constituting only the general framework of the community. To find the answer to his problem the ecologist must be able to trace out the ramifications of sustenance activities and ascertain the degree to which they affect and are in turn affected by other kinds of activities.

It has been maintained that a crucial assumption of human ecology is that organization "arises from sustenance-producing activities" (Duncan, 1959:682), and that sustenance organization constitutes the fundamental subject matter of human ecology (Gibbs and Martin, 1959:34). Although in theoretical terms many contemporary ecologists seem to have found sustenance organization a useful point of departure, empirical analysis of the concept has been neglected (or ignored [see Gibbs and Martin, 1959:30]), except for the early taxonomic work of Gibbs and Martin. However, recent research has, via conventional factor analytic methods, identified several configurations or modes of sustenance activities, developed indices, and demonstrated the contribution of the concept to empirical explanations of variation in population change in general, and in net migration in particular (Frisbie and Poston, 1975; 1976; 1978). While this research has uncovered certain consequences of the presence of different modes of sustenance activity and of the degree of differentiation among them, numerous other dimensions of the concept remain to be operationalized. As an illustration, the effects observed must be partially a function of differential levels of productivity as these vary by type of sustenance activity. Unfortunately, absence of relevant data prevents a full examination of this assumption, for although information exists that bears directly on the productivity of some sustenance activities such as manufacturing and retail service functions, for other modes, such as educational and public administration services, no comparable data are available. Nor is it clear how productivity should be conceptualized with respect to the latter. In recent taxonomic research Poston (this volume) has developed several important dimensions of sustenance organization which may serve as a model guiding both the methodological and substantive extensions of research dealing with the concept. Hopefully, future research will identify other dimensions and indicators which will prove useful in exploring the construct further. One dimension of sustenance organization that has received extensive treatment is the degree of differentiation evident in a population.

THE DIVISION OF LABOR

Given the fundamental significance of sustenance organization, it is logical to find the division of labor defined as "differences among members of a population in their sustenance activities and the related functional interdependence (Gibbs and Poston, 1975:469; see also Clemente, 1972).

Although there is room for debate concerning the specific nuances of the substantive definition, there is widespread consensus as to the theoretical significance of the concept. Yet, until a series of seminal articles by Gibbs and several co-authors (Gibbs and Martin, 1962; Labovitz and Gibbs, 1964; Gibbs and Browning, 1966), it could be said that (at least since Durkheim) insufficient attention had been given to empirical analysis of the division of labor (Lampard. 1968:100) and that attempts to operationalize the concept had "employed ad hoc procedures devoid of an adequate conceptual rationale, possessing questionable face validity and lacking...methodological import" (Clemente, 1972:31; see also Clemente and Sturgis, 1972: 176).

Gibbs and his colleagues developed a measure of the division of labor sometimes denoted the Measure of Functional Dispersion (Clemente, 1972), the Measure of Industrial Diversification (Clemente and Sturgis, 1972), an indicator of sustenance differentiation (Frisbie and Poston, 1978), and simply as $M_1$ (Gibbs and Poston, 1975). Regardless of nomenclature, which varies with the focus of analysis (e.g., intraindustry versus interindustry differentiation), the measure is computed:

$$M_1 = 1 - (\Sigma X^2 / (\Sigma X)^2)$$

where X is the number of individuals in any one of two or more categories. The measure has been shown to be related in a theoretically consistent manner to other variables of ecological interest, including urbanization, population size, size of productive association, and level of technology (Gibbs and Martin, 1962; Gibbs and Browning, 1966; Clemente and Sturgis, 1972; Frisbie, 1975b).

Nevertheless, certain methodological criticisms of $M_1$ have been raised (some by the developers of the measure) including the following:

(1) A problem of comparability arises when the number of categories (k) varies from unit to unit since while the lowest score possible is zero, the maximum varies directly with k.

(2) The measure reflects only the distribution among a given number of categories and can make no finer distinction.

(3) The measure is not sensitive to functional interdependence.

The first problem is easily resolved via standardization achieved through use of

$$M'_1 = M_1/M_{max} \text{ where } M_{max} = 1 - 1/k.$$

(The standardized index is referred to as $M_2$ by Gibbs and Poston, 1975). As a further interpretation, Rushing and Davies (1970) have shown that $M'_1 = 1 - A/A_{max}$ where A is the variance of a particular distribution and $A_{max}$ is the maximum variance possible.

Although $M_1$ gets at distributive differentiation, i.e., the uniformity of the distribution across categories, it does not reflect what Gibbs and Poston (1975:470) term structural differentiation. i.e., "the number of categories or types of sustenance activities in a population" and also does not possess the desirable quality of varying between 0 and 1. Thus Gibbs and Poston (1975) have proposed other measures that resolve either one or the other of the two problems just mentioned. The interested reader is referred to that source for details.

More recently, Smith and Snow (1976) have offered an alternative set of measures based initially on the coefficient of variation, with adjustments so that their indexes also reflect the proportional distribution regardless of the number of categories and with variation between 0 and 1. Smith and Snow conclude that certain of their indicators, expressed in terms of relative variability as a function of maximum variability, behave more appropriately than the more conventional indicators under conditions where distributions vary as to means, frequencies, and number of categories.

Regardless of the comparative utility of either set of measures, three issues remain unresolved. First, while several indexes tap both variation in the number of categories and dispersion among them, neither set reflects degree of functional interdependence or integration, a crucial aspect of the conceptual definition. Hence some authors (Frisbie and Poston, 1978) have preferred to refer to the underlying concept as "sustenance differentiation" rather than the "division of labor." Second, despite the definite theoretical import of variation in the number of functional categories, the substantive meaning of scores is ambiguous unless such differences ensue from real diversification of function instead of from record-keeping peculiarities based on considerations of practicality and convenience.

Third, a related question pertains to any of the measures, especially as applied to interindustry dispersion. To illustrate, most countries now report distributions according to International Standard Industrial Classification categories. Since the number of categories is the same for all countries, a question of validity is apparent. At the stage of development when a nation's labor force is being redistributed from a concentration in extractive industry across other industrial classes, the measure seems clearly appropriate. However, at some point, there may be a "reconcentration" in certain tertiary industries which, without addition of new categories, must result in a deflation of scores that is at least partly artifactual. Would the fact that the U.S., e.g., at one point in time, might come to have a score below that recorded at an earlier point (or below that of certain developing nations), indicate a regression in the degree of division of labor? Likely not. Just as evident, of course, is the fact that such an anomaly stems from less than adequate data resources and not from a flaw in the measure per se.

It is obvious that considerable methodological progress has occurred with respect to the division of labor construct. While not desiring to play down the contribution of Smith and Snow, it is fair to say that the Gibbs, et al. measures have much to recommend them in that they have produced sensible results when related to an impressive number of variables at different levels of analysis including cities (Clemente and Sturgis, 1972), counties (Frisbie and Poston, 1978) and societies (Gibbs and Martin, 1962; Gibbs and Browning, 1966).

## URBAN STRUCTURE AND PROCESS

One widely accepted view of human ecology is that it is the "study of the form and development of the human community" (Hawley, 1950·68; 1968:329). While community is defined generically as a "territorially localized system of relationships among functionally differentiated parts" (Hawley, 1968:329), the urban community has, from ecology's inception, been a primary locus of attention. Hence, in this section several notable themes of urban ecological analysis are discussed along with particular methodological problems associated with each.

### Intraurban Organization

Schwirian (1974:3-31) has identified several prominent models applied by ecologists in the study of intraurban form and growth. Methods of analyzing most of these are discussed under rubrics essentially the same as those employed by Schwirian.

*Classic Models.* Among the best known approaches in human ecology are theories of urban form and growth, including Burgess' Concentric Zone hypothesis (1925), Hoyt's Sector model (1939), and Harris and Ullman's theory of multinucleation (1945). All contemplate patterns of land use as related directly or indirectly to land values, relative complementarity (or lack thereof) of different functions, and socioeconomic competition in the land market (Hawley, 1971a; Schwirian, 1974). Each is so familiar that we need not pause to describe their substance in detail. Apparently less well recognized is the fact that all are theories of how and why urban *growth* proceeds as it does. Despite the palpable longitudinal thrust of the models, most research has persisted in testing their implications with cross-sectional designs (but see B. Duncan et al., 1962). Much early criticism of Burgess' hypothesis, for example, stemmed from the failure of other investigators (e.g., Davie, 1937; Caplow, 1952) to find circular, homogeneous zones corresponding to inverse gradients (or positive in the case of socioeconomic indicators) between distance from the center of the city and variables such as density, delinquency rates, and incidence of broken families. Although a regular spatial pattern may not be apparent in many cities, the underlying model based on gradients reflecting functional specialty, intensity of land use, and competition for space, all mediated by developing transportation and communications facilities in an expanding city, remains quite viable. The decline in intensity of residential land use has been formalized by Colin Clark (1951) as:

$$d_x = d_o e^{-bx}$$

where $d_x$ is the population density at some point d that is at distance x from the center and where $d_o$ is the central density, e is the natural logarithmic base, and b is the density gradient. The conceptual rationale for this expression, which has been found without exception to fit data drawn from most areas of the world at numerous points in time for over 150 years, is based on land use theory central to urban ecology (Berry and Kasarda, 1977: Chapters 5-6).

The most significant methodological and analytical advances in testing these models involve a move away from a simple search for spatial regularities to: (1) longitudinal and trend investigations consistent with the processsual character of the models (e.g., Haggerty, 1971; Salins, 1971); (2) the expansion of analytic designs to include factors which may "distort" expected spatial arrangements such as topographical features (Gilmore, 1944), cultural and symbolic factors (Firey, 1947), and institutional influences (e.g., real estate interests and regulations imposed by local governmental agencies; see Form, 1954); and (3) techniques of data analysis used to show the complementarity of models. For example, analysis of variance methods indicate that differentials in family life cycle stage tend to conform to the concentric zone pattern (distance gradient) and economic status to a zonal model (Anderson and Egeland, 1961). These findings were supported by Schwirian and

Matre's (1974) analysis which employed factor analytic methods. Similar results and, in addition, a race/ethnic multinucleated pattern are reported on the basis of computer mapping techniques (Salins, 1971).

*Social Area Analysis/Factorial Ecology.* Social Area Analysis assumes that three primary bases of social differentiation--socioeconomic status (social rank), family status (urbanization, familism), and ethnic status (segregation)--reflecting structural changes in a social system serve to identify urban subpopulations with distinctive attributes and behavior (Shevky and Bell, 1955). The concentration on only three categories of variables in Social Area Analysis has largely given way to contemporary factorial ecology which searches for latent structure among a much wider range of variables.

With more sophisticated techniques have come more complex methodological questions. Given the variety of computational procedures and alternative types of factor rotation, comparability of findings may be difficult to achieve. Put differently, results may not be "method independent." A reasonable strategy is to apply different factor solutions, rotations and weighting techniques and compare results. Schwirian reports on both orthogonal and oblique rotations based on factors extracted from data for Mayaguez and Ottawa. In both cities, *orthogonal* rotation produced three distinct configurations corresponding roughly to the three Social Area dimensions. In Ottawa, *oblique* rotation produced analogous results, but in Mayaguez, oblique rotation allowed a more "parsimonious" solution in that all variables except one loaded highly on a single factor, an indication of the "undifferentiated nature of the urban subareas" of the latter city (1974:22). In a study of U.S. nonmetropolitan counties, Frisbie and Poston (1976, 1978) factor analyzed sustenance organization variables using (1) orthogonal rotation following simple principal components (without iteration) and (2) principal components with iteration as well as (3) oblique rotation. The factor structures obtained were nearly identical in all three instances with no interfactor correlation greater than .25. It may be, as Schwirian suggests, that level of societal development is an important consideration in regard to whether different findings with respect to dissociation of factors will obtain with different methods.

It is also true that different sets of input variables will lead to dissimilarity of factor structures (cf. Schwirian, 1974:9). Nevertheless, it is significant that the relatively frequent (relative to most other areas of ecological interest) factorial analyses of cities in nations

other than the U.S. (e.g., Copenhagen [Pedersen, 1967];
Helsinki [Sweetser, 1965]; Cairo [Abu-Lughod, 1969]; 11
Canadian cities [Schwirian and Matre, 1974]; 7 Indian cities
[Berry and Spodek, 1971, also Berry and Rees, 1969]) generally uncover configurations corresponding to economic
status, family life cycle, and ethnic status, though with
varying degrees of dissociation and differential contribution of factors to explained variation (see Johnston, 1971:
316).

While this discussion has concentrated on the factorial
ecology of urban areas (because such analyses seem to have
been of greatest interest to ecologists in sociology), it is
clear that other observational units may be employed. To
illustrate, factorial ecologies of the structural aspects of
nation-states have yielded results of considerable ecological interest, including the finding of distinct factors
indexing size, degree of economic development, and the distinction between intensive and extensive agriculture (Rees,
1971:225).

Extensions of factorial ecology that might be pursued to
good effect include the further investigation of the stability of factors in different subareas of cities and over
time. Such work has been initiated by Sweetser (1969) and
Hunter (1971). In particular, Hunter, in a study of Chicago
from 1930 to 1960, introduces the distinction between
*changes in ecological structure,* determined by separate
factor analyses at different points in time, and the *structure of ecological change,* determined by factor analysis of
differences in variables across several time intervals.
Hunter concludes that "the first method most clearly eluci-
dates stable and persistent ecological structure, while the
second method is more sensitive to short-run ecological
change..." (1971:425).

Another topic that warrants continued exploration has to
do with the tenability of the linearity assumption underlying factor analysis. Of course, orthogonal rotations tend
to be the rule. But, even with oblique rotations, factors
may be uncorrelated without being independent, if the relationship is nonlinear. Johnston (1971:321) recommends two
methods of detecting nonlinearity: (1) The first involves
simply "plotting the scores on each pair of factors" and
inspecting the plots. Also, regression of factor scores
might be used in a test for interaction. (2) "The second
method involves producing a typology of social areas from
the factor scores." If cross-tabulations of cases according
to the typologies result in "certain groups (that are) very
large, very small, or even absent, then independence does
not exist and the pattern of groups would indicate the
dimensional structure."

*Residential Segregation.* Segregation of residence by race, ethnicity, occupation, education, etc. has long been of interest to ecologists for the same reason that other spatial patterns are, namely, they are a manifestation of social differentiation and functional interrelationships. In other words, "social distances tend to be expressed in physical distances" (Hawley, 1971a:187). Whenever spatial patterns, such as segregation by race, persist over extended periods of time, the reason may be that these patterns help to create or maintain a competitive advantage for one or more groups (Hawley, 1944a).

Evidence of functional differentiation is found in the segregation of population by occupation. Most interesting is the relatively low degree of separation of clerical workers on the one hand and craftsmen and foremen on the other, which mirrors the ambiguous position of these groups in the stratification system. Clerical workers are accorded upper level (white collar) status, yet often have lower earnings than highly skilled blue collar workers such as craftsmen and foremen (Duncan and Duncan, 1955b; Hawley, 1971a:187). More recently, informative studies have appeared that focus on occupational residential segregation both within and between racial categories (Simkus, 1978) and on the much neglected area of segregation by age and family life-cycle stage (Guest, 1972, 1977; Pampel and Choldin, 1978).

Methodological sophistication came early to analyses of segregation (mainly focused on racial distributions) in the form of the Duncan's "Methodological Analysis of Segregation Indexes" (1955a) following discussions by Jahn et al. (1947), Jahn (1950), and Cowgill and Cowgill (1951). In their classic analysis, Duncan and Duncan demonstrated that several segregation indexes proposed to that point could all be defined with reference to the "segregation curve" in which cumulative percentages of the proportion white and nonwhite are plotted in the form of a Lorenz curve (see also Taeuber and Taeuber, 1965:203). Of these, only the Index of Dissimilarity, the Index of Segregation, and the Gini Index have been used extensively. In this context, the Gini Index is simply "the area between the segregation curve and the diagonal..., expressed as a proportion of the total area under the diagonal" (Duncan and Duncan, 1955a:211), and, of course, it has been frequently used to measure inequality of distributions in regard to other variables, such as income. The most widely employed measure continues to be the Index of Dissimilarity, D, which is expressed as:

$$D = \frac{1}{2} \Sigma \mid N_i/N - W_i/W \mid$$

where $N_i$ and $W_i$ symbolize the number of persons (or households) in each of two groups in a given area i, and N and W the total number of persons (households) in each group in the entire ecological unit (city, SMSA, etc.). In the case of polychotomous categorizations, the Index of *Segregation* allows the measurement of the segregation of one group from all others. It is computed simply as:

$$S = \tfrac{1}{2} \Sigma \mid X_i/X - Y_i/Y \mid /(1-p)$$

where $X_i/X$ is the proportion of persons in a particular group in area i, $Y_i/Y$ is the proportion of all groups combined in area i, and p is the proportion of X in the total population.

Despite what Taeuber and Taeuber (1965:197) term "insurmountable problems of measurement," a great deal of progress is observable in the study of segregation, longitudinally as well as in the cross-section (e.g., Taeuber and Taeuber, 1965; Farley and Taeuber, 1968). Likewise it has been demonstrated that conflicting evidence indicating both recent increases (Clemence, 1967; Farley and Taeuber, 1968) and declines (Sorensen et al., 1975; Roof, et al., 1976) in residential segregation by race may be explained in methodological terms. In particular, conclusions that segregation increased during the 1960s were based on the analysis of small and, perhaps, unrepresentative samples further complicated by shifting boundaries of analytic units. On the other hand, much of the overall decline is attributable to the addition of new SMSAs with low segregation scores in the 1960-70 interval (Van Valey, et al., 1977).

While progress is obvious, basic methodological issues continue unresolved. In their early article, Duncan and Duncan note that, in spite of the palpable centralization of the black population, some of the more commonly used indicators rely on the erroneous assumption "that segregation can be measured without regard to the spatial pattern of white and nonwhite residents in a city" (1955a:215). The same problem is given extended attention by Taeuber and Taeuber (1965). A measure of concentration proposed by Duncan and Duncan in their study of occupational stratification (1955b) is "formally identical with the index of urbanization" developed previously bv O.D. Duncan (1952). Computation of this quantity is according to the formula:

$$\Sigma \, X_{i-1} Y_i - \Sigma \, X_i Y_{i-1}{}'$$

where $X_i$ is the cumulative proportion of one group in a given area, and $Y_i$ the corresponding cumulation for the other group, with areas ordered according to the well-known segregation curve (Duncan and Duncan, 1955a, 1955b). In other words, the measure is the "Gini Index." Although employed for other purposes, the Gini Index, in comparison with the Index of Dissimilarity, has been used rather infrequently in subsequent work on racial segregation.

Other methodological difficulties accruing to D are currently calling forth additional methodological/statistical contributions. D gives the proportion of one group or the other which would have to move from present area of residence (tract, block) to another in order to achieve a perfectly even distribution, under the assumption that the "movers" are not replaced by members of the other group (Taeuber and Taeuber, 1965:30). Under such an assumption, a tract that is 100% black would have to be totally evacuated to achieve a nonsegregated situation (Cortese et al., 1976: 633). Perhaps a more meaningful measure would be qD or $(1-q)D$, where q is the proportion of the minority in a population. The measure $(1-q)D$ can be viewed as "the proportion of minority population which would have to be *exchanged* while keeping the number of households constant," with qD the corresponding proportion for majority households, and $2q(1-q)D$ the analogous figure for the total population (Cortese et al., 1976:633, 635, emphasis in the original). The latter has been termed the "replacement index" (Farley and Taeuber, 1968).

Another problem has to do with the impact of q on intercity comparisons. Duncan and Duncan expressed doubt "that a meaningful comparison can be made...of two cities with greatly different q's" (1955a:216), as did the Taeubers (1965:211). Recently, Cortese et al. showed that, within categories of q, the expected value of D is inversely related to the number of households. Accordingly, Cortese et al. propose a standardized D given by:

$$Z = \frac{D - \mu D}{\sigma D}$$

i.e., the difference between D and its expected value ($\mu D$) based on *random* placement expressed in standard deviation units ($\sigma D$).

Even acknowledging the utility of the "standardized $D_1$," it remains unclear whether measuring deviation from randomness or from evenness is the more appropriate procedure. The matter may be better considered in theoretical rather than purely methodological terms. Apparently independent of Cortese et al., Winship also has recommended an "adjusted" D to "serve as a measure of deviation from random segregation" (1977:1058). Further, Winship suggests that if one is interested in the *effects* of segregation, it is the fact of isolation that is significant, and thus it makes little difference whether the segregation is random or non-random. In such a case, D is an appro¬riate indicator. But if one is interested in the *causes* of segregation, "it is necessary to know how much segregation there would be if people chose where they wanted to live randomly" (1977: 1065). In the latter case, the adjusted D is viewed as preferable.

For the sake of completeness, one other point of mild controversy that has emerged in the literature should be mentioned. It has been amply demonstrated that scores on all conventional segregation indices increase in magnitude as attention shifts to smaller units of analysis (e.g., from tracts to blocks; see Taeuber and Taeuber, 1965:220-231; Roof and Van Valey, 1972). There seems to be some sentiment that analyses of block data come closer to representing the "real" degree of residential segregation, but there is no inherent reason why this should be so. Presumably, all units of analysis "have spatial meanings that represent particular levels of generalization" (Bogue and Bogue, 1976:56), although the boundaries of units dictated by official data-gathering agencies rarely circumscribe areas possessed of "unit character" in the ecological sense, and homogeneity of contiguous units may make statistical interpretations difficult (O.D. Duncan et al., 1961:128-129). Nevertheless, the most crucial problem of comparability would seem to be "matching the unit of area to be employed with the level of generalization desired" (Bogue and Bogue, 1976:56). Based on this criterion, tracts have at least as great a claim to legitimacy as blocks.

Directions for future research should include analyses of both determinants and effects of segregation comparing the results of alternative indexes measuring deviations from both evenness and randomness, as well as the causes and consequences of clustering. The latter issue to a large extent seems to underlie the discussion by Bogue and Bogue (1976) of quantity versus intensity of segregation.[2] In addition, these authors point to the need to consider and distinguish three other dimensions: whether segregation is to be measured in terms *absolute or relative*, whether to make reference to *traits or variables*, and whether measurement should be on a *"parcel" or community-wide* basis.

*Density*. Ecological interest in density initially resides in the consistent finding that density of settlement declines with distance from the core of the city. The declining gradient reflects land values and competition based on varying ability to make intensive use of land and to bear the costs of overcoming the friction of movement over space. Thus the slope of the gradient may be employed as an indicator of the efficiency of local transportation in intercity comparisons or in studies of the same city over time (Hawley, 1971a:102-103).

One problem here (and perhaps with all areal-based studies) is that of disparate degrees of homogeneity within areas. Two areas (say counties or SMSAs) may have the same average number of persons per acre, but in one case the average may reflect a combination of very high and very low densities, and in the other, an even spread of population across the unit of analysis. While it is not necessary to achieve perfect homogeneity, it is nevertheless true that "criteria for adjudging a 'suitable' degree of homogeneity have not been elaborated" (O. D. Duncan et al., 1961:37-38). In a sense, the problem is the same as that encountered with any summary measure; some information is invariably lost. If the loss is considered too great, other measurement strategies should be implemented or smaller and more homogeneous units of analysis should be selected if possible.

One might, e.g., focus sequentially on several density "components," the measurement of which depends on different "areal" bases. In addition to persons per acre, one might also observe "the number of persons per room (overcrowding),

---

[2] *For example, a community may possess only 100 Negroes, all of whom live in one census tract, along with 1,000 white residents. In such a community, the intensity of Negro segregation would be low (only one resident in 11 is Negro in the tract where Negroes live) while the quantity of Negro segregation would be very high, because all of the Negroes are confined to one small part of the community* (Bogue and Bogue, 1976:46).

the number of rooms per housing unit, the number of housing units per structure, and the number of residential structures per acre" (Galle et al., 1972:26), literally the components of density measured as persons per acre (P/A) since:

$$P/A = P/R \times R/H \times H/S \times S/A.$$

More important, various social and individual pathologies relate differently to the several components (Schmidt, 1966; Galle et al., 1972). It is difficult to make unqualified statements regarding such relationships however, due to the difficulty in separating the effects of density per se from alternative social, economic, and demographic explanations (Galle et al., 1972).

## Interurban Organization

*Functional Specialization.* As a natural outgrowth of ecology's emphasis on functional interdependence, a large amount of research has been devoted to developing classifications of metropolitan communities according to functional specializations that serve to integrate areas into the larger urban system (Kass, 1973). Five approaches to identifying functional specializations have been summarized by Kass (1973:428):

> ...(1) a taxonomy based on absolute constraints (Harris, 1943); (2) a classification system based on the normal distribution (Nelson, 1955); (3) a system based on the minimally necessary level of activity for a community's viability (Alexandersson, 1956); (4) a system based on the relative proportion of activity in the community (Duncan and Reiss, 1956); and (5) a system based on the industrial profile of the community (Duncan et al., 1960).

The list represents something of a delineation of methodological process in this area. Harris (1943), Alexandersson (1956), and Duncan and Reiss (1956) used reasonable, but rather arbitrary and often shifting criteria for determining placement of cities in functional categories. Nelson's scheme (1955) does not generate mutually exclusive categories. An important advance then was the Duncan et al. (1960) use of location quotients, i.e., the proportion of the labor force employed in a given industry in a city divided by the proportion of the national labor force employed in that industry. Location coefficients greater than unity were taken to indicate that a city was a net exporter

of a given good or service, though Duncan and his collaborators were careful to claim only that "the technique is
sensitive to major axes of specialization in the industry
structure" (1960:211).

Location quotients yielding functional profiles have
recently been manipulated via cluster analysis in order to
distinguish groups of cities characterized by similar types
of activities (Kass, 1973; 1977). This approach allows identification of patterns of all functions as opposed to
earlier work based on a single function approach. Finally,
Wanner (1977) has demonstrated the use of a continuous,
rather than categorial, approach to measuring functual
specialization.

*Functional Integration*. The ecological perspective on
metropolitan systems is basically hierarchical in character.
Expressed in "central place" terminology, a rank-size
ordering of cities is expected in which each successive
class has "a specific group of central functions" and a
somewhat distinct population level (Berry and Garrison,
1958:145-154). Inherent in the hierarchical model are the
notions of *dominance* of large metropolitan centers in an
overall *functionally interdependent* system. Only limited
progress has been made in quantifying either the concept of
dominance (Gibbs and Erickson, 1976:610) or the degree of
functional integration. However, Bogue (1949) suggested that
density gradients may serve as indicators of metropolitan
dominance. Vance and Sutker (1954) derived an index of dominance from a standard score ranking on six variables: wholesale and retail sales, business service receipts, number of
manufacturing branch offices, bank clearings, and value
added. More recently Abrahamson and DuBick (1977) have distinguished among three dimensions of dominance, national
(international), regional and local, and offered indicators
of each. Although intended as a step toward a more elaborate
conceptualization through an emphasis on "noneconomic"
dimensions, the latter research continues (appropriately, I
think) to rely heavily on measures which directly or indirectly index financial and commercial transactions (e.g.,
import duties, clearinghouse exchange, transportation and
communications variables). One difficulty in the work by
Abrahamson and DuBick is the seeming inconsistency in the
measurement which ranks cities such as New York and Boston
high on the dimension of national dominance, but low in
regional and local influence.

Methods of determining the degree of functional integration have yet to be determined. One might speculate that
combining the notions of centrality, isolation, and connectedness viewed as properties of the division of labor

(Kemper, 1972) with methods of nonmetric scaling such as smallest space analysis (Kruskal, 1964a, 1964b; McFarland and Brown, 1973) might yield interesting results. (See, for instance, Duncan and Lieberson's [1970] use of smallest space analysis based on industrial dissimilarity among major urban centers in 1960.) Such techniques allow scaling according to any type of proximity or dissociation (Kruskal, 1964a, 1964b) including frequency or rate of interaction. Suitable data for this sort of analysis might be information on location of branch offices, connections among corresponding banks and so on.

## SOME NEGLECTED AREAS

In the previous sections, attention has been concentrated on measurement and methodological issues associated with theories of ecological organization. This focus is "natural" in the sense that the mainstream of ecological research has remained fairly close to Hawley's perspective that "human ecology...is concerned with the general problem of organization, conceived as an attribute of population" (1968:329). It must be admitted that, although the concept of environment (both social and physical, natural and man-made) looms large in general theoretical formulations, it has been rather neglected in empirical analysis (Duncan, 1959:702; Michelson, 1970, Chapter 1)—a situation which may be partially remedied by students of population ecology (e.g., Hannan and Freeman, 1977).

Finally, while ecologists have investigated certain manifestations of technological advance, particularly transportation and communications technology, few have attempted to deal empirically with the more general construct. Interest has been confined mainly to the societal level, and even then, analysis has usually proceeded with only a single indicator, energy consumption per capita (Gibbs and Browning 1966:158). Hence it is appropriate to suggest that one avenue for future research in human ecology would involve the development of measures of other dimensions of the ecosystem (Duncan, 1959; 1964) possibly along the lines suggested by the current work of Sly (1972) and Micklin (1973: 2-19).

## METHOD AND MEASUREMENT IN THE
## ANALYSIS OF ECOLOGICAL RELATIONSHIPS

It is argued here that the explanatory power of ecological theory can best be established by demonstrating its applicability in as wide a variety of situations as possible. In other words, methods need to provide for tests of ecological hypotheses at different points in time and space and across diverse levels of analysis. To illustrate briefly, conclusions reached on the basis of research at one level of analysis may not hold at another level. Likewise, clear interrelationships among variables in one society and/or at one point in time may become ambiguous or diminish in cross-national, diachronic analysis. (See Berry and Kasarda's [ 1977 ] review of cross-national, factorial ecology and Lieberson and Hansen's [ 1974 ] cross-national, longitudinal study of mother tongue diversity.)

In assessing the present state of methodology in human ecology, there is an apparent need for broadly comparative research designs in each of the three senses just mentioned, accompanied by methods of analysis appropriate to each. In subsequent sections of this chapter, this line of thought is elaborated and examples of potentially fruitful methodological strategies are suggested. The word "suggested" is used advisedly. While concrete examples are given for illustrative purposes, the intent is not to offer a definitive program for future research, but to indicate broad areas where additional work seems most needed. Put differently, important questions need to be posed even though satisfactory answers are not readily available.

## MULTILEVEL ANALYSIS

### *Discrete Analysis at Different Levels*

Increased emphasis on multilevel analysis constitutes a promising direction for future ecological research. Such research might take more than one form, depending on the interests of the researcher. One type consists of examination of the relationship between the same (or similar) variables at different levels of aggregation, but with no analysis across levels. Since selection of analytic units may make a great deal of difference in the outcome of an analysis, and even partially determines the body of literature brought to bear (Hannan and Freeman, 1977:933), it makes sense, where practical, to conduct inquiries at multiple levels. An obvious advantage of this methodology is, as Scheuch puts it: "A research design becomes more

powerful when it provides for direct measurements of phenomena on different levels" (1969:143). If it is found that
socioeconomic status is inversely related to fertility in
aggregates as well as on the individual level, the dual con-
firmation certainly makes a stronger case for the hypothesis
than if the result were unique to one level or the other.

Relationships observed at one level of a social system
(say formal organizations) may not exist or may reverse
direction at another level (say societies) as Kasarda (1974)
so competently demonstrates in his multilevel analysis of
the structural implications of system size. Kasarda found a
correlation of -.43 between size and the managerial structural component at the institutional level. Among societies,
the correlation was .36, while at the community level, virtually no relationship existed. It is possible that correlates of other basic ecological concepts such as the degree
of the division of labor may be relative to the units of
analysis (Gibbs and Poston, 1975·469). Again, as mentioned
above, it is well known that the magnitude of all conventional indexes of segregation varies with the unit of analysis selected (Taeuber and Taeuber, 1965:230: Roof and Van
Valey, 1972). It would also be illuminating to examine part-
whole (i.e., parcel versus community-wide) differences in
segregation (Bogue and Bogue, 1976·43-84). The point is not
that one unit may somehow be found more appropriate than
another (though that is a possibility), but rather that the
evidence so far is that changes in analytic units sometimes
eventuate in different conclusions, and it would be instructive to know if and why such variation occurs.

An obstacle to multilevel research when larger units are
simply congeries of smaller ones has been termed aggregation
bias. The problem is that "grouping units somehow changes
variation in the variables of interest" primarily because
'shifting from one unit of analysis to another (may) affect
the manner in which potentially disturbing influences are
operating on the...variable under consideration" (Hannan,
1971:489, 491; see also Blalock, 1964:98). However, at least
in cases where models can be precisely specified it is
possible that "aggregation bias will represent only a minor
inconvenience." At any rate, it may be possible to estimate
the extent of the bias which may exist (Hannan, 1971:503).

*Contextual Analysis*

Another type of multilevel design attempts to implement
empirically Scheuch's call for more complex theoretical
specifications:

Theories in the social sciences that maintain a dependency between the state of a higher-order collectivity and the characteristics of the units within the collectivity should specify the processes of interchange between system levels (1969:143).

What is being suggested is a *contextual* analysis in which the properties of groups or collectivities are examined for their effect on individually measured variables. Formally, the relationships might be expressed as:

$$Y_{ij} = a + b_i X_{ij} + b_2 \bar{X}_j$$

(neglecting error) where $Y_{ij}$ and $X_{ij}$ are individually measured dependent and independent variables and $\bar{X}_j$ represents an ecological or aggregate variable. The ecological variable might be derived by aggregating the properties of individuals (e.g., percent Black in an area), in which case the effect may be termed *compositional*. More interesting to ecologists, $\bar{X}_j$ might represent a "structural" effect which has no counterpart on the individual level (such as the division of labor, the structure of sustenance organization, the level of technology, etc.).

Cross-level hypotheses, coupled with appropriate cross-level methods might be expected to yield rich substantive dividends. The method has a venerable tradition in sociology (e.g., Blau, 1960; Davis, et al., 1961; David, 1966: assis, 1977). In fact, studies which posit a causal relationship between density, overcrowding, an overload of stimuli in a heterogeneous urban setting and various individual and social pathologies (e.g., Wirth, 1938; Galle et al.,1972 fall within the purview of contextual analysis. Juan Linz (1969:107, 108) concisely describes the general rationale for attempting such research:

> *Structural-functional* analysis, on the one hand, and the emphasis on *social interaction,* on the other, have stressed that the individual and his behavior cannot be studied in isolation from his social context.. To emphasize this contextual element in social relations was one of the great contributions of Emile Durkheim's *Suicide* (emphasis in original).

Specifically, contextual analysis would seem to hold an especially high degree of promise for ecologists because it (1) refuses to view micro and macro-level analyses as competing, but rather takes them to be complementary; (2) brings to bear the explanatory power of ecological variables i accounting for individual behavior; and (3) may have the potential to convert the so-called "ecological fallacy" from statistical embarrassment to theoretical advantage. (The term "ecological fallacy," of course, refers to the fact amply demonstrated by Robinson [1950] that correlations obtained with aggregate data cannot normally be substituted for individual correlations, and that relationships typically increase in magnitude as the units of analysis become fewer and larger.)

For example, one source of bias arises from the situation where the relationship between individual variables "is a function of the level of the independent variable," i.e., where there is a contextual effect (Hammond, 1973:770). A prime illustration is found in Robinson's treatment of the race/illiteracy correlation. A plausible explanation of the "bias" in the inference from the aggregate to the individual relationship is the contextual effect of the variable percent Black. Hammond (1973), building on earlier work by Key (1949), shows that Robinson's statistical demonstration may be given a substantively meaningful interpretation, *viz.*, that illiteracy is higher (for both races) where the proportion of Blacks is greatest. If percent Black may be taken as an indicator of state and regional inequalities in the level of services and educational opportunities, illiteracy can be viewed as "a function not only of an individual's race, but also of the racial composition of a state or region" (Hammond, 1973:770).

However, the utility of contextual analysis has been sharply questioned in a number of respects. The debate has revolved principally around the use of contextual variables measured in terms of aggregated individual attributes that presumably reflect normative climate as embodied in reference groups. This procedure has led to a number of cogent critiques such as that by Hauser (1970, 1974) who argues that the psychologically based propositions attaching to the concept of normative climate are not testable with aggregated individual-level variables and, therefore, constitute a "contextual fallacy." Thus, a crucial issue is raised regarding the meaning of contextual effects specified as residuals (Hauser, 1974:366-367).

A related critique is that "the contextual effect may be an artifact of explicit selection on the dependent variable" (Hauser, 1974:375), a connection not made clear in the work of Hammond (1973). Other criticisms summarized by Hauser include the typically small magnitude of observed contextual effects, the possibility that inclusion of other explanatory individual-level variables would result in the disappearance of the contextual effect (see also Sewell and Armer, 1966a,

1966b), and problems of measurement error (1974:366). The latter difficulty arises because "when an individual variable and the corresponding contextual variable have effects of the same sign, random measurement error in the individual variable will inflate the estimated contextual effect, deflate the estimated individual effect, and vice versa" (Hauser, 1974:372). Hauser quite reasonably regards the first two issues as the most damaging. The question of magnitude of effect is an empirical question that remains open with each new piece of research and which is subject to arbitrary assessment besides. The problems of measurement error (though not necessarily of the type mentioned by Hauser) and the possibility that other variables added to the equation would significantly alter the results are by no means unique to contextual analysis.

Counter-arguments include Farkas' contention that certain operational definitions (e.g., Bowers' aggregation of individual normative sentiments) "avoid the untested social-psychological mechanisms whose imputation Hauser calls the contextual fallacy" (cited in Farkas, 1974:339-340). Farkas also believes that contextual effects emanating from grouping on the dependent variable either are not causal in the conventional sense or reflect the effects of other "group-level" variables (1974:361, n. 20).

What then is to be made of the two opposing positions as they relate to ecological research? Both authors whose works serve as the basis of the brief summary of the controversy, although holding to their avowed positions, admit there is room for differences of opinion. As Hauser correctly states,

> The question is not whether group composition affects anything. Of course it does, and that is why you need statistical control of variables measured on individuals in contextual analysis.
> The issue is whether there are net or direct effects of group composition which persist above and beyond those of individual variates and which are susceptible to unambiguous and distinctively sociological interpretation (1974:369).

One approach might be to press forward with further examinations of composition to determine if, indeed, the effects persist and can be interpreted in a fashion acceptable to the majority of the social science community. Preliminary work by the present author attempting to estimate the relationship between ethnicity and income as affected by the relative size of the ethnic group resulted in findings which support Hauser's contention regarding the difficulty of substantive interpretation and the minor contribution of the aggregate variable to explained variation in the dependent variable measured at the individual level. (All coefficients were significant, but sample size was quite large, and little theoretical meaning could be attached to the link between ethnic proportion and ethnicity as an individual attribute.) Farkas, on the other hand, seemingly dismisses "variance accounted for" as a relevant criterion.

The strongest argument for ecologists to continue to engage in contextual analyses involves a shift of focus away from compositional effects to truly ecological variables, which are *not* simply aggregates of individual characteristics and which, in fact, have no individual-level counterpart; i.e., they are emergent in the Durkheimian sense. Examples are the degree of the division of labor, modes of sustenance organization, productivity of key economic functions, and level of technological advance. To illustrate, efficiency of technology, rates of capital investment, and the complexity of the division of labor may affect the overall productivity of a system and thereby directly influence the productivity of individuals and, indirectly, individual income. Such system-level contextual variables exercise influences and constraints which do not depend on social-psychological interpretations. And, since they are not operationalized in terms of group composition, the problem of grouping on the dependent variable does not directly arise. Thus, there is no necessity in many instances of relying on concepts like normative climate or on measurement tied to group composition. However, it is still possible that system-level variables might, in some way, be related to selection of individuals according to characteristics which are to be explained.

At this juncture, it may be well to remind those who may be concerned that human ecology remain at a strictly macro-level, paying no attention to individuals, that the discussion has merely taken the literature in which individual *persons* are the units of interest as a convenient point of departure. That is, the term "individual level" can refer to the lower in any pair of levels of analysis (Hammond, 1973: 1973:765, n. 3). It is possible, e.g., to conceive of individual organizations existing in the context of populations of organizations with system-level as well as compositional attributes (Hannan and Freeman, 1977:933-934).

On the one hand, the present author, along with numerous other human ecologists, is attracted to the view that "the ecological mode of analysis remains at one level (macro) with respect to the variables it employs" (Schnore, 1961: 136). On the other hand, it can be argued that, today, human ecology is well enough developed and secure enough in its contributions that it can afford to apply its explanatory framework in various types of multi-level and cross-level analyses. Theoretical and empirical implementations following from the second argument would seem to be quite consistent with Duncan's statement (1961:141) regarding the systemic approach:

> When we elect wittingly or unwittingly, to work *within* a level...we tend to discern or construct-- whichever emphasis you prefer--only those kinds of system whose elements are confined to that level. From this standpoint, the doctrine of levels may not only fail to be heuristic, it may actually become anti- heuristic, if it blinds us to fruitful results obtain- able by recognizing *systems that cut across levels* (emphasis in original).

In proceeding along these lines, it is necessary to bear in mind Burgess' caveat (quoted in Schnore, 1961:138), that while both micro- and macro-level "approaches can be brought together to produce significant findings on particular prob- lems, their joint use should be conscious and deliberate." This implies that considerable thought be given to alterna- tive methodological procedures, which, in essence, is the primary point of the current discussion.

*Cross-Level Analysis: The Ecological Fallacy*

Contrasting with, but clearly not altogether unrelated to, multi-level analysis is the issue of cross-level gener- alization; i.e., attempts to infer relationships at one level from analysis performed at another level. No discus- sion of methods of human ecology would be complete without reference to the "ecological fallacy." Until fairly recently the familiarity of the problem would have suggested that only a passing reference was required. However, current methodological developments reported by Hammond (1973) and Bogue and Bogue (1976) warrant more than superficial con- sideration.

Briefly, the history of the ecological fallacy has pro- ceeded from an early caution that the magnitude of correla- tions may inflate as the size of the unit of analysis in- creases (Gehlke and Biehl, 1934), to a well-taken statisti- cal caveat against aggregate-to-individual inference accom- panied by a misconception of the analytical interests of human ecology (Robinson, 1950), to several impressive efforts to develop techniques for reducing error in making inferences from ecological data to individual behavior by (1) determining the bounds of individual-level relationships based on aggregate marginals (Duncan and Davis, 1953), (2) areal weighting (Robinson, 1956; see also Thomas and Anderson, 1966), and (3) application of regression techniques (Goodman, 1953, 1959; Blalock, 1964, Chapter 4; Shively 1969; Bogue and Bogue, 1976). Another thrust is seen in attempts to identify in mathematical and statistical terms the source of bias (Alker, 1969; Hammond, 1973; Firebaugh, 1978). These analyses are most useful when considering the *substantive* basis of bias in social processes. Finally, certain scholars have sought to define the so-called ecological fallacy in theoretically meaningful terms. rather than as a statistical aberration (Allardt, 1969; Valkonen, 1969; Alker, 1969; Hammond, 1973). Some of the latter work is contextual in the sense critiqued earlier.

The position taken in this paper is that the notion of "ecological fallacy" is, and has too long remained, a false issue in a number of respects. This does not in any way deny either the importance or the accuracy of Robinson's statement (1950:356) that "the ecological will be greater than the individual correlation whenever the within-areas individual correlation is not greater than the total correlation, and this is the usual circumstance." Instead, the point is simply that the warning sign hoisted by Robinson has led to an almost phobic anxiety and to a fixation on the specific statistical issue raised rather than to a consideration of the broad implications and promise of cross-level research. Put differently, the argument is that:

> The real issue...does not seem to be the ecological fallacy but rather the technique used in analyzing data from many levels of social organization (Allardt, 1969: 45).

For the sake of completeness and as a basis for the discussion of recent progress in the area, it may be well to mention certain erroneous implications of Robinson's statement which have been long and widely recognized.

*Who Says the Fallacy is Ecological?* The term "ecological fallacy" is a misnomer to the extent that it implies that the only difficulty lies in trying to generalize from aggregates to individuals. Clearly, the problem may be present whenever attempts are made to move from one level of aggregation to another and regardless of direction. For instance, one cannot assume that the magnitude or even the direction of a relationship will be the same for states as for SMSAs or counties or census tracts. Furthermore, it is perfectly possible to commit an *"individualistic* fallacy." An example of the latter is given by Alker who cites the case of "ideologically motivated social scientists (who) try to generalize from individual behavior to collective rela-tionships" (1969:78).

*Aggregate Analysis Does Not a Fallacy Make.* Robinson concluded explicitly that:

> In each study which uses ecological correlation, the obvious purpose is to discover something about the behavior of individuals. Ecological correlations are used simply because correlations between the properties of individuals are not available (1950:352).

The invalidity of this conclusion was pointed out by Menzel (1950). Indeed, it should be transparent that many of the more meaningful constructs of the social sciences, both theoretical (e.g., the division of labor) and operational (e.g., vital rates), have no individual counterpart and relate strictly to collectivities.

Having said this, at least two reasonable views of the situation are possible. On the one hand, it is perfectly legitimate to focus solely on aggregates possessed of a more or less unit character such as counties, SMSAs, nations, etc. Given my own interests, I would certainly be content to remain within the boundaries of the perspective that human ecology represents a distinctly macro-level approach which takes populations (not individuals) as units of analysis. On the other hand, purely ecological variables (division of labor, level of technology, the structure of sustenance or-ganization, relative size of the coordination/control sector of the labor force [either society-wide or within formal organizations]) may contribute substantially to our under-standing of individual behavior. This approach seems per-fectly congruent with Hawley's perspective as expressed in his comment on causes of migration:

> For an understanding of the general phenomenon, it is important to know not why the migrant thinks he has moved but the conditions or characteristics common to all instances of migration and lacking in situations from which there is not migration (1950: 328).

It would be unfortunate, indeed, if the potential explanatory power of ecological variables were to go unexplored because of a hasty and before-the-fact foreclosing of the possibility of multi-level analysis.

*The Care and Feeding of the Ecological Fallacy.* Once one gets past purely statistical considerations, the ecological fallacy may be viewed, not as an obstacle, but as an opportunity for specifying important social processes which manifest themselves in what have at times been referred to as structural effects. This means that multi-level research will necessarily be a focus of attention. When referring to *cross-level inferences,* the discussion proceeds from the aggregate to the individual. That is, the concern here is with *disaggregation* bias rather than aggregation bias (see Hannan, 1971). Others, e.g., Hammond (1973), use the term aggregation bias simply to refer to the lack of congruence between relationships estimated at different levels of aggregation regardless of direction of the inference.

From one perspective, the ecological fallacy *is* simply a statistical problem. Unfortunately, most ecologists have apparently been content with (or have failed to look beyond) the purely statistical perspective. In a way, even Robinson's statistical interpretation is something of a false issue. As Goodman (1953, 1959) suggested earlier, and as the Bogue's reiterated (1976), Robinson's comparison was of the phi ($\phi$) coefficient with the Pearsonian product moment correlation, and "there is no mathematical necessity for the values of Pearson correlation coefficients computed from grouped (quantitative) data to be exactly equal to the (qualitative) $\phi$ coefficient, even if the ecological and the individual relationships were identical" (Bogue and Bogue, 1976:6-7). Without doubt, the statistical aspect of the issue must be taken into account. For instance, Alker (1969), by elaborating on the covariance theorem, defined a set of cross-level fallacies as a beginning step in the development of cross-level hypotheses. Hammond (1973) shows that, although the ecological correlation will generally exceed the individual correlation, regression coefficients from aggregate data may, under certain limited conditions, provide unbiased estimates of individual relationships. Bias will occur, however, when there is grouping by the dependent variable and when the aggregate variables are systematically related to the individual level independent variable (contextual effect). Without denying the significance of such work, it is my contention that it is time to deemphasize *purely* statistical approaches. In the first place, a sort of Catch-22 situation exists. While the statistical sources of bias have been amply demonstrated, it is impossible to be sure, on purely statistical grounds, if the bias is operative in any given instance unless data are available on *both* the individual and aggregate levels. In such a case, of course, one would not be interested in making cross-level generalizations in the first place.

Second, we are much closer to identifying the sources and extent of bias than we are to finding ways to minimize it. Duncan and Davis (1953) provide a means of determining the possible maximum and minimum magnitudes of individual relationships consistent with aggregate level marginals (see also Shively, 1969). Moreover, it has been demonstrated, to my satisfaction at least, that a single rule suffices to define the circumstances in which one can, without bias, infer individual relationships from aggregate regression coefficients. The rule, mentioned by Shively (1969) is elegantly elaborated and shown to apply in both the bivariate and n-variable cases by Firebaugh (1978:557) as follows: "bias is absent when, and only when, the group mean of the independent variable (X) has no effect on Y, with X controlled," where X and Y are individually measured variables. (The rule does *not* apply in this form to inference from individuals to aggregates.)

Given the general agreement as to both the statistical nature of the problem and the impossibility of its resolution in purely statistical terms, it would seem time to move in the direction of reasonable methodological strategies that can be applied in empirical research in such a way as to reduce bias and, more importantly. to develop theoretical models that inform methods of multilevel research. A method designed explicitly for dealing with cross-level inferences has been proposed by Rogue and Bogue (1976) building on Goodman's earlier work.

*Cross-Level Inference: The Goodman-Bogue Technique.* This procedure involves development of methods for arriving at ecological approximations of individual correlations, a process begun by Goodman (1953; 1959) and extended in impressive fashion by Bogue and Bogue (1976). A detailed description of the approach will not be given here since the necessary specifics appear in the work of the authors cited. Basically, Bogue and Bogue (1976) suggest practical procedures by means of which bias can be detected and seemingly substantially reduced when making cross-level individual relationships but no suitable data on individuals are available.

As noted above, appropriate comparisons between aggregate and individual estimates must involve comparable statistical tests. It makes little sense to compare product-moment correlations derived from ecological analysis with $\phi$

based on information on individuals (as Robinson did). Essentially, the Goodman-Bogue method applies regression techniques to arrive at estimates of the dependent variable of interest which, in turn, are used to derive an estimate of frequencies in a contingency table. The latter may then be directly compared with the frequencies cumulated from individual data. In brief, the method consists of stratified, weighted, multiple regression, though it may not be necessary both to stratify and to weight.

The logic of the procedure is illustrated in Goodman's (1953) conversion of the problem to a regression format. To illustrate (employing Goodman's notation in an example from the present author's research), let X be the proportion Mexican American and 1-X the proportion not Mexican American. Assuming aggregation over several units, p = the average proportion of Mexican Americans with low income and r = the average proportion non-Mexican Americans with low income. Then the expected proportion of persons with low income in the total sample, E(Y), is:

$$E(Y) = Xp + (1 - X)r.$$

This may be rewritten as:

$$E(Y) = r + (p - r)X,$$

which is an expression equivalent to the familiar regression equation: Y = a + bX. The importance of Goodman's demonstration is that it indicates that, if from aggregate data we know the average probability (proportion) of the X and Y variables, we can, if certain assumptions are met, estimate the proportion of all persons with low income from a single regression equation. Since a = r and a + b = p, the unknown values r and p can be estimated by obtaining several samples and regressing Y on X, if the usual least squares assumptions are met and if p and r do not differ significantly from sample to sample (Goodman, 1953). In other words, "Goodman suggested the use of a conventional bivariate regression equation to estimate the value of one variable ...given pre-selected values of the other variable" (Bogue and Bogue, 1976:8). A solution can be generated by substituting values of zero (or one) for the independent variable.

The Bogues suggest the extension of Goodman's work to include stratified, weighted, multiple-regression equations. Multivariate, rather than bivariate, analysis is required because it is almost always the case that "several variables are simultaneously affecting the behavior of the dependent variable," so that "if the researcher is able to introduce indicators of other independent variables..., the resulting estimate will never be worse and usually will be superior to the results of simple bivariate regression" (Bogue and Bogue, 1976:13).

Stratification into more homogeneous groups is viewed as a means of control over potentially extraneous effects. Thus, "if stratification significantly reduces the variance of p and r (as defined above) and/or their covariance, the resulting estimate will tend to be closer to the unknown individual effects than one made for all ecological areas without stratification" (Bogue and Bogue, 1976:15). Weighting is recommended in order to take into account unequal size of ecological units (i.e., the fact that individual relationships are determined mainly by data from the larger units).

The conclusion is that, in many instances, it may be possible to significantly reduce the bias in cross-level inference from aggregate to individual relationships by employing this simple regression method. Additional guidelines designed to insure valid application of the method are presented in Bogue and Bogue (1976:31-34), and these should be consulted when engaging in research of the type illustrated here. For instance, close ecological approximations to individual relationships seem more likely to be forthcoming when smaller ecological units are employed (e.g., counties instead of SMSAs). Also, the procedures described work best where the proportion of variation accounted for in the ecological regression is high. Finally, even if most or all recommended precautions are taken, and although the methods outlined seem generally to bring one closer to the actual individual relationship, it is still possible for estimates to be substantially in error. Hence, it is well to close this section with this comment from Bogue and Bogue:

> This does not mean, however, that researchers may return to their past uncritical use of grouped data, provided only that they throw in a few additional independent variables, use weighted regressions, and possibly stratify the ecological units along some hastily contrived basis. Instead, an effort should be made to formulate some guidelines which would curtail improper use while encouraging greater use of these techniques under conditions favorable to obtaining valid results (1976:31).

DIACHRONIC ANALYSIS

The dynamic quality of human ecological theory constitutes one of its more useful features. From the classical
interest in the growth of cities described in terms such as
invasion, succession, concentric zones (e.g., McKenzie,
1924; Burgess, 1925; Park, 1936) to Hawley's perceptive
linking of change and spatial movement (1950: Chapter 17),
as well as his definitive statement on cumulative change and
the principle of expansion (1968), to the recurrent focus on
population redistribution as seen in urbanization, suburbanization, metropolitanization (e.g., Schnore, 1965; Hawley,
1971b) and now "nonmetropolitanization" (cf. Beale and
Fuguitt, 1975), the emphasis has continued to be on process
and the dynamics of society. In particular, it has been suggested that "communal adaptation constitutes the distinctive
subject matter of ecology..." (Hawley, 1950:31) and that
adaptation, in turn, is "the most important dynamic concept
in human ecology" (Klausner, 1971:27). Micklin concludes
that:

> Adaptation as well as related terms such as adjust-
> ment and accomodation have been part of the vernacular
> of sociology for many years, (but) they do not appear to
> be among its core concepts. *On the other hand, concep-*
> *tual frameworks for the study of human ecology fre-*
> *quently stress the central importance of adaptation as*
> *an ecological process* (1973:5). - Emphasis added.

Even so, human ecologists have been no more likely (and
perhaps even less likely) than others to subject their hypotheses to diachronic test. (As always, there are notable
exceptions [e.g., Haggerty, 1971; Hunter, 1971] ). This is
especially surprising in light of widespread recognition
that research methods which entail generalization to process
from cross-sectional data can lead to a fallacy rather analogous to (and which can be specified in statistical terms in
a manner similar to) the so-called ecological fallacy
(Alker, 1969). Thus, in order to approach realization of the
dynamic potential of human ecological theory and to demonstrate its broad applicability, more attention must be paid
to methods of handling data with a temporal dimension in research designs relevant to both temporal sequence of cross-
sectional comparisons and to true longitudinal studies of
process. Given the present state of the art, the following
discussion will raise many more difficult issues than there
are presently solutions for. Nevertheless, as will be
pointed out below, progress has been made (though by no
means always by ecologists).

*The Promise and Problems of Diachronic Analysis*

A primary benefit of diachronic analysis is that it permits a more direct study of social change and thereby circumvents the problems of making cross-temporal inferences. Although it may often be the case that none but cross-sectional data are available, attempts to generalize from such data to change processes are subject to serious error (Duncan, et al., 1961) as Lieberson and Hansen (1974) clearly demonstrate in their investigation of mother tongue diversity and national development (see also Hage, 1975).

Perhaps the most persuasive reason for interest in diachronic analysis lies in its potential for determining causal priority or direction. If X and Y are significantly related and X is temporally prior to Y, Y can scarcely be a cause of X and, thus, the case of X———→Y, as opposed to Y———→X, is considerably strengthened. Unfortunately, the methods involved in carrying out analyses over time are rarely as straightforward as this simple logic would indicate.

*Availability and Quality of Data.* A common problem in diachronic analysis is the lack of high quality data over extended time periods for a large number of units of analysis. This, along with measurement problems, has led Davis (1976:1) to conclude that, in sociology, "full-blown time series analysis is seldom appropriate." Instead, Davis offers a sensible procedure based on linear flow graph methods for use with "a handful of time points" (as few as two).

Other researchers have sought alternatives which, hopefully, allow some of the benefits of time series analysis to be realized in the absence of observations over numerous points in time. One approach is simply to forge ahead with a minimally acceptable number of observation points while attempting to make adjustments for lack of longitudinal depth. For example, in an effort to test the "push-pull" migration hypothesis, Frisbie (1975a:3-13) examined lagged correlations between changes (first-differences) in a set of economic variables over a given time interval and changes in the Mexican illegal migrant apprehension rate over the next interval for the years 1946-1965. Because of the lag, one time interval was "lost" so that N = 18. Although only a few predictor variables (never more than six) were employed in achieving $R^2$ values above .6, the number of independent variables can be considered large relative to N, thereby creating the potential for artificial inflation of $R^2$. Indeed, in this case, the author's adjusted coefficients (based on McNemar, 1962) were deflated from twelve percent to about twenty-five percent, depending on the number of variables in the equation.

Another strategy recently applied by Speare, et al.
(1975, in a study of residence histories of Rhode Island
residents from 1955 to 1967 obtains N as the product of time
intervals covered and the number of respondents. Since there
were 2233 respondents and thirteen intervals, the analysis
of residential mobility was "based on 22,644 one-year life
segments" (Speare, et al., 1975:107; see also Speare, 1970:
449-458). The maximum product was not obtained since some
histories were incomplete. While possessing a definite appeal, especially given the resemblance of the "inflated N"
to the life table function, $T_x$, this method raises serious
questions concerning the independence of observations which
were used to compute mobility rates and analyzed via a modified dummy variable technique.

Lieberson and Hansen (1974:523-541) suggest a procedure
which combines cross-sectional and diachronic analysis in a
way that takes into account the problem of lack of temporal
depth while seeking to preserve the advantage in terms of
causal inference afforded by longitudinal analysis. The
recommendation is for use of diachronic case studies "to
examine the inferences drawn from cross-sectional results"
(for which significantly larger amounts of data are apt to
be available [1974:539]). What is suggested is a sort of
cross-temporal analysis in which inferences from data at one
point in time are checked against findings from time-series.
Limitations due to nonrepresentativeness of a small number
of case studies notwithstanding, it is clear that "causal
inferences based on cross-sectional data will be far more
convincing if they are at least consistent with the available longitudinal results" (Lieberson and Hansen, 1974:539).

*Causal Inference.* A primary stimulus to diachronic
research is its "theory probing" potential (Campbell, 1963),
and Hannan and Young note that "the central methodological
problem of panel analysis is to exploit intertemporal variation in such a way as to simplify causal inference" (1977:
54). In particular, time-series data afford much needed
leverage in attempts to determine causal priorities. Campbell (1963) and Pelz and Andrews (1964) proposed "cross-
lagged" correlation models for detection of causal direction
between two variables. The method basically relies on the
assumption that if A is a cause of B, and not vice versa,
the correlation $A_t B_{t+k}$ will exceed the correlation
$A_{t+k} B_t$, where k is some measurement interval and controls are imposed for stability. Unfortunately, the potential of this procedure has turned out to be considerably
less than was originally supposed. The results of early
efforts to establish causal direction were equivocal at best

(Rozelle and Campbell, 1969:79-84). In fact, quite strong *a priori* assumptions are required in order for the models to shed any light on causal priorities (Duncan, 1969:177-182). In particular, Hannan (1971:54), citing Duncan, points to a number of estimation problems associated with lagged dependent variables.

Heise, on the other hand, recommends that reliance be placed on regression coefficients obtained from time-lagged models, since they, unlike correlation coefficients, "are estimates of parameters in a specified model of change" (1970:10), and suggests a design which seems superior to the simple cross-lagged model illustrated above. Yet, even with Heise's significant extension (which he applied to panel designs), it is necessary to make strong assumptions concerning lag-times. The problem is concisely put by Davis (1976):

> Here the definitive paper seems to be Heise's (1970)....Heise is optimistic about establishing directions from panel designs. However, his argument require that one know the *causal lag exactly*. Causal lag (Heise, 1975, Chapter 6) is the time required for influence to occur....But how likely is it we would know lag but not causal direction (e.g., not know whether marijuana usage produces depression or depression produces marijuana usage, but knowing whichever it is, it takes 10 days to two weeks?). Extremely unlikely, in my opinion. (Emphasis in original.)

It should be noted that Heise's method requires a close approximation, but not completely exact knowledge, of lag-time. Further, there would seem to be no question that diachronic analysis can yield rich dividends in understanding change relationships irrespective of the direction of causation. Thus, it would appear that ecologists, who presumably have as much or more to gain as anyone from analysis of change, should be in the forefront of those attempting to devise better methodological and statistical approaches for use with time-series data.

Of course, numerous problems exist besides those mentioned. For example, even if the causal lag can be precisely determined, appropriate data may not be available at the intervals required. Other difficulties include "simultaneity bias" and autocorrelation.

*Levels, Change Score, and Simultaneity Bias.* Before engaging in analysis of variables measured at more than one point in time, one must first determine just what type of relationship is of major interest. One might observe, e.g., how levels of X at time t are related to levels of Y at time t + k. Alternatively, interest might be in the relationship between levels of X at t and the change in Y between t and t + k or how changes in X over an interval are associated with changes in Y over the same period of time. In interpreting regression coefficients, we often say that a given change in Y is associated with a certain unit change in X even though the data are purely cross-sectional. There is certainly no harm in using this terminological convenience—as long as we do not convince ourselves and others that we are talking about process when what we really have are static relationships. On the other hand, if we are really interested in whether a change in X is related to a change in Y, the most logical procedure would be to make use of change scores (first differences). Moreover, unless we believe that a change in X *concurrently* produces a change in Y, one might logically turn to lagged change scores.

As with other methods considered thus far, this procedure is not as easy to implement as it is to describe. A number of authors have voiced a caution that, with either change scores or ratio variables with common components, built-in definitional dependencies may exist such that the observed relationships are partially spurious (i.e., due to the common elements; see Schuessler, 1973; Freeman and Kronenfeld, 1973; Fuguitt and Lieberson, 1974). However, the issue of complex variables and definitional dependency may not be anywhere near as severe as some scholars have envisioned (Kasarda and Nolan, 1979; MacMillan and Daft, 1979). In analyses of the type under consideration here, this particular problem does not exist since they do not contain common terms. That is, attention is being directed to correlations of the type:

$$r_{X_1 Y_2}$$

or

$$r_{X_1 (Y_2 - Y_1)}$$

or

$$r_{(X_2 - X_1)(Y_2 - Y_1)}.$$

By contrast, issues of definitional dependency might arise with correlations of the type:

$$r_{(X - Z)(Y - Z)} \text{ or } r_{(X - Y)X}$$

(Fuguitt and Lieberson, 1974).

Lieberson and Hansen (1974) do caution that problems may also exist with correlations of the type:

$$r_{(X_2 - X_1)(Y_2 - Y_1)},$$

but the difficulty they have in mind seems to be that of stability effects due to the serial correlation of Y with itself. The latter problem can apparently be handled by partialling out the stability effect in the manner mentioned above. And, in fact, Lieberson and Hansen (1974:525) follow a somewhat similar procedure as evidenced by their statement describing how the effects of levels of predictor variables measured in 1930 affect levels of mother tongue diversity in 1960, net of the effect of the latter variable in 1930. However, Miller (1971:291) cautions that, while this method may often be a satisfactory solution, it may result in reversal of the direction of the true relationship "in some cases where the effect of X on Y is immediate and temporary." Problems of serially correlated errors, of course, pose even more serious difficulties.

When the dependent variable is operationalized in terms of change scores and the equation is estimated using change scores and/or end-of-period variables as predictors, problems of simultaneity may plague the analysis since changes in Y may engender changes in the independent variables and, therefore, impact end-of-period levels of the independent variables as well (Greenwood, 1975). In such an event, OLS single equation regression may yield biased estimates of parameters. This observation should occasion little or no difficulty in many cases, since Greenwood concludes from his examination of migration data that a model in which levels of X at time t are used to predict changes in Y between times t and t + k can be estimated via OLS inasmuch as the levels of X at the beginning of the period cannot be affected by changes in Y over the period (1975:530). With other kinds of analyses where change scores in X are related to change scores in Y, and "if significant interactions are expected" between them, OLS may be inappropriate. However, simultaneous equation models and techniques for their estimation are available (e.g., see Greenwood, 1975, and Hannan and Young, 1977).

*Autocorrelation.* A major obstacle in arriving at causal inferences from time-series data is the frequent occurrence of serially-correlated error terms, i.e., autocorrelation (Blalock, 1969; Heise, 1970; Hibbs, 1974). With autocorrelated disturbances, ordinary least squares (OLS) will yield unbiased estimates of regression coefficients, but serious underestimates of sampling variances and standard errors are likely (Johnston, 1972:246). As Hibbs (1974: 257) points out. given the typically negative bias in regard to error variance, values of $R^2$, t, and F will tend to be inflated.

Techniques designed to deal with nonindependent disturbances have been developed primarily in the econometrics literature (see Nakamura, et al., 1976). Perhaps the most common approach has involved differencing and other transformations of data. "The rationale for the use of first differences" depends on the assumption that the coefficient of autocorrelation "is *close* to one" (Aigner, 1971:132, emphasis in the original). Even if such an assumption can safely be made, it may be argued that, when we test for the significance of a linear relationship of first differences of two series, "we are not testing exactly the same hypothesis as when we test for a linear relation between the two series themselves" (Nakamura, et al., 1976:218). On the other hand, it would quite often seem to be the case that primary theoretical interest really is in whether a *change* in X between two points in time is associated with a *change* in Y over the same (or a later) interval.

Tests on which to base decisions regarding autocorrelated series are available. the most prominent being the Durbin-Watson d-statistic (Durbin and Watson, 1950, 1951). A conventional approach is to test for autocorrelation applying the Durbin-Watson test "to the computed residuals from the least-squares regression" (Johnston, 1972: 249). If autocorrelation is detected, the data may be transformed, and subsequent residuals may then be tested for autocorrelation (Aigner, 1971; Johnston, 1972·262-263).

In actual practice, the procedure may not turn out to be so simple. For example, use of the Durbin-Watson statistic presumes a first-order autogressive series, but it is certainly possible that higher-order processes are at work. Further, if lagged endogenous variables appear in the system, OLS no longer yields unbiased estimates (Hibbs, 1974·290), and the Durbin-Watson statistic itself is "biased *against* finding serial correlation" (Aigner, 1971:136, emphasis in the original).

Hibbs (1974:260) argues persuasively for expanded use of generalized least squares (GLS) and "pseudo-GLS" techniques since they provide an "unbiased estimate of the error variance." Hannan and Young (1977) conclude that even in the face of problems of the sort outlined above, it may still be possible to employ lagged variables. These authors mention three alternative methods:

(1) "Average observations over time and analyze the averages" is rejected since the procedure increases standard error and "grouping over time or over units gives rise in many cases to complicated aggregation problems" (p. 57).

(2) "Conduct separate analyses for each lag period."
This may be useful since it "avoids aggregation
problems" and "may uncover changes in the causal
structure over time" (p. 57).

If changes in causal structure over time are not observed, a
further alternative is:

(3) "Pool the lag structures into a single model." The
third technique might consist of pooling the scores for
several time periods, T, for all N units of analysis.
Although acknowledging that the technique does not produce NT independent outcomes, Hannan and Young (p. 59)
conclude that "the pooling method yields a considerable
gain in efficiency" and allows "explicit consideration
of autocorrelation problems." Whether or not such an
effort is worthwhile naturally depends on the availability of time-series data of the sort required for
sophisticated techniques to bear substantive fruit, as
well as obtaining a reasonable approximation of lag-
times. In sociology, at least, it would seem that the
nature of the data will often preclude even initial
steps along these lines (Davis, 1976:1). Whatever the
case, the implication is that conclusions from time-
series based on conventional OLS procedures are highly
questionable in the absence of tests (and/or adjustments) for autocorrelation. Interestingly, Hannan and
Young (1977:78) find that OLS estimates are "actually
improved" in the presence of both autocorrelation and
simultaneity in that "the biasing effect of simultaneity
can be considerably offset by the presence of autocorrelation." With the increasing availability of appropriate time-series data, a further implication is that
the new directions (new at least to most sociologists)
proposed by Hibbs and others (e.g., Mayer and Arney's
[1974] explication of spectral analysis) seem well worth
pursuing.

The major conclusions reached on the basis of the foregoing discussion are, first, that the centrality of dynamic
concepts for human ecology strongly suggests that we pay
more attention to the methodology of cross-temporal research
and, second, that although problems exist in such research
above and beyond conventional static analysis, techniques
are available which would seem to permit significant substantive returns from diachronic analyses. Finally, it
should be kept clearly in mind that diachronic designs will

in some instances be inferior to cross-sectional models. In particular, this will be the case where confounding influences vary more over time than over units (Hannan and Tuma, 1979:303).

## CROSS-NATIONAL RESEARCH

Just as with cross-level and cross-temporal analyses, consistent findings (or theoretically meaningful interpretations of divergent results) across societies bolster claims for the generality of the ecological perspective. Ecological theory argues for convergence toward isomorphism of urban structure as "increasing participation by initially differentiated societies in a common technology, common markets, and a common universe of discourse exerts a powerful generalizing and standardizing influence" (Hawley, 1971ʰ·294). An empirical illustration of the point is the consistent emergence of configurations reflecting socioeconomic status, family life cycle, and ethnic (minority group) status in cross-national factor analyses and reasonable explan tions of divergencies in structure where these have occurred (Berry and Kasarda, 1977, Chapter 7; Schwirian, 1974:21-23).

At least as consistent are the findings from "almost a hundred cases..., with examples drawn from most parts of the world for the past 150 years," (Berry and Kasarda, 1977:87, 94-95) that testify to the regularity with which urban population densities conform to Colin Clark's (1951) equation:

$$d_x = d_o e^{-bx}$$

which expresses the decline in population density d at distance x from the city's center and where $d_o$ is the center density, and b represents the density gradient.

Since ecologists seem to have made greater strides in cross-national analyses, especially of urbanization, economic development, and the division of labor (e.g., Gibbs and Martin, 1962; Schnore, 1969; Gibbs and Browning, 1966; Berry and Kasarda, 1977: Chapters 7 and 17-20) than has been the case in regard to cross-level and time-series comparisons, only a brief discussion of problems in cross-national research is presented.

Among the more vexing difficulties in cross-national research are the questionable quality and comparability of data (see Davis, 1965). Systematic bias may enter an analysis if, as is usually the case, data from developing countries are less likely to be available and more likely to be inaccurate. Problems of gaps in the data and diminution of sample size can be partially remedied by the substitution of means (generally a "conservative" strategy, cf. Heise, et al., 1976:324) or estimation of missing values through regression involving the fully covered variables. If consistent results are obtained with a variety of methods, the case that the observed relationships are "method-independent" is strengthened.

It may be impossible to adequately handle inaccurate data, but Scheuch (1966) recommends opting for rougher measurement by collapsing categories in order that "the threshold of sensibility to error"... will be greater "than the possible errors in the data." He also indicates that, even if there are inaccuracies in the data, comparisons of nations may be relatively safe over time if (and it is a large "if") the error can be assumed to remain relatively constant over the intervals studied.

Lack of comparability of data creates further difficulties. The effort by the United Nations to standardize data reporting is far from complete success, as a cursory inspection of the wide variety of definitions of "urban" will attest. In addition, changes in definitions and improvements in data collection and reporting sometimes make for noncomparability. In some cases, it is of course possible to create comparability by simple manipulation of the data.

Scheuch (1966:148) summarizes a set of strategies for handling or ameliorating problems of cross-national data such as those delineated above as follows:

> In general, and especially for such varied, unstable, and heterogeneous units as polities, we would recommend as a strategy: (1) reliance on several descriptions in addition to averages (at least a measure of dispersion); (2) in many cases averaging between repeated observations over a short period of time; (3) grouping cases into comparable classes; and (4) discarding units that are not units in terms of the inferences drawn.

Despite the difficulties involved in cross-national study, the alternative of no research at all seems to be a case of the cure being worse than the disease. Further, when cross-national and cross-temporal analyses can be combined in the same research design, the dividends are apt to be considerable.

## SUMMARY

An attempt has been made to raise in summary form a fairly large number of methodological and statistical issues in human ecology, to comment on the progress made in dealing with these issues and, finally, to suggest possible avenues along which further progress might be achieved. No attempt has been made to compare the methodological progress in ecological research with that achieved in other areas of sociology or in other disciplines. Overall, ecologists probably fare little better or worse than other sociologists. But the latter point is hardly worth debating. What is important is that the methods of human ecology be adequate for the realization of its theoretical potential.

168

Abrahamson, M., and M. A. DuBick (1977). "Patterns of urban dominance: the U.S. in 1890." American Sociological Review 42 (October):756-768.

Abu-Lughod, T. T.. (1969). "Testing the theory of social area analysis: the ecology of Cairo, Egypt." American Sociological Review 34 (April):198-211.

Aigner D. J. (1971). Basic Econometrics. Englewood Cliffs: Prentice-Hall.

Alexandersson, G. (1956). The Industrial Structure of American Cities. Lincoln, Nebraska: University of Nebraska Press.

Alihan, M. (1938). Social Ecology: A Critical Analysis. New York: Columbia University Press.

Alker, H. R., Jr. (1969). "A typology of ecological fallacies." Pp. 69-86 in M. Dogan and S. Rokkan (eds.), Quantitative Ecological Analysis in the Social Sciences. Cambridge: MIT Press.

Allardt, E. (1969). "Aggregate analysis: the problem of its informative value." Pp. 53-68 in M. Dogan and S. Rokkan (eds.), Quantitative Ecological Analysis in the Social Sciences. Cambridge: MIT Press.

Anderson, T. R., and J. A. Egeland (1961). "Spatial aspects of social area analysis." American Sociological Review 26 (June):392-398.

Bassis, M. S. (1977). "The campus as a frog pond: a theoretical and empirical reassessment." American Journal of Sociology 82 (May):1318-1326.

Beale, C. L., and G. V. Fuguitt (1975). "The new pattern of nonmetropolitan population change." Working Paper 75-22 (Revised, 1976). University of Wisconsin Center for Demography and Ecology.

Berry, B. J. L., and W. L. Garrison (1958). "The functional bases of the central place hierarchy." Economic Geography 34:145-154.

Berry, B. J. L., and J. D. Kasarda (1977). Contemporary Urban Ecology. New York: Macmillan.

Berry, B. J. L., and P. H. Rees (1969). "The factorial ecology of Calcutta." American Journal of Sociology 74 (March):445-491.

Berry, B. J. L., and H. Spodek (1971). "Comparative ecologies of large Indian cities." Economic Geography 47 (June):266-285.

Blalock, H. M., Jr. (1964). Causal Inferences in Non-experimental Research. Chapel Hill: University of North Carolina Press.

Blalock, H. M., Jr. (1969). Theory Construction. Englewood Cliffs: Prentice-Hall.

Blau, P. M. (1960). "Structural effects." American Sociological Review 25:178-193.

Bogue, D. J. (1949). The Structure of the Metropolitan Community: A Study of Dominance and Subdominance. Ann Arbor: University of Michigan Press.

Bogue, D. J., and E. J. Bogue (1976). Essays in Human Ecology. Chicago: University of Chicago Community and Family Study Center.

Rurgess, E. W. (1925). "The growth of the city." Pp. 37-62 in R. E. Park, E. W. Burgess, and R. D. McKenzie (eds.), The City. Chicago: University of Chicago Press.

Campbell, D. T. (1963). "From description to experimentation: interpreting trends as quasi-experiments." Pp. 212-242 in C. W. Harris (ed.), Problems in Measuring Change. Madison: University of Wisconsin Press.

Caplow, T. (1952). "Urban structure in France." American Sociological Review 17 (October):544-549.

Clark, C. (1951). "Urban population densities." Journal of the Royal Statistical Society, Series A, 114: 490-496.

Clemence, T. G. (1967). "Residential segregation in the mid-sixties." Demography 4(2):562-568.

Clemente, F. (1972). "The measurement problem in the analysis of the division of labor." Pacific Sociological Review 15 (January):30-40.

Clemente, F., and R. B. Sturgis (1972). "The division of labor in America: an ecological analysis." Social Forces 51 (December):176-182.

Cortese, C. F., R. F. Falk, and J. K. Cohen (1976). "Further considerations on the methodological analysis of segregation indices." American Sociological Review 41 (August):630-637.

Cowgill, D. O., and M. S. Cowgill (1951). "An index of segregation based on block statistics." American Sociological Review 16 (December):825-831.

Davie, M. R. (1937). "The pattern of urban growth." Pp. 133-161 in C. P. Murdock (ed.), Studies in the Science of Society. New Haven: Yale University Press.

Davis, J. A. (1966). "The campus as a frog pond: an application of the theory of relative deprivations to career decisions of college men." American Journal of Sociology 72 (July):17-31.

Davis, J. A. (1976). "Studying categorical data over time." Paper presented at the Conference on Strategies of Longitudinal Research on Drug Use. San Juan, Puerto Rico (April).

Davis, ᴛ. A., J. L. Spaeth, and C. Hudson (1961). "A technique for analyzing the effects of group composition." American Sociological Review 26:215-225.

Davis, K. (1965). "La comparacion internacional en las ciencias sociales: problemas y soluciones." America Latina, 8 (January-March):61-75.

Duncan, B., G. Sabagh, and M. D. van Arsdol (1962). "Patterns of city growth." American Journal of Sociology, 67 (January):418-429.

Duncan, B., and S. Lieberson (1970). Metropolis and Region in Transition. Beverly Hills, California: Sage.

Duncan, O. D. (1952). "Urbanization and retail specialization." Social Forces 30 (March)·267-271.

Duncan, O. D. (1959). "Human ecology and population studies." Pp. 678-716 in P. M. Hauser and O. D. Duncan (eds.), The Study of Population. Chicago: University of Chicago Press.

Duncan, O. D. (1961). "From social system to ecosystem." Sociological Inquiry 31(2):140-149.

Duncan, O. D. (1964). "Social organization and the ecosystem." Pp. 36-82 in R. E. L. Faris (ed.), Handbook of Modern Sociology. Chicago: Rand McNally.

Duncan, O. D. (1969). "Some linear models for two-wave, two-variable panel analysis." Psychological Bulletin 72 (September):177-182.

Duncan, O. D., R. P. Cuzzort, and B. Duncan (1961). Statistical Geography. Glencoe, Illinois: Free Press.

Duncan, O. D., and B. Davis (1953). "An alternative to ecological correlation." American Sociological Review, 18:655-666.

Duncan, O. D., and B. Duncan (1955a). "A methodological analysis of segregation indexes." American Sociological Review 20 (April):210-217.

Duncan, O. D., and B. Duncan (1955b). "Residential distribution and occupational stratification." American Journal of Sociology 60 (March):493-503.

Duncan, O. D., and A. J. Reiss (1956). Social Characteristics of Urban and Rural Communities, 1950. New York: Wiley.

Duncan, O. D., R. W. Scott, S. Lieberson, B. Duncan and H. H. Winsborough (1960). Metropolis and Region. Baltimore: Johns Hopkins University Press.

Durbin, J., and G. S. Watson (1950). "Testing for serial correlation in least-squares regression. Biometrika 37:409-428.

Durban, J., and G. S. Watson (1951). "Testing for serial correlation in least-squares regression." Biometrika 38:159-178.

Farkas, G. (1974). "Specification, residuals and contextual effects." Sociological Methods and Research 2 (February):333-363.

Farley, R., and K. E. Taeuber (1968). "Population trends and residential segregation since 1960." Science (March 1): 953-956.

Firebaugh, G. (1978). "A rule for inferring individual-level relationships from aggregate data." American Sociological Review 43 (August):557-572.

Firey, W. (1945). "Sentiment and symbolism as ecological variables." American Sociological Review 10 (April):140-148.

Firey, W. (1947). Land Use in Central Boston. Cambridge, M.A.: Harvard University Press.

Form, W. (1954). "The place of social structure in the determination of land use: some implications for a theory of urban ecology." Social Forces 32 (May):317-323.

Freeman, J. H., and J. E. Kronenfeld (1973). "Problems of definitional dependency: the case of administrative intensity." Social Forces 52 (September):108-121.

Frisbie, W. P. (1975a). "Illegal migration from Mexico to the United States: a longitudinal analysis." International Migration Review 9 (Spring):3-13.

Frisbie, W. P. (1975b). "Measuring the degree of bureaucratization at the societal level." Social Forces 53 (June):563-573.

Frisbie, W. P., and D. L. Poston, Jr. (1975). "Components of sustenance organization and nonmetropolitan population change: a human ecological investigation." American Sociological Review 40 (December):773-784.

Frisbie, W. P., and D. L. Poston, Jr. (1976). "The structure of sustenance organization in nonmetropolitan America." Rural Sociology 41 (Fall):354-370.

Frisbie, W. P., and D. L. Poston, Jr. (1978). Sustenance Organization and Migration in Nonmetropolitan America. Iowa City, Iowa: Urban Community Research Center.

Fuguitt, G. V., and S. Lieberson (1974). "Correlation of ratios or difference scores having common terms." Pp. 128-128-144 in H. L. Costner (ed.), Sociological Methodology, 1973-1974. San Francisco: Jossey-Bass.

Galle, O. R., W. R. Gove, and J. M. McPherson (1972). "Population density and pathology: what are the relations for man?" Science 176 (April 7):23-30.

Gehlke, C. E., and K. Biehl (1934). "Certain effects of grouping upon the size of the correlation coefficient in census tract material." Journal of American Statistical Association (Supplement) 29:169-170.

Gibbs, J. P., and H. L. Browning (1966). "The division of labor, technology, and the organization of production in twelve countries." American Sociological Review 31 (February):81-92.

Gibbs, J. P., and M. L. Erickson (1976). "Crime rates of American cities in an ecological context." American Journal of Sociology 82 (November):605-620.

Gibbs, J. P., and W. T. Martin (1959). "Toward a theoretical system of human ecology." Pacific Sociological Review 2 (Spring):29-36.

Gibbs, J. P., and W. T. Martin (1962). "Urbanization, technology, and the division of labor: international patterns" American Sociological Review 27 (October):667-677.

Gibbs, J. P., and D. L. Poston, Jr. (1975). "The division of labor: conceptualization and related measures." Social Forces 53 (March):468-476.

Gilmore, H. W. (1944). "The old New Orleans and the new." American Sociological Review 9 (August):385-394.

Goodman, L. A. (1953). "Ecological regressions and behavior of individuals." American Sociological Review 18 (December):63-64.

Goodman, L. A. (1959). "Some alternatives to ecological correlation." American Journal of Sociology 64 (May):610-625.

Greenwood, J. M. (1975). "Simultaneity bias in migration models: an empirical examination." Demography 12 (August): 519-536.

Guest, A. M. (1972). "Patterns of family location." Demography 9 (February):159-172.

Guest, A. M. (1977). "Residential segregation in urban areas." Pp. 268-336 in K. Schwirian (ed.), Contemporary Topics in Urban Sociology. Morristown, NJ.: General Learning Press.

Hage, J. (1975). "Theoretical decision rules for selecting research designs: the study of nation-states or societies." Sociological Methods and Research 4 (November): 131-165.

Haggerty, L. J. (1971). "Another look at the Burgess hypothesis: time as an important variable." American Journal of Sociology 76 (May):1084-1093.

Hammond, J. L., Jr. (1973). "Two sources of error in ecological correlations. American Sociological Review 38 (December):764-777.

Hannan, M. T. (1971). "Problems of aggregation." Pp. 473-508 in H. M. Blalock, Jr. (ed.), Causal Models in the Social Sciences. Chicago: Aldine-Atherton.

Hannan, M. T., and J. Freeman (1977). "The population ecology of organizations." American Journal of Sociology 82 (March):929-964.

Hannan, M. T., and N. B. Tuma (1979). "Methods for temporal analysis." Pp. 303-328 in A. Ikeles, J. Coleman, and P. H. Turner (eds.). Annual Review of Sociology. Palo Alto: Annual Reviews, Inc.

Hannan, M. T., and A. A. Young (1977). "Estimation in panel models: results on pooling cross-sections and time series." Pp. 52-83 in D. R. Heise (ed.), Sociological Methodology (1977). San Francisco: Jossey-Bass.

Harris, C. D., and E. L. Ullman (1945). "The nature of cities." Annals of the American Academy of Political and Social Science 242:7-17.

Harris, C. E. (1943). "A functional classification of cities in the United States." Geographical Review 33 (January):86-99.

Hauser, R. M. (1970). "Context and consex: a cautionary tale." American Journal of Sociology 75 (January): 645-664.

Hauser, R. M. (1974). "Contextual analysis revisted." Sociological Methods and Research 2 (February):365-375.

Hawley, A. H. (1944a). "Dispersion versus segregation apropos of a solution of race problems." Papers of the Michigan Academy of Science, Arts, and Letters 30:667-674.

Hawley, A. H. (1944b). "Ecology and human ecology." Social Forces 22 (May):398-405.

Hawley, A. H. (1948). "Discussion of Hollingshead's 'community research: development and present condition.'" American Sociological Review 13 (April):153-156.

Hawley, A. H. (1950). Human Ecology. New York: Ronald.

Hawley, A. H. (1968). "Human ecology." Pp. 323-332 in D. L. Sills (ed.), International Encyclopedia of the Social Sciences. New York: Crowell-Collier and Macmillan.

Hawley, A. H. (1971a). "The structure of social systems." Department of Sociology mimeo. University of North Carolina.

Hawley, A. H. (1971b). Urban Society. New York: Ronald.

Heise, D. R. (1970). "Causal inference from panel data." Pp. 3-27 in E. F. Borgatta and G. W. Bohrnstedt (eds.), Sociological Methodology, 1970. San Francisco: Jossey-Bass.

Heise, D. R. (1975). Causal Analysis. New York: Wiley.

Heise, D. R., G. Lenski, and J. Wardwell (1976). "Further notes on technology and the moral order." Social Forces 55 (December):316-337.

Hibbs, D. A., Jr. (1974). "Problems of statistical estimation and causal inference in time-series regression models." Pp. 252-308 in H. L. Costner (ed.), Sociological Methodology, 1973-1974. San Francisco: Jossey-Bass.

Hoyt, H. (1939). The Structure and Growth of Residential Neighborhoods in American Cities. Washington, D.C.: U.S. Government Printing Office.

174

Hunter, A. (1971). "The ecology of Chicago: persistence and change, 1930-1960." American Journal of Sociology 77 (November):425-444.

Jahn, J. A. (1950). "The measurement of ecological segregation: derivation of an index based on the criterion of reproducibility." American Sociological Review 12 (February):100-104.

Jahn, J. A., C. F. Schmid, and C. Schrag (1947). "The measurement of ecological segregation." American Sociological Review 12 (June):293-303.

Johnston, J. (1972). Econometric Methods. New York: McGraw-Hill.

Johnston, R. J. (1971). "Some limitations of factoral ecologies and social area analysis." Economic Geography 47 (June):314-323.

Kasarda, J. D. (1974). "The structural implications of system size: a three-level analysis." American Sociological Review 39 (February):19-28.

Kasarda, J. D., and P. D. Nolan (1979). "Ratio measurement and theoretical inference in social research." Social Forces 58 (September):212-227.

Kass, R. (1973). "A functional classification of metropolitan communities." Demography 10 (August):427-445.

Kass, R. (1977). "Community structure and the metropolitan division of labor." Social Forces 56 (September): 218-239.

Kemper, T. D. (1972). "The division of labor: a post-Durkheimian analytical view." American Sociological Review 37 (December):739-753.

Key, V. O., Jr. (1949). Southern Politics in State and Nation. New York: Vintage Books.

Klausner, S. F. (1971). On Man in this Environment. San Francisco: Jossey-Bass.

Kruskal, J. B. (1964a). "Multidimensional scaling by optimizing goodness of fit to a nonmetric hypothesis." Psychometrika 29 (March):1-27.

Kruskal, J. B. (1964b). "Nonmetric multidimensional scaling: a numerical method." Psychometrika 29 (June): 115-129.

Labovitz, S., and J. P. Gibbs (1964). "Urbanization, technology, and the division of labor." Pacific Sociological Review 7 (Spring):3-9.

Lampard, E. (1968). "The evolving system of cities in the United States." Pp. 81-139 in H. Perloff and L. Wingo (eds.), Issues in Urban Economics. Baltimore: Johns Hopkins University Press.

Lieberson, S., and L. K. Hansen (1974). "National development, mother tongue diversity, and the comparative study of nations." American Sociological Review 39 (August):523-541.

Linz, J. J. (1969). "Ecological analysis and survey research." Pp. 91-131 in M. Dogan and S. Rokkan (eds.), Quantitative Ecological Analysis in the Social Sciences. Cambridge: MIT Press.

MacMillan, A., and R. L. Dapt (1979). "Administrative intensity and ratio variables: the case against definitional dependency." Social Forces 58 (September):228-248.

Mayer, T. F., and W. R. Arney (1974). "Spectral analysis and the study of social change." Pp. 309-355 in H. L. Costner (ed.), Sociological Methodology, 1973-1974. San Francisco: Jossey-Bass.

McFarland, D. D., and D. J. Brown (1973). "Social distance as a metric: a systematic introduction to smallest space analysis." Pp. 213-253 in E. O. Lauman (ed.), Bonds of Pluralism. New York: Wiley.

McKenzie, R. D. (1924). "The ecological approach to the study of the human community." American Journal of Sociology 30 (November).

McNemar, Q. (1962). Psychological Statistics (3rd Edition). New York: Wiley.

Menzel, H. (1950). "Comment on Robinson's 'ecological correlations and the behavior of individuals.'" American Sociological Review 15 (October):674-675.

Michelson, W. (1970). Man and His Urban Environment. Reading, MA.: Addison-Wesley.

Micklin, M. (1973). "A framework for the study of human ecology." Pp. 2-19 in M. Micklin (ed.), Population, Environment and Social Organization: Current Issues in Human Ecology. Hinsdale, IL.: Dryden Press.

Miller, A. D. (1971). "Logic of causal analysis: from experimental to nonexperimental designs." Pp. 273-294 in H. M. Blalock, Causal Models in the Social Sciences. Chicago: Aldine.

Nakamura, A. O., M. Nakamura, and G. H. Orcutt (1976). "Testing for relationships between time series. Journal of the American Statistical Association 71 (March):214-222.

Nelson, H. J. (1955). "A service classification of cities." Economic Geography 31 (July):189-210.

Pampel, F. C., and H. M. Choldin (1978). "Urban location and segregation of the aged: a block-level analysis." Social Forces 56 (June):1121-1139.

Park, R. E. (1936). "Human ecology." American Journal of Sociology 42 (July):1-15.

Pedersen, P. O. (1967). Modeller for Befolkningsstruktur og Befolkningssudviklingi Storbymorader Specielt med Henblik pa Storkobehavn. Copenhagen: State Urban Planning Institute. (As cited in Berry and Kasarda, 1977).

Pelz, C. D., and F. M. Andrews (1964). "Detecting causal priorities in panel study data." American Sociological Review 29 (December):836-848.

Rees, P. H. (1971). "Factorial ecology: an extended definition, survey, and critique of the field." Economic Geography 47 (June):220-233.

Robinson, A. H. (1956). "The necessity of weighting values in correlation analysis of areal data." Annals of the Association of American Geographers 46:233-236.

Robinson, W. S. (1950). "Ecological correlations and the behavior of individuals." American Sociological Review 15 (June):351-357.

Roof, W. C., and T. L. Van Valey (1972). "Residential segregation and social differentiation in American urban areas." Social Forces 51 (September):87-91.

Roof, W. C., T. L. Van Valey, and D. Spain (1976). "Residential segregation in southern cities: 1970." Social Forces 55 (September):59-71.

Rozelle, R. M., and D. T. Campbell (1969). "More plausible rival hypotheses in the cross-lagged panel correlation technique." Psychological Bulletin 71 (January): 74-80.

Rushing, W. A., and V. Davies (1970). "Note on the mathematical formulation of a measure of division of labor." Social Forces 48 (March):394-396.

Salins, P. D. (1971). "Household location patterns in American metropolitan areas." Economic Geography 47 (June): 234-248.

Scheuch, E. K. (1966). "Cross-national comparisons using aggregate data: some substantive and methodological problems." Pp. 131-167 in R. L. Merritt and S. Rokkan (eds.)., Comparing Nations. New Haven: Yale University Press.

Scheuch, E. K. (1969). "Social context and individual behavior." Pp. 133-156 in M. Dogan and S. Rokkan (eds.), Quantitative Ecological Analysis in the Social Sciences. Cambridge: MIT Press.

Schmidt, R. C. (1966). "Density, health and social organizations." Journal of the American Institute of Planners 32:38-40.

Schnore, L. F. (1958). "Social morphology and human ecology." American Journal of Sociology 63 (May):620-634.

Schnore, L. F. (1961). "The myth of human ecology." Sociological Inquiry 31:128-139.

Schnore, L. F. (1965). The Urban Scene. New York: The Free Press.

Schnore, L. F. (1969). "The statistical measurement of urbanization and economic development." Pp. 91-106 in W. A. Faunce and W. H. Form (eds.), Comparative Perspectives on Industrial Society. Boston: Little, Brown and Company.

Schuessler, K. (1973). "Ratio variables and path models." In A. S. Goldberger and O. D. Duncan (eds.), Structural Equation Models in the Social Sciences. New York: Seminar.

Schwirian, K. P. (1974). "Some recent trends and methodological problems in urban ecological research." Pp. 3-31 in K. P. Schwirian (ed.), Comparative Urban Structure. Lexington, MA.: Heath.

Schwirian, K. P., and M. Matre (1974). "The ecological structure of Canadian cities." Pp. 309-323 in K. P. Schwirian (ed.), Comparative Urban Structure. Lexington, MA.: Heath.

Sewell, W., and J. M. Armer (1966a). "Neighborhood context and college plans." American Sociological Review 31 (February):159-168.

Sewell, W., and J. M. Armer (1966b). "Reply to Turner, Michael and Boyle." American Sociological Review 31 (September):707-712.

Shevky, E., and W. Bell (1955). Social Area Analysis. Stanford: Stanford University Press.

Shively, W. P. (1969). "Ecological inference: the use of aggregate data to study individuals." American Political Science Review 63 (December):1183-1196.

Simkus, A. A. (1978). "Residential segregation by occupation and race in ten urbanized areas, 1950-1971." American Sociological Review 43 (February):81-93.

Sly, D. F. (1972). "Migration and the ecological complex." American Sociological Review 37 (October):615-628.

Smith, D. L., and R. E. Snow (1976). "The division of labor: conceptual and methodological issues." Social Forces 55 (December):520-528.

Sorensen, A., K. E. Taueber, and L. Hollingsworth, Jr. (1975). "Indexes of racial segregation for 109 cities in the United States, 1940 to 1970." Sociological Focus 8 (April): 125-142.

Speare, A., Jr. (1970). "Home ownership, life cycle stage, and residential mobility." Demography 7:449-468.

Speare, A., Jr., S. Goldstein, and W. H. Frey (1975). Residential Mobility, Migration and Metropolitan Change. Cambridge, MA.: Ballinger.

178

Sweetser, F. L. (1965). "Factor structure as ecological structure in Helsinki and Boston." Acta Sociologica 26: 205-225.

Sweetser, F. L. (1969). "Ecological factors in metropolitan zones and sectors." Pp. 413-456 in M. Dogan and S. Rokkan (eds.), Quantitative Analysis in the Social Sciences. Cambridge, MA.: MIT Press.

Taueber, K. E., and A. F. Taeuber (1965). Negroes in Cities. Chicago: Aldine.

Thomas, E. N., and D. L. Anderson (1966). "Additional comments on weighting values in correlation analysis of areal data." Annals of the Association of American Geographers 55 (December):492-505.

Valkonen, T. (1969). "Individual and structural effects in ecological research." Pp. 53-68 in M. Dogan and S. Rokkan (eds.), Quantitative Ecological Methods in the Social Sciences. Cambridge, MA.: MIT Press.

Vance, R. B., and S. S. Sutker (1954). "Metropolitan dominance and integration." Chapter 6 in R. B. Vance and N. J. Demerath (eds.), The Urban South. Chapel Hill: University of North Carolina Press.

Van Valey,T. L., W. C. Roof, and J. E. Wilcox (1977). "Trends in residential segregation: 1960-1970." American Journal of Sociology 82 (January):826-844.

Wanner, R. A. (1977). "The dimensionality of the urban functional system." Demography 14 (November):519-537.

Winship, P. C. (1977). "A revaluation of indexes of residential segregation." Social Forces 55 (June):1058-1066.

Wirth, L. (1938). "Urbanism as a way of life." American Journal of Sociology 44 (July):1-24.

# Part II

## THE THEORY AND SUBSTANCE OF ECOLOGICAL KNOWLEDGE

# Introduction

*the Editors*

While Part I dealt with the epistemological bases of human ecology, Part II presents some results of ecological analysis. It surveys a large number of studies conducted between 1950 and the late 1970s. Each of its four chapters sets forth the objectives of research at a particular societal level, exhaustively reviews several studies, and concludes with some suggestions for needed research. Chapters 6, 7, and 8 deal with units of analysis which have been examined since the beginnings of human ecology: communities of smaller or larger scale, cities (which are covered in all three chapters), and regions. But the first chapter in Part II attempts to bring a new type of social unit, the large-scale organization, under the ecological umbrella.

John Kasarda and Charles Bidwell, authors of Chapter 5, take seriously Hawley's argument that organization is the principal adaptive mechanism of human populations. Generally they follow Duncan's inclusion of social organization as one of the four main elements of the ecosystem. Literally, Kasarda and Bidwell examine the organization itself as a unit of ecological analysis. Thus, they attempt to liberate ecology from its traditional attachment to community studies, implicitly suggesting that an ecological perspective can have far broader sociological utility. Drawing from their empirical studies of large-scale educational bureaucracies, the authors incorporate the vocabulary of systems theory more explicitly into ecological analysis. Simultaneously, though, they use concepts from bioecology, such as the *niche,* in a new and potentially fruitful content. They lead ecologists toward an open systems perspective, suggesting that the model of a bounded system, as might have been used in community research, is not appropriate. In general, Kasarda and Bidwell, by helping to open a new field--organizational analysis--to ecological analysis and by explicitly bringing systems theory into combination with ecological concepts offer new possibilities to sociological human ecology.

Like Kasarda and Bidwell, Choldin, in Chapter 6, is attempting to build bridges between main-line ecology and other theories and units. Working toward a micro-ecology, Choldin argues that places and populations smaller than communities may be better understood by means of ecological analysis. In particular, he suggests that suburbs and neighborhoods, which are not complete communities in any sense,

179

can be analyzed ecologically as subcommunities. The residential area is no longer a tightly-knit primary group, if it ever was one. Nonetheless, it does represent the locus of important social activities, from childrearing to consumption and expression of life styles. Choldin reviews and endorses a series of recent attempts to forge a combination of human ecology and social psychology, harkening back to the origins of human sociology at the University of Chicago. He argues that human ecology should be combined with social psychology to understand the subcommunity as a unit of contemporary community life.

In Chapter 7, Avery Guest moves the level of analysis to a familiar point, that of the city itself. Rejecting the year 1950 as a beginning, Guest starts his discussion in 1925, evaluating Burgess' model of urban growth and form in the contemporary context. He asks whether the ideas of the Chicago school should now be taken seriously or simply regarded as artifacts of a bygone era. He formalizes Burgess' famous essay into a series of propositions and considers their current applicability, concluding that they applied well to the streetcar city, but now require revision. Guest concludes that once the Central Business Districts stopped expanding spatially in the automobile-freeway era, the Burgess model lost its central dynamic. He then reviews a number of studies of the contemporary metropolis, on residential movement and dispersal, population composition and decentralization. The chapter concludes that a new paradigm is needed for the multinucleated metropolis, a paradigm which comes to terms with current transportation systems and with the new place of the metropolis in "an increasingly integrated and centralized national society."

Chapter 8, by Dudley L. Poston, Jr., concludes Part II with an exhaustive review of studies of regional ecology. Even more than the other authors, Poston takes a strictly macroscopic perspective, dealing consistently with large territorial and demographic units, usually employing the county as a unit of analysis. Like the other contributors to this volume, Poston argues that ecological analysis falls within the mainstream of sociological analysis, legitimating this claim by showing that much regional ecology represents a continuity of interest in concerns first set forth by Emile Durkheim in his theory of the division of labor. He also shows that current research in regional ecology continues to pursue questions set forth by some of the founding fathers of sociological human ecology. In addition to reviewing studies on the division of labor, Poston discusses literature on the relationship between race and sex in the allocation of occupations, the relationship between ecological change--particularly technological and organizational-- and demographic change as reflected by migration and fertility, and studies of nodal and homogeneous regions. In his review of nodal regions, Poston covers a series of studies on the metropolitan community and systems of cities. Like some of the other authors in this section, Poston enriches his chapter by reviewing his own research, particularly on the ecological structures of nonmetropolitan counties, in the context of previous theories and research.

# 5
# A Human Ecological Theory of Organizational Structuring

*John D. Kasarda*
*Charles E. Bidwell*

A basic objective of modern sociological human ecology is to account for the organizational forms that arise in social systems as their populations adapt to varying environmental, technological, and demographic opportunities and constraints. Adaptation is construed as a structuring process by which analytically distinguishable subunits and routinized activities evolve in the system that serve to increase the productivity (or efficiency) of a given function or set of functions. The structuring process involves the differentiation or dedifferentiation of the system's subunits and activities and their integration into a complex of relationships possessing unit character.

As a heuristic framework for interpreting the structuring process under various external conditions, human ecology takes its fullest form in the notion of the human ecosystem (Duncan, 1959, 1961, 1964; Duncan and Schnore, 1959; Hawley, 1968, 1973; Schnore, 1958, 1961; Berry and Kasarda, 1977). The human ecosystem framework is a dynamic open-system formulation addressing how changing social organization is shaped by and shapes changing aspects of environment, technology, and population. This framework has not been applied extensively beyond territorial facets of social organization, however, and scarcely at all to formal organizations. Nevertheless, if human ecology is to help us understand the organization of modern society, its framework must be specified and applied beyond the territorial unit. Of special importance, we believe, is the formal organization, the most central organizational unit of modern society.

In this chapter we develop a human ecological theory of structural dynamics in formal organizations. Our theory is presented as an open-system model of morphological change and feedback in organizations and as a substantive contribution to human ecology. We will specify how variation in the environment, technology, and demography of an organization (separately and in interaction) affects its emerging structure under the fundamental assumption that structuring is an adaptive process. We will also consider how the emergence of structure in an organization affects outputs to its environment. Finally, we will consider how organizations, as they become structured, act on their environments to foster feedback that modifies the content and volume of resource inputs to their sustenance activities.

## THEORETICAL ANTECEDENTS:
## FROM CLOSED TO CONTROL SYSTEM THEORIES OF ORGANIZATIONS

In classic organizational theory, formal organizations appear as closed systems. This approach, which originated in Weber's (1947) theory of bureaucracy, views the organization as if it were a machine. To account for the existence and survival of the organizational machine, one assumes a "prime mover," whose actions remain unanalyzed. In the case of organizational mechanics, the prime mover is an actor who gives the organization its mandate to perform certain functions, sets its goals, and endows it with a supply of resources sufficient to attain these goals.

The closed-system approach occurs in both a behavioral and a structuralist variety. Closed-system theories of behavior in organizations include Taylorism (Taylor, 1911) and the more recent "human relations" approach to management (e.g., Mayo, 1933; Roethlisberger and Dickson, 1939; Dubin, 1951; Sofer, 1962; Caplow, 1964). In this behavioral literature, the worker is viewed as a component of the organizational machine. The intellectual and practical problem addressed by these theories is to understand how human components can be adjusted to the inexorable requirements of the machine's operation, which itself, thanks to the prime mover, is regarded as given.

The objective of the structuralist version of closed-system theory is to explain variation in organizational form --the parts that an organization has and relationships among them (see Blau, 1970; Blau and Schoenherr, 1971; Etzioni, 1961; Hall et al., 1967; and Meyer, 1972). If, at a given time, organizations look different from one another morphologically or if organizations change morphologically from one time to another, the closed-system explanation regards these differences as arising *sui generis*. Variable organizational form (whether considered statically or dynamically) is explained in closed-system theory as the result of varying capability between parts of the organizational machine --either interdependencies among its structural variables or consequences for organization structure of properties of the organization's member population.

Closed-system theory imparts implicitly a strong managerial bias to the study of formal organizations. The prime mover turns out to be some sort of policymaker--whether ruler, cabinet minister, or entrepreneur--who is the sole link between the formal organization and the environment. Any adaptation or adjustment to environmental change is accomplished by this prime mover, who completely determines the structure and activity of the organization. By assuming a prime mover, closed-system theory can take as given the genesis and continued existence of an organization, the goals it pursues, and the resources it consumes. These aspects of functioning organizations, which include such critical matters as organizational legitimacy, maintenance, and effectiveness are therefore not addressed.

But, more importantly, since closed-system theory views formal organizations primarily as machines that lack the ability to provide their own impelling force (a force provided instead by the unanalyzed prime mover), the result is inevitably a theory of organizational statics. Thus, closed-system theory is of limited value for identifying the processes by which organizational form arises, is maintained, and changes.

Realization of these limitations has fostered new theoretical approaches to the study of formal organizations (see Burns and Stalker, 1961; Cyert and March, 1963; Katz and Kahn, 1966; Lawrence and Lorsch, 1967; March and Simon, 1958; Perrow, 1970; Thompson, 1967; and Woodward, 1965, 1970). For the most part, they are attempts to capitalize on open-system approaches to account for variable organizational form. These new approaches, however, have been less than successful. Their limitations are due in some degree to their failure to exploit fully the open-system perspective.

By retaining certain assumptions akin to those of closed-system theory—namely, that organizations are strongly bounded, that stability is essential within this boundary, and that organizational form is primarily the consequence of managerial decisions—these theories treat organizations not as open systems, but as control systems (cf., Boulding, 1968).

Control systems, generally speaking, have two principal components: operators and regulators. The operator is the machine (like the furnace, pipes, and radiators in a heating system or the production roles or structure of an organization). The regulator (like the thermostat or organizational decision-maker) receives information about the state of the system's environment (e.g., the temperature level of the surrounding air or the level of demand for the organization's product). It responds by altering the operator's level of activity, or, if necessary, rebuilding the operator to a new design, so that its output satisfies some pre-determined criterion.

In the study of formal organizations, control-system theorizing has led in two rather different directions. One direction has been to study the behavior of individual actors in organizations. The other, in the closely related forms of socio-technical and contingency theories, attempts to relate the structure of organizations to technological and environmental constraints.

The behavioral theory of the firm (Cyert and March, 1963; March and Simon, 1958) represents the most significant advance of theories developed at the social action level. By asking how decision-makers in economic organizations behave and under what conditions, Simon, March, and Cyert demonstrate the inadequacy of the mechanistic underpinnings of closed-system theory and turn from static to explicitly dynamic analysis. The quintessential trait of an organization's decision-makers is imperfect formation and, of the organization, the conflicting purposes and choices of its decision-makers.

The behavioral theory of the firm centers not on the operator—the organizational machine of closed-system theory—but on the regulator, which is the set of managerial decision-makers within the firm. This regulator is an uncommonly interesting one. It may adjust the operator by changing levels or rates of organizational activity (e.g., the amount of a given product turned out in a given amount of time). It may also rebuild the machine by changing its structure (e.g., adding new operating units to make a new product or shifting sequences of activity within a production process). Most important of all, the regulator sets its own goals—it is a thermostat that decides on the temperature setting and can rebuild the furnace if it cannot meet this criterion.

The prime source of imperfect information is the inscrutability of the organization's environment and consequent costs of information-gathering. The prime source of conflict is the collective nature of the regulator. Thus, the regulator's input to the organizational machine results from processes of conflict resolution.

In one stroke, Simon, March, and Cyert presented a dynamic theory, moved from a closed-system to an explicit control-system perspective, opened the possibility of a political analysis of organizational control (in contrast to the assumed rationality of the prime mover), and thus showed the impossibility of explaining organizational dynamics without taking into account how organizations receive, process, and adapt to information about events outside their boundaries.

But the behavioral theory of the firm is not a theory of organizations. Its attention is almost entirely on the regulator, which is analyzed as a system of individual actors rather than as part of an organizational system. How this regulator acts on the organizational operator (the machine), with what effects, and under what conditions, and how the attributes of the operator may affect the action of the regulator go unexplained. In short, the behavioral theory of the firm is a theory of the behavior of decision-makers in organizations—behavior that remains only weakly linked in either causal direction to organizational form.

Socio-technical and contingency theories do try to explain structural variation among organizations (see Woodward, 1965, 1970; Perrow, 1970; Thompson, 1967; Lawrence and Lorsch, 1967). However, these theories, which center on either technological determinants or environmental constraints of organizational structure, despite the fact that some have been welcomed as open-system formulations, differ markedly in their assumptions from general theories of open systems. Indeed, socio-technical and contingency theories retain the essential of a closed-system formulation:

1. that stability is an essential condition for the effective operation of the production process;

2. that as a result, at least the production sector of an organization must be strongly-bounded;

3. that organizational form (both in the production sector and at the boundary) is the consequence of managerial decision; and

4. that managers make these decisions on rational premises in the light of clearly defined goals or targets that apply to the *entire* organization.

Stability in either the socio-technical or contingency formulation is by definition a necessary condition of effective production, since the production machine cannot itself adapt to changes of input. The regulator adapts the machine, by altering its rate of operation or by rebuilding it. The impact of changing input on structure, therefore, can occur only through the medium of information (about the state of these inputs and their sources) processed and responded to by some agent that is capable of altering the activity or structure of the production machine (i.e., an authoritative or powerful agent). This latter assumption leads directly to the notion of the manager or decision-making collective as the sole adaptive link between organization and environment.

Control-system theory represents an advance over closed system theory because environment does enter as a key factor and dynamic analysis, in principle, is possible. However, when control-system theory takes a truly dynamic character, it becomes a theory of interpersonal behavior in organizations. As such it fails to account for the emergence of organizational structure from interpersonal behavior. Otherwise, it is a theory of concomitant variation between structural and either technological or environmental variables connected by an unanalyzed regulatory mechanism. In practice, if not in principle, control-system theories sustain the static, cross-sectional character of the closed-system approach. The emphasis remains on how organizations differ from one another, not on how and why they change.

### ORGANIZATIONAL ECOLOGY: OPEN-SYSTEM THEORY RECAPTURED

The signal difference between control-system and open-system theory is the latter's abandonment of the mechanistic assumptions that boundary maintenance and internal stability are necessary conditions for effective system performance. It does not assume that stability is the normal state of organizations or that a rigorous separation can be made between organization and environment. An open system, contrary to widespread belief among organizational theorists, does not maintain stability *despite* diversity or instability of inputs. Obeying the Law of Limited Variety, it exhibits no more variety than is present in the input from its environment. It does so precisely because what commonly are treated as elements of organization *or* environment (e.g., administrative and production units versus suppliers and consumers) are themselves systemically related. In Schrödinger's phase (1968:146), an open system maintains and changes form "...by sucking orderliness from its environment." Nonuniform inputs (e.g., inputs that are qualitatively diverse or that vary in the rates at which they are received) result in differentiated form. Change in the uniformity of inputs is a major source of change of form. In fact, only nonuniform inputs can counteract entropy--the tendency of systems (including organizations) to move toward an undifferentiated state as they consume and eventually exhaust the resources needed to sustain their differentiated parts or as random variation works toward simple structure.

Clearly, then, an open-system theory of organizations must show how openness occurs. It does this by assuming that organization-environment boundaries are highly permeable and fluid, so that the effect of the environment is felt at all points of the organization rather than solely at the organizational apex. Internal stability, order, and coordination thus become highly problematic. Hence, while closed and control-system theories tend to emphasize the organizational mechanisms which maintain the internal stability of the system and buffer it from external influence, open-system formulations focus on the processes which elaborate, differentiate, and transform organizational structure in response to both internal and external influences.

Open-system theory provides an orienting framework, but this framework must be elaborated and specified to apply to a particular area of analysis. We must provide a detailed account of those elements of environment and structure most pertinent to the study of organizations. We also must account for the processes through which these elements are related and act on one another. For this purpose, we have turned to a human ecological view that treats formal organizations and their environments as ecosystems.

The human ecological perspective on social organization is a "social realist" rather than a "social nominalist" view, in which social form is analyzed as an emergent attribute of a human collectivity (see Wolff, 1959; Schnore, 1961:135-136). The realist-nominalist distinction is important because a realist view allows us to seek causes and consequences of social organization in a wide range of variables to which the *collectivity* is exposed and to which it may make a *collective* response--demographic properties of its population, technology in the form of knowledge, procedures and tools for conducting its activities, and the availability of resources to sustain these activities. Indeed, these forces themselves most often are appropriately measured at the aggregate level (e.g., the size or age composition of population, rates of invention, or the absolute amount of a given resource available to the collectivity). Moreover, these forces can be analyzed as reciprocally related, for example, population size as a constraint on resource scarcity, and resource scarcity as a constraint on population size, or rates and kinds of invention as responses to resource scarcity—where scarcity is defined in terms of population size and the absolute amount of the resource available. These forces also can be treated as reciprocally related to social form, for example, technological change as both a cause and consequence of the division of labor. Finally, because organization is seen as an emergent collective property—a response or adaptation to those forces to which it is related—the ecological perspective is inherently dynamic. An ecological theory of formal organization will, we believe, have wide scope and promises great power.

Before we begin, we should be clear about the precise level of ecological analysis at which we shall work. Focusing on ecological communities composed of populations of organizations, Hannan and Freeman (1977) have presented a theory of the population ecology of organizations. Their theory seeks to explain the limited variety of form displayed in these populations through an application of central propositions of modern population biology. It asks how competition between organizations affects the comparative survival rates of organizational forms in differing environments.

Hannan and Freeman do not ask whether or how formal properties of organizations themselves emerge. This is not their problem, but it is the central question that our theory addresses. Our theory focuses on structuring *within* individual organizations. We ask how variation in the environment affects stability and change in an organization's formal structure. We ask further how the formal structure of an organization affects its environment.

Level of analysis is a principal difference between our theory and that of Hannan and Freeman. They take as given the form of organizations; we take as given the form of populations of organizations and pertinent to our theory only to the extent that it is a property of the organization's environment. It will become clear by the end of this chapter that this difference requires us to treat environment in different terms and to be more explicit and detailed about the processes by which organizational niches emerge and about the ways in which structure--the pattern of relationships between these niches--emerges.

## Assumptions, Axioms, and Constructs

The working assumptions upon which our ecological theory of organizational structuring rests are the central assumptions of modern sociological human ecology. These are:

1. *Social systems are open systems whose organizational morphology is adapted to the conditions confronting the system, including the nature of its physical and social environment, the size and composition of its membership, and the repertory of tools, techniques, and information at its command.* The full set of relationships among these variables is known as the ecological complex. Each variable within the ecological complex is presumed to be interdependent with every other variable. Hence, it is possible to regard the ecological complex as a system-- Duncan's (1959) "ecosystem." Not all of these relationships can be examined at once. Some will be of greater theoretical interest than others; some will prove significant on a sheer empirical basis. While we have selected organizational form as the set of variables to be explained, the assumption of interdependence and our interest in dynamics dictate sensitivity to feedback from formal variables to other components of the ecosystem--if only because these feedback effects in turn may lead to the further emergence of new structure.

2. *The elementary structural unit of analysis (seen as emerging in an organization's population) is the "pattern of activity."* Organization, then, is "an organization of activities, arranged in overlapping and interpenetrating series of activity constellations or groups" (Duncan and Schnore, 1959:136). The activity pattern is a property of the population; hence, it consists of physically observable relationships between specific activities characteristic of the niches (junctional subunits) in which population members are located. Activity pattern describes relationships between niches, such as the degree of differentiation or interdependence. The description of those relationships constitutes the description of organizational structure. In the study of

organizational populations, the principal niche-
activities are those involved in production, the coordination of production activities, and the coordination of input and output exchanges between the organization and its environment. The analysis of the activity
pattern, or organizational structure, is the analysis of
relationships within and among these three sets of
activities.

3. *Organization is exclusively a property of the population taken as a whole and exhibits structural characteristics that can be examined apart from the personal
characteristics of its individual actors.* Thus, in an
ecological model, the aggregate, rather than the individual, is the unit of analysis. Explanation is centered
on relationships among aggregate phenomena (demographic,
technological environmental, and organizational), and
their properties are regarded as emergent at this level
without recourse to mechanisms conceived to operate at
the individual level. In line with its macrosocial perspective, human ecology analyzes the structure of
organized activities without reference to the motives,
attitudes, or sentiments that individual members may
entertain in their roles. No attempt is made, for
example, to explain the individual's feelings or commitment to his role, the anxiety or stress he suffers while
engaged in conflicting roles, or his personal motives or
interests behind his actions. As an emergent property of
the aggregate, organizational structure transcends the
personal characteristics of its members. This social
fact is demonstrated regularly in bureaucracies, communities, and larger sociopolitical units where individuals of quite different personal characteristics
periodically replace others in particular roles without
disrupting the observable pattern of organized activity.
It is this important property of social systems which
provides for their continuity in development over time.

The above axioms and assumptions indicate four principal
and significant ways in which our ecological theory of organizations differs from closed- and control-system
theories. First, to repeat, there is no assumption that the
organization is strongly bounded. Structural boundaries
remain to be determined empirically and should vary according to specified conditions in the organization's ecosystem.
That is, because the location and permeability of boundaries
are determined by gradients of interdependence between
niches, if we regard organization as an emergent population

attribute, boundary properties (as organizational variables) also must be emergent population attributes. Hence, boundary location and permeability are taken in our theory as variable, rather than constant, properties of organizations; they are properties to be explained.

Second, in our human ecological theory, the Law of Limited Variety is itself axiomatic. Organizational structure should only be as complex as the variety of demographic, technological, and environmental inputs to sustenance activity. The degrees of differentiation and interdependence of niche activities are to be explained in terms of the size and composition of the available work force (population) and the relative availability of resources needed for alternative activities, as these resources can be acquired and transformed through technologies available to administration and production. We shall consider the form of this function later.

Third, the input-output axioms of ecosystem and modern human ecology's heuristic concern with organization as an independent as well as a dependent variable will direct our theory beyond explaining structuring exclusively as reactive organizational adaptation. We will also consider the significance of organizational outputs to the environment and conditions that foster the emergence of specialized activity patterns in certain organizations that, in turn, act on the organization's environment to modify or otherwise affect demographic, technological, and resource inputs to the organization's sustenance activities. Thus, we will explore whether organizational complexity is, in part, self-creating through the feedback mechanisms of the organization's actions on these inputs (or their environmental sources).

Fourth, because our ecological theory makes no appeal to any attribute of individual actors, it does not require cognitive analysis of members for whom certain goals, motives, or intentions are imputed (e.g., empire building, profit maximization, or rationality). To be sure, structural emergence can be viewed as the aggregate outcome of intentional activity by members of the organizational population. But if one's objective is to explain organizational morphology, as ours is, there is no analytical requirement to refer to the motives of the organization's founder or to the individual interests, personalities, or values of its membership. In this regard, we adhere firmly to the principle that powerful theories to account for events at a given level of social aggregation can be stated in terms that refer entirely to that level of aggregation. We do not rule the social actions of individual organizational members out of the empirical organizational field. Rather, we rule the social actions out of our theoretical purview. We work from the assumption that demographic properties of the membership of organizations (such as size and skill composition), the attributes of the technologies that organizations use to do their work, and the content and structure of their physical, demographic, social, and cultural environments powerfully constrain social action at the individual level, so far as this action produces variation in organizational form. Hence, the structure of organizations can be explained economically by reference to the constraining forces, without central attention to the specific individual social actions constrained.

In fact, even at the time an organization is founded, its enactment by an individual or group is both stimulated and constrained by ecosystem variables (Aldrich, 1979). These stimuli and constraints are the main point of Stinchcombe's (1965) analysis of the variety of organizational form. Markets for products, manpower, materials, and capital, he argues, have distinctive characteristics at different historical times. These characteristics foster enacted organization (for example, to satisfy a demand or use a technology), while they also limit the probability that a given production process or organizational form will occur (for example, more or less capital intensive techniques, and, consequently, greater or lesser degrees of routinization and direct administrative control of production).

Thus, from an ecological perspective, the only assumption required about organizational enactment is materialistic: that a market (demand) for a product exists and that resources are assembled, in the broadest terms the main factors of production--capital, labor, technology, and materials--so that the organizational population receives a flow of raw material and engages in activities that represent technologically consistent procedures through which this material is changed into a product.[1] Beyond specifying the organizational population, its technology, and its environment, we do not need to specify a priori the product or any other result that the founder or workforce members intend product-making to accomplish.

---

[1]*The term technologically consistent, applied to the activities of the organization's population, means only that one activity does not undo the results of another--so that some product, in fact, is made.*

*The organizational population.* Hence, we shall begin our theory with a discussion of the organization's population. This population is an aggregate of persons defined or bounded by the fact of common membership in the organization. That is, we take as given the *initial* (but not necessarily the enduring) existence of the organization only to the extent that its initial existence is required to prescribe the class limit that defines the population in which we are interested.[2]

As we have asserted earlier, for our theoretical purposes, it is not, in fact, the organization itself for which a boundary is assumed. The only assumed boundary is the class boundary of the organizational population. This approach contrasts to usual practice in human ecology in which the class limit of population is spatial. But in principle there is no reason why the defining attribute of a population must be shared location in space, especially in those cases where advanced transportation and communication technologies have substantially reduced the friction of space. In terms of our theory, this assertion is tantamount to saying that technological variables define the importance of spatial variables.

We make the usual assumptions of human ecologists concerning the properties of an organization as a population, *namely,*

1. that within the boundary of membership "regularly operating interdependence is feasible,"

2. that its members are independently mobile,

3. that they are replaceable and interchangeable, and

4. that neither the longevity nor the size of the population is a *priori* limited (Hawley, 1968).

The first two assumptions are obviously necessary for the population to become organized, since independent mobility is required for functional differentiation, while

---

[2]*If an organization loses structural integrity to the point that it no longer can be said to exist, membership in the organization no longer defines a population; it is no longer a useful class limit.*

organization cannot occur if it is not possible for the differentiated parts to be dependent on one another. The remaining assumptions are not, strictly speaking, necessary for organization, but they are necessary if the organized population is to endure. With respect to the demography of this population we will be concerned especially with the size and skill composition of an organizational population considered as a work force--that is, with the representation among its members of various kinds and levels of productive and administrative skill and with the relative size of these skill components. Demographic composition on so-called ascriptive attributes (age, sex, race, and the like) need be attended to only as these compositional properties may affect the specific sustenance activities of the organizational population. In other words, our principal concern is for the ability of an organizational population as a systemic unit to support its principal activities--production, the coordination of production, and the coordination of organization-environment exchanges.

The total size of the labor market sets an upper limit on the size of its production organization (and, of course, on its administrative organization as well). But more important are constraints imposed by the sizes of specific labor market sectors on the relative sizes of specific categories of production niches. A given division of production labor cannot be sustained without a supply of labor sufficient to the activities of its niches. In effect, an organization's production workers comprise intraorganizational pools of labor qualified (whether by evaluated performance or otherwise) to undertake one or another of the activities in the division of production labor--population in another guise. These pools may overlap, may be more or less restricted, or may be empty depending on the composition of the production work force and the formalization and specialization of production tasks. The absolute and therefore the relative size of each such internal pool is a function of the availability of recruits and thus of the composition and structure of the organization's labor markets.

We asserted earlier that an organization will be just as complex (in structural terms will have just as intensive and interdependent a division of labor) as are the stimuli from the inputs it receives (in our terms both technological and environmental). We expect the skill composition of an organizational population to modify this relationship. An organizational population cannot adapt to stimuli of greater structural complexity if it does not contain the requisite skills in the requisite numbers. Alternatively, it is likely to be slow to adapt to stimuli for less complex structure to the extent that it contains members with skills that would thereby be rendered redundant. In other words, we expect that for any organizational population there is a demographically determined zone of adaptability that will bracket and constrain structural adaptation to varying technological or environmental input. The boundary of this zone, for the specific case, should be determined by the observed skill requirements of the given change stimulus.

*Technology.* We define technology in broad and basic terms—as the knowledge, tools, and procedures involved in performing the activities observed in a human population (in the present case, an organizational population). In contrast to the convention in organizational studies, we do not limit the purview of technology to "production" activities. Administrative activities also use technologies such as doctrines of management or methods of persuasion as well as such tools as telephones, typewriters, and electronic computers. In short, every niche in an organizational population contains its own activities, which sustain that niche through the application of some technological elements to certain inputs (which may come either from the environment or from other niches within the population). We assume, therefore, that all organizational niches, whatever their functions, are related reciprocally to some technological elements, whether they are concerned with production activities, with the coordination of production activities, or with the coordination of organization-environment exchanges.

We take these elements and their interrelationships as variables and shall be concerned especially with their differentiation and their lateral and vertical integration. Differentiation denotes the extent to which knowledge, tools, and procedures are broken down into discrete parts. Integration denotes the prevalence of dependencies among the parts of a technology. Integration may be lateral (among parts of knowledge, tools, or procedures) or vertical (dependencies among knowledge, tools, and procedures).

Turning first to differentiation and lateral integration, knowledge is differentiated to the extent that it consists of analytical statements about specific activities. It is laterally integrated to the extent that there also are analytical statements about dependencies between these activities. Tools are differentiated to the extent that they are activity specific and laterally integrated to the extent that the use of any given tool either depends upon or subsequently requires the use of another. Procedures are differentiated to the extent that they cannot be substituted for one another in performing a given activity. They are strongly integrated laterally to the extent that they form interdependent (reciprocal) sets, moderately integrated to the extent that they form serially dependent sets, and weakly integrated to the extent that they can occur independently of another.

We expect technology to affect structure, in particular the division of labor, through procedures. That is, variable properties of knowledge and tools should influence organizational form only because of their effects on procedures. We expect an isomorphism between procedure and structure. The more differentiated the procedures, the more differentiated should be the population niches, while the strength of lateral procedural integration should be paralleled in the integration of niches—interdependent procedures accompanied by interdependent niches, and so on.

We postulate that this effect of procedures on organization is a function of the strength of vertical integration of technology. By vertical integration, we mean the dependence of the differentiation and lateral integration of procedures on the differentiation and lateral integration of knowledge, tools, or both. We regard vertical integration as imperfectly correlated with the differentiation and lateral integration serially of knowledge, tools, and procedures. It is entirely possible, for example, for highly differentiated and laterally-integrated bodies of technological knowledge or tools not to be translated into differentiated or laterally-integrated procedures. Thus, knowledge about building construction and the corresponding tools until recently were much more highly differentiated and laterally integrated than the procedures actually used in the construction industry.

We expect that the stronger the vertical integration of technology, the stronger the effects of the differentiation and lateral integration of procedures on structure because vertical integration limits the degree to which procedures can be adapted to constraints of structure. The weaker the vertical integration of technology, the more likely are procedural adaptations to structural constraint and the greater the likelihood that the connectedness and specialization of procedures will mirror the division of labor among niches in an organizational population.

The dependencies among these seven technological variables and between these variables and structural complexity are shown in Figure 1. Overall, this model (and the analytical formulations upon which it rests) implies that the more differentiated the technology of an organization, the more likely is each of the parts to be incorporated within a specific niche's activity. In this way, the differentiation

199

Figure 1.

Technology and Structural Complexity

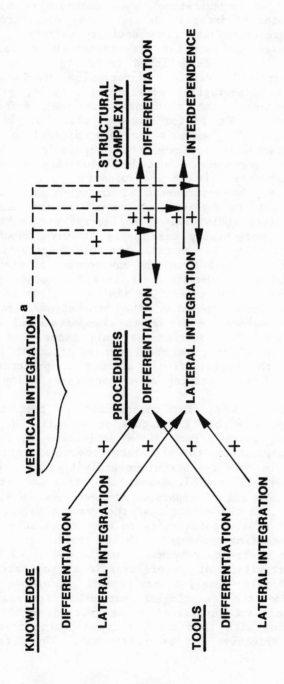

a Dotted lines depict the modification of bivariate relationships by the action of a third variable.

of technology (itself a function of the variety of technologies available in the organization's environment) is a
powerful force behind growing specialization of activity
patterns in an organization. When technology is differentiated, lateral integration promotes symbiotic (interdependent) relationships among activity patterns situated in
the specific niches that technological differentiation
fosters (as in the long-linked technologies that Thompson
[1967] describes). Vertical integration should alter the
strength of technological effects on activity patterns of
different niches in the organization and their symbiosis.

   *Environment.* We follow Hawley (1968:330) in defining
environment as all phenomena that are external to and potentially or actually influence the population under study.
Accordingly, environment must be theoretically respecified
for each separate unit of investigation. For our theoretical purposes, the environment of an organizational population comprises its physical and human resources and whatever
set of external individual or collective actors that either
supplies or potentially can supply it with inputs of resources necessary to sustain its niche-activities. At a
later point, we shall treat the environment of niches within
an organizational population as including other population
niches, but, for the moment, we limit ourselves to the population considered *in toto*. The conventional set of resources to be considered is the components of the three
major factors of production--capital, labor, and materials
--but, in our theory, we shall expand this set to include
demand for the organization's product or products and the
legitimacy of its standing as a corporate entity within a
society.

   We assume no spatial constraints on the location of
source suppliers--they are actual or potential suppliers if
they can be reached from niche activities in the organizational population to stimulate resource input *and* if
that input in turn reaches niche activities in this population (Hawley, 1973:1198). Hence, the costs of communicating
with suppliers and of transporting resources to the population niches, to the extent that they cannot be externalized,
form a part of the total costs to the organizational population of conducting exchanges with its environment.

   Because we treat environment as the source of sustenance
for the activities of an organizational population, it is
not possible to analyze environment independent of the
action of certain technological variables. For example, more
spatially distant suppliers can be reached as the ways for
communicating with them and for transporting resources become more effective and cost-efficient. Thus, the spatial

concentration of an organizational population's environment is an inverse function of the availability of effective, cost-efficient means of overcoming the friction of space (on this and related matters, see Stinchcombe, 1968:265-292).

As we stated earlier, location does not necessarily bound either system or environment. Moreover, each of the organization's constituent activity patterns may be located in a substantially distinctive environment, according to its ability (largely technologically determined) to reach resources that it needs. In fact, as activity patterns of different niches within the organization are related symbiotically, each must encounter a different environment because its sustenance needs and suppliers thereby differ.

It follows, then, that the more differentiated the activity patterns in an organization and the more symbiotic their relationships, the more differentiated the environments in which each is situated. Of course, not every activity pattern in an organization finds the resources that it requires entirely outside the organization itself. Activity patterns within a factory assembly line may serially supply one another with required material inputs, while personnel managers and purchasing agents supply them with the required labor, tools, and raw materials. But these administrative activity patterns require information about labor and materials that comes from outside the organization. Top level management requires information about capital and product markets that again comes from outside the organization. Similarly, they must transmit information about their demand for labor, materials, or capital beyond the network of activity patterns that comprise the organization. As means of transportation and communication become increasingly cost-effective, space becomes less and less constraining on these exchanges.

Consequently, it is perfectly possible to think of certain activity patterns in an organization as being more tightly bound into exchanges outside rather than inside the organization. In short, the organization's nominal boundary does not by necessity constrain such exchanges. For many organizational activity patterns, this boundary may be highly permeable and shifting (that is, not specified in simple locational terms). If a top manager or entrepreneur negotiates for capital or labor in the office of a banker or union official, has he crossed the organization's boundary to do so, or does the boundary move as the location of such exchanges move?

The above obviously is an unproductive question. Rather than worry about the spatial location or organizational boundaries, it makes better sense to assume their permeable and shifting character, expanding and contracting as activity patterns engage in input and output exchanges across varying distances and in relationships that involve actors who have extra-organizational locations.

We now shall enumerate the chief environmental variables that will enter our theory and discuss how, interacting with aspects of technology, they may constitute stimuli to the structural complexity of organizational populations. We shall discuss these environmental variables as global properties of the environment, that is, as averages calculated for all actual or potentially reachable inputs to the population (or for actual and potential inputs combined). But note that each of these variables also may be disaggregated, as appropriate, as measures specific to given resources or suppliers, or jointly by resource and supplier.

*Environmental Properties and*
*Stimuli to Structural Complexity*

SCOPE. The first of these environmental properties is the scope of the environment, which as our discussion already has suggested, is determined by the "reachability" of resources. Reachability can be measured by the size of the increments per unit of spatial distance from a population niche to any supplier (whether actual or not) in the combined costs of communication and transportation required to obtain a unit of resource input. Thus, the scope of the environment may change over time, as the marginal utility of a resource to the activities of the organizational population increases or decreases.

Composition, structure, and carrying capacity can be measured for an environment of given scope. Together, the three sets of variables comprise environmental parameters that set a ceiling on the level of activity that is possible within the niches (functional subunits) of an organizational population. Interacting with elements of technology, these environmental parameters also limit the possible range of activities of an organizational population and thereby the content and the intensity of its niche differentiation.

The central compositional properties of environment are *heterogeneity*—the number of different resources actually or potentially supplied to the population—and *diversity* —the number of different suppliers that the environment contains. For any organizational population, heterogeneity can be specified by content, according to the observed requirements of technological procedures. In this regard, heterogeneity has two aspects: the number of qualitatively different resources that an organization consumes (e.g., coal and iron ore) and quantitative variation in a given quality of input (e.g., coal or iron ore of varying grade). We assume for each aspect of heterogeneity an optimal condition for the efficiency of production.

Focusing on heterogeneity of materials, if production procedures require qualitatively different materials, they will be sustained only if they receive these specific inputs. (Here, for the sake of simplicity, we treat substitutable but qualitatively different materials as if they were, in fact, identical.) Above this minimal threshold, the relative volume of input also affects production efficiency, a relationship to which we turn in a moment.

We assume that as production procedures and niches specialize, they tend to consume qualitatively different materials (e.g., the different drugs used by different medical specialties; the different textbooks used by teachers of different subjects; the different metals, plastics, fabrics, etc., used to make different parts of an automobile). Thus, to the degree that the optimum range of materials is available, the production organization should tend to specialize up to the limit set by the available technological procedures. In addition, the availability of heterogeneous materials may foster technological innovation, if the aggregate marginal productivity of the production organization can thereby be increased, changing the optimum range of material heterogeneity. If, however, one or another of these sustaining inputs is not available, then an organization must either change to a different line of production or adapt its production procedures to the available input, despite its technological capacity to handle more qualitatively heterogeneous materials.

If the qualitative heterogeneity of materials input exceeds the optimum range, so that the production organization receives materials that its procedures are not designed to treat (e.g., a common school that is required to enroll children with severe learning disabilities or a public general hospital that must treat patients with exotic diseases), the efficiency of its production activities will be lowered in two ways. The out-of-range materials will not be transformed properly, while factors of production will be diverted to some degree from work on within-range materials to deal with those that are out-of-range.

Quantitative heterogeneity of materials input refers to the degree to which these inputs exceed the tolerance built into its production procedures. These tolerances then set outer limits that define the optimal range of quantitative heterogeneity. The more routine the production activities, the narrower these tolerances and the optimal range are likely to be. Moreover, the more interdependent the activities, the more widespread should be the disturbances to production produced by excessive quantitative heterogeneity of materials.

As our discussion already has implied, variation in both the qualitative and quantitative heterogeneity of materials inputs should affect the structure of the production organization. In addition, the ability of the administrative organization to coordinate inputs of materials so that they come within their optimal ranges of heterogeneity will have powerful effects on the direction and strength of these relationships. If input coordination in this way is effective, the qualitative and quantitative heterogeneity of materials input will fit the requirements of technological procedures. Thus, if the coordination of materials input is effective, qualitative heterogeneity should foster the specialization of the division of production labor (and, thereby, indirectly the interdependence of the production organization). In effect, in this case qualitative heterogeneity heightens demand for specialized production procedures, activities, and niches.

If input coordination is ineffective and materials inputs are below the optimal range of qualitative heterogeneity, short of the extreme dedifferentiating response of shutting down a line of production, the organization may respond by technological innovation to reset the optimal range according to the available heterogeneity of materials. Whether such innovations will affect the level of specialization of the production niches is not clear *a priori*, since the effect should depend primarily on the specific content of the innovating response. Thus we would expect low qualitative heterogeneity to depress the specialization of the division of production labor, but only below a threshold representing the failure of technological innovation.

If input coordination is ineffective and materials inputs are above the optimum range of qualitative variation, several adaptations are possible. Technological innovation again may substitute for effective input coordination, resetting the optimum range to fit the high level of qualitative heterogeneity and, thereby, fostering the specialization of production labor.[3] To the degree that the new

---

[3]*Thus, note the ineffective input coordination may be a stimulus to technological change in an organization when it fails to buffer production activities from either insufficient or excessive qualitative heterogeneity of materials inputs.*

technological procedures cannot be integrated into existing networks of production niches, they may be established as separate lines of production, so that the organization's output moves toward multiproduct form.

Otherwise, newly specialized niches may be incorporated within existing networks of production niches so that the out-of-range material is, during early stages of production activity, brought within the optimum range (i.e., the aggregate qualitative heterogeneity of materials is reduced), and the organization's production mix is not altered. These specialized niches are devoted to reducing the heterogeneity of raw material (e.g., the successive stages of metals refining). This adaptation is another source of supportive specialization linked asymmetrically to a focal production niche.

Adaptation through supportive specialization, however, requires an appropriate analytical knowledge base and the consequent differentiation of technological procedures. So does response to qualitative heterogeneity by establishing a separate production line. If the knowledge base is lacking, excessive qualitative or quantitative heterogeneity should simply increase the unpredictability of production activities and through this intervening variable have a de-differentiating effect on the division of production labor.[4]

The former adaptation is more likely the more interdependent the production niches because destabilization of existing production activities arising from the introduction of new activities and niches will be more widespread, and the more intense interdependence should amplify further the destabilizing effect.

The latter adaptation is apt to occur not only as a response to qualitative heterogeneity, under the conditions that we have just noted, but also as a response to quantitative heterogeneity. Changes in technology, of course, may

---

[4]*This discussion is not meant to suggest an iso- morphism between the heterogeneity of materials and the differentiation of tools or procedures in technology. To be sure, a differentiated technology cannot be implemented if materials of optimal heterogeneity are unavailable. But homogeneous materials input can be transformed into multiple products through differentiated technological tools and procedures. This pattern characterizes, for example, such continuous process industries as petroleum refining.*

allow an organization to adapt to the problem of tolerance (again with indeterminate effects on the division of production labor) but to the extent that these changes cannot be made or are expensive to make, the division of production labor may be used to reduce quantitative, as well as as qualitative, heterogeneity of materials.

The foregoing argument regarding heterogeneity of materials can also be applied to inputs of labor, capital, and consumer demand. Consumer demand, however, is better treated as an indirect rather than direct resource input. Demand generates varying flows of liquid capital into the organization, which, we argue, is the key means of organizational sustenance.[5] Demand changes just as does direct resource supply (whether in level or kind), again partly as a result of technological change. Chandler (1962) provides an elegant account of the way in which more efficient communication and transport of goods expands markets for the products of economic organizations, thereby inducing structural changes in these organizations (e.g., decentralization of management in response to heterogeneity within the expanded market).

Change in environing populations--whether of other organizations or of individuals--is another obvious source of change in demand. The effects of demographic alterations surely need no discussion. With respect to changes in populations of organizations, however, note that the effects occur primarily because organizations consume each other's products; indirect effects occur as the number of organizations that supply a given product affect the intensity with which a given level of demand is felt by any one of these organizations (Williamson, 1975).

This leads us to the one central structural property of environments--the *connectedness* of resource suppliers. Connectedness refers to the degree to which individual suppliers of a given resource act in concert with respect to the organizational population. Connectedness is important because it modifies the diversity of suppliers. In the terms of market structure, environments become more connected and thus less effectively diverse as they progress from perfect, through imperfectly competitive and oligopolistic, to monopolistic resource markets.

---

[5]*The argument here is simple. Most direct resource inputs (e.g., materials, tools, skilled labor) cannot be obtained if there is no money to buy them.*

Diversity, as is modified by connectedness, is important because it determines the degree to which an organizational population is dependent for a given resource input on one or a few suppliers, rather than a relatively autonomous actor with respect to many suppliers (Williamson, 1975). For any resource, the more diverse the environment (and the less connected the suppliers), the more autonomous the organizational population. To the degree that inputs from a given supplier become disrupted or perturbed—a point which we shall explicate in a moment—the perturbation (disruption) can be offset by inputs from another supplier. But to the degree that suppliers are connected, such perturbations are more difficult to offset.

Technology also affects diversity. To the degree that a given niche-activity is differentiated procedurally, it is less likely to allow one resource to be substituted for another (for example, plastics for metals or capital-intensive for labor-intensive procedures). Perturbations in the supply of a given resource can be offset not only by turning to a different supplier of that resource, but also by replacing the resource with another. Substitutability of resources, however, permits such adaptations only to the extent that substitutability is isomorphic with diversity. If, for example, the same corporation controls supplies of coal, gas, and oil, it may not be possible for a fuel-consuming organizational population to offset increasing oil prices by substituting gas or coal. All three prices may well have risen.

In addition, the differentiation and lateral integration of technological procedures affect the consequences of diversity for the autonomy of an organizational population. The more differentiated the procedures, the greater the heterogeneity of the environment, therefore, the greater the probability that its average diversity will be high and the organizational population an autonomous actor. But to the degree that technological procedures are laterally integrated, perturbations in any one resource that sustains a component of the laterally integrated set of procedures will affect the activities of several population niches rather than of a single niche. As a result, variation in the environmental diversity of any of these niches becomes, in effect, variation in the diversity of the environment of all of them, thereby immediately affecting the organizational population's autonomy in its environment.

CARRYING CAPACITY refers to the relative abundance of the resources supplied to sustain an organizational population's niche activities. Relative abundance denotes the

ratio of the amount of a resource supply (both actual and
potential) to the level of demand for this resource generated by the activities of the population. On the supply
side, relative abundance is a function of the scope of the
environment, that is, the reachability of the resource. On
the demand side, it is in part a function of the rate of
activity within the niches of the organizational population.
The higher the rate, the stronger the demand.

GENERALIZABILITY is another important technologically
induced property of resource input. It acts on the autonomy
of an organizational population with the same effect as
lateral integration of procedures. Inputs are generalized
according to the number of separate niche activities that
they sustain. They may sustain these activities either
directly or indirectly by virtue of the integration of the
procedures. So far as direct sustenance is concerned, the
more differentiated the population's technological procedures, the less generalized its resource inputs. But when
differentiation is accompanied by lateral integration, differentiation and generalizability are likely to be positively related. Capital, however, is a universally generalized resource. To the extent that elements of technology
(whether they are items of knowledge, information about procedures, or tools) must be purchased, capital inputs are
generalizable, whatever the degree of procedural differentiation and lateral integration. Consequently, capital is a
highly generalized resource in all organizational populations. But whatever the genesis of generalizability, the
more generalized a resource, the more widespread the effects
of environmental diversity on niche activities, and the
greater the effects on the autonomy of the population in its
environment.

Relative abundance, or carrying capacity, also is a
function of the generalizability of the resource. The more
generalized a resource, the greater the number of niche activities sustained and, holding constant the rates of niche-
activity, the stronger the demand for the resource. To the
extent that a resource is generalized, because demand is
likely to be strong, relative abundance is likely to be low.
As this condition emerges, the niches of the organizational
population compete with growing intensity for the now-scarce
resource.

Figure 2 schematically outlines a major portion of our
theoretical specifications. It summarizes our expectation
that the structural complexity of an organizational population is a function of the heterogeneity of its environment,
as it is of the differentiation and lateral integration of

209

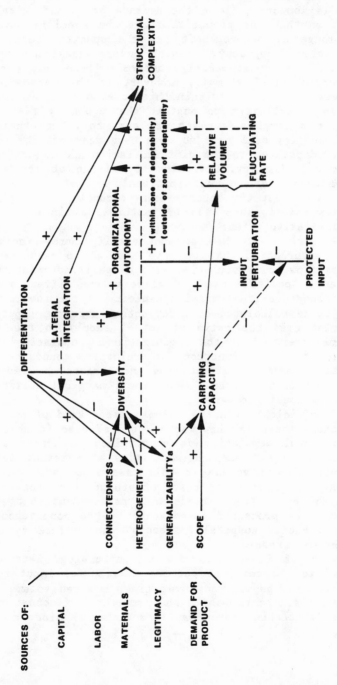

Figure 2.

TECHNOLOGICAL
PROCEDURES

a Generalizability has a constant high positive value for inputs of capital. Dotted lines depict the modification of bivariate relationships by the action of a third variable.

technological procedures. Each is a necessary but not sufficient condition for structural complexity. Together, we predict, they are necessary and sufficient. It is, of course,
not sheer heterogeneity that is at issue, but heterogeneity
that is isomorphic with the demands of technological procedure, so that our proposition must be specified by content
and range of heterogeneity to the specific case. As with
population demography, so with environmental heterogeneity.
There is an environmentally determined zone of adaptability
to technological stimuli. However, if the heterogeneity of
the environment lies within this zone, but the volume of input is insufficient to sustain the consuming niche activities at a level sufficient at least to return their costs,
heterogeneity will have no more than weak effects on structural adaptation to the differentiation and lateral integration of technology. Diversity, by virtue of its effect on
the autonomy of an organizational population, lessens the
likelihood that the heterogeneity-technology structural complexity relationship will be perturbed by input of insufficient relative volume.

   *Perturbation.*  Now we can specify more precisely the
term *perturbation* that we have applied to resource inputs.
Inputs flow to a population with a specified relative volume
and at a specified rate. Relative volume differs from relative abundance (the carrying capacity of the environment) in
that it is calculated only for actual resource inputs. It is
calculated as the ratio of actual supply to the level of
demand generated by the organizational population's activities. It is a function of relative abundance because
relative abundance affects the unit prices and reachability
costs of resources, and, thus, their marginal utility to the
organizational population.

   Insufficient relative volume is one kind of perturbation
of input. There is, however, a special case in which an organizational population is constrained to accept a greater
volume of input than its activities at existing levels can
consume. Excess volume in this case also is a perturbation
if only because of the costs of stockpiling, but especially
when the constraint extends to a requirement that all units
of input be processed immediately by the population's activities. Public hospitals, schools, and welfare agencies are
well-known examples.

   Rate of input also may be perturbing. Rate of input
refers to the temporal pattern of resource input to an organizational population. Over time, a given volume of input
may be characterized by either smooth or fluctuating rates,
while fluctuating rates may form either regular or irregular

cycles. Smooth rates of input do not, in themselves, constitute perturbations, while fluctuating rates do. We expect
fluctuating rates of input to weaken the effect of heterogeneity on structural adaptation, as does insufficient
volume, to the extent that the population's niche activities
cannot tolerate variation in input volume because they consume resource stocks rapidly. This effect should be especially marked if these activities are, in addition, tightly
interdependent. Fluctuating input, then, may perturb an organizational population in two ways: (1) by braking levels
of any given niche activity and thus potentially reducing
its productivity and (2) by inducing instability into interdependent activities that presses toward lowered interdependence and probably, in the long run, makes a high level of
differentiation less viable.

However, regular cycles of input will be perturbing only
to the extent that an organizational population (1) lacks a
surplus supply of capital to ride out these fluctuations
(whether in capital input itself or in purchased resources),
(2) lacks the technological means to store surplus resources, or (3) because of low environmental diversity
cannot offset irregular rates of input by changing suppliers. Irregular input cycles, by contrast, are unpredictable, so that the availability of a resource surplus at
appropriate times is likely to be fortuitous. Irregularity,
too, may be offset by changing suppliers, but when the
diversity of the environment is low, it should be a strong
and escapable perturbation.[6]

Let us specify some important structuring consequences
of perturbations in inputs of materials, labor, and capital.
For any given production organization there is an optimal
flow of raw material, above and below which production activities are inefficient because of overloaded or idle
capacity. If an organization cannot maintain inputs of raw
material within this optimum range--which may result, for
example, from such legal constraints as those requiring
public welfare agencies to accept all qualified clients or
from inability to stockpile inputs or expand the scope of
diversity of the supplying environment--it can adapt by

---

[6]*Parallels between the approach that we have taken to
environment and that taken in the behaviorist literature to
environmental "predictability," "turbulence," or "instability" (e.g., Thomspon, 1967; Terreberry, 1968) and in the
interorganizational literature (e.g., Levine and White,
1961; Evan, 1972) should be clear.*

increasing or decreasing the number of persons who occupy production niches sustained by the input (assuming sufficient revenue and flexibility in budgeting). Thus, we expect a positive direct effect of the relative volume of material input on the size of the production organization. Moreover, this adaptation will be more widespread in the production organization the more interdependent the production niches. Increase or decrease in the volume of output of a given niche, as its population rises or falls, will affect the relative volume of their inputs to the other production niches that they sustain, so that the populations of these other niches also are likely to grow or shrink. Hence, the relationship between the relative volume of input to the production organization and the size of the production organization should be stronger the more interdependent the production niches.

Irregularity of materials input should have destabilizing and deintegrating effects on the division of production labor, according to technological constraints. Irregular materials input should lower the predictability of production activities, making it more difficult to apply formalized procedures and increasing reliance on the judgment of production workers (e.g., forcing them to reschedule their activities to fit fluctuating inputs). One likely response to these effects of irregular input is to insulate resulting instabilities of production activities within production niches—moving toward a more segmental division of production labor in which coordinative problems induced by these instabilities are contained with the broad scope of the corresponding activity patterns.

If this response is not feasible technologically (for example, because the production tools are too highly differentiated to be used efficiently within a single production niche), the reduced level of formalization induced by irregular input should foster a level of interdependence higher than that expected on the basis of the level of niche specialization alone.

Similar arguments can be made for inputs of labor and capital. When the relative volume of the supply of labor is insufficient to sustain the division of production labor, the organization must adapt. Of the various possible adaptations, two are especially significant for the form of the production organization. One of these is formalization. By making tasks more routine, formalization expands the effective labor pool from which to recruit; thus we expect a negative direct effect of the relative volume of labor input on task-formalization. The other adaptation is specialization. As a means of coping with labor scarcity, specialization capitalizes on routine tasks. By reducing the scope of each production niche, it reduces the variability of performance. Thus, there should be a negative direct effect of the relative volume of labor input on specialization of the production organization, but only when production activities are themselves differentiated and predictable.

Thus, we are arguing that in the general case, the larger the carrying capacity of the environment—here the total size of an organization's labor market—the more likely it is that the relative volume of input of specific labor skills required to sustain production activities would be adequate. This general proposition, of course, can be specified to particular cases if one can measure the skill requirements of its production activities. The causal chain then would lead from specific aspects of the skill composition of the labor market through the specific composition of the organization's internal labor pool, to the emergence of specific activity patterns and niches in the division of production labor.

We should note also that technological change—for example, the technological adaptation to materials input of the kind that we have discussed—is contingent on the availability of the requisite labor skills either inside the organization or available at an acceptable level of marginal cost from the environment. Therefore, technological innovation generally should be more frequent the larger an organization's labor market (or the more abundant the supply of labor within the organization). More specifically, to the degree that these innovations involve departures from formalized and specialized production activities, the smaller the labor market the less likely they are to occur. For example, if a school wishes to handle slow readers among its students by adding specialist remedial reading teachers, it can do so only if a supply of appropriately trained or experienced persons is in its labor market.

Perturbations in capital input likewise have pervasive effects on organizational structure. We turn here to effects of capital input on production organization.[7] We

---

[7]*Capital here refers only to liquid capital. It does not include capitalization (e.g., in the form of investments in tools, plant, or stocks of materials), though the capitalized value of an organization's holdings can be used to secure loans or be sold. In this sense, any of an organization's physical resources can be converted to liquid capital.*

expect the relative volume of an organization's capital input to have a positive direct effect on the size of the production organization (as, indeed, on the total size of the organization) and, when technological procedures require worker judgement, on its specialization.

In addition, the relative volume of capital input should have an important mediating effect on the predicted relationships between all other input variables and the elements of production organization. The higher the relative volume of an organization's capital input, the more flexible its response to input variation--for example, hiring more workers to meet increased raw material input or consumer demand, or increasing specialization to deal with heterogeneous raw material. When the relative volume of capital input is low, this flexibility is reduced and an organization must respond to increased demand from its niches for sustenance mainly by rationing.

Of course it is true that decreased income or revenues often accompany decreased demand for an organization's product and depressed levels of production activity. In such cases, although income or revenues decline, the relative volume of capital input may decline even though demand for the product is stable or rising. Such variation may be short run, as in the case of cash flow problems that, for example, accompany escalations of demand for product before increased demand can be realized in increased profits. However, insufficient relative volume of capital input may be of longer duration. For example, organizations may find themselves in markets for labor, materials, or technology in which rising unit prices of these inputs outrun even increasing prices of products. Or, fixed interest charges for borrowed capital may reduce an organization's flexibility of response to rising demand for products or rising unit costs of factors of production. These longer run constraints are of interest here. They lead us to predict that when change in the relative volume of capital input is secular, decline should weaken all relationships between input and production organization, while increase should strengthen them.

*Environment, Inputs, and the Emergence of Key Functions among Administrative Niches*

Our theory implies that the morphology of administrative organization is a function not only of the form of the production organization, but also of the attributes of inputs to an organization and then of characteristics of its environment. Indeed, these input variables and environmental characteristics are the major factors that shape the form of upper-level administration. We turn now to these relationships, a discussion that will lead us directly to a consideration of the emergence of key functions among an organization's administrative niches.

We begin our discussion of the growth of administrative components of organizational structure with what Hawley (1968) calls *key functions*. In our theory, a key function is an activity within a specific niche that makes a disproportionately large contribution to the sustenance of a population.[8] Populations are sustained by supplies of whatever resources their niche-activities consume. Resource supplies are maintained by a population in two ways: (1) by acquiring resource inputs to replace resources con- sumed or to add to the supply, and (2) by the efficient use of resources in the population's niche-activities. Thus, key functions are activities that have disproportionately large effects on the relative volume or predictability of inputs or on their efficient use. Proportionality here is calculated as the ratio of the productivity of a *specific* niche, in either or both of these two senses, to the total productivity of all niches in an organizational population. So, for example, the aggregate contribution of production niches to an organization's sustenance may be a large fraction of the organization's total productivity, while the fractional contribution of each of these niches is small. The opposite

---

[8]*The populations that we consider, of course, are populations of members of organizations. In our concern with the sustenance of these populations and the contribution to sustenance of key functions, we side with those organizational theorists who argue that organizational form is constrained more by the maintenance of an organization than by goal attainment. That we should take this stand follows from our ecological premises, especially the exclusion of intentionality from our theory. We find it intuitively appealing and theoretically clarifying to denote by the maintenance of an organization the sustenance of its member population through its structured activities and exchanges with its environment. The survival of an organization, a term sometimes used as a synonym for criterion of maintenance, is a trivial concept, since it refers to nothing more than the persistence of the class limit that defines an organizational population.*

situation may obtain for the organization's administrative niches. We would regard the latter, but not the former, as key functions.[9]

*Productivity and Key Functions.* It should be clear that productivity is central to the maintenance of an organization's capital surplus—especially (1) the productivity of production niches as they add value to the materials they transform, (2) the productivity of exchanges with consumers as value added in production is realized as income,[10] and (3) the productivity of exchanges with suppliers of factors of production as the prices paid for the factors obtained are low in relation to the factors' value to the organization's niche-activities.

Production niches will be productive to the extent that their activities combine the factors of production in a way that optimizes the aggregate marginal productivity of these factors, while organization-environment exchanges will be productive to the extent that market opportunities are known or created and input-acquiring activities are fitted to the location and timing of these opportunities. In short, an organization's aggregate productivity should depend disproportionately on coordination—of both production and organization-environment exchanges. We expect that *administrative niches* (i.e., niches in which coordinating activities are located) will be more numerous than production niches, however, only in those rare situations where the relative volume of communication is greater than the relative volume of resource inputs to the organization's production niches.

---

[9]*In our discussion of key functions, we thus depart from Hawley's (1968) principal criterion for the emerging location of these functions: the directness of a niche's contact with the environment. We shall argue that the emergence and location of key functions depends on technological and environmental conditions. Directness of contact with the environment seems to us to derive from the niche activities that these conditions induce, not to forerun them.*

[10]*Organizations to some degree realize nonmonetary income (e.g., legitimacy) from exchanges with consumers. For organizations that enjoy protected inputs, nonmonetary income is especially significant. We shall discuss these organizations later in this section.*

In organizations with very simple production activities, both coordination and production may be combined within segmentally ordered niches. But as production becomes more complex, coordination of production activities and of inputs to production becomes more problematic. It follows that the emergence of key functions in an organization, and the subsequent differentiation of administrative niches, should tend in general to center on the coordination of production activities, the coordination of exchanges with suppliers of factors of production, and the coordination of exchanges with consumers. These tendencies, however, should be affected in specific ways by attributes of the organization's technology and division of production labor and by attributes of inputs to the organization's production niches.

These several attributes introduce complexity into production activities and into the conduct of organization environment exchange. As a result, they affect the emergence of coordinating activities of one or another kind within an organization's overall activity pattern. We shall see that forces accelerating or retarding the emergence of a given kind of coordinating activity work in the same direction to magnify or reduce the relative size of the activity's contribution to organizational productivity. Hence, they also work in the same direction to affect its chances of becoming a key function. These processes are important because, as we shall argue, the differentiation of coordinating activities is the principal source of the differentiation of administrative labor and the interrelationships among administrative niches should be affected powerfully by the location of key functions among an organization's array of coordinating activities.

*The coordination of production.* The contribution of the coordination of production activities to organizational productivity should be affected primarily by an organization's production technology, as this technology influences the division of production labor. The coordination of production is concerned especially with phenomena intrinsic to production activities—their scheduling and stability and the allocation and combination of factors of production within and among production niches. The more highly specialized an organization's production procedures *and* the stronger their lateral integration, the more likely are production niches to be specialized (differentiated) and interdependent. Interdependence in turn magnifies the negative effects on organizational productivity of instabilities or temporal disarticulation of production activities because these effects travel through the entire set of interdependent niches. Stabilization and scheduling must deal with the entire set of production activities rather than with each of them separately. In this way, interdependence generates scheduling and stabilization problems that cannot be handled within the production niches themselves. Thus, interdependence fosters the emergence of activities specifically concerned with the coordination of production niches and amplifies the consequences of these coordinative activities for organizational productivity.

In addition, the allocation of resources to any one production niche necessarily affects all other niches that the resource sustains, since supplies always are to some degree limited. The consequences of resource allocation for the productivity of production niches, however, are magnified to the degree that these niches are interdependent.[11] In this way, too, interdependence fosters the emergence of activities that coordinate production and amplifies the contribution of these activities to organizational productivity.

Further, to the degree that production activities are difficult to predict (i.e., are nonroutine), these activities tend to be destabilized and disarticulated. The coordination of production then is more exigent and more likely to make a disproportionately large contribution to organizational productivity. However, these effects of unpredictability should be larger when the production activities also are interdependent. When interdependence is low, decisions about combining factors of production can be made primarily within the production niches themselves, whether or not the niche-activities are routine.

Although we expect the emergence and subsequent productivity contribution of production coordination to be affected primarily by technology and the division of production labor, attributes of inputs (of factors of production and demand) also should have certain effects. For example, the more generalized an input is across segmentally ordered production niches, the greater is the aggregate influence of

---

[11]*Even when the division of production labor is segmental, to the extent that inputs are generalized (and especially when they also are perturbed), some coordination will be required to allocate inputs among production niches. (Resource generality thus is central to what Thompson [1967] calls "pooled interdependence.") We argue only that the proportionate size of the contribution of production coordination to organizational productivity should covary with the interdependence of production activities, not that it will disappear entirely below some threshold of interdependence.*

its allocation among these niches on the organization's productivity. This impact should be still greater when the input also has a relatively high marginal utility. Thus, when the division of production labor is segmental, the generality and marginal utility of inputs to production niches should foster the emergence of production coordinating activities and increase the relative size of their contribution to organizational productivity. But, when the division of production labor is specialized and interdependent, these effects at best should be minimal. Interdependence in effect makes all inputs to production generalized, even though they may sustain directly only a small fraction of the production niches.

Perturbed input, however, should foster the emergence and proportionate productivity contribution of production coordination whatever the division of production labor, although these effects should be stronger the more interdependent the production activities. When a factor of production has a low relative volume, priorities must be set for allocating the factor among the production niches. Such allocation becomes urgent the more generalized the input and the greater its marginal utility in production. Moreover, when a factor of production has low relative volume, its use must be highly efficient. Thus, production coordination becomes more exigent and its relative contribution to organizational productivity should be enhanced.

In addition, when input of a factor of production has an irregular rate, production activities are hard to coordinate because uncertain supply upsets production schedules and lowers the stability of production activities--again, the more so the more generalized the input and the higher its marginal utility. Here, too, pressures toward specialized activities to schedule and stabilize production are strengthened, while such activities should increase the productivity of production niches at a faster rate than when input is unperturbed.

Similarly, when the relative volume of demand is low, and demand therefore is inelastic, it is difficult to realize value added to finished products, with consequent pressures toward the efficient use of resources in production activities. Unpredictable demand makes it hard to schedule production activities. Thus, perturbed inputs of demand for an organization's product should generally promote the emergence of production coordinating activities and raise their relative contribution to organizational productivity.

There is an additional interesting possibility in the case of perturbed demand. If the product consuming environment is heterogeneous—that is, if there are many different tastes that might be satisfied by products to which the organization's factors of production could be applied—multiproduct output often can increase the scope and diversity of this environment. In effect, multiproduct output, by increasing the diversity of demand, makes it possible to smooth out perturbations of demand for any one product and thus to maintain the aggregate productivity of exchanges with consumers.

Therefore, the more heterogeneous the product-consuming environment, the more likely is an organization to engage in multiple lines of production. As a result, the coordination of production becomes more complex—for example, calculating the marginal productivity of the several factors of production becomes more difficult. Here again, we see pressure toward the emergence and subsequently magnified productivity contribution of activities coordinating production.

*The coordination of organization-environment exchanges.* We should observe distinctive activity patterns that coordinate organization-environment exchanges (for either factors of production or demand) in direct relation to (1) the generality of the input and (2) its aggregate marginal utility in the organization's niche-activities. Similar effects also should be observed on the relative size of the productivity contribution of these activities. The reasoning behind these assertions is simple. The more widely used or the more valuable an input, the greater the aggre- gate effects of differences per unit (of a factor of produc- tion or of a product distributed) between the cost of obtaining or distributing the unit and the resulting gain to the organization's sustenance. Hence, the productivity of organization-environment exchanges becomes more consequen- tial for the aggregate productivity of an organization as the input involved is more generalized and as its marginal productivity rises. As the productivity of organization en- vironment exchange becomes more consequential, activities centered on coordinating these exchanges, which for brevity we will call *input coordination,* should be observed more often in organizations. Their subsequent contributions to organizational productivity also should increase in relative size.

As in the case of production coordination, perturbed in- put should affect the emergence and productivity contribu- tions of input coordination—and to the same effect. When the relative volume of input of a factor of production is low, even though production coordination allocates the factor effectively, certain production niches still are likely to receive less of the factor than they require. Such shortages should lower the organization's productivity. This adverse effect, which should create pressures toward specialized coordination of the scarce factor, will be stronger the more generalized the factor or the greater its marginal utility. Input coordination that raises the productivity of exchanges with suppliers of the scarce factor thereby should raise the productivity of production niches at a faster rate than when relative volume is high.

We already have noted the likely adverse effects of irregular inputs of factors of production on an organization's production niches. These adverse effects should promote coordinating activities that seek a more regular rate of input. The stronger the adverse effect (as we have seen in part a function of the generality and marginal utility of the input), the greater the relative size of the productivity contribution of these coordinating activities because of their effects on the productivity of the organization's production niches.

So, too, when inputs of demand are of low relative volume or irregular rate, the coordination of these inputs (e.g., the management of product sales or transportation) may increase the number of consumers or the aggregate strength and consistency of their preferences for the organization's product. To the degree that these activities succeed, disturbances to the stability and scheduling of production activities that perturbation induces should diminish and thus contribute to the organization's productivity, at a rate roughly proportional to the degree of perturbation. In addition, if an organization's lines of production become more numerous, the coordination of exchanges with consumers, like the coordination of production, becomes more complex because it requires a search for new consumer tastes that the organization's factors of production can satisfy, while it also raises the difficulty of calculating the probable income returns from different combinations of products. Thus, multiple lines of production should foster activities coordinating exchanges with consumers and, as the product mix becomes more complex, also magnify the productivity contribution of these coordinating activities.

Perturbed input (whether of factors of production or of demand) should, therefore, foster a specific set of coordinating activities which together comprise input coordination: (1) activities that increase the heterogeneity of the environment by searching for substitutable factors of production or consumer tastes, (2) activities that increase the scope and diversity of the environment by searching for new suppliers or consumers and for cost-effective means of communicating with them and transporting factors of production or finished products, (3) activities that stabilize exchanges with existing suppliers or consumers at higher levels of input, and (4) activities that schedule inputs at a more regular rate. The first and second of these activities, by increasing the relative volume of input and the autonomy of an organization vis-à-vis suppliers or consumers, raises the marginal utility of an input (by lowering the price of a factor of production or the elasticity of demand). This effect should thereby further increase the productivity of these exchanges and the relative size of the productivity contribution of input coordination.

*The institutional environment.* To this point we have described the environment as a dynamic array of resource suppliers and product consumers and have postulated the emergence of specific patterns of activity (structure) in our organizational population in response to various environmental stimuli. But most notably for organizations, the environment also is institutional. The principal manifestation of the institutional environment of organizational populations is law, in its statutory, judicial, and administrative forms. The very enactment of an organization-- which establishes it as a population category, a combination of resources, and a primordial division of labor--is made possible and shaped by laws governing the formation of corporate groups.

Similarly, transactions between organizational populations and the two other principal components of their environments--direct resource supply and demand for products --occur through legally defined mechanisms, such as laws of contract, laws governing the transmittal of property, or laws regulating the establishment and conduct of organized labor or limiting the employment of children. In addition, activities within the organizational population to some extent will be constrained by law, for example, laws or governmental rules that impose standards of product quality or workers' safety.

Potential diversity and complexity of the institutional environment is great, but our theoretic interest is specific. It centers on the degree to which the institutional framework that surrounds an organization protects its access to sustenance resources (direct and indirect) and to technology. We will refer to this consequence of institutional arrangements as *protection*.

The more protected an organization's access to a given resource, the greater its total share of the supply. Therefore, the less vulnerable it is to changes of resource costs (including costs of inducing demand), the lower these costs are likely to be, and the less vulnerable the organization to changes in the size of the supply or the intensity of the demand. Thus, carrying capacity ultimately is constrained not only by the aggregate productivity of an organization's populations and by demand for its outputs, but also by the degree to which the organization's access to resources (whether direct resources or the indirect resources of capital and demand) is protected.

Protected inputs are especially likely among organizations whose products are defined institutionally as exempt from market exchange, primarily because of their status as public goods.[12] This exemption is more likely to be complete when the public good is indivisible--for example, police or fire protection, the maintenance of standing armies, or common education--and partial when the public good is divisible but of high symbolic value--for example, museums, universities, ballet companies, or orchestras. One might make the case that the completeness of protected input is a function of the value of an organization's product as an indivisible public good; government bureaus and other governmentally sponsored organizations are typical cases of protected input.

As protection of input exchanges grows more prevalent and complete, an organization's sustenance will depend increasingly on its entitlements to protection--for example, its charter as a unit of government or regulated public utility, laws or governmental rules (e.g., laws providing it with subventions of public funds), or less formal understandings (e.g., that an organization's efforts to gain a protected product market will not lead to antitrust action). Entitlements, in turn, are grounded on the *legitimacy* of the organization. As more of an organization's inputs become protected and as this protection becomes more complete, legitimacy becomes a more generalized sustenance resource.

Legitimacy can have several bases--among them the value of an organization's product as a public good, the symbolic value of its primary functions (e.g., common education or health care), attributes of its technology or population (e.g., a hospital's equipment or staff qualifications), or the symbolic value of the organization itself (e.g., a

---

[12]*Public goods are products whose consumption cannot be restricted by the provider and whose benefits generally accrue to the citizenship at large.*

museum as an object of civic pride). Moreover, the legitimacy of an organization is a variable outcome of the preferences or values of actors in the environment, or of individual actors as their preferences are politically aggregated. These actors are an organization's constituents. The relative volume and predictability of an organization's inputs of legitimacy result from the central tendency and dispersion of the aggregate preferences of these constituents, to which the preferences can be mobilized (e.g., as interest group action or plebiscitary voting). Like any environment, the legitimacy-supplying environment of an organization can be more or less heterogeneous (i.e., variation in the value bases of legitimacy) and diverse (i.e., the number of constituents), with the consequences for input that we outlined earlier (see Figure 2).

As input protection becomes more complete, so that legitimacy becomes a more generalized resource sustaining an organization, three new activities to coordinate organization-environment exchanges should appear among its activity patterns. These activities center (1) on the mobilization of legitimacy inputs to support protection entitlements, (2) on their use to maintain and expand the completeness of entitlements, and (3) on the melioration of the environmentally located regulation of organizational activities that is characteristically entailed by the protection of inputs.

Regarding key functional status, we propose that as protection becomes more complete, extending across the full array of factors of production, and consumer demand and, as well, fixing the volume and rate of input, the productivity contribution of activities coordinating inputs of legitimacy and exchanges with entitling agencies should outrun the contribution of any other form of input coordination. Similarly, the productivity contribution of activities coordinating exchanges with regulatory agencies should increase, at a sharper rate the more vulnerable the organization's capital surplus to regulation (e.g., regulation of rates for service vs. regulation of staff qualification). Under these conditions, the triad of activities that coordinate exchanges for constituent support, protection entitlements, and benign regulation should tend more strongly than activities coordinating exchanges with suppliers or consumers to emerge as specialized activities and to make disproportionately large contributions to organizational productivity.

*Organizational Output and Feedback from the Environment*

The final portion of our theory completes specifications of the flow of information and resources through an organizational ecosystem. We return now to an organization's

relationships with its constituents, since these relationships are central to the structures through which an organization receives signals from its environment about the
conditions that will govern its continued sustenance.

We already have discussed the two principal sustaining
or supporting components of an organization's environment.
One of these is the carrying capacity of the environment
with respect to the factors of production, although the
realization of carrying capacity in the form of input is
affected by the structure of markets and the technologies of
communication and transportation.

The other is the set of individual and collective constituents that can be mobilized (either by the organization
itself or some other actor) in response to attributes of the
organization or its product. We have argued that this "political" aspect of the supporting environment can be characterized according to the distribution and intensity of preferences among constituents and the effectiveness of means
for aggregating and expressing these preferences (to the
organization, and in the case of protected organizations, to
entitling and regulating agencies).

We have argued further that these preferences may center
on the organization's product, on specific organizational
attributes as technology or population, or globally on the
organization itself. Depending on the institutional structure of the environment (in this case its involvement in or
exemption from market exchange as the medium for distributing its product), these preferences may be aggregated and
expressed in the form of demand for the product--more precisely, the elasticity of demand in relation to price--or as
legitimacy inputs and associated political support expressed
through various representative processes.

Although market mechanisms for aggregating and expressing constituents' preferences should be more significant for
economic organizations and political mechanisms for others,
in modern societies all organizations to some degree are
subject to the latter form of feedback from constituents.
Their environments to an extent are all institutionally
structured to provide one or another kind of input protection and performance regulation. Nevertheless, we would
expect noneconomic organizations to be more responsive to
political inputs than to revenue, economic organizations to
show the opposite pattern. Among the former organizations,
the significance of output to nonconsuming publics is a
major aspect of support. Among the latter, because of the
dominant market process of support aggregation, nonconsumer
preferences are usually expressed through governmental or

other third-party regulation. Thus, for noneconomic organizations, revenue may be more responsive to nonconsumer publics. Indeed, these organizations are financed through third-party arrangements (e.g., governmental appropriations or philanthropy).

Among our basic assumptions is the centrality of surplus capital to the sustenance of organizations. From this assumption it follows that for all organizations (economic, noneconomic, or whatever) the principal link between aggregated and expressed constituents' preferences and the structuring (and the performance) of organizations is the effect of these preferences on capital input—whether in the form of profits (the realization of value added in production) or of revenues (the fiscal subvention of the organization outside of economic markets).

These elements of our theory, then, imply the following chain of events that constitutes the chief feedback loop that opens an organization to its environment:

1. Any organization sends multiple outputs to its environment—its product or products, its technological means of production, the size and composition of its population (or certain of its sub-populations), attributes of its production or administrative organization, or its nominal existence as a corporate body performing certain specialized functions in the society.

2. Each of these outputs becomes more or less salient in the feedback process according to the content and distribution of preferences among an organization's constituents. The more heterogeneous this supporting environment, the more numerous the salient outputs.

3. Any of these outputs can be valued by constituents in either or both of two ways—as a sign of organizational effectiveness (the absolute number of more or less preferred units of output and the proportion of such units among all units of output—e.g., the sheer number of Nobel laureates on a university faculty or their ratio to the total number of faculty members) or as a sign of organizational efficiency (the ratio of the number of units of preferred outputs to the cost to the organization of maintaining them—e.g., the intensity of specialization of a hospital's medical staff in relation to house staff salaries and the costs of supporting services). The degree to which effectiveness or efficiency criteria are salient in the feedback process again is a function of the content and distribution of constitutents' preferences.

4. Information about salient outputs of an organization, which may be more or less regular, accurate, and complete depending on market imperfections and the effectiveness of means of communication between the organization and its constituents, is acted on by these constituents in the form of decisions to consume or not to consume the product, or to provide legitimacy inputs (either positive or negative) or to remain inactive.

5. The results of these decisions are then fed back to the organization as information about the level of constituents' support. This feedback can take three main forms: (a) as the rate of product sales; (b) as expressions of support (varying in direction and intensity) directly to the organization or its entitlement granting and regulating agencies; or (c) as variation in the absolute volume of capital input (i.e., net profits or net outcomes of organization-environment exchanges affecting the protection of inputs of factors of production).

6. The absolute level of capital input, then, should be a function of the aggregate direction and intensity of constituents' preferences, their potential level of mobilization (in political terms a function of the pervasiveness and effectiveness of interest group organization, in economic terms a function of the freedom of consumers to enter product markets), and the rate and accuracy of feedback to the organization or its entitling and regulating agencies (in political terms the effectiveness of representative organs of the polity, in economic terms the elasticity of the product market).

7. Thus, feedback of information from constituents affects organizational structure primarily through its effects on the absolute volume of capital input--either directly in the form of profits or revenues or indirectly in the form of varying completeness of protection of capital input and in the completeness and pervasiveness of inputs of other factors of production (since protection of these inputs influences the organization's aggregate productivity).

8. The range of variation in the absolute volume of capital input, however, will be limited by the availability of inputs from the environment—primarily of capital and secondarily of other factors of production. As we have seen, the availability of these inputs is a function of the environment's carrying capacity, scope, diversity, and heterogeneity. Thus, the toal amount of wealth in the environment of an organization is an ultimate and central constraint on the effectiveness of feedback from an organization's constituents.

9. Furthermore, the net efficiency of an organization, in addition to its function as an organizational attribute of potential value to constituents, affects an organization's responsiveness to absolute variation of capital input. At any level of such input, the more efficient an organization, the greater the relative volume of input. Therefore, the more efficient an organization, the wider its structural tolerance of variation in the absolute volume of capital input and the less immediate should be its structuring response to this variation. Indeed, increased efficiency may be a less costly adaptation than structural change, but only within environmentally imposed limits to the availability of substitutable inputs of technology, labor, or materials of varying cost. Once factors of production are recombined to increase efficiency, restructuring is stimulated, as our earlier discussion has indicated.

10. Organizations are likely also to respond directly to constituents' preferences, as a function of the effectiveness of environmental monitoring by input coordinating (especially upper level administrative niches) and the degree to which feedback is channeled directly to the organization (e.g., feedback through product markets or local rather than regional or national organs of political representation). These reponses are decisions about how to cut costs, in the case of declining capital input, or about the use of increased relative volume of capital input to increase the value to constituents of a salient output.[13] Rising profits

---

[13]These may be outputs not yet generated in significant volume by the organization. This process underlies Chandler's (1962) analysis of decisions by economic firms to diversify their product lines.

or increased actual or potential legitimacy inputs, as these inputs are grounded on evaluation of an organization's product, are likely to result in increases in the level of production activities and in the size of the production organization. These changes, in turn, should foster the specialization of production niches and their interdependence—within limits set by technological procedures and tools and by the supply of labor and materials. Alternatively, preferences for specific organizational attributes should foster re-allocation of capital toward the supply of valued attributes. The net outcome of such re-allocations is not possible to predict in the general case, nor is the net outcome of responses to global preferences for the organization itself. These strategic adaptations depend on the specific content of the preferences, on the one hand, and administrative interpretation of the grounding of global preferences, on the other. In any event, these specific adaptations should have their structuring effects through the impact of entrepreneurial decisions on the allocation of surplus capital.

## SUMMARY AND THEORETICAL IMPLICATIONS

In this chapter, we have utilized the axioms, assumptions, and constructs of modern sociological human ecology to develop a dynamic open-system theory of organizational structuring. We have defined the principal causal parameters in our ecological theory of the emergence of organizational structure—the size and skill composition of an organizational population, its technologies, and its institutional and resource-supplying environment. We have specified the variable properties of these parameters that we expect to be the most potent sources of variation in the emergence of organizational form.

Our theory brings the Law of Limited Variety to bear on the structural analysis of organizations. We expect them to be no more complex than the stimuli to complexity from the variety of demographic, technological, and environmental inputs to their sustenance activity. Why should this be? Why should organizations not grow in complexity as an autonomous process, at least up to some relatively high threshold of scale, whatever the characteristics of their inputs of resources, technologies, or demography?

The answer, we propose, rests on the fact that formal organizations are truly open systems that are themselves functioning components in a societal division of labor in which they perform specialized activities. As nodes in a complicated network of input-output exchanges with other specialized producers, organizations receive the material resources, the labor, and the technical means of production necessary to sustain their own specialized activities—that is, capital surplus and, through the use of this surplus in a series of market exchanges, the factors of production that they require.

Thus, formal organizations, though they can be analyzed in ecosystem terms, are not the relatively closed communities that have tended to preoccupy ecologists. They do not, except in unusual circumstances, generate ancillary activities to reproduce their populations, extract or fabricate their materials, or invent or develop their technologies. Rather, formal organizations seek so far as possible to externalize costs. They attempt to do so with respect to all activities that their specialized tasks involve, but ancillary activities provide an unusually good opportunity for such externalization. Hence, organizations characteristically acquire labor that to some degree already is trained to the skills that their production and administrative activities require. They purchase materials from other organizations that extract or fabricate them. They borrow technology from the cultural stock of their environing societies. They distribute their products in markets that function largely through activities of other organizations (e.g., the chain of distribution from extracting organizations, through manufacturers, wholesalers, and retailers, to the "final" consumer).

Only when the marginal utility of internalizing any activity is greater than that of externalizing it will the activity come to be located among an organization's niches. Hence, the complexity of an organization's structure should correspond closely to attributes of its inputs of resources, technology, and population requirements (viewed over a fairly long run of time) and of the institutional structure of its environment, since these attributes affect the marginal utility of the internal or external location of activities, whether ancillary to or more directly involved in its specific production tasks.

It is precisely these inputs that counteract the entropic tendency toward simple structure. Thus, we have given little attention to the problem of equilibrium that is central to so much of ecological and system-theoretic analysis. Organizations as open subsystems of a society are subject to continuing destabilizing shocks as a consequence of the exchanges that yield their supplies of the factors of production. We are concerned with systematic properties of these shocks, with structural adaptations to them, and with the conditions under which organizations attain greater or lesser degrees of enduring structure within their highly dynamic environments. It might be said that the more structurally stable organizations attain dynamic equilibrium, but the dynamics more than the equilibrium interest us.

Our theory presents the processes and conditions under which organizations retain or lose, and perhaps regain, adaptability to the exigent problems of sustenance that their environments present. It shows that the principal stimuli to structural change—the sources of destabilizing shocks—are to be found in the heterogeneity of the environment and in the perturbation of the inputs that it provides. This same point can be put in a slightly different way. Organizations should change structure as a correlate of the variety of activity patterns that their environments potentially can sustain. Sustenance involves both a level of input sufficient to the consumption requirements of these activity patterns (the relative volume of input) and to the persistence of this level long enough to allow for feedback to the organization from the environment and the restructuring and reintegration of the organizational population that this feedback promotes (the regularity of input).

Now we must make explicit a point that heretofore has been implicit in our theory. Organizations will be dynamic morphologically according to the rates at which environmental heterogeneity and input perturbation change. These changes are, in turn, a function of the dynamic properties of the environing society itself. The more rapid the rate of social change, the more dynamic should be the structuring processes that characterize the society's organization subsystems.

This general proposition, however, does not tell us whether the changes will move toward greater or lesser structural complexity in specific organizations within a society, nor the rates at which these changes should occur. Within any society and historical period, we observe organizations that seem relatively stable structurally, others that are growing and declining in complexity, and at quite different rates. Moreover, the same organization, at different times, will display markedly different rates and directions of structural change. How are these phenomena to be understood?

Our theory suggests that the key to these dynamic variations is the productivity of the organization. The greater an organization's productivity, the larger will be its supply of surplus capital and the more likely it is to respond to whatever stimuli to complexity its environment provides. Further, our theory suggests that organizational productivity is a function of properties of input from the environment—its heterogeneity and degree of perturbation—and of organizational structure itself—the degree of isomorphism between technological procedures and production organization, and the elaboration of administrative organization according to differentiation and interdependence in the production organization and the perturbation of inputs.

The ultimate limits to the structural complexity of organizations are set by the carrying capacity of the environment, fundamentally by its wealth (which constrains the absolute volume of capital input), and the content and distribution of constituents' preferences (which constrain the ability of an organization to realize value added in production as capital input and thus to realize the environment's carrying capacity as sustenance).

Entropy sets in, so that an organization loses complexity and, over the long run, integral identity (the basis of the class limit of its population) primarily when it creates value through producation that cannot be realized in the form of surplus capital. Entropy also is fostered when the environment cannot provide the labor or materials to sustain production, or when the cultural stock of its society cannot provide the technology of which these activities are constituted—at least not at a sufficiently regular rate for integral structure to emerge in the organizational population.

Nevertheless, as the absolute volume of capital input declines, an organization can counteract entropy. It can raise its aggregate productivity. We have suggested that specific productivity-increasing adaptations will vary with the technologies, raw materials, and labor force characteristics that the organization can reach. Certain of these adaptations may occur in the production organization—for example, specialization and formalization of tasks when labor is unskilled. Others may occur in the administrative organization—for example, the emergence of input coordinating niches to counteract perturbed inputs of factors of production.

Thus, declining capital input may foster structural complexity, but only to the degree that these structural changes are indeed adaptive—changes that in fact raise organizational productivity and thus restore the relative volume of capital input to an adequate sustenance level. Productivity is indeed the central constraint on such adaptations, within the limits set by the carrying capacity of the environment and those structural aspects of the environment that affect the perturbation of inputs. If aggregate organizational productivity cannot be increased, entropy cannot be counteracted.

By contrast, as the relative volume of an organization's capital input rises, whether as a result of rising organizational productivity or more intense positive preferences among an organization's constituents, the organization is stimulated to new levels of structural complexity. These stimuli may be created by environmental heterogeneity (which capital surplus allows the organization to reach), but the ability of the organization to counteract perturbed inputs by structural means, or by increased levels of production activity (or its functional equivalents in the intensification of organizational attributes valued by constituents) required to satisfy the preference distribution to which it is exposed.

Moreover, structural specialization itself stimulates still greater specialization, especially as the emergence of upper level, entrepreneurial administrative niches creates capacity to explore the environment, increase its scope and effective carrying capacity, and reform the production and administrative organization accordingly.

Thus, we can expect organizations to grow in structural complexity up to the ultimate limits on the sustenance that its environment can provide, and as a consequence of the heterogeneity of the sustenance resources that the environment contains, but only to the degree that the organization maintains or increases its productivity. Therefore, within these limits, we may expect organizations--whether compared with one another or viewed longitudinally--to change more rapidly the more rapid the fluctuations in environmental heterogeneity and, more basically, in the one fundamental sustenance resource, surplus capital. These changes should be centered on those organizational niches where productivity gains will be greatest--where entropy not only will be counteracted, but net increments to sustenance capacity absorbed by the organization.

REFERENCES

Aldrich, H. E. (1979). Organizations and Environments. Englewood Cliffs, NJ.: Prentice-Hall, Inc.

Aldrich, H. E., and J. Pfeffer. (1976). "Environments of organizations." Annual Review of Sociology 2:79-105.

Berry, B. J. L., and J. D. Kasarda. (1977). Contemporary Urban Ecology. New York: Macmillan.

Blau, P. M. (1970). "A formal theory of differentiation in organizations." American Sociological Review 35:201-218.

Blau, P. M., and R. Schoenherr. (1971). The Structure of Organizations. New York: Basic Books.

Boulding, K. (1968). "General systems theory: the skeleton of science." Pp. 3-10 in W. Buckley (ed.), Modern Systems Research for the Behavioral Scientist. Chicago: Aldine.

Burns, T. R., and G. M. Stalker. (1961). The Management of Innovation. London: Tavistock Institute of Human Relations.

Caplow, T. (1964). Principles of Organization. New York: Harcourt, Brace, and World.

Chandler, A. D., Jr. (1962). Strategy and Structure: Chapters in the History of American Industrial Enterprise. Cambridge, MA.: MIT Press.

Cohen, M. D., and J. G. March. (1974). Leadership and Ambiguity. New York: McGraw-Hill.

Cyert, R. M., and J. G. March. (1963). A Behavioral Theory of the Firm. Englewood Cliffs, NJ.: Prentice-Hall.

Dubin, R. (1951). Human Relations in Administration: The Sociology of Organization. Englewood Cliffs, NJ.: Prentice-Hall.

Duncan, O. D. (1959). "Human ecology and population studies." Pp. 678-716 in P. M. Hauser and O. D. Duncan (eds.), The Study of Population. Chicago: University of Chicago Press.

Duncan, O. D. (1961). "From social system to ecosystem." Sociological Inquiry 31:140-149.

Duncan, O. D. (1964). "Social organization and the ecosystem." Pp. 37-82 in R. E. L. Faris (ed.) Handbook of Modern Sociology. Chicago: Rand-McNally.

Duncan, O. D., and L. F. Schnore (1959). "Cultural, behavioral and ecological perspectives in the study of social organization." American Journal of Sociology 65:132-146.

Etzioni, A. (1961). A Comparative Analysis of Complex Organizations. New York: Free Press.

Evan, W. M. (1972). "An organization-set model of inter-organizational relations." Pp. 181-200 in M. Tuite, R. Chisholm, and M. Radnor (eds.), Interorganizational Decision Making. Chicago: Aldine.

Hall, R. H., et al. (1967). "Organizational size, complexity, and formalization." American Sociological Review 32:903-912.

Hannan, M., and J. H. Freeman. (1977). "The population ecology of organizations." American Journal of Sociology 82:929-964.

Hawley, A. H. (1968). "Human ecology." Pp. 328-337 in D. L. Sills (ed.), International Encyclopedia of the Social Sciences. Volume 4. New York: Macmillan Co. and Free Press.

Hawley, A. H. (1973). "Ecology and population." Science 179:1196-1201.

Katz, D., and R. L. Kahn. (1966). The Social Psychology of Organizations. New York: Wiley.

Lawrence, P. R., and J. W. Lorsch. (1967). Organization and Environment: Managing Differentiation and Integration. Cambridge, MA.: Division of Research, Graduate School of Business Administration, Harvard University.

Levine, S., and P. E. White. (1961). "Exchange as a conceptual framework for the study of interorganizational relationships." Administrative Science Quarterly 5:583-601.

March, J. G., and H. A. Simon. (1958). Organizations. New York: Wiley.

Mayo, E. (1933). The Human Problems of an Industrial Civilization. New York: Macmillan.

Meyer, M. W. (1972). Bureaucratic Structure and Authority: Coordination and Control in 254 Government Agencies. New York: Harper and Row.

Perrow, C. (1970). Organizational Analysis: A Sociological View. Belmont, CA.: Wadsworth .

Roethlisberger, F. J., and W. J. Dickson. (1939). Management and the Worker. Cambridge, MA.: Harvard University Press.

Schnore, L. F. (1958). "Social morphology and human ecology." American Journal of Sociology 63:620-634.

Schnore, L. F. (1961). "The myth of human ecology." Sociological Inquiry 31:128-139.

Schrodinger, E. (1968). "Order, disorder, and entropy." Pp. 143-146 in W. Buckley (ed.), Modern Systems Research for the Behavioral Scientist. Chicago: Aldine.

Sofer, C. (1962). The Organization from Within. Chicago: Quadrangle.

Stinchcombe, A. L. (1965). "Social structure and organizations." Pp. 142-193 in J. G. March (ed.), Handbook of Organizations. Chicago: Rand McNally.

236

Stinchcombe, A. L. (1968). Constructing Social Theories. New York: Harcourt, Brace, and World.

Taylor, F. W. (1911). The Principles of Scientific Management. New York: Harper.

Terreberry, S. (1968). "The evolution of organizational environments." Administrative Science Quarterly 12: 590-615.

Thompson, J. D. (1967). Organizations in Action. New York: McGraw-Hill.

Weber, M. (1947). The Theory of Social and Economic Organization. Trans. T. Parsons and A. M. Henderson. New York: Oxford University Press.

Weick, K. E. (1969). The Social Psychology of Organizing. Reading, MA.: Addison-Wesley.

Williamson, O. E. (1975). Markets and Hierarchies: Analysis and Antitrust Implications. New York: Free Press.

Wolff, K. H. (1959). "The sociology of knowledge and sociological theory." Pp. 557-602 in L. Gross (ed.), Symposium on Sociological Theory. New York: Harper and Row.

Woodward, J. (1965). Industrial Organization: Theory and Practice. London: Oxford University Press.

Woodward, J. (ed.) (1970). Industrial Organization: Behaviour and Control. London: Oxford University Press.

# 6
# Subcommunities:
# Neighborhoods and Suburbs
# in Ecological Perspective

*Harvey M. Choldin*

In the early years of human ecology, urban sociologists often studied local "communities" within the city. These researchers viewed the city as a collection of smaller "natural areas," which were highly differentiated by land use, population composition, and function. Zorbaugh (1926: 222-223), for example, stated that the city is broken up

> ...into numerous smaller areas which we may call natural areas, in that they are the unplanned, natural product of the city's growth... A natural area is a geographical area characterized both by a physical individuality and by the cultural characteristics of the people who live in it.

Even in the 1920s, though, some sociologists said that the local area was disintegrating as a social unit. McKenzie (1923) stated that population mobility coupled with modern communications and transportation technologies would weaken the local community. Wirth (1938) said that the ecological imperatives of urban settlement would tend to destroy such primary groupings as families and neighborhoods. Later, three empirical studies (Hatt, 1946; Form, et al., 1954; Glass, 1948) tended to undermine the validity of the natural area concept and these studies supported the abandonment of the concept by urban ecologists. Indeed, eventually there was no agreement upon a definition of neighborhood or upon a procedure for delimiting one in an existing city. Ecological theory de-emphasized local community life within the metropolis on the grounds that the smaller areas had lost most of their functions. Hawley (1971:198) stated that "the tendency is for small territorial units to be absorbed and stripped of their identities by the larger universe of activity."

Some urban theorists have argued that the local area has lost its social significance in contemporary urban life. There is an ongoing debate in which one group contends that the metropolis has become one large potential social field and that social networks transcend locality (Craven and Wellman, 1974; Webber, 1962). On the other hand, Kasarda and Janowitz (1974) and Hunter (1974, 1975), maintain that sub-communities have enduring functions for many urban residents. It will be necessary to deal with this issue in order to evaluate the function of the residential area.

Sociologists studying neighborhoods abandoned ecological theory. One substitute for the natural area was the personal neighborhood (Sweetser, 1941) which consisted of an individual's network of close social contacts and the locations of the people in the network. Some sociologists (Fava, 1959; Keller, 1968) focused upon neighboring as the defining feature of neighborhood life. Others (Foley, 1959; Hunter, 1975) investigated localized activity patterns within the city. These various approaches reflected a theoretical fragmentation, although most were closer to social psychology than to ecology in that they emphasized the qualities of interpersonal relationships and attitudes toward the locality.

The social science literature on residential areas has been fragmented also as researchers have looked upon neighborhoods and suburbs in and of themselves, apart from the larger community context. The neighborhood literature is composed mostly of individual case studies (i.e., Kornblum, 1974; Suttles, 1968; Hunter, 1974; Gans, 1962). Studies by

Hunter, 1974 and Bradburn, Sudman and Gockel, 1970, which statistically examined large numbers of residential areas are notable exceptions. Suburban studies are also typically of individual cases (see, for example, Gans, 1967). The neighborhood and suburban literatures are separate and rarely recognize similarities between these parts of the metropolis.

It is an error to look at the residential area, in and of itself, apart from the metropolitan community of which it is a part. Few sociologists have heeded Burgess' (1925:148) warning: "To think of the neighborhood or the community in isolation is to ignore the biggest fact about the neighborhood." Now it is necessary to see "neighborhood" and metropolis together. First, though, it is necessary to recognize city and suburban residential areas as equivalent units. They are both *subcommunities,* residential areas, parts of the metropolitan community.

Unfortunately, ecologists have eliminated such units from the field of ecological inquiry, even though their theories may be effectively applied. Thus, one task is to argue that subcommunity is an ecological unit of analysis.

This chapter suggests an ecological approach to the sub-community within the modern metropolis. The chapter draws together ideas from ecology and urban sociology. It suggests that neighborhoods and suburbs will be better understood as parts of a metropolitan whole, that part-whole relationships will reveal the functions of the subcommunity. The approach uses the analytical framework of the ecological complex (Duncan, 1959) and looks explicitly at the demography, organization, and technology of the community and subcommunity. Another part of the approach is to ask what effect the subcommunity has upon the sustenance base and general adaptivity of the greater community. The approach will help to show a fruitful pairing of ecology and social psychology. This approach will also help answer the question of whether it matters whether subcommunities exist or whether neighborhoods have disappeared as features of residential areas.

## PROBLEMS IN DEFINITION AND MEASUREMENT

A variety of names have been suggested for local residential areas within the city, including natural area, community area, neighborhood, social area, microcommunity and subcommunity, among others. Each of these has some conceptual or empirical deficiency, but, for reasons elaborated below, subcommunity is the most satisfactory.

The Chicago School urban sociologists introduced two loosely related concepts to represent sections of the city: natural area and community area. These sociologists viewed Chicago as a collection of smaller communities which were integral to some degree. A community area had identifiable and agreed-upon boundaries, a community name and a history. Burgess and his students examined the city in the 1920s and divided it into 75 areas (Hunter, 1974:20-25). They then published the local community fact book with the histories and statistics of the areas (Wirth and Furez, 1938). These definitions of the community areas were adopted by many city governmental units and endured in local culture over the decades. Some community areas differentiated into smaller areas and others fused into larger districts over time (Hunter, 1974).

Community areas were much larger than neighborhoods in any conventional sense of that term. Burgess (1925:148) stated that the zones of the city contained communities which in turn "subdivide into smaller areas called neighborhoods." By 1950, when the city grew to a population of 3.6 million, the average population of an area was more than 48,000 (Hauser and Kitagawa), which is much greater than either popular or planners' conceptions of neighborhood size.

The Chicago urban sociologists conceived of the community area as a natural area (Zorbaugh, 1926), which was a territory bounded by some prominent features of the terrain such as rivers, highways, railroad embankments, industrial zones and the like. Presumably, within a natural area there was uniformity of social class, ethnicity and housing type.

The viability of the concept natural area/community area became doubtful in the 1940s and 1950s when research was unable to validate it. Studies were unable to find a method to delineate natural areas. Hatt (1946) delineated what should have been a natural area in Seattle and found several social types within it. Even a prominent Chicago study of a natural area, *The Gold Coast and the Slum* (Zorbaugh, 1929) showed considerable diversity within its borders. Studies in England (Glass, 1948) and the U.S. (Form, et al., 1954) failed to find consistency between physiographic boundaries, sociodemographic uniformities and activity distributions.

Hunter (1974), Molotch (1972), Kornblum (1974), and other University of Chicago students in the 1960s "revived" community areas in a series of local field studies. Hunter found that over 80 percent of the residents in any given area knew its name and more than two-thirds knew its conventional boundaries. Less than half the survey respondents said they had positive feelings or some attachment to it.

Some areas were fusing; others were subdividing still further Blacks tended to discard local names of formerly white areas. Kornblum (1974) described an area with distinct boundaries and considerable self-consciousness as did Molotch (1972).

The weakness of the community area concept is that the boundaries are unclear and shifting, the resident populations change, and the areas are not necessarily uniform in composition and many inhabitants have no awareness of a community identity.

*Neighborhood* is the most common name used for the residential area, both in sociological discussions and in ordinary English. Carpenter (1933:356) provided a serviceable definition of neighborhood.

> The most distinctive characteristics of a neighborhood are its relation with a local area sufficiently compact to permit frequent and intimate association and the emergence out of which association of sufficient homogeneity and unity to permit a primary or face-to-face social grouping endowed with a strong sense of self-consciousness and capable of influencing the behavior of its several constituents.

This defines an ideal-typical neighborhood. The definition includes the elements most often found in such definitions: a small residential area, a homogeneous population, intimacy of social relations and some social psychological effects: common behavior patterns, self-consciousness, loyalty, etc. There are numerous definitions of neighborhood; see, for examples: Park (1916:579); McKenzie (1923:344), McClenahan, (1929:107), Keller (1968:12, 87); (Greer, 1968: 121); Gans, (1968b:50); Sweetser (1941).

In reality, though, such ideal-type neighborhoods were rarely found in contemporary cities. Carpenter (1933:356) said that they occur in rural places but only occasionally in urban areas. He said that there are "pseudoneighborhoods," residential areas with homogeneous populations which condition the residents' behavior, but these areas have too many people for primary group relationships. Like McKenzie (1923), McClenahan (1929), Wirth (1938), Park (1916:97), and other contemporaries, he said that urban conditions and forces tend to undermine neighborhoods.

Keller (1968) emphasizes the special quasi-primary relationship between neighbors. This relationship is based largely upon proximity. Neighbors ordinarily engage in neighboring: reciprocal chatting and visiting as well as the exchange of help and advice on a limited scale. Gans (1968b: 40) also states that the contemporary relationship between neighbors is quasi-primary: "interaction is more intimate than a secondary contact, but more guarded than a primary one."

Fischer (1976:120) says that "urbanism tends to reduce the role of neighbor toward its bare essence." (1) "Be ready to assist your neighbor at those times when physical proximity is important," and (2) "don't be offensive."

Neighborhood and neighboring depend heavily upon population stability. Small size and homogeneous population, by socioeconomic level or ethnic culture, would also promote this type of relationship. None of these conditions obtains in the typical modern metro community and thus, this type of organization is rare. In the U.S., the only neighborhood organization of this type is the "ethnic village," which has been described by Gans (1962) and Suttles (1968). Other studies have shown relatively little neighboring in areas of apartment buildings, and somewhat more of it in low density areas (Fava, 1959). Neighborhood, then, is not a useful term to describe the social reality of the urban residential area.

Social area analysis (Shevky and Bell, 1955; Shevky and Williams, 1949) offers another term, the social area. This type of analysis is based upon the division of metropolitan communities into census tracts and the measurement of each tract with regard to three dimensions, socioeconomic status, race/ethnicity, and family status. These give rise to a typology of census tracts (Sweetser, 1974). An example of one type of tract/social area would be middle class, white, non-ethnic, familistic. Social area analysis sidesteps the problem of boundary delineation in that a single tract or a set of contiguous or noncontiguous tracts of the same type forms a social area (Shevky and Williams, 1949:61-64). However, the method may generate a statistical geographical artifact. Social area analysis does not indicate that there is any internal organization or integrity to a social area. It relies on the vagaries of the determination of tract boundaries for its own boundaries. Since the social area is not necessarily a discrete subarea of the city—it may be several scattered places with the same social properties—it does not prove useful in an attempt to examine a functional part of the larger community. A more useful concept will refer to a place in a city rather than to a location in an attribute space. (Social area analysis was heavily attacked as being atheoretical by Hawley and Duncan, 1957). The concept of social area, then, also fails to be useful for the definition of a meaningful social unit within the metropolis.

A new term to represent the local residential area is microcommunity (National Research Council, 1975:67). The social scientists who introduced this term defined it as the nonecological concept of community. They suggested that microcommunity should represent the social-psychological element of community. They rely upon a "traditional" definition of community for which the village has been the model, a grouping of people who live close to one another and are united by common interest and mutual aid. Relying upon sentiment to represent what occurs locally or what should occur, however, ignores that fact that residential areas are parts of the metropolis and have functional relationships to it.

*Subcommunity* is the most useful term to represent the local residential area. The residential area is "sub" because it is less than a community, not having a sustenance base. Since residence and work are spatially divided, residential areas do not have industry or other major employment establishments within them. Residential areas are completely dependent upon other parts of the community for subsistence. They are less than communities because they do not have governments; they depend upon citywide or suburban governmental systems and bureaucracies for decision-making as well as for police, educational, sanitation and other community services. The term subcommunity is connotatively neutral, unlike neighborhood which has a gemeinschaft flavor. Subcommunity is denotatively accurate, though, referring to a part, something less than a complete community. This term will be used throughout the balance of this chapter.

Individual suburbs, which also lack sustenance bases, are also subcommunities. The only exceptions are satellite cities which have industry or some other employment base which is not dedicated to local service functions (Schnore, 1957). Even though many employers have decentralized, suburbs are still divided between those which are principally residential and those which include both jobs and houses (Muller, 1976). In employing suburbs, the term subcommunity applies only to the residential areas.

Drawing the boundaries of individual subcommunities has proven to be difficult. Early studies of urban social life did not find this to be problemmatical. McKenzie (1923) and McClenahan (1929) were able to define boundaries for individual neighborhood studies and Burgess was able to delineate community areas (Hunter, 1974). But later investigators were unable to find clear boundaries of neighborhoods. Form, et al., (1954) attempted to find natural physical boundaries which coincided with areas of population homogeneity and sociability but found that they did not coincide. Glass (1948) also found that agency service areas, homogeneous areas and natural boundaries did not coincide in an English city. Hunter (1974) also found that the boundaries of many of Burgess' community areas had shifted over the decades. In general, studies of cognitive maps (Lynch, 1960) show that people divide urban space and define their neighborhoods differently.

Thus the current use of the subcommunity concept will have to omit the specification of boundaries. The subcommunity is simply a residential area, large or small. The search for boundaries could go on indefinitely with limited intellectual return. Nonetheless, it is possible to understand local life in cities and suburbs without specifying precisely the limits of any given residential area.

Children and mothers are among the heaviest users of the subcommunity and their activities have been studied more extensively than those of other groups. (Roper, 1963; Foley, 1959). Roper (1963) noted that "Much of the play time of small children is used in informal activities around the home, in the local neighborhood, on the streets, in the alleys, etc." Foley, (1959) found that children under age 12 made the most use of local facilities and, among adults, females used them more than males did. Households with children made more use of local facilities than those without (Foley, 1952).

Other groups who are heavy users of local facilities are the elderly and the very poor. The aged are restricted in their movement and have many of their social contacts near their residences. They also use nearby parks and shops. The very poor have limited mobility due to lack of money and information. Individuals without cars also tend to use local facilities (Foley, 1959).

Hunter (1975) replicated Foley's study in the same area of Rochester after an elapsed time of 25 years; he discovered a somewhat changed pattern of local activities. Residents in the early 1970s were less likely to use local facilities for instrumental purposes--shopping, medical care, etc.--than their counterparts a quarter-century earlier had. But they were more likely to conduct their informal social life within the area and they had more of a sense of involvement and commitment to the area. More people had friends in the area and there was more neighboring than there had been 25 years earlier.

Duration of residence and stage in the family life cycle are highly related to local participation. Long-term residents are much more likely to be involved in local social networks and to be members of local voluntary associations

(Janowitz, 1952; Kasarda and Janowitz, 1974; Hunter, 1974). Parents are more likely than others to be involved in local networks and organizations. Young adults without children are likely not to be involved in the local social life and not to use local facilities. Organizational participation declines after the age of 55. (Voluntary associations are discussed in a later section of the chapter.)

AN ECOLOGICAL APPROACH

*Subcommunity as a unit of analysis*

Human ecology views the ecosystem as the main object of investigation (Duncan 1959, 1964) and the community as the smallest ecosystem (Hawley, 1950). Community has been a difficult concept to define in sociology and ecology for several decades, giving rise to as many as 94 sociological definitions (Hillery, 1955). Human ecologists have introduced a satisfactory definition, as expressed by Schnore (1967):

> [Community is ] the localized population which is interdependent on a daily basis, and which carries on a highly generalized series of activities in and through a set of institutions which provides on a day-to-day basis the full range of goods and services necessary for its continuity as a social and economic entity.

With this definition, ecologists reject another sociological view of community which emphasizes sentiment and common interests (Gusfield, 1975). Clearly, town, city and even metropolis satisfy the ecological definition of community. The metropolis comprises a single commuting field, a single retail distribution market, a single economic network for such other economic activities as banking. It is also a single communications field for newspapers and radiotelevision broadcasting (Meier, 1962). The metropolitan area contains the daily life of its inhabitants.

The metropolitan community can clearly be seen as an ecosystem. It is a population occupying a habitat, carrying on a set of sustaining activities. It has a cyclical flow of energy with systemic properties (Tilly, 1974). It is analyzable within the framework of the ecosystem as laid out by Duncan (1959).

Duncan (1959:684), however, implies that the community itself may be too small a unit for ecological analysis. He states:

Recent statements on ecological theory have moved toward the assumption that the *community* is the smallest ecological complex with properties approaching those of a system (Hawley, 1950; Dice, 1955). But it is only in a limiting case that the community approximates a closed or isolated system. The trend of social evolution is toward the elaboration of organization at the intercommunity or supralocal level to such an extent that it becomes necessary, for some purposes, to take account of a fabric of interdependence with planetary scope-the "world community," for want of a better term.

He does grant, though, that the community exhibits the full range of relationships postulated for the "ecological complex." Hawley (1968) also states that "the community is regarded as the smallest microcosm in which all the parameters of a society are to be found."

It is overly restrictive to view the community as the smallest social system amenable to ecological analysis. Some very small units have been examined fruitfully in general ecology and these have been much smaller than communities as denoted conventionally. Two examples of extremely small ecosystems are a single rotting log and a single piece of cow dung (Mohr, 1943). Ecologists have studied these small habitats, enumerating the populations occupying them over time. Biologists have described the succession sequences and the trophic dynamics of these little ecosystems. They showed an interaction between the inhabitants and the environment as the populations modified the habitats setting forth conditions which accommodated the next inhabitants.

In these examples, the habitat defined the ecosystem-- the populations were passing through. There is no reason why habitat should not be used to define ecosystem within sociological human ecology. Researchers could attempt ecological analysis of any reasonable habitat, including urban ones. There could be an ecological analysis of a suburb, a housing project, an industrial district, etc. Each habitat would be seen as the environment of a "chunk" of the community. It could be examined in relation to the larger ecosystem of which it is a part.

Michelson (1970), an urban sociologist, implies that the environment may define the social unit. He enumerates criteria for concepts with which to analyze urban environments in conjunction with social phenomena. Michelson states that social life in relation to environment should be analyzable at several scales, from the dwelling to the city, and he employs the Ekistics Grid (Ekistics, 1972) for this purpose. He argues further that the concepts developed to analyze man-environment relationships should be applicable at any scale of environment or population.

Granted that it is possible to conduct an ecological analysis of some social unit smaller than a community, it is necessary to find a theoretically defensible unit which is also fruitful for the understanding of social life at the local level. This requires a delineation of the parts of the metropolitan community. Although Hawley notes that the constituent members of a population are individuals, he states (1968) that the community "is construed as a territorially localized system of relationships among *functionally differentiated parts...*" (emphasis mine.) What are these parts and how can they themselves be subjected to ecological analysis?

## Parts of the metropolitan community

The metropolitan community may be viewed as a whole, composed of several interrelated parts. Schnore (1966:60) once proposed an analogy comparing a city to a biological organism.

> There is a territorial or geographic division of labor between the sub-areas making up the city. Most broadly, the division is between homes and workplaces, producing and consuming areas, between which there is a continuous flow of commodities, information, and people. On a finer grain, there is also a division between areas devoted to different land uses-industrial, commercial and recreational.

Some structural features are clearly represented in the spatial arrangements of parts. Different areas such as residence and work represent parts like "organs" which are bound together by flows of commodities, information and individual persons (1966:62-64).

This analogy is consistent with the conventional dissections of the metropolis into constituent parts including specialized areas in which particular activities, types of organizations, and land uses and types of structures are concentrated. These include specialized areas such as Central Business Districts, manufacturing zones, large retailing areas, transportation and warehousing districts, and the like. In addition, great portions of the metropolis are built-up into residential areas differentiated by social characteristics such as socio-economic status and by environmental features such as density and age of housing.

The community is an ecological whole, an ecosystem composed of functionally and spatially differentiated interdependent parts. Residential areas are one category of functional spatial parts.

In employing an ecological perspective, the analyst (1) views the community as an ecosystem and uses the "POET" analytical framework; (2) examines the flows of energy and information through the ecosystem; and (3) looks particularly at the sustenance activities of the ecosystem and its adaptivity in regard to its environment.

(1) Duncan's (1959) analytical framework includes four principal variable clusters, population, social organization, environment, and technology. It guides the analyst to examine the interrelationships among these four to understand ecological processes within the ecosystem.

(2) The flow of energy throughout an ecosystem is central to the general ecological paradigm. The ecologist looks at the place of various member species of an ecosystem to see the ways in which they gather and transform energy and their relationships to other occupants and to the environment. Duncan (1964) shows that in human ecosystems it is necessary to look also at the flow of information through the system.

(3) Sociological human ecologists are particularly concerned with the sustenance activities of social units (Gibbs and Martin, 1959). (See Chapter 8 in this volume for an elaboration.) Ecologists look at the ways in which human aggregates organize themselves for sustenance, and ultimately, for survival (Berry and Kasarda, 1977:12). Emerging from evolutionary theory, ecology is concerned with the adaptivity of populations. Thus, the ecologist becomes a functionalist, looking at the relevance of particular social patterns, institutions, units for system adaptivity.

The following examination of urban subcommunities will be guided by this conception of human ecology.

*Sustenance functions*

In relation to the sustenance base of the metro community, the subcommunity has two major functions: to house workers and to bring workers into the economic system. The pejorative appelation, "bedroom community," is quite accurate; the residential area, by definition, houses adult workers, among others. Obviously, housing is necessary, and the functional question is simply, does the housing contribute to the productivity of the workers? The health of the populace must be related to its productivity.

Housing shelters its occupants from climate (Fitch, 1966; Hole, 1966) and protects them from injury from human and nonhuman sources (Rainwater, 1966). It also has some effects upon health, disease and recovery, promoting or impeding the transmission of contagious diseases and providing suitable environments for recovery from illness or injury (Cassel, 1971). It allows rest and recovery between work periods. There has been some research in public health and social science fields on the effects of housing, regarding such variables as crowding and comparing slum housing with government housing projects but North American studies have not shown marked effects of different quality housing. Wilner, et al., (1962) were not able to discern more than minor differences in the health and morale of workers in slum and project environments. Booth (1976) also found trivial differences in the health and morale of adults in crowded and uncrowded housing in a Canadian city. Schorr (1963) on the other hand, in a review of the literature on slum housing, concluded that deteriorated environments had harmful effects on health, morale, child development, and family life.

Two categories of people are socialized into the community and economy at the local level: adult migrants and children. At least since the period of the great Atlantic immigration, large U.S. cities have had "port of entry" immigrant sections. Within these poor areas, the nationality groups organized to survive and to receive kinfolk. They formed special-purpose organizations for mutual aid, schools, insurance groups, newspapers, etc. Some of the immigrants started businesses or purchased real estate within the immigrant area. Churches also met the needs of these immigrants. The net effect of such subcommunities was to receive new members of the population and socialize them into the host society and inject them into the workforce. After the end of these migrations, at the middle of the twentieth century, newer migrant groups in the larger cities continued to form such "port of entry" subcommunities.

Socialization of children, which also takes place at the local level, will be discussed later in the section on social organization.

The flow of energy is a central concern in a proper ecological analysis and this is most important in understanding the relationship of subcommunity to community. The subcommunity is the context for the ultimate consumption of many products of the economy—this is the place where energy is used.

Food and heating fuels are simply consumed or burnt in residential areas. Any number of consumer products get used up in the subcommunity. They are only returned cyclically in the form of wastes. The other productive return is in the maintenance of workers who are returned to the economy to do additional productive work and in the socialization of new workers. The subcommunity has typically been designed for consumption activities. Retail distribution is spatially distributed for maximum accessibility from residences. Subcommunities also contain retail shops, schools and churches in addition to residences. In older cities residential areas contained secondary and tertiary shopping areas for most kinds of retail distribution. In newer residential areas they contain small and large-scale shopping centers for the same purposes, which are accessible mainly by automobile.

## TRANSITIONS OF THE LOCAL COMMUNITY

In earlier historical epochs the local community was a more-or-less complete unit within the larger urban settlement. There have been types of cities in which the component spatial units were not functionally differentiated. The early industrial city presented a clear model of a "cellular city," according to Hawley (1971). In it, the parts were functionally equivalent, each nucleated by a factory surrounded by a residential slum and ancillary shops and services. This was a city without a center; the round of daily life was contained within the cell. Intracity transportation was based upon pedestrian and animal movement. Large preindustrial cities were also cellular or segmental, except without the factories (Sjoberg, 1960). Small medieval towns had a mix of activities over space and manufacturing; buying, selling and dwelling were conducted in the same area.

The trend of urban development in the nineteenth and twentieth centuries has been to divide activities into different subareas. Intercity transport and warehousing are separated from office work which in turn is separated from residences. The division of land uses is extensive. City planning theory supports such division saying that it is best not to have activity areas mixed. Thus, the residential area in the twentieth century becomes an increasingly partial segment of the urban whole, first separated from work and more recently from retailing and other activities as well.

*Population*

Several of the early urban sociologists recognized demographic processes as inimical to traditional neighborhood life. In particular, they saw transiency or geographic mobility undermining stable primary group relationships. For example, McKenzie (1923:157-158) wrote:

> Perhaps the most obvious effect of the mobility of the population within a city is the striking instability of local life... Rapid community turnover also plays havoc with local standards and neighborhood mores.

McClenahan (1929) also stated that population instability and turnover tended to undermine the stable neighborhood. Park (1916:97) asked, "What part of the population is floating? How many people live in hotels, apartments and tenements? How many people own their own homes?" He said that anything which makes the population unstable tends to weaken the neighborhood. But all three of these sociologists recognized that mobility is a fundamental feature of modern urban life.

Mobility was misunderstood in two ways: it was not evenly distributed across households or across subcommunities. There is differential migration within the population. Some groups move more than others. Young and poor people move; upwardly mobile people move. But some types are quite stable--the population is divided among "movers" and "stayers." (Morrison, 1971). The oft-cited statistic that one-fifth of U.S. households move annually masks the fact that many of the moves are made by repeat movers while a majority of households stays in place over years or decades. Subcommunities also differ in the transiency of their populations, from highly mobile to quite stable. Berger (1960) showed that the "suburban myth" that people were just passing through the suburbs did not apply to working class residents. There are some types of subcommunities in which people are transient, for example slums and singles projects. But, even among New York City welfare recipients, surveyed in 1970, more than half had lived in the current quarters for at least two years (Sternlieb and Indik, 1973: 83).

Population composition, especially by age and racial-ethnic characteristics, is also very important in urban subcommunities. Many sociologists have pointed out the importance of ethnic homogeneity in urban subcultural development, (Wirth, 1928; Gans, 1961; Fischer, 1975). Park (1961) hypothesized that ethnic heterogeneity would tend to weaken neighborhood cultural cohesiveness. Sociological depictions of the early twentieth century U.S. city showed a patchwork quilt of immigrant neighborhoods with distinctive names. (See the descriptions of localities in Wirth and Furez, 1938). Even this image was overdrawn; the immigrant slums always had mixtures of nationalities within them. (See for example the detailed 1895 Hull House maps showing nationalities house-by-house in a Chicago immigrant slum, Duis, 1976: 66.)

Race, of course, continues to divide the city and metropolis. After early decades of scattered black settlement, the cities moved toward patterns of perfect segregation, first in the North and later in southern cities (Spear, 1967; Rose, 1969; Taeuber and Taeuber, 1965). In recent decades, the cities have tended to remain almost perfectly segregated. Segregation has declined very slightly each decade since 1940 (Sorenson et al., 1975). (Southern cities have become more segregated since 1940). What may have appeared to be integration was simply expansion of the ghetto (Molotch, 1972). The slight movement of middle-class blacks to suburbs has produced black enclaves rather than suburban integration (Farley, 1970).

Despite the population melting pot theory, ethnicity still differentiates subcommunities to a considerable degree. Kantrowitz (1973) has shown that identifiable ethnic groups in the New York City area are still spatially concentrated and are segregated from other groups to some extent. Case studies in Chicago show traditional groupings of ethnic groups at different socioeconomic levels (see Suttles, 1968 and Kornblum, 1974, for poor and working-class examples and Molotch for middle-class examples). Suburban ethnicity has not been explored effectively, but there is reason to believe that suburbs have identifiable ethnic concentrations.

Both the youthful and the aged segments of subcommunities affect local social life. Populations throughout the metropolitan areas are aging, with the exception of new suburban areas at the periphery which house young families. (The pattern of zonal distribution of families with children was presented by Anderson and Egelund, 1961). Declining fertility levels for several years have been having dramatic effects on subcommunities, the most dramatic being the lack of children to populate the schools. School closings are a major community issue throughout the nation. Entry of women into the workforce has also changed patterns of childrearing and local social life, leaving many households empty during the daytime.

Although the depiction of "geriatric ghettoes" is over-drawn, there are more elderly persons toward the metropolitan center than at the periphery (Pampel and Choldin, 1978). Now there are projections of the aging of the suburban population also as middle-aged couples retain their houses or move into suburban apartments.

The principal demographic patterns affecting subcommunities are complex. The urban population is mobile, but not uniformly so. Most subcommunities have a considerable proportion of long-term stable residents. The urban population is heterogeneous, but there is clearly a sorting process by socioeconomic status and race/ethnicity. Individual subcommunities are clearly identifiable by status and race/ethnicity. The metropolitan population in general is aging, but subcommunities are also clearly differentiated by age and stage in the family life cycle, higher proportions of young families with children at the periphery and somewhat higher proportions of older persons toward the center.

*Impact of technology*

Technological developments, especially in transportation and communications, have powerfully affected the urban subcommunity over the course of the past century. In the nineteenth century, major changes in intracity and long distance transportation—introduction of the trolley and the railroad—brought forth dominant centers in cities of all sizes (Tunnard and Reed, 1955). The Central Business District emerged during this epoch. Governmental and administrative activities became centralized along with transport-related activities, warehousing, and light manufacturing. The division between residence and workplace was accentuated during this period (Schnore, 1965). Thus, the residential area became just that, as fewer men carried on their work at home shops.

The strong center gave way to decentralization in the twentieth century. This transition moved many of the centralized activities out to the periphery. Manufacturing, transport and warehousing, wholesaling and many other subsistence-related activities were redistributed throughout the suburban areas. Major retail activities also located in the suburbs as secondary retail areas within the city declined. The separation of work and residence continued, perhaps accentuated.

In the twentieth century there were also two major technological developments in transportation and communications. Personal automobile ownership increased rapidly and truck usage increased among business establishments. This was accompanied by massive street, road and highway investments. The most important communications innovation was the telephone which diffused widely among commercial and household units.

The early urban sociologists recognized that changing transportation and communications systems would affect traditional neighborhoods. "The easy means of communication and of transportation, which enable individuals to distribute their attention and to live at the same time in several different worlds, tend to destroy the permanency and intimacy of the neighborhood," wrote Park (1916:98). McKenzie (1923: 167) similarly stated, "The automobile, streetcar, telephone, and press, together with increased leisure time, have all contributed greatly to the breakdown of neighborhood ties." McClenahan (1929) also argued that citywide transportation liberated people from their neighborhoods.

Cars and trucks changed the patterns of everyday activities, which had been highly localized. For example, shopping was formerly limited by the distance groceries could be carried. In contrast, automobile owners can shop at a greater distance from their residences, depending upon the amount of time they are willing to travel. In addition, the reorganization of retail distribution into large chain store operations has diminished the number of retail outlets in older residential areas. Newer low density residential areas are designed without scattered shops, but have shopping centers instead. Other formerly local facilities such as professional offices and recreation--movies, bars, etc.--have also been taken out of the residential areas and relocated along major streets with parking.

The automobile permitted the full development of the low density city. Unlike Europeans who had always built dense urban communities with apartments or other multifamily buildings, North Americans built cities with vast areas of single-family dwellings. This distinctive way of building cities included large residential areas of single family detached dwellings with individual yards. These residential areas are built at what became a new dominant density level (DeChiara and Koppelman, 1969)--approximately 22 persons per acre--which is very low for urban areas by world standards.

Developers and city planners introduced local service institutions such as schools and shops with service radii much larger than those which predominated in the earlier high-density pedestrian city. (See DeChiara and Koppelman, 1969, for examples of planning standards.) Church-goers also switched to cars, thus freeing the church from the locality.

Changes in communication technology also diminished the need for the local community. Two different types of media became prevalent and both of them, in very different ways, have bypassed the local area. The telephone creates a communications net which frees message transmission from physical location. This facilitates the maintenance of primary ties, regardless of location. Kinsfolk and close friends need not live in the same neighborhood to have frequent interactions. The medium is personal, accessible and cheap. Certain types of computer systems, if they diffuse like the telephone, will further accentuate this potential. The metropolis in which each household, office, and other establishment has a telephone connection may be named a "fully-wired community." Wellman (1977:221) suggests other devices such as conference calls and cable systems which might also free social relationships from locality.

Radio-television has also affected formerly localized activity patterns. Rather than establishing a net, this type of communications system has a central broadcast point from which messages are sent to individual receivers. The signal covers an entire metro area and thus it may have the effect of integrating the larger community while bypassing local areas. Such systems transmit various kinds of messages including news, entertainment, and advertising from the international to the metro level. Broadcasting goes directly from sender to receiver, bypassing the local community and its communications systems.

The broadcast system suggests a mass audience and mass society, with messages and influence beamed from a central elite to an atomized populace. Mass communications research, however, discovered that the audience is not atomized and that primary groups within the larger society mediate between broadcasters and individuals (Katz, 1957).

The telephone system is congruent with aspatial social networks within urban communities. The network concept arose in English studies of family and kinship (e.g., Bott, 1957). These studies led to a view of urban people tied together in numerous networks, some composed of kinfolk, others of friends, and has led at least two sociologists to characterize the new urban community as the "network city" (Craven and Wellman, 1974). Theoretically, networks are not spatially limited; they may be localized or spread over a large territory. Spatial dispersion is independent of the intensity of relationships within networks which may vary between primary and secondary and which may have differing substantive contents including kinship, friendship, occupational interests and many others.

It is possible that networks could provide the basis for a reconceptualization of the metropolis. The titles of two essays imply as much: "Community without propinquity," (Webber, 1963), and "Who needs neighborhoods?" (Wellman, 1972).

## Environment

The residential environment evolves and changes over time; it is both cause and effect of some local processes. Environment has been ignored in subcommunity analyses and its influences are not well known. (For exceptions, see Michelson, 1970, 1977; Popenoe, 1977). The urban environment is special in that it is a built environment, extremely heavily influenced by human products.

The evolution may follow two courses, one ending in destruction and the other leading to stability. Guest (1972) has shown that residential areas have life cycles involving environment and population. Starting with open land at the periphery of a built-up area, a residential area is constructed. Over time, the land is covered with structures. Population density rises along with the number of structures and it finally peaks and begins to decline. At this point, residential areas either stabilize or go into a phase of abandonment and destruction. Central city areas are more likely to go into the destructive process (Sternlieb and Burchell, 1973), while most suburban areas stabilize (Farley, 1964; Guest, 1978). Some declining residential areas are redeveloped through urban renewal, and some are totally reconstructed after slum clearance (Suttles, 1972).

Environmental sociologists reject deterministic ideas and look for more complex and subtle relationships between environment and social life. They ignore the environment in general, the potential environment, and focus on the "effective environment," those environmental features which seem to make a difference in social relation (Gans, 1968). They look for congruence or incongruence between environmental features and patterns of social life (Michelson, 1970).

House type and age and condition of housing seem to be the most important environmental features of the subcommunity. Most Americans prefer single-family detached dwellings for family life and childrearing (Zuiches and Fuguitt, 1972). It is widely thought that the high-rise apartment building is incongruent for family life (Wallace, 1952). Many consumers reject older forms of urban housing, particularly walk-up apartment buildings and this rejection leads toward abandonment. Newer forms of apartment development are particularly conducive to assaults, muggings and other crimes (Newman, 1973). High-rise apartment buildings sited away from streets are unlikely to generate "defensible space" which suppresses crime. Environmental forms cannot be considered apart from social characteristics. Population composition makes a difference: high-rise apartments seem to be particularly unsuitable for poor young families while they may be quite acceptable for older persons or even for families with higher incomes (Michelson, 1977). Building management policies and procedures also strongly affect the satisfaction of the residents.

Residential areas of single-family houses have higher levels of informal interaction than apartment areas (Fava, 1959). Given homogeneous middle-class populations, they generate a "quasi-primary" style of interaction (Gans, 1962). Beyond this, the housing type has little influence on the social life of its residents. The suburban myth was effectively debunked by Berger (1960), who showed that the suburban environment did not necessarily produce a homogenized suburban life style. He showed that social class made more of a difference than environment and that working class people could carry their life style and attitudes into the suburban setting.

Environmental changes and disruptions can affect the social composition of an area. Large scale demolition for slum clearance or highway construction simply removes resident populations. Urban renewal projects in declining subcommunities typically remove only the poor segment. Abandonment and arson and the violent activities which often accompany them frighten residents and drive them from the area. The recent progress of "gentrification," in which middle-class persons buy and remodel old structures in central city areas also displaces their lower-class residents.

Community organization is often a response to some environmental problem. Subcommunity groups may organize to deal with banks which are "redlining" residential areas and refusing to invest in them. They may acquire and improve buildings themselves, with governmental or foundation assistance. They may demand environmental improvements like parks or traffic lights from city administrations. Indeed, one report says that the environment is the principal concern of local groups (National Research Council, 1975:75-76).

## Social organization

Three aspects of social organization will be discussed: stratification, formal organizations, and local networks. Each section will begin with a discussion of subcommunity itself and then its relationship to the larger community.

*Stratification.* Although most residential areas are by no means perfectly homogenous they are clearly differentiated and stratified by socioeconomic status and minority status. This is a basic fact of the social geography of the city and metropolis which has long been recognized. Social area analysis and factorial ecology have found socioeconomic status differences among subcommunities in scores of cities, throughout the world (Rees, 1972; Timms, 1971). In U.S. cities, members of high and low status occupational groups are residentially segregated from each other. This pattern is replicated within racially segregated areas: in black districts occupational groups are also segregated from each other (Simkus, 1978).

Processes of choice and constraint in the housing market yield these patterns of differentiation. "Real estate values distribute a city's population into various residential sections of different economic and social status" (McKenzie, 1923:145). Middle-class households have a variety of choices in the metropolis (Michelson, 1977) and many choose the suburban environment for childrearing (Gans, 1967; Zuiches and Fuguitt, 1972). The very poor have limited choices and must accept old housing in slums or newer housing in projects--"Federal Slums," as Rainwater (1970) has called them.

Residential areas are stratified by reputation and prestige as well as by income and housing value (Felson, 1978; J. Duncan, 1976; McClenahan, 1929). Families seek to locate in respectable residential areas (Gans, 1977). Individuals know the ranking of their own residential area (Taub, et al., 1977). Slum areas are disreputable and this fact is recognized by the residents and by the community at large (Suttles, 1968).

Housing markets and plus reputation processes tend to produce relatively homogeneous populations within residential areas. Most city and suburban subcommunities surveyed in 1967 showed low variability in socioeconomic status (Bradburn, et al., 1970:163). There is some evidence that income inequality is greater in poor than in middle-class areas (Bell, 1970:45), but inequality within subcommunities has not been extensively researched. According to Gans (1961), most people seek homogeneous areas, looking for neighbors of their "own kind." People in some nationality groups form ethnic villages in old residential areas despite the ability to acquire newer housing because of a desire to be among their own kind. In sum, although subcommunities are not perfectly homogeneous, most have identifiable social groups within them, at least by status and ethnicity.

Stratification among subcommunities is a manifestation of broader inequalities within the society (Gans, 1977). Slum dwellers, particularly in well-identified public housing projects are stigmatized by the community at large (Moore, 1969). Most suburban areas are spatially and politically removed from the lower classes. Muller (1977) argues that the suburbs have been developed to segregate the wealthier classes from the working class and the poor.

The concept of the caretaker expresses the low rank and subordinate status of the slum relative to the larger community. The caretaker is a functionary of a municipal bureaucracy such as a social worker, policeman, teacher, who deals with slum residents. This term has been introduced relatively recently in sociological and social welfare writings (Gans, 1962:142). Its connotations are clear, especially in contrast with the older terminology which referred to the helping professions. The term, caretaker, implies that the function of such workers is to maintain the poor and keep them in their place.

Subcommunities are segmental to each other (Suttles, 1968): they are equivalent and not interdependent. This means that the life or death of one need not necessarily affect the condition of others. A whole residential area may be razed without seriously disrupting nearby subcommunities and certainly without affecting distant ones.

Two issues which divide city and suburb--housing and schools--may be seen in relation to the stratification of subcommunities. Suburbs resist the construction of low-cost housing and integration of schools with the central cities for fear that the contact with lower class or minority groups would lower the status of their subcommunity. Property values are tied to status levels. Furthermore, residents of wealthy suburbs are unwilling to share the benefits of expensive educational investments with residents of poorer areas.

*Formal organizations.* Social life in subcommunities is rather diffuse and not tightly organized. "The neighborhood exists without formal or;anization," according to Park (1916:96). There are organizations in local areas, but they have not been well studied.

Control of the principal structures of community has been lost to higher-level institutions. Government, communications, education, religion, police, maintenance and construction of infrastructure: all have been transferred completely or in part to the city, (Zorbaugh, 1929), county or state. This trend applies to communities in general (Warren,

1972), not just to subcommunities. The subcommunity has become an outpost of the local agencies of the city government and its bureaucracies. Suburbs retain more local control, but are still constrained, particularly by state governments.

There are several types of local organizations: neighborhood improvement associations; community centers and associated sports programs; parent-teacher organizations; churches and church-related groups. There are also more specialized organizations such as businessmen's associations.

Urban theory states that urban vitality is tied to local organization, that it is good for subcommunities to be organized. Some liberal thinkers advocate community control, neighborhood government, a transfer of power from center to periphery (Kotler, 1969).

Shaw and McKay (1942) argued that social disorganization at the subcommunity level was the key to high levels of juvenile delinquency. They said that some subcommunities were internally organized so that the dominant American value system pervades various institutions including school, church and family. Other disorganized subcommunities have no such linkage and reinforcement of values. Without a locally enforced value system, the subcommunity was anomic. In such areas there was no pervasive system of informal social control over the behavior of the young. Subcommunities with transient or heterogeneous populations also tended to be disorganized.

It is not possible to say whether subcommunities are now less organized than they were a half-century ago. Some organizational forms are gone; the settlement house is no longer a prominent local institution. Contemporary priests and rabbis do not seem to be as central to local groups as their predecessors in immigrant neighborhoods were. The party functionary plays a different role now than in earlier times. Newer voluntary associations have appeared, such as "little league," PTAs, etc. Settlement houses are replaced by YMCAs and community centers.

A small number of studies indicate the extent to which subcommunities are organized. Janowitz's city study (1952), now almost three decades old, provides some of the best information. It showed two forms of local organization: businessmen's associations and subcommunity newspapers. The latter served to communicate local news and advertising and to help integrate the households into a subcommunity. Suttles (1968) demonstrated the way in which the Catholic church helps integrate an Italian subcommunity. His study and other have shown boys gangs to be organizations at the subcommunity level. School-related and church organizations are also persistent forms of subcommunity organizations.

Duncan, Schuman and Duncan (1973) reviewed a series of Detroit Area Surveys and reported on trends on local participation from 1959 to 1971. They showed that about twenty percent of the adults in the metropolitan area were members of parent-teacher associations in both years. Membership in "neighborhood improvement associations" declined from 12 to 8 percent over the twelve-year period, but membership in neighborhood clubs or community centers rose from 8 to 10 percent, so perhaps the local participation level is fairly stable. Church participation fluctuated over the years, but it seemed lower in 1971 than it had been in the 1950s. In Chicago, Hunter (1974:145) discovered that 29% of the adults belonged to local voluntary associations.

The interests of local organizations center about schools, recreation, religion, and local environment. There seems to have been an increase in the number of subcommunity organizations in cities in recent years although they appear to be rather short-lived (Hawley, 1971; see Hunter, 1974: 203-206 for a listing of over one hundred local organizations in Chicago). Many local organizations have been dedicated to the resistance of blacks, but others have worked toward environmental improvement, racial integration, and other goals. A new type of organization is the externally-induced voluntary association (Taub, et al., 1977). These associations are sponsored by exogenous organizations, such as city and federal bureaucracies, to facilitate some sort of local action. The external bureaucracies need them because they do not find strong local networks or associations with which to link.

Suburbs are evidently more highly organized than city areas, although this seems to be a function of status rather than community. Early suburban social studies showed a proliferation of clubs and voluntary associations (Whyte, 1956; Gans, 1967), but recent observers say that participation rates have diminished. There were many organizations in the early years as the new subcommunities were getting settled. Higher status groups tend to join more organizations, so the status differences between city and suburban areas account for participation differences.

The voluntary associations support the basic activities of the local area. School and church-related organizations, as well as community centers and recreational programs support socialization of the young. These same organizations support adult recreation and mental health more generally. Local organizations also attempt to maintain or improve the quality of the environment as residents organize to prevent housing deterioration and conversion and to get acceptable city services such as park maintenance, trash collection, and the like. The organizations may also work to improve the level of public safety, particularly in suppression of crime, but also to promote traffic safety.

In effect, these activities also support the status level of the subcommunity. These organizations aim to maintain the reputation of an area. They attempt to retain residents of the same status as the current population and to attract new households of equivalent status. They resist attempts of minority or low status groups to enter the area. They also resist the attempts of real estate operators to interfere with the class composition of the area.

D. I. Warren (1977) has outlined a typology of subcommunities based upon their levels of mobilization and organization. He says there are six types of subcommunities ("neighborhoods") which differ along three dimensions: level of organization, orientation toward the larger community, and whether or not the residents see the subcommunity as a positive reference group. He suggests that informal and formal organization tend to be tied to each other--subcommunities which have high levels of informal interaction also have high levels of formal organization. There are three types of subcommunities which are highly organized: "integral," "parochial," and "stepping-stone." Integral neighborhoods are organized and are tied into the city at large through the personal connections and involvements of their residents. Parochial neighborhoods are organized, but are cut off from the larger community. Stepping-stone areas are similar to parochial neighborhoods, but they are essentially places which house in-migrants who are passing through in the course of social mobility. There is an implicit social class dimension to the scheme, in that the parochial neighborhood is likely to be working-class and the integral is likely to be upper-middle class. The city-wide connections of the residents of the integral neighborhood are a function of their professional occupational networks and their memberships in voluntary associations. The union memberships of the South Chicago workers (Kornblum, 1974) would not qualify them as non-parochial in Warren's scheme.

Suttles (1972) has also defined types of subcommunities, including the "defended neighborhood," and the "contrived neighborhood." The former resembles Warren's parochial neighborhood. A subcommunity becomes a defended neighborhood when its residents mobilize to resist some external threat. Many white subcommunities have become defended neighborhoods to resist the entry of blacks. Other subcommunities have mobilized against threats from governmental units which would disrupt the local environment: demolition for highways, for example.

The contrived neighborhood is quite a different matter in which real estate developers and residents promote an attractive image of the residential area. One objective is to draw new residents of a particular social class into an area. Part of this effort may be to create new organizations and activities within the area. The image-making characterizes a particular life-style for the area.

Federal urban programs of the post-World War II era demonstrate the subordinate status of the subcommunity. This is particularly true of the central city areas which were subjected to programs to uplift the poor or to prevent neighborhood decay. These programs, urban renewal and the Community Action Programs of the "War on Poverty" may be taken as natural experiments to test the strength of the subcommunity.

Urban renewal, in most instances, gave rise to externaly imposed pseudo-organizations. (For a case study of an internally organized grass-roots unit, see Rossi and Dentler, 1961; and Tax, 1959). Urban renewal legislation called for a neighborhood committee to work with the city administrators and other parties, but these tended to be weak ephemeral organizations of selected local business leaders. Certainly, the poor residents of the deteriorated housing scheduled for demolition went unrepresented on the local committees. The main decisions were made extralocally: the city political leaders and planners chose areas for renewal and then the local population could only react.

Locals were ineffectual at reactive organization in the early years of urban renewal, but over the course of the decade and a half of the program, they became more vociferous and sophisticated in their tactics. It is ironic that while Gans' ethnography, *The Urban Villagers,* endures as sociology, the "village" itself was torn down in a large urban renewal program. The interstate highway program was in full swing during the years of urban renewal and there was slum clearance to make way for expressways. In this process also the local residents had no voice at the outset, but became effective in resistance after a decade of large scale demolition.

Community organizing was a high-priority activity in the Community Action Program of the "War on Poverty." This was followed by the Model Cities Program based on some of the same reasoning. Many federal programs introduced during this era included citizens' advisory boards to generate local participation in programmatic decision-making. The logic behind all these efforts was that the people to be affected by a program should participate in its formulation and administration. Older forms of social welfare and reform were deemed inadequate because poor people had to relinquish control to outsiders, professionals. During this period the community organization approach of Saul Alinsky became quite fashionable. Alinsky, a former labor union organizer, with trained organizers from his Industrial Areas Foundation, aided many local groups throughout the nation to organize themselves. The Alinsky approach was based upon conflict as a means of organizing. The idea was that the poor would mobilize most readily against some perceived enemy. Thus, a subcommunity would organize against some party external to itself: the school board, a slum landlord, a university, etc.

Ultimately, most of this urban organizing came to naught. Even the most effective of the community groups failed (Molotch, 1972). The external community would not tolerate attacks by local groups. Mayors prevented the federal government from channeling additional funds directly to these insurgent groups as it had in the first years of the poverty program. This operation of the higher-order groups—city hall and the federal government—illustrates the lack of control of the subcommunity over its own affairs.

The school "community control" experiment in New York city also demonstrated the limits of subcommunity autonomy within the urban community. The purpose of the experiment was to transfer control of the subcommunity's public schools to a local board of education, while leaving finance in the hands of the central administration (Berube and Gittell, 1969). The local board was to handle personnel, textbook selection, and other matters. However, the attempt of one local board to manipulate teaching personnel ran into conflict with the teachers' union and precipitated a citywide strike. Indeed, the ramifications of the conflict spread rapidly and disrupted intergroup relations between two large minority groups, blacks and Jews. This shows that the local school is a branch of the centralized bureaucracy and it cannot simply be cut out of that system without disrupting many of the community's systems. Power and control are centralized and they cannot be released to the periphery without disturbing numerous established intersystemic connections throughout the community.

The relationship between the black ghetto and the city at large remains problemmatic and a matter of deep controversy. Blauner (1969) argues that the ghetto is a colony within the city, exploited by the majority just as colonial peoples were exploited by metropolitan powers. This implies that ghetto people should organize and revolt and control their own areas and institutions. Bell (1970), an economist, argues that independent economic development of the ghetto is futile and counterproductive. She says that the economic betterment of blacks will come through their absorption into the wider economy, as workers and consumers. While she has no objection to black entrepreneurship, she says that the ghetto itself has very little potential for independent and separate economic development.

Suburbs are far more effective than city subcommunities at independent organization because they maintain individual governments. They are able to conduct many governmental activities: they can levy taxes, pass ordinances, and zone their land. They have the police power and can build and maintain streets and civic buildings. Nonetheless, even these powers are circumscribed by higher levels of government.

State, county, and federal government limits the powers of the suburb to govern itself. The state specifically limits the tax levels of municipalities and it controls local budgets through various grant programs in education, roads and other areas. Even education may not be controlled by the municipality as many suburbs are in consolidated school districts. Many federal urban and environmental programs require municipalities to conform to regional plans in order to qualify for aid.

Nonetheless, suburbs have been highly effective in controlling their own environments. They control the class of people they admit through the use of zoning restrictions which enforce a minimum standard for buildings, amenities, and lot sizes. The effect of this is to keep new development up to the general level of the existing environment. This keeps housing prices at a certain level and determines the SES of new residents. More recently, some suburbs have joined into the "no-growth" movement to prevent continued expansion. Most suburbs have been adamant at resisting the location of low-cost housing and at school integration with central cities. They also resist other forms of metropolitan government, both for specific purposes such as transportation and for overall government.

## SUMMARY AND CONCLUSIONS

The residential area is one of the differentiated parts of the metropolitan community. Subcommunity is the best term to represent residential areas, in preference to older terms such as neighborhood and community area. Central city and suburban residential areas should be seen as equivalent.

Subcommunities are differentiated by socioeconomic status, race/ethnicity and familism. Familism represents the age and household composition of an area and varies from familistic, including families with children, to individualistic, including young adults and older people. The differentiation of subcommunities is by no means perfect; it does not approach the patchwork of highly individuated social worlds which was portrayed in some early sociological images of the city. There are concentrations of particular types in various sections of the metropolitan area which can be detected statististically by means of segregation indexes and other measures. Although the typical subcommunity houses a mix of people, usually one socioeconomic status group and one family type predominates. Ethnic concentrations are to be found at various locations in the metropolis including the suburbs. Racial segregation is very high in most cities.

The major functions of the subcommunity are socialization, consumption, and status differentiation. The subcommunity socializes children as well as in-migrants into the community. Many products are ultimately consumed in the subcommunity. The subcommunity is a place of rest and recreation for adults. Individuals seek residential areas with good reputations as they shop in the housing market. The environment is often used to project an image of the local status of its occupants.

Subcommunities are loosely organized with localized networks and voluntary associations. There are local social networks and the main participants are children, mothers, and older people. Local networks also tend to be more pervasive in poor areas. Voluntary associations support the basic functions of the area. School- and church-related organizations support socialization activities, among others. Businessmen's associations support the distribution functions which eventuate in local consumption. Homeowners' associations and similar organizations attempt to maintain the environment, which supports the reputation and status of the area. Such organizations may also be mobilized to maintain status by rejecting outsiders.

Politically, subcommunities have very little capacity for independent action. They are dependent parts of the larger community. Their networks are not politically oriented and they are not easily mobilized for action. Even the externally imposed voluntary associations are short-lived and very weak. Those who envision a revitalization of the old cities should not base their hopes on powerful action at the neighborhood level.

Sociological analyses of urban social life by Janowitz, Suttles, Hunter, and Kasarda offer a bridge between human ecology and social psychology. The local area has some significance to a considerable fraction of the urban populace. People look to it for reputability, for some part of their social life. Even though it is not the highest priority element of their lives, it is not trivial. It has at least a symbolic significance. This is a social psychological input to the social organization of the area in its networks and voluntary associations. The activities of the local area also have social psychological outputs. One is the socialization of children and newcomers and the other is the sense of belonging to a comprehensible part of the larger community. This is certainly far less than the sense of belonging to a primary group, but, at least for some residents of the metropolitan community, it occurs.

The subcommunity is an enduring feature of the urban community if for no other reason than that people must have places to reside. It is no longer the tightly-knit primary group neighborhood, if there ever was one. It is also not the "ethnic quarter" of the immigration period. It is a loosely-knit part of the metropolis where children grow up, where people care for their residences and their possessions, where many people take their rest and recreation, and where they express their life styles.

## NEEDED RESEARCH

Despite the voluminous literature on urban subcommunities, there are many gaps and unanswered questions. Major developments in U.S. society are likely to produce changes at this level. In addition, the ecological perspective suggests some questions which have not been asked before.

1. Transformations of family life and childrearing patterns are likely to change subcommunity life. Decreasing fertility, increasing proportions of women in the labor force and rising divorce rates have been accompanied by increasing numbers of daycare centers. The division of child care and housekeeping responsibilities between husbands and wives in some segments of the U.S. population may change the daytime population of the subcommunity.

Do the changing family patterns mean that young mothers will be decreasingly involved in primary groups, voluntary associations and other activities of the subcommunity? Will fathers become increasingly involved? Will children's social lives be less localized if daycare is not near the residence?

The aging of the U.S. population is also likely to change subcommunity life. Over the next two decades, U.S. metro areas are likely to gain millions of persons aged 65 and over. Many of them will be highly localized in their daily activities; how will the community deal with them? What effect will they have upon their local areas?

2. Technological and environmental changes may impact upon the local area. Even the impact of the telephone and radio-television upon urban social life is not well understood. The "fully-wired" community, with computer terminals in all residences and businesses, cable systems, etc., is an emerging possibility. What effects would such technology have upon subcommunity life? Such systems could change patterns of retail distribution, dissemination of news, banking and investment and many other types of interactions.

The flow of information at the local level needs more research. Are local newspapers (Janowitz, 1952) and local informal networks (Katz and Lazarsfeld, 1955) as efficacious as they were when they were studied in the 1950s? Do suburban patterns replicate city ones? What is the connection between the local and the metropolitan networks and channels?

Rising costs of energy could have powerful effects upon urban form and patterns of social life. Growth at the suburban periphery could diminish or cease because of energy and the increasing effectiveness of the community no-growth movement. Commuting could become expensively unattractive. Higher density development might become more feasible. Such trends might lead toward intensified subcommunity life or in various unanticipated directions.

More broadly, the energy nexus between subcommunity and community needs exploration. What are the energy flows and exchanges between these social levels? How is energy transformed locally; what is the subcommunity's output? (What are the politics of this flow: does city administration use trash collection as a resource for hiring more workers who join into the local machine, etc.?)

3. Urban social organization needs continuing research, both within the subcommunity and between the subcommunity and other units. What are the forms of organization within city and suburban subcommunities? Is there local leadership? Is it true that local organizations, especially neighborhood improvement associations, are ephemeral? What precipitates local organization; how effective is it?

The social organization of suburbs appears to be less understood than that of city areas. Suburban subcommunities need additional research, but it should be done in combination with city research. The dichotomy between city and suburban studies is artificial and need not continue. It will be interesting to learn the degree to which suburbs are divided into differentiated areas and the ways in which they are organized. Differences among types of subcommunities should be studied.

Finally, the relationships among subcommunities and between them and the community at large need to be illuminated. How segmental are subcommunities--which types, if any, are least interdependent with the larger community? What are the connections among subcommunities, what formal or informal ties do they have? How clear is the stratification of subcommunities? Where do central areas fit into the ranking?

What are the exchanges between the subcommunity and the community at large--is there an exchange of votes for services, for example? What is the relationship between city government and subcommunity?

## REFERENCES

Anderson, T. R., and J. A. England (1961). "Spatial aspects of social area analysis." American Sociological Review 26:392-399

Bell, C. S. (1970). The Economics of the Ghetto. Indianapolis: Pegasus.

Berger, B. (1960). Working Class Suburb: A Study of Auto-Workers in Suburbia. Berkeley: University of California Press.

Berry, B. J. L., and J. D. Kasarda (1977). Contemporary Urban Ecology. New York: MacMillan.

Berube, M. R., and M. Gittell (eds.) (1969). Confrontation at Ocean Hill-Brownsville. New York: Praeger.

Blauner, R. (1969). "Internal colonialism and ghetto revolt." Social Problems 16:393-408.

Booth, A. (1976). Urban Crowding and Its Consequences. New York: Praeger.

Bott, E. (1957). Family and Social Network. London: Tavistock.

Bradburn, N. M., S. Sudman and G. Gockel (1970). Racial Integration in American Neighborhoods. Chicago: National Opinion Research Center.

Burgess, E. W. (1925). "Can neighborhood work have a scientific basis?" Pp. 142-155 in R. E. Park and E. W. Burgess (eds.), The City. Chicago: University of Chicago Press.

Carpenter, N. (1933). "Neighborhood." Pp. 356-357 in Encyclopedia of the Social Sciences, Volume 11. New York: MacMillan.

Cassel, J. (1971). "Health consequences of population density and crowding." In Rapid Population Growth: Consequences and Policy Implications. National Academy of Sciences. Baltimore: Johns Hopkins University.

Craven P., and B. Wellman (1974). "The network city." Pp. 57-88 in M. P. Effrat (ed.), The Community: Approaches and Applications. New York: Free Press.

DeChiara, J., and L. Koppelman (1969). Planning Design Criteria. New York: Van Nostrand Reinhold.

Dice, L. R. (1955). Man's Nature and Nature's Man: The Ecology of Human Communities. Ann Arbor: University of Michigan Press.

Duis, P. (1976). Chicago: Creating New Traditions. Chicago: Chicago Historical Society.

Duncan, J. S., Jr. (1976). "Landscape and the communication of social identity." Pp. 391-404 in A. Rapoport (ed.), The Mutual Interaction of People and Their Built Environment. The Hague: Mouton.

Duncan, O. D. (1959). "Human ecology and population studies." Pp. 678-716 in P. M. Hauser and O. D. Duncan (eds.), The Study of Population. Chicago: University of Chicago Press.

Duncan, O. D. (1964). "Social organization and the eco-system." Pp. 37-82 in R. E. L. Faris (ed.), Handbook of Modern Sociology. Chicago: Rand-McNally.

Duncan, O. D., and B. Duncan (1955). "Residential distribution and occupational stratification." American Journal of Sociology 60:493-503.

Duncan, O. D., H. Schuman and B. Duncan (1973). Social Change in a Metropolitan Community. New York: Russell Sage Foundation.

Ekistics (1972). "The Ekistic Grid." Ekistics 34 (December): Inside Front Cover.

Farley, R. (1964). "Suburban persistence." American Sociological Review 29:38-47.

Farley, R. (1970). "The changing distribution of Negroes within metropolitan areas: the emergence of black suburbs." American Journal of Sociology 75:512-29.

Fava, S. F. (1959). Contrasts in neighboring: New York City and a suburban county. Pp. 122-130 in W. E. Dobriner (ed.), The Suburban Community. New York: Putnam.

Felson, M. (1978). "Invidious distinctions among cars, clothes and suburbs." Public Opinion Quarterly 42:49-58.

Fischer, C. S. (1975). "Toward a subcultural theory of urbanism." American Journal of Sociology 80:1319-1342.

Fischer, C. S. (1976). The Urban Experience. New York: Harcourt Brace Jovanovich.

Fitch, J. M. (1966). American Building (Vol.2): The Environmental Forces That Shape It. Boston: Houghton Mifflin.

Foley, D. L. (1952). Neighbors or Urbanites? Rochester: University of Rochester.

Foley, D. L. (1959). "The use of local facilities in a metropolis." Pp. 607-616 in P. Hatt and A. Reiss (eds.), Cities and Society. New York: Free Press.

Form, W. H., J. Smith G. P. Stone, and J. Cowhig (1954). "The compatibility of alternative approaches to the delimitation of urban sub-areas." American Sociological Review 19:434-440.

Gans, H. (1961). "The balanced community: homogeneity and heterogeneity in residential areas?" Journal of the American Institute of Planners 27:176-184.

Gans, H. (1962). The Urban Villagers. New York: Free Press.

Gans, H. (1967). The Levittowners. New York: Random House-Vintage.

Gans, H. (1968a). "The potential environment and the effective environment." Pp. 4-11 in H. J. Gans, People and Plans, Essays on Urban Problems and Solutions. New York: Basic Books.

Gans, H. (1968b). "Urbanism and suburbanism as ways of life: a reevaluation of definitions." Pp. 34-52 in H. J. Gans, People and Plans, Essays on Urban Problems and Solutions. New York:Basic Books

Gans, H. (1977). "Why exurbanites won't reurbanize themselves." New York Times 126 (February 12):21.

Gibbs, J. P., and W. T. Martin (1959). "Toward a theoretical system of human ecology." Pacific Sociological Review 2:29-36.

Glass, R. (1948). The Social Background of a Plan: A Study of Middlesborough. London: Routledge and Kegan Paul.

Greer, S. (1968). "Neighborhood." Pp. 121-125 in International Encyclopedia of the Social Sciences, Vol. 11. New York: MacMillan.

Guest, A. M. (1972). "Urban growth and population densities." Demography 10:53-69.

Guest, A. M. (1978). "Suburban social status." American Sociological Review 43:251-264.

Gusfield, J. R. (1975). Community: A Critical Response. New York: Harper and Row.

Hatt, P. (1946). The concept of natural area. American Sociological Review 11:423-427.

Hauser, P. M., and E. M. Kitagawa (1953). Local Community Fact Book for Chicago, 1950. Chicago: Chicago Community Inventory, University of Chicago.

Hawley, A. H. (1950). Human Ecology. New York: Ronald.

Hawley, A. H. (1968). "Human ecology." Pp. 329-337 in D. Sills (ed.), International Encyclopedia of the Social Sciences, Vol. 4.

Hawley, A. H. (1971). Urban Society. New York: Ronald.

Hawley, A. H. (1972). "Population density and the city." Demography 9:521-529.

Hawley, A., and O. D. Duncan (1957). "Social area analysis: a critical appraisal." Land Economics 33:337-344.

Hillery, G. A. (1955). "Definitions of community: areas of agreement." Rural Sociology 20:111-123.

Hunter, A. (1974). Symbolic Communities, the Persistence and Change of Chicago's Local Communities. Chicago: University of Chicago Press.

Hunter, A. (1975). "The loss of community: an empirical test through replication." American Sociological Review 40: 537-553.

Janowitz, M. (1952). The Community Press in an Urban Setting. Chicago: University of Chicago Press.

Kantrowitz, N. (1973). Ethnic and Racial Segregation in the New York Metropolis. New York: Praeger.

Kasarda, J. D., and M. Janowitz (1974). "Community attachment in mass society." American Sociological Review 39: 328-340.

Katz, E. (1957). "The two-step flow of communication: an up-to-date report on a hypothesis." Public Opinion Quarterly 21:61-78.

Katz, E., and P. Lazarfeld (1955) Personal Influence. New York: Free Press.

Keller, S. (1968). The Urban Neighborhood. New York: Random House.

Kornblum, W. (1974). Blue Collar Community. Chicago: University of Chicago Press.

Kotler, M. (1969). Neighborhood Government. Indianapolis: Bobbs-Merrill.

Krebs, C. J. (1972). Ecology: The Experimental Analysis of Distribution and Abundance. New York: Harper and Row.

Lynch, K. (1960). The Image of the City. Cambridge, MA: MIT Press.

McClenahan, B. A. (1929). The Changing Urban Neighborhood. Los Angeles: University of Southern California.

McKenzie, R. (1923). The Neighborhood: A Study of Local Life in the City of Columbus, Ohio. Chicago: University of Chicago Press.

Meier, R. L. (1962). A Communications Theory of Urban Growth. Cambridge: MIT Press.

Michelson, W. H. (1970). Man and His Urban Environment. Reading, MA: Addison-Wesley.

Michelson, W. H. (1977). Environmental Choice, Human Behavior, and Residential Satisfaction. New York: Oxford University Press.

Mohr, C. O. (1943) "Cattle Droppings as Ecological Units." Ecological Monographs 13:275-298.

Molotch, H. (1972). Managed Integration. Berkeley and Los Angeles: University of California Press.

Molotch, H. (1975). Review of: Black Power/White Control, by J. H. Fish. American Journal of Sociology 80: 1481-1483.

Moore, W., Jr. (1969). The Vertical Ghetto: Everyday Life in an Urban Project. New York: Random House.

Morrison, P. A. (1971). "Chronic movers and the future redistribution of population: a longitudinal analysis." Demography 8:171-184.

Muller, P. O. (1976). The Outer City: Geographical Consequences of the Urbanization of the Suburbs. Washington, D.C.: Association of American Geographers.

274

National Research Council. Social Science Panel of the
Significance of Community in the Metropolitan Environment.
(1975). Toward an Understanding of Metropolitan America. San
Francisco: Canfield Press.

Newman, O. (1973). Defensible Space. New York: MacMillan.

Pampel, F. C., and H. M. Choldin (1978). "Urban location
and segregation of the aged: a block level analysis." Social
Forces.

Park, R. E. (1916). "The city: suggestions for the investigation of human behavior in the urban environment."
American Journal of Sociology 20. Reprinted in R. Sennett,
(ed.), Classic Essays in the Culture of Cities. New York:
Appleton-Century-Crofts.

Popenoe, D. (1977). The Suburban Environment: Sweden and
the United States. Chicago: University of Chicago Press.

Rainwater, L. (1966). "Fear and the house-as-haven in
the lower class." Journal of the American Institute of
Planners 32:23-31.

Rainwater, L. (1970). Behind Ghetto Walls, Black Family
Life in a Federal Slum. Chicago: Aldine.

Rees, P. H. (1972). "Problems of classifying subareas
within cities." Pp. 265-330 in B. J. L. Berry (ed.), City
Classification Handbook. New York: Wiley-Interscience.

Roper, M. W. (1963). "The city and the primary group."
Pp. 231-244 in E. W. Burgess and D. J. Bogue (eds.), Con-
tributions to Urban Sociology. Chicago: University of
Chicago Press.

Rose, H. M. (1969). Social Processes in the City: Race
and Urban Residential Choice. Washington, D.C.: Association
of American Geography, Commission on College Geography,
Resource Paper No. 6.

Rossi, P. H., and R. A. Dentler (1961). The Politics of
Urban Renewal. New York: Free Press.

Schnore, L. F. (1957). "Satellites and suburbs." Social
Forces 36:121-127.

Schnore, L. F. (1963). "The social and economic characteristics of American suburbs." The Sociological Quarterly
4:122-134.

Schnore, L. F. (1965). "The separation of home and work:
a problem in human ecology." Pp. 33-45 in L. F. Schnore, The
Urban Scene. New York: Free Press.

Schnore, L. F. (1966). "The city as a social organism."
Urban Affairs Quarterly 1:68.

Schnore, L. F. (1967). "Community." Pp. 79-150 in N. J.
Smelser (ed.), Sociology: An Introduction. New York: Wiley.

Schorr, A. L. (1963). Slums and Social Insecurity.
Washington, D.C.: U.S. Government Printing Office.

Shaw, C. R., and H. D. McKay (1969). Juvenile Delinquency and Urban Areas, Revised Edition. Chicago: University of Chicago Press.

Shevky, E., and W. Bell (1955). Social Area Analysis. Stanford, CA.: Stanford University Press.

Simkus, A. A. (1978) "Residential segregation by occupation and race." American Sociological Review 43:81-92.

Sjoberg, G. (1960). The Preindustrial City. New York: Free Press.

Sorensen, A., K. E. Taeuber, and L. Hollingsworth Jr. (1975). Indexes of racial residential segregation for 109 cities in the United States, 1940 to 1970. Sociological Focus 8:125-142.

Spear, A. H. (1967). Black Chicago: The Making of a Negro Ghetto, 1890-1920. Chicago: University of Chicago Press.

Sternlieb, G., and R. W. Burchell (1973). Residential Abandonment: The Tenement Landlord Revisited. New Brunswick, NJ.: Rutgers University, Center for Urban Policy Research.

Sternlieb, G., and B. Indik (1973). The Ecology of Welfare: Housing and the Welfare Crisis in New York City. New York: Transaction.

Suttles, G. D. (1968). The Social Order of the Slum. Chicago: University of Chicago Press.

Suttles, G. D. (1972). The Social Construction of Communities. Chicago: University of Chicago Press.

Sweetser, F. L. (1941). Neighborhood Acquaintance and Association: A Study of Personal Neighborhoods. New York: Columbia University Press.

Sweetser, F. L. (1974). "The uses of factorial ecology in classification." Pp. 317-343 in M. S. Archer (ed.), Current Research in Sociology. The Hague: Mouton.

Taeuber, K. E., and A. F. Taeuber (1965). Negroes in Cities: Residential Succession and Neighborhood Change. Chicago: Aldine.

Taub, R. P., G. P. Surgeon, S. Lindholm, P. B. Otti, and A. Bridges (1977). "Urban voluntary association, locality based and externally induced." American Journal of Sociology 83:425-442.

Tax, S. (1959). "Residential integration: the case of Hyde Park in Chicago." Human Organization 19 (Spring):22-27.

Tilly, L. (1974). "Metropolis as ecosystem." Pp. 466-472 in C. Tilly (ed.), An Urban World. Boston: Little Brown.

Timms, D. W. G. (1971). The Urban Mosaic: Toward a Theory of Residential Distribution. Cambridge: Cambridge University Press.

Tunnard, C., and H. H. Reed (1955). American Skyline: The Growth and Form of Our Cities and Towns. Boston: Houghton Mifflin.

Wallace, A. F. C. (1952). Housing and Social Structure. Philadelphia: Philadelphia Housing Authority.

Warren, D. I. (1977). "Neighborhoods in urban areas." Pp. 224-237 in R. L. Warren (ed.), New Perspective on the American Community. Chicago: Rand-McNally.

Warren, R. L. (1972). The Community in America. Chicago: Rand-McNally.

Webber, M. M. (1963). "Order in diversity: community without propinquity." Pp. 23-56 in L. Wingo, Jr. (ed.), Cities and Space. Baltimore: Johns Hopkins University Press.

Wellman, B. (1972). "Who needs neighborhoods?" Pp. 94-100 in A. Powell (ed.), The City: Attacking Modern Myths. Toronto: McClelland and Stewart.

Whyte, W. H. (1956). The Organization Man. New York: Simon and Schuster.

Wirth, L. (1928). The Ghetto. Chicago: University of Chicago Press.

Wirth, L. (1938). "Urbanism as a way of life." American Journal of Sociology 44:3-24.

Wirth, L., and M. Furez (Eds.). (1938). Local Community Fact Book. Chicago: Chicago Recreation Commission.

Wilner, D. M., R. P. Walkley, T. C. Pinkerton, and M. Tayback (1962). The Housing Environment and Family Life. Baltimore: Johns Hopkins University Press.

Zorbaugh, H. (1926). "The natural areas of the city." Pp. 219-232 in E. W. Burgess (ed.), The Urban Community. Chicago: University of Chicago Press.

Zorbaugh, H. (1929). The Gold Coast and the Slum. Chicago: University of Chicago Press.

Zuiches, J. J., and G. V. Fuguitt (1972). "Residential preferences." Pp. 617-631 in S. M. Mazie (ed.), Population, Distribution, and Policy. Vol. V., Research Reports, U.S. Commission on Population Growth and the American Future. Washington, D.C.: U.S. Government Printing Office.

# 7
# The City

*Avery M. Guest*

Ecological concern with the city may be traced back to what has become known as the Chicago School of Sociology, a group which flourished in the 1920's and 1930's (Carey, 1975). Its leading theoreticians such as Ernest Burgess, R.D. McKenzie, and Robert Park did not intend ecological theory to apply only to the study of the city. But the human ecologists repeatedly turned to the city for the presentation of examples to support the theoretical perspective (for instance, see McKenzie, 1925) and for a laboratory of social research (Hunter, 1973:3-22).

The reason for this emphasis may be traced back to the basic concerns which human ecology was intended to study. As expounded by Park (1967), human ecology concerned itself primarily with two orders of analysis, the biotic and the social, the second necessitated by the first. Park argued that the basic nature of community life involved the biotic or competitive level, focusing on the drive of each individual or group to maximize its goals and advantages, particularly in economic terms. The ecologists were quick to perceive that the biotic level, if left unchecked, would

277

evolve shortly into a state of cutthroat anarchy. It was clear that the dominant pattern of social life, stability and gradual change, required an explanation. As a result, the social or moral order was perceived as arising out of the biotic, and involved the development of communications, consensus, and mores to regulate the conflict.

The city became a central focus for expounding the theory, for within its relatively limited spatial area was concentrated a variety of diverse groups with contrasting interests. Spatial analysis provided an excellent opportunity to observe the biotic struggle as employment and residential groups struggled for prized spatial locations. In turn, the study of local community areas—their organizations, friendship patterns, political conflicts—became an important means of illustrating the development of the moral or social order; daily activities in the community area were frequently perceived as developing out of the need to regulate the conflict among competing groups and to protect group interests (Stein, 1970:13-16).

The crux of the ecological perspective is well stated in Park's (1967:68) famous dictum:

> It is because social relations are so frequently and so inevitably correlated with spatial relations; because physical distances, so frequently are, or seem to be, the indexes of social distances, that statistics have any significance whatever for sociology. And this is true, finally, because it is only as social and physical facts can be reduced to, or correlated with spatial facts that they can be measured at all.

Some of the ecologists, most motably McKenzie and Burgess, also became concerned with specifying the structural (environmental) characteristics of cities which influenced the development of their spatial patterns, and presumably biotic orders. Factors such as community population growth and technological development were seen as basic constraints (perhaps causal factors) on the types of spatial orders which developed. This concern, as the elaboration of the basic physical-social relationships in the city, led the ecologists to a particular emphasis on the study of social organization among aggregates. In their studies of the city, the human ecologists were creating sociology as a discipline with very different emphases than the more established social sciences such as economics and psychology, which, among various differences, have tended to emphasize the individual as a unit of analysis.

Unfortunately, the Chicago "urban" tradition went into eclipse after World War II. Critics found fault in its emphasis on economic values (Firey, 1947) and its failure to consider a variety of spatial patterns other than concentric zones (Davie, 1938; Hoyt, 1939). Studies of spatial distribution continued to some extent, but unfortunately, they too often were merely descriptive accounts of the location of this or that group. They had lost the perspective which bound them to sociological theory and gave them a larger relevance.

Hawley's (1950) post-World War II volume on human ecology showed perhaps the closest affinity to the urban concerns of the Chicago ecologists. By defining the central concern of ecology as community structure, he aligned himself, to some extent, with the original ecological perspectives which had been presented by Park and Burgess. Other viewpoints on human ecology, such as Duncan and Schnore (1959), seemed to lead human ecology away from its urban concerns. They defined ecology as the study of the interrelationships among population, organization, environment, and technology, a scheme which permits the study of cities but seems to lead in much broader and too diffuse directions. Within this conception, human ecology could (and did) become the study of any number of attributes of population, organization, environment or technology. In fact, though, Duncan and Schnore were two of the few ecologists who were doing exciting research on the organization of cities.

Several decades have now passed since the great flowering of the Chicago school, and a crucial question is whether the perspective should be treated as a historic relic--with more reverence than seriousness--or as a base upon which to build contemporary theories of the city. In evaluating this issue, I focus primarily on the biotic level, encompassing studies of the internal spatial organization of the metropolis. My orientation is toward the densely settled core of our great American urban agglomerations. This choice has been made because one colleague (Choldin) is concentrating on what the Chicago school defined as the moral order at the local community level. And another colleague (Poston) is analyzing the region.

In this paper, I argue that the assumptions and hypotheses of the Chicago ecologists were amazingly accurate for describing a type of city--organized around streetcar transportation. But the theories badly need revision for understanding the development of post-World War II ecological structure. Since 1950, massive changes have occurred in the transportation and communications network of the metropolis—the continued diffusion of the motor vehicle, electronic communications, and new methods of building construction. The challenge for human ecologists is using the classical assumptions and hypotheses as a basis for building a new theory of how cities grow and develop. It is too early to know whether success will greet this effort at a new theory within the classical framework. We must contemplate the possibility that the city is becoming organized in new patterns which cannot be explained by our classical research and interpretations.

My presentation is organized in two parts. First, I shall discuss the basic theories of the Chicago ecologists about the internal spatial development of cities, sketching the major points, problems, and strengths. Second, I shall discuss the applicability of important ideas and concepts of the classical ecologists to understanding the emergence of modern metropolitan America. Much of the discussion will focus on the well-known Burgess hypothesis, the viewpoint which I see as the major organizing focus of the ecological literature.

In the following pages, many issues and studies in the urban ecology literature will be touched only briefly or even ignored, due to limitations of space. The paper is particularly parochial by emphasizing the work of sociologists, a sin necessitated by the fact that human ecology's concerns about the city have traditionally centered in this academic area.

## The Burgess Hypothesis

Some of the basic tenets of the ecological perspective are found in early published work by Park and McKenzie, but the central organizing conception of ecological work—the tour de force—was Burgess' (1925) paper, "The Growth of the City." It brought together many important but uncodified ideas of other Chicago school members. It served subsequently as the major blueprint for empirical research by the Chicago school. Because of its centrality, the Burgess paper is a useful device for discussing the Chicago school approach and subsequent developments in our understanding of urban structure. Burgess' paper may be read at two levels, as a rather prosaic description of major land use patterns within a typical American city or, more correctly, as an insightful analysis of the ways in which social forces affect the organization of urban space.

Like many human ecologists, Burgess was primarily interested in the development of the spatial order through the biotic struggle. In his theory, urban population growth was the primary environmental factor which intensified this struggle. Cities started with a relatively formless pattern, and then growth produced a pattern of functional differentiation, which at least at the spatial level, was similar to segregation of activities. All patterns of segregation, at least ideally, would become organized on a central-peripheral basis.

Burgess' theory, consistent with much of ecological work, was indebted to biologists who studied the organization of plant and animal communities. Just as the plant and animal communities changed in response to major environment forces, the urban community altered its character in response to population growth. A whole series of terms such as invasion and succession, commensalism, and symbiosis were essentially extracted from the biological literature as tools for analyzing the urban system. It also seems likely that Burgess was familiar with the work of land economists, such as van Thunen (Hall, 1966), who had suggested zonal conceptions of spatial organization, although none had applied it in the same manner to the internal organization of cities.

At the descriptive level, Burgess suggested that the spatial organization of the mature city could be portrayed in a series of concentric zones, emanating from the Central Business District. His theory represented (1925:50):

> An ideal construction of the tendencies of any town or city to expand radially from its central business district...Encircling the downtown area there is normally an area in transition, which is being invaded by business and light manufacturing (II). A third area (III) is inhabited by the workers in industries who have escaped from the area of deterioration (II) but who desire to live within easy access to their work. Beyond this zone is the 'residential area' (IV) of high-class apartment buildings or of exclusive 'restricted' districts of single-family dwellings. Still farther out, beyond the city limits, is the commuters' zone —suburban areas, or satellite cities—within a thirty to sixty-minute ride of the central business district.

The Burgess theory was attractive because it was testable and suggested further research projects. Unfortunately, Burgess never attempted a more complete theoretical explanation of the theory. The ingredients of theoretical rationales are found in his publications, but the task of making them explicit was left to others, particularly Hawley (1950: esp. 382-395). Since Burgess never fully clarified the links in his theoretical perspective, it is not surprising that a variety of interpretations have developed (Davie, 1938; Quinn, 1940; Schnore, 1965a).

I have identified at least five major "general" arguments in the Burgess theory of the "Growth of the City." Some apply primarily to the CBD, although having a more general potential applicability. These arguments are worth presentation and discussion as a basis for understanding the Chicago school perspective, both its strengths and weaknesses. I am sure that others will have different interpretations, but these arguments help me order much of Burgess' work, and the subsequent studies by his students and colleagues.

The arguments are:

> (1) Accessibility is the most important factor in the location of employment and residential activities.

The Chicago ecologists saw the final location of activities in the city as a serious version of "Musical Chairs" in which activities jockeyed for position. The goal of each activity was the maximization of economic self-interest, which might also be termed maximization of survival possibilities or maximization of sustenance possibilities. For employment activities, several types of accessibility were important: (a) to major transportation points and depots, both intra- and inter-urban; (b) to potential suppliers of goods and services; (c) to potential consumers or purchasers of goods; (d) to sources of information and knowledge which would help increase their sales and efficiency. For residential activities, two types of accessibility were emphasized: (a) to work places, and (b) to desirable neighborhoods and housing.

Activities emphasized different locational goals, a problem which causes difficulty in summarizing neatly the importance of various kinds of accessibility. As an example, for the clothing manufacturer, downtown locations were prized primarily because information could be exchanged on the latest trends in an industry with rapidly changing fads. For the newspaper, downtown locations were sought because of proximity to news sources and the distribution of residential purchasers.

Problems of accessibility led to two types of relationships in the city, symbiotic (the attraction and mutual interdependence of unlike) and commensalistic (the attraction and mutual interdependence of like). Thus, prostitutes and red-light districts depended symbiotically on the existence of deteriorated housing areas, for no other part of the city would permit their continued functioning. Higher status persons depended commensalistically on the continued residence of other higher status persons in their neighborhoods as a means of protecting property values and the quality of the area.

(2) Competition for accessibility leads to differential land values in the city.

While activities emphasized many different interests in their search for location, some parts of the city served one function which was crucial to many activities or a variety of functions which were important to selected activities. As a result, land would assume different values, based on its general accessibility qualities.

The classic case of a highly accessible site was the Central Business District (CBD). In the city of the early 20th century, it was most notable as the urban transportation hub, both for inter-city travel by water and railroad and also intra-city travel by streetcar. The CBD also served other functions. Due to the great concentration of work places, it was valuable for interests which depended on the exchange of goods or information with other activities. Furthermore, it attracted activities which depended on accessibility to the entire metropolis. Finally, it also exerted some attraction for the location of residences in close proximity to work places.

As the most accessible site in the city, the CBD became the primary node for gradients in land values. Each mile of distance from the center was marked by a progressive decrease in land value. Other accessibility nodes might develop their land value gradients but these were only ripples in the general pattern.

(3) The most valuable pieces of land attract those activities with the greatest demand and the greatest willingness to pay the high prices.

A variety of activities might desire a location in the city, but only those with a particular need for the land and the ability to pay would dominate that territory. On the grounds of ability to pay alone, commercial users generally occupied the most valuable land. Individual residential users typically lacked the economic resources to compete with larger commercial organizations.

Location patterns around the CBD particularly exemplified this argument. Commercial uses predominated, but within this general category, selective patterns of location could be discerned. Highly specialized service and information-processing activities particularly sought the center because related activities were nearby, little space was typically consumed, and customers were frequently drawn from the whole metropolis. Activities of control and administration (such as governmental administration) also concentrated in the CBD, if for no other reason than its centrality. In contrast, many types of manufacturing might desire the center, but the potential advantages did not compare with those of other activities. Besides, the frequent requirements for large amounts of operating space made very costly central locations.

Residential users were least able to compete for centrality. This does not mean that no residential activities would be found around the center. But central residential activities were disproportionately of three types: those for whom the cost of land was no impediment, such as the super-rich; those who had very small households such as the child-less and thus could afford small amounts of space, and those who lived temporarily in transition areas which were being turned into commercial uses.

> (4) Metropolitan population growth intensifies the demand for central land and increases the differentiation of the metropolis.

As the metropolitan population grew, the potential competitors for central land increased but the amount of central land remained relatively constant. Central land prices rose, and two ecological processes occurred: first, a greater functional differentiation of activities occurred, as a smaller, more specialized number of activities was willing to occupy the most central space; second, the central commercial district began to expand outward to accommodate the increased demand. As the CBD expanded, property owners held their residential property for resale to potential employment users at a higher price than could be obtained from residential users. Since the commercial users were paying primarily for the land, the owners allowed their residential structure to deteriorate.

Over time, the process of differentiation was indicated by a life cycle or invasion and succession process for neighborhoods (Burgess, 1925:50). Community areas would start their histories on the periphery of the city, with low density, primarily residential, users. Over time, as the urban community expanded geographically, individual neighborhoods would become relatively closer to the metropolitan center, and thus eligible for what became known as the invasion and succession process. Settlement patterns would become more intense, and residential users would gradually yield to non-residential users. The cross-sectional city zones were replicated on a longitudinal basis in each neighborhood.

While the Burgess hypothesis reduced the organization of cities to a study of concentric distributions, this does not mean that other patterns were unimportant. Burgess himself was clear that the pattern could be distorted by other factors, and other ecologists suggested important forces in the alternation of community characteristics. For instance, McKenzie (1925:75) suggested that the invasion and succession process could be stimulated by some of the following: (a) changes in forms and routes of transportation; (b) obsolescence resulting from physical deterioration or from changes in use or fashion; (c) the erection of important public or private structures, buildings, bridges, institutions, which have either attractive or repellent significance; (d) the introduction of new types of industry, or even a change in the organization of existing industries; (e) changes in the economic base which make for redistribution of income, thus necessitating change of residence; and (f) real estate promotion creating sudden demands for special location sites, etc.

Finally, the Burgess hypothesis contains a last, crucial argument:

(5) The process of land-use changes affects the distribution of population groups.

The Chicago ecologists clearly saw the morphological structure of the city as having a dominant effect on the types of persons who would live in a community. The most basic distinction could be made between distribution by status and family composition. As the city grew, higher status persons and families in the childbearing stage were increasingly located on the metropolitan outskirts. Three major morphological factors can be cited as crucial in the location of higher status persons away from the center. First, the center of the city was generally more congested than other parts of the metropolis; other things being equal, high-status persons would prefer to live in parts of the city where they could obtain large homes and spacious lots. Second, the center of the city included significant non-residential activities which were often visually un-attractive and polluting. Finally, commercial expansion from the metropolitan center led indirectly to large amounts of obviously undesirable deteriorated housing. Similar factors could be cited for families in the childbearing stage. In particular, childbearing families needed large homes and lots for their large households, and these could be found disproportionately on the metropolitan outskirts.

Racial and ethnic groups were treated largely in terms of their social status (Guest and Weed, 1976). It was felt that recent migrants to the city from abroad or from rural parts of the United States were characterized by relatively low status and difficulties in competing in the employment market, factors which consigned them to areas around the CBD. As these groups became assimilated over time, however, they would move upward in the job and educational structure, assuming the residential distribution of all higher status groups.

*Criticism and Comment*

The Burgess perspective, as the heart of the Chicago school perspective, has attracted an immense amount of dis-cussion from sociologists. A number of criticisms of the Burgess theory are discussed cogently by Schnore (1965b: 347-358), and need not detain us. The major criticisms of the Burgess model by sociologists have generally focused on three major points. First, activities locate in the metro-polis in terms of goals other than maximizing their economic interests; these are sometimes known as cultural or symbolic factors. Second, other major patterns of land use are found in cities, such as location by sectors or pie-shaped wedges. Third, many cities, in fact, do not seem to fit the Burgess model in one or several attributes.

The assumption that urbanites maximized their economic interests in locational choices was challenged in a series of papers by sociologists such as Firey (1947), Alihan (1938), and Strauss (1961). As a counter-theory, they sug-gested that locational choices were often made on the basis of non-economic or cultural values. In other words, eco-nomics couldn't explain everything. Even if correct, these perspectives seemed to have limited usefulness from an empirical, theory-testing standpoint. Various "cultural" factors were cited as important in the location of different groups, but these were never tied together into a clearly integrated, coherent theory which would explain major patterns of urban development. That is, the culturalists never posed a theoretical alternative to the "Growth of the City"; they only suggested the cultural ingredients of such a theory.

The most persuasive "culturalist" studies focused on Boston (Firey, 1947). Firey pointed out that "uneconomic" uses such as public gardens and burial grounds remained in the downtown area; that an old Italian section of Boston persisted even though some time had passed since the arrival in the United States of the ethnic group, and many of its members had economically succeeded; that a high-status neighborhood (Beacon Hill) persisted near the downtown area, presumably in contradiction to the Burgess hypothesis (Beacon Hill allegedly served familial, historic, and aesthetic functions for the city's upper-middle class and thus persisted in status). A full discussion of Firey's perspective would require more space than can be reasonably devoted here, but it does seem that Firey failed to consider two major points: first, some supposedly cultural functions may also serve economic purposes; second, "culture" costs money. As an example of the first point, it may be noted that having public gardens and burial grounds in downtown areas serves as an attraction for the tourist dollar. Downtown businesses are not indifferent to cultural attraction if it enhances the use of their facilities. The desire of ethnic groups to live together has certain economic functions, for they may occupy similar roles in the occupational division of labor and depend upon each other for financial support and economic opportunities (Hechter, 1971). In regard to the second point, it should be pointed out that persons can enjoy living on Beacon Hill and soaking in the atmosphere because of a willingness to pay the high rents for housing. The Chicago school never suggested that high-status neighborhoods would be completely absent from the center of larger cities; it only suggested that they would be absent as long as high-status persons lacked an extreme willingness to pay the high housing rents found there. In fact, most high status neighborhoods have disappeared from the center of Boston.

Another set of criticisms centered on the importance of non-concentric modes of spatial organization in the metropolis. In particular, the land economist Homer Hoyt (1939) attacked the Burgess view, arguing that higher status groups were organized in residential sectors or pie-shaped wedges in the metropolis. The geographers Harris and Ullman (1945) portrayed cities as organized in multiple nuclei or districts of various sorts. These districts presumably exerted an unspecific influence on the pattern of activities around them. Few would challenge the idea that cities have sectors and nuclei in them; in fact, these patterns of location may coexist with concentric zonation. The exact importance of these various patterns is a matter which is still unanswered empirically

Attacks on the Burgess model for not "holding" in individual cities have been frequently made (Anderson and Egeland, 1961; Quinn, 1940). In my opinion, these generally failed to perceive that the Chicago school perspective was applicable to growing or large industrial cities. Thus, Davie's (1938) finding that the Burgess pattern did not hold in the relatively small New Haven metropolitan area could be interpreted as supportive of the basic theoretical premises, rather than contradictory.

Amidst all the discussion of the Burgess model, there were actually few adequate empirical tests. Almost no one bothered to determine whether cities changed their ecological structure in the predicted manner as they grew in population size. And almost no one bothered to compare cities on a cross-sectional basis to determine if large and rapidly growing cities differed in the predicted manner from other cities.

*Historical Relevance*

From the perspective of a metropolitanite of the 70's, I believe that the Burgess theory was largely accurate for describing the streetcar city of the early 20th century. The evidence is not definitive, but in recent years, various historical case studies have suggested empirical patterns of urban development in the period from 1890 to 1920 (the heyday of the electric streetcar) which largely reflect the predictions made by Burgess (Ward, 1971; Warner, 1962, 1972). Streetcar lines were developed in fixed radial patterns, emanating from the CBD, and tended to make the center of the metropolis its clear focal point. At the same time, the streetcars were a vast improvement in the speed of travel over the horse and human foot and, as a result, permitted some expansion of the urban geographic area. The Burgess theory and the streetcar were made for each other, because the streetcar encouraged the central processes which were described in the Growth hypothesis, while simultaneously permitting the development of new residential areas on the urban outskirts to accommodate the activities being pushed out of the metropolitan center. As Winsborough (1963) has shown, the city of Chicago, at least in its early streetcar days, showed both an increasing congestion of activities at its center and also an increasing geographical dispersal of activities, or average distance of activities from the center.

The streetcar and the Burgess theory were not a perfect match, however. The fixed radial lines of the streetcar encouraged the metropolis to expand in a star-shaped pattern, but concentric zonation could still be discerned, particularly around the urban center.

The immense usefulness of the Burgess hypothesis for understanding contemporary metropolitan America can be quickly discerned by viewing metropolitan areas which achieved a large population size during the streetcar era. Particularly concentrated in the East and Midwest, these urban concentrations developed urban structures which are consistent with the Burgess theory and have persisted for several decades. In fact, much of what is perceived as an "urban crisis" in these metropolitan centers stems from the continued existence of outmoded land use patterns which are in many ways disfunctional for the automobile era.

The importance of the Burgess theory is strongly suggested by comparative research on metropolitan spatial patterns which almost inevitably finds that "old" areas differ from "new." Age has typically been defined as the census decade in which the metropolitan area's central city first reached 50,000 population. In effect, the age variable distinguishes metropolitan areas which were rapidly growing in the early 1900's from those which have achieved a large size in recent decades. Contemporary population size of metropolitan areas seems to have little effect in understanding metropolitan structure, once age is controlled. This suggests that the effects of population growth or size on ecological structure have probably varied in different time periods (Guest, 1972b, 1973).

The value of the old-new distinction has been most thoroughly pursued by Schnore and his students (1965:201-252). In a series of pioneering studies, Schnore compared social status differences between central cities and peripheral suburban residents in Standard Metropolitan Statistical Areas (SMSAs) and Urbanized Areas (UAs). While a majority of urban regions had higher status suburbanites, a large number of central cities were characterized by relatively high status. The expected "Burgess pattern" was most frequently found in the oldest metropolitan areas, while infrequently found in the new areas.

It is also clear that old metropolitan areas differ in other aspects of ecological structure. They are disproportionately characterized by central cities with older,

multiple unit, deteriorated housing, and also by large concentrations of manufacturing activity. The congestion,
deterioration, and commercial activity should all be expected in the Burgess-type city. In fact, it has been shown
that the tendency of higher status persons to disproportionately live in the suburbs of older metropolitan areas
may be at least partially explained by the unattractive
housing and living conditions found in the central cities
(Guest, 1976b; Schnore and Winsborough, 1972).

Even with urban renewal and construction, patterns of
ecological structure in metropolitan areas seem to change
slowly. Historical patterns persist by themselves, and they
may also shape the subsequent types of development. It seems
likely that the Burgess viewpoint, as symbolized by the old-
new distinction, will remain valuable for some time as a
tool in distinguishing contemporary American differentials
in metropolitan structure.

*The Motor Vehicle*

The most crucial test of value for the Burgess theory is
its ability to predict the recent development of metropolitan America. In this, it must be labeled a failure. The primary explanation was the development of the motor vehicle,
which radically altered patterns of location within the city
after World War I, but particularly after World War II. Unlike the streetcar, the automobile had relatively flexible
movement patterns; it could and did go into the downtown
areas, but it was useful as well for many other parts of the
metropolis. While activities had some trouble settling at
long distances from the limited streetcar lines, the automobile could travel almost anywhere and had the potential of
creating new, important sub-centers. The streetcar had permitted some dispersal of population, but the motor vehicle
was, on the average, at least twice as fast, and had the
potential of at least quadrupling the functioning area of
the metropolis (Ward, 1971: 125-146).

The effect on the metropolis only became clearly evident
after 1910, particularly after World War I. Motor vehicles
had been mass produced before World War I, but the general
boom conditions of the 20's apparently made its purchase
feasible for middle-income groups; eventually, it became a
tool of the vast majority of the population.

Once started, the diffusion of the automobile was rapid
(Tobin, 1976). In 1916, 83 percent of the persons entering
the CBD of St. Louis arrived by streetcar, with 17 percent
entering by automobile. In 1926, 26 percent used cars, 7
percent buses, and 57 percent the streetcar. By 1937, 45

percent used cars, 12 percent buses, and 27 percent street-cars. Even during the Depression, automobiles and motor trucks were sold on a large-scale basis, and ownership of the motor vehicle increased in the U.S. population (Tobin, 1976:104).

Cars, of course, require highways, and these also developed in large numbers after World War I. Zimmer (1975): 43-46) shows that the early highways (post-1920) around Flint, Michigan, were all-weather but heavily gravel, pre-sumably restricting the speed of travel. The major achieve-ments in highway construction occurred after World War II, when multi-lane limited-access highways pierced the suburban territory within an extensive range from the central city, and almost all highways became hard-surfaced. Belts and downtown-oriented expressways became a prominent feature of the urban landscape.

In the United States, the period from 1920 to 1950 could probably be described as transitional from the streetcar to the motor car. Both systems of transportation co-existed, and changes in metropolitan structure probably reflected this dualism. That is, the effects of both streetcar and automobile technology were evident in the development of metropolitan structure. The strong effects of the automobile became evident after World War II.

The development of the automobile directly confronted two of the most basic arguments of the Burgess hypothesis: the importance of accessibility in location, and the exis-tence of strong land value gradients in relationship to the metropolitan center. As the speed of transportation in-creased, activities no longer depended so much on close physical proximity. This is well-illustrated by data on the relationship between home and workplace which show a gra-dually increasing distance (Catanese, 1970). Accessibility did not end as an important factor with the development of the automobile, but it declined in importance (Zimmer, 1964:332-333). In other words, a theory based only on accessibility as a factor in urban location seems to be an incomplete, although still important, method of theory building.

A more serious problem was the changing value of land with distance from the center. Trucking facilities appeared on the urban outskirts, and water and rail transit declined as modes of intra- and inter-urban movement. The automobile went anywhere at any time, and the center of the metropolis became one of many major points of access. As Yeates (1965) nicely demonstrates, the Chicago of 1910 had a very close relationship between distance from the center and the value of land, but this relationship dramatically altered by 1920 and 1930, and has decreased ever since. By 1960, the relationship between distance from Chicago's center and the value of land had become very small, although consistent with the original Burgess theory.

The importance of the automobile in altering ecological relationships was, of course, not ignored by the early Chicago school. A reading of McKenzie's classic study, *The Metropolitan Community* (1933), and his other work (1929) will quickly indicate that the importance of this technological change was clearly perceived. Ecologists tended to focus only upon the significance of the automobile in the development of metropolitan regions. McKenzie, for instance, primarily concentrated on the role of transportation in altering ecological relationships in the metropolitan hinterland, in the areas within marginal commuting range or beyond the commuting range of the metropolitan center. His analysis of the metropolitan community within close distances of the center recognizes such trends as the coming automobile era, nucleation of employment, and changes in metropolitan building techniques, but his theoretical understanding of spatial development within the dense urban core goes little beyond the Burgess conception.

Two other technical factors might be mentioned in explanations of why the Burgess theory seemed limited to a period in American history. First, revolutions in building construction by World War II permitted the vast upward expansion of structures and reduced much of the pressure for the central activities to expand outward. As long as buildings could be constructed with only a few stories, demand for central land had to be accommodated by outward movement; but when buildings could have dozens of floors, the area size of the center may remain constant while its intensity of utilization changes. Second, the revolution in electronic communications removed much of the impetus for face-to-face contact which had made the urban center so valuable. With the development of advanced telephone and computer equipment, persons no longer had to meet face-to-face to learn the latest in the world of business. Related activities could be miles away in space but only seconds away from communications. Consistent with this, Zimmer (1975:49-50) shows that the area of toll-free telephone communication in Providence, Rhode Island, has expanded dramatically since 1935.

The other major problem with the Burgess theory is its inability to account for changes in organizational relationships both within urban agglomerations and also between cities and the larger society. The Burgess theory assumes that the allocation of urban space is determined by the actions of hundreds of individualistic competitors. Yet, the decades since World War II have involved the impressive growth of large bureaucracies—governmental, economic, service—which undoubtedly have important influences over the political processes in determining the allocation of land. Rather than a free market of supply and demand for land, we may have developed complex versions of oligopoly and monopoly in the urban spatial market. Sociologists such as Form (1954) have pointed to the importance of these issues, but unfortunately few have provided clear theories to guide our understanding.

The period since World War II has seen the federal and state governments become increasingly involved in the organization of cities. While federal intervention is still relatively minor in our cities as opposed to the world system (compare urban with so-called defense expenditures), few can doubt that the growth and development of metropolitan areas are affected by policies from distant points. Programs such as urban renewal, housing rehabilitation, and Model Cities have left lasting (but not well understood) impressions on the physical structure of metropolitan areas (Zimmer, 1964). Furthermore, the decision of the federal government to subsidize new, single-family housing in the United States through loans to contractors and buyers has undoubtedly played an important role in the suburbanization of population. In the following sections, we would like to discuss the effect of these organizational transformations in urban structure, but our knowledge seems limited and diffuse; as a result, I concentrate more on the effects of the revolution in transportation.

In summary, the Burgess theory was based on the notion that population growth, within the context of streetcar transportation, led to the differentiation of the metropolis. In my opinion, the technological and organizational revolution has produced a situation in which growth has, if anything, just the opposite effect. That is, growth is an opportunity for the metropolis to further break down its mono-centered structure which has been inherited from an outmoded age. The exact emerging structure is unclear, but will be discussed in the next sections and the end of the paper.

Another possible alternate position to the classic Burgess theory is that population growth itself is really a very unimportant variable in understanding the development of urban structure. Rather, technological and organizational factors are the primary causes of the urban development within the United States. That is, rather than assuming the primacy of population growth and the subordinate role of technology and organization (as Burgess did), we might emphasize the dominant role of technology and organization and the subordinate role of population growth.

*Dispersal*

The most impressive demographic fact about the development of contemporary metropolitan America since World War II is its dispersal. All contemporary theories of urban structure must recognize that the "push" toward the center in the Burgess theory has turned into a pull toward the outskirts. The Burgess theory posited a commuters' zone on the metropolitan periphery, but it came almost as an after-thought, and little time or effort was spent in clarifying the nature of the suburbanization. By 1970, more than half of the population of metropolitan areas lived in the heart of the commuters' zone, the suburbs (U.S. Bureau of the Census, 1971: Figure 38), and the trend showed little abatement.

The Burgess hypothesis had emphasized varying patterns of change across metropolitan areas as a consequence of differential population growth, but what seems clear from the post-World War II automobile era is that recent patterns of population and employment dispersal have been nearly universal across all metropolitan areas. This dispersal has primarily resulted from the changing functional value of the metropolitan center with alterations in the technological and organizational character of the metropolis. It is worthwhile to examine the dispersal of employment and residence in some detail.

The streetcar metropolis had led to the development of some employment activity at points away from the CBD. Small retail shopping centers were often established at major transfer points for the streetcar lines (Warner, 1962), but these were generally collections of a few small stores. On the periphery of metropolitan areas, a few industrial satellite cities had appeared, but these seemed to be more or less self-contained (Taylor, 1915). That is, persons both worked and lived in the same community, and a high degree of daily interchange between communities was lacking.

After World War II the CBDs were not ever-expanding as the growth model had predicted. It was expected that commercial activities would completely pre-empt the centers of metropolitan areas and then move outward. What seemed to happen was that the commercial areas did, in fact, drive out almost all non-commercial uses, but the geographic size of the commercial center did not noticeably expand (Guest, 1975a). Much of the demand for central space was accommodated by the construction of multi-story skyscrapers

(Manners, 1974). In Seattle, a large hill near the downtown area was removed by 1910 to make way for commercial expansion, but the CBD was never really expanded to engulf this area (Sale, 1976:75-76). Rather than zones in transition, metropolitan centers developed gray areas with obsolescent and undesired structures. Until government intervened in terms of urban renewal, the area around the CBD could be described as the Zone in Rot.

The most thoroughly researched area of employment redistribution is retailing. In the post-World War II period, from 1948 to 1967, the average CBD showed an absolute decline in the level of retail sales, and this decline occurred nearly universally across all metropolitan centers (Guest and Cluett, 1974). At the same time, metropolitan areas saw an explosion of shopping centers, particularly of the planned variety. In the period 1958 to 1967, the number of shopping centers recognized by the U.S. Census in 73 metropolitan areas increased from an average 5.0 to 12.9 (Guest and Cluett, 1974).

A complex new commercial structure was created in this era, which is still not well understood. In one interesting effort to grapple with this transition, Berry (1963) has used some of the ideas of central place theory, normally applied to studies of inter-urban retail structure, to understand the emerging commercial structure of the modern metropolis. Berry's primary notion is that a hierarchy of shopping centers in the metropolis may be described, ranging at the bottom from small centers which serve the most general convenience functions for small geographical areas to the CBD at the top, which serves all the general functions of the lowest order center for the immediate neighborhood plus the most specialized functions of shopping and luxury goods for the entire metropolis. In between are found a variety of district and regional shopping centers, each with its own geographic sphere of influence.

If Berry's theory has value for understanding longitudinal change, the CBD (the highest-order center) should be shedding some of its less-specialized functions, but post-World War II data suggest that the rate of exodus of both general convenience and more specialized shopping goods from the CBD has been relatively equal (Guest and Cluett, 1974).

Two major theories of current changing employment structure in the automobile era may be suggested.

One viewpoint (what we call the traditional ecological perspective) focuses on the continued functional differentiation of the metropolis in regard to the location of employment. Best represented by the work of Birch (1970), this perspective argues that the center is increasingly becoming the site of white collar-service-administrative jobs while the suburban ring is increasingly becoming the site of manufacturing goods-producing activity. This process is presumably occurring most rapidly in the largest, fastest growing SMSAs. This theory would be best supported by showing that the distribution of specific jobs or industries between central cities and suburbs is becoming increasingly dissimilar, particularly because of changes in location for the goods-service dichotomy. What Birch actually emphasizes is that the central cities are gaining absolutely in white collar service jobs while losing absolutely or showing little change in manufacturing jobs. What he fails to emphasize is that suburban rings, while gaining absolutely in manufacturing jobs, are gaining at an even faster rate in white collar service jobs. It is thus unclear how well this viewpoint has sorted out general changes in the overall industrial-occupational composition of metropolitan society from specific changes in parts of the metropolis.

In contrast, other work (Guest, 1977c) suggests that most major employment activities are engaged in a headlong flight from our central cities. Since 1940, a dramatic trend of absolute losses in various types of central city employment has developed in metropolitan areas with relatively constant central borders. The exceptions tend to be professional and governmental work which are growing absolutely in both central cities and suburban rings. On the whole, this suburbanization has not been particularly selective of specific industries (also see Kasarda, 1972). The net result has been that the metropolis maintains its center-periphery contrast in the distribution of specific types of activities. Service-informational processing-administrative activity tends to remain relatively centralized; only the average distance of all activity from the center has shifted outward. These data do suggest, however, some slight trend in functional differentiation. Over time, the central cities do seem to become very slightly more specialized in service-professional work, but this differentiation seems relatively unimportant compared to the broader pattern of general dispersal.

Unfortunately, we do not know much about the changing location patterns of more specific types of industries or occupations, as great variations in location occur within broad industrial categories. For instance, specific types of manufacturing establishments still have widely varying spatial locations: activities such as clothing and electrical manufacturers tend to be located relatively close to the center, while durable goods industries involving such activities as chemical and metals tend to be more peripheral in location (Guest, 1976a).

In general, the location of employment within the metropolis has been treated as a consequence of intrametropolitan constraints, but the development of a national system of cities should alert us also to the constrains of intermetropolitan factors. In one major study, Pappenfort (1959) shows that manufacturing firms with extra-local administrative offices and economic relationships tend to locate on the metropolitan periphery. It is an interesting, but unexplored, question of the extent to which suburbanization of employment can be attributed to locational patterns for firms which are increasingly extra-local in their orientation.

With the decline of the metropolitan center as the dominant employment site, it seems likely that new nodal employment structures are being created. The existence of sectors of industrial activity and multiple nuclei for various employment activities has been recognized for a long time. Everyone can observe the numerous industrial parks and beltline centers of employment which have appeared in our major metropolitan centers. Unfortunately, little empirically documented theory has appeared which leads to an understanding of this new structure in the post-World War II period. Do land values and patterns of activity use decline with distance from these nodes? Some affirmative but limited evidence on this point is found in Yeates (1965).

The changing function of the metropolitan center and the dispersal of activities outward has been a truly dramatic social change. Contrary to some theorists (Greer, 1966; Hawley, 1972), I am unwilling to argue that the center has been relegated only to those lacking the resources to get out. The center may be assuming a new equilibrium with its metropolis by serving some, albeit limited, functions for the metropolis. Many metropolitan cores seem to be sites of strong and recent activity by major corporations, government agencies, and cultural facilities. All these activities still draw clients from wide geographic areas, and depend on the close exchange of information among a number of suppliers and customers. The center may also serve as a major regional center for a part of the metropolis.

While the Burgess theory of center-periphery functional differentiation within the conventional metropolis may have limited usefulness, it may have more contemporary relevance if the scale of analysis shifts to core and periphery of the metropolitan region (Guest, 1977a). With technological and organizational development, the size of functioning social and economic urban units may have expanded much behond the conventional notion of a central city and its inner suburbs. Whole regions of the country may have become integrated, so that the major contrasts should be made between the densely settled cores (containing the central cities and inner suburbs), and the periphery (containing what are generally considered non-metropolitan counties). In short, the new core may serve many of the same functions, only on a larger scale, as the old core (consisting of the CBD and its immediate environs). Consistent with this, Wilson (1975) claims that metropolitan cores, as total units, are now capturing the primary service-information functions so that they control large regions; the periphery is assuming, in contrast, a goods producing function.

*Residential Movement*

Some social scientists have delighted in pointing out that the suburbanization of residential population is really nothing new (Jackson, 1975; Schmitt, 1956). They have shown that residential population has increasingly been settling on the periphery of metropolitan areas for several decades and, in this sense, are correct. Schnore (1965b:98-113) has demonstrated that some suburban rings of metropolitan areas, particularly on the east coast, were growing faster than their central cities by the late 1800's. It also seems clear that the peripheral movement of residences predated the large-scale movement of employment, a finding which is compatible with what we know about the streetcar city. From an ecological standpoint, though, calculations of central city versus suburban growth rates as indicators of suburbanization should be used cautiously. The same point could be made about the study of employment dispersal. Central city and suburban boundaries vary among metropolitan areas, and also across time, due to central city annexation of territory.

The most useful way of charting the pattern of population suburbanization is through the density gradient. This is described as

$$D_x = D_0 e^{bx}, \text{ or in natural logarithms} \qquad (1)$$

$$LnD_x = LnD_0 + bx, \qquad (2)$$

where $D_x$ equals the population density of an area x distance from the center; $D_0$ equals the predicted density of the city at its center, and b is a measure of the change in density with each mile from the center. The equation may be calculated over small areal units, such as census tracts. This function may also be applied to employment distribution, but little work has proceeded in this direction due to a lack of data for small areal units (for an exception see Mills, 1972). Winsborough (1963) has shown that values of $D_0$ measure congestion, or average density levels at which a population lives. Values of b measure the concentration or average distance of populations from the center of the metropolis. Using this conception, suburbanization may be described as involving both changes in the overall level of density for the metropolis ($D_0$) and the distribution of population in relationship to the center (b).

Within this framework, suburbanization in the automobile era is something new. Winsborough (1963) shows that values of $D_0$ were increasing in Chicago until the early 1900s, and values of b were declining only slowly in the late 1800s and early 1900s. Both began to decline clearly only after the automobile became rapidly adopted by the population (after 1910).

Since World War II, changes in values of b and $D_0$ have been dramatic. While they showed moderate declines in most metropolitan areas in the 1940s, they began an impressive decline in the 1950s. Guest (1975a) demonstrates that values of b and $D_0$ declined by at least 50 percent in the period 1950 to 1970. By 1970, density patterns were becoming weakly related to distance from the center in most metropolitan areas, suggesting the declining importance of land values from the center in ordering the structure of the metropolis. The changing dispersal of population is also indicated by the fact that once annexation was controlled, the average central city showed no growth in residential population during the 1960s (Kaufman and Schnore, 1975).

Changes in patterns of population dispersal have been essentially universal across metropolitan areas (Guest, 1975a). In 1950, large metropolitan areas had a clear tendency to have a gradual decline of density (b) from the center of the metropolis, but by 1970, this relationship had changed so that large and small metropolitan areas were increasingly similar in their patterns of population distribution.

In studying central city versus suburban rates of population growth, researchers have found that central cities are more frequently losing population in the older, eastern metropolian areas (Schnore, 1965:114-133). Some have interpreted this to indicate that suburbanization is more rapid in this section of the country, and, at least by this measure, the conclusion is correct. Central city boundaries are much more constrained in the East, though, and it is probable that this pattern heavily reflects different distances from the center over which the measures are made. Traditional ecological theory suggested that neighborhoods in the metropolis passed through a life cycle in population density. They started off with a low density, and then, as they became relatively closer to the center and land values increased, they became more intensively settled. Eventually, commercial uses would begin pre-empting the residential land, and the residential population density would decline (Hoover and Vernon, 1962). One consequence of the changing technological-organizational character of the metropolis, however, is that this life cycle pattern need not occur to the same extent. With the decline in competition for centrality, urban neighborhoods need not pass through a rapid period of building up and then a decline in population density.

In elaborating on this point, Guest (1973) has shown that neighborhoods established in recent decades in Cleveland have built up to much lower levels of density than older neighborhoods, and also have passed very slowly through the neighborhood life cycle process. That is, once built up, the newest neighborhoods have changed little in population density. Population density is primarily explained by the density of housing units, and housing units have shown a somewhat greater pattern of increasing concentration in newer neighborhoods, but still the evidence for life cycles has not been strong. Population density has remained relatively constant in the newer neighborhoods because increasing numbers of housing units have been counterbalanced by declining household size.

Studies of neighborhood life cycles really require data on changes in both residences and employment (lacking in Guest's study), but it does seem likely that the traditional life cycle process, described by the Chicago ecologists, is relatively unimportant in comparison to the past. What seems more likely is a type of leap-frogging process in cities. Rather than activities competing strongly against each other for the same established location, activities select new and different locations in unsettled peripheral territory. Not only do activities leap-frog across the metropolis, but large chunks of land, with some proximity to the metropolitan center, are probably passed for more peripheral areas.

What are the underlying factors behind this great suburbanization of residential population? An answer to this question has been sought for several decades now, but with little consensus. Most analysts agree that the size and quality of suburban housing are dominant factors (Clark, 1966; Gans, 1967). This explanation is consistent with the primary attitudinal rationales which have been found in studies of intra-urban mobility (Rossi, 1955; Simmons, 1968). More conflict occurs on the relative importance of broader contrasts between central cities and suburbs in such factors as neighborhood quality, schools, noises, and racial composition (Berry et al., 1976; Guterbock, 1976). While these factors undoubtedly play some role in the "flight" to the suburbs, I tend to minimize their importance for two reasons. First, I have yet to find any study which demonstrates their strong importance. Second, the process of suburbanization is nearly universal across all metropolitan areas, which have significantly different central cities in terms of various environmental qualities.

The move to the suburbs in search of desirable housing --new, single-unit, and spacious--has been facilitated by three major factors. First, the transportation orientation of the metropolis has permitted the development of previously inaccessible tracts of land. Second, housing construction has increasingly become a large-scale mass production industry in which large tracts of land (generally found disproportionately in the suburbs) are crucial. Finally, the federal government has increasingly intervened in the housing market to subsidize suburban housing. Federal loan policies have encouraged the development of new housing, either by direct subsidies to contractors or guaranteeing mortgage payments for potential purchasers.

The great suburbanization of population probably has some spatial limits, of course. The motor vehicle does not permit an indefinite commuting range around the metropolitan center, and at some point it is likely that further outward development will simply be constrained by the distance that persons are willing to travel. Some constraints are suggested by the fact that the growth of metropolitan suburbs has primarily occurred within a ring about 20 miles from the central city (Guest, 1976d). Suburbs beyond this point have actually been declining in their share of the suburban, and perhaps metropolitan, population although not in absolute number of residents.

Some relevant information on this question has developed as a result of studies on the redistribution of population among counties since 1970. The finding that counties outside SMSAs are growing disproportionately (Morrison and

Wheeler, 1976) contradicts a general trend in the 20th
century for population to be increasingly concentrated within metropolitan areas. One possible explanation of this
trend is economic conditions in the United States. In the
30s, a period of economic hard times, metropolitan areas
also showed relatively low population growth. Apparently, a
booming economy creates jobs in metropolitan areas, and a
stagnant economy encourages people to stay down on the farm
and in the rural areas. Another explanation of the trend is
the possibility that residential suburbanization has simply
overflowed conventional metropolitan area borders. One of
the major predictors of population growth in nonmetropolitan
counties is commuting rates to central metropolitan counties
(Morrison and Wheeler, 1976:12). Areas with high commuting
rates are clearly showing the high rates of residential
population growth.

What ties have developed between the suburbanization of
employment and residence? One viewpoint is that the location of workplace currently exerts little effect on the
location of residence for individuals (Stegman, 1969). This
conclusion has been heavily based on survey data showing
that the location of workplace is infrequently cited as an
important cause of residential choice or movement. While the
exact location of workplace may not exert a strong direct
effect on the location of residence, workers may consider it
an underlying constraint. Thus, persons may pick a residence
within a certain tolerable range of distances and times from
workplace (Brown, 1975).

Cross-sectional data on the location of home and workplace in metropolitan areas suggest that the clear majority
of central city residents also work in the central city
(Guest, 1975b), and a clear majority of suburban ring residents also work in the suburban ring. The image of the typical suburbanite as a long-distance commuter to the central
city and CBD is incorrect. While the exact process is not
well understood, persons seem to establish some type of tie
between home and workplace.

Some longitudinal data suggest that workplace may exert
more of an effect on the residential location of suburbanites than central city residents. For instance, central city
workers were particularly apt to suburbanize their residences in the 1960 to 1970 period, while there was less
change in the residential location of suburban workers
(Guest, 1976f). Michelson (1977:284) has shown that suburbanites indicate a greater concern about locating homes
near workplaces than central city residents. These studies
suggest that workers are willing to live away from their
workplaces if they find immediate areas to have unattractive

residential environments (as is probably the case for central city workers), while workplace location has a more important direct effect if the surrounding residential area is attractive.

The other "major" interpretation of emerging journey to work patterns is that a separation of homes and workplaces is developing in the metropolis. One ecologist, Schnore, calls the functional division of labor "extreme" (1965:108) in the modern metropolis and argues that "homes and workplaces are developing in different sectors" (1965:328). While the individual length of the journey to work may have increased, the location of homes and workplaces may remain relatively close in relationship to each other. At least in large suburban communities (over 50,000 residential population), almost 40 percent of workers typically live in the same community as their employment site (Guest, 1976a). In another study (Guest, 1978b) growth rates of employment and residential populations were strongly related in a positive direction in a sample of American suburbs which were studied between 1947 and 1970 (Guest, 1978b). The dissimilarity in distribution between employment and residential activities over these communities slightly decreased, on average, during the time period.

Development of theory in this area should recognize the functional interdependence of homes and workplaces. While the length of the journey to work (if not necessarily the time) is increasing for the average worker, there is still some effort to minimize the journey to work. Many industries depend on the proximity of residential population for their economic livelihood. This is particularly true of the rapidly expanding service sector. Finally, residential populations may heavily depend on the location of employment for the support of governmental structures (Logan, 1976). Many communities may find at least some types of employment desirable because they help support the tax base.

*Population Composition*

The most accurate descriptive summary of residential distributions in American metropolitan areas would be in terms of a basic racial dichotomy, with blacks and whites largely occupying separate communities which rarely overlap except when one community is expanding into another (generally black into white). Within each racial community, patterns of social status and family segregation emerge. The white community is also crosscut by patterns of segregation among European origin groups. Some like to perceive neighborhoods as highly or almost completely segregated by family, white ethnic, or status factors. While neighborhoods of homogeneously rich or poor and childbearing or nonchildbearing do exist, data on levels of segregation suggest that they are rare (Guest, 1976c). That is, many neighborhoods in cities have a mixture of rich and poor, old and young, childbearing and non-childbearing. This would be expected since few neighborhoods are homogeneously composed of one type of housing.

As noted earlier, the ecologists primarily believed that differences in residential distribution among social groups occurred because of differences in the urban morphology or basic spatial structure. Thus, factors such as the distribution of different types of housing, and the location of workplaces were emphasized as crucial. Underlying these causes were group differences in income which permitted access to various areas of the city. Thus, the decentralization of higher status persons was primarily seen as a product of the distribution of deteriorated housing, spacious housing, and the location of business and industry. The high income of high status persons permitted them to select their residential neighborhoods, and they therefore became segregated from lower status persons.

One way to think about the ecologists' perspective is in terms of two major causes of segregation which can, in turn, be divided into two subtypes (Guest, 1976c). Most basically, we may consider residential segregation to arise from personalistic or non-personalistic factors. The first refers to a desire by one group to live specifically near or far from another group, regardless of housing or morphological characteristics of an area. Thus, the choice of residence, say, by a Pole, will heavily hinge on how many other Poles live in the neighborhood, or perhaps negatively, on how many blacks live in the neighborhood. Personalistic segregation may result from either individual or institutional action. The individual may specifically seek out a residence which is close or distant from a specific person or group. Alternatively, institutions such as banks, realtors, government, may create segregation because they interpret some popular desire for it. Thus, realtors may refuse to show housing to blacks because they perceive that white people in the neighborhood would not desire it. Or banks may refuse to make loans for residential construction in a neighborhood because they perceive it as a place which will primarily be used for commercial purposes.

In contrast, non-personalistic factors refer to segregation resulting from the morphological structure of the city, as primarily emphasized by the Chicago ecologists, or from the role of cultural traditions (sentiment and symbolism) as

Firey (1947) argued in his study of Beacon Hill. Thus, higher status persons dominate certain neighborhoods because they particularly prize a certain type of housing there or the more elusive but, perhaps, important cultural factors.

My view is that the Chicago ecologists' emphasis on explaining population composition of metropolitan sub-areas, by morphological characteristics has a high degree of usefulness. This is particularly true of family location patterns which can be closely related to types of housing which are needed at various stages of the life cycle. While the evidence is more controversial, patterns of status location also indicate a close dependency on the housing and environmental character of neighborhoods. The Chicago school perspective seems least useful for investigating patterns of segregation by ethnicity or race. It seems though, as if most conventional explanations of segregation do not fit well with patterns of ethnic and racial distribution.

The importance of morphological factors in explaining residential segregation by family or life cycle composition is suggested by various studies of intra-urban mobility. These show that changes in family composition, such as marriage, childbearing, the attainment of adulthood by children are very important in the decision to seek a new home and the type of home which is sought (Simmons, 1968; Speare et al., 1974). A study (Guest, 1972c) of census tracts in the Cleveland SMSA in 1960 demonstrated that patterns of residential segregation among six types of families (differentiated by the presence of a spouse, children, and age of the household head) could be primarily explained by housing features of the areas, particularly the age and density of housing. This research also demonstrated that the concentration of new, low-density housing on the outskirts largely explained the tendency of childbearing families to be found there. Broken and childless households were more frequently centrally located, a pattern which seemed attributable to the spatial distribution of high-density, older housing. Similar patterns were found in 16 other SMSAs in 1960 (Guest, 1970).

The best-known support for the ecologists' morphological explanation of status segregation is the Duncans' (1955) study of occupational segregation in Chicago. They found that prestige differences among groups were closely related to differences in residential distribution. But just as importantly, income differences were perceived as the major underlying explanation of differences in residential distribution, permitting workers differential access to desirable housing and neighborhoods. Certain anomalies were evident, however. Even though relatively low in average income, clerical workers had residential distributions more similar to other white collar workers (professional, managerial, and sales) than blue collar craftsmen.

In followup to the Duncans, Feldman and Tilly (1960) have argued that differences in residential distribution among occupational groups are primarily due to educational distinctions, presumably in reflection of cultural or life style dissimilarities. Apparently, workers seek out their "own kind" in choosing a residence. An adequate resolution of these conflicting views would evaluate the simultaneous importance of differences in education, income, and other factors (say, workplace location and age composition) in explaining differences in residential distribution among occupational groups.

Another perspective on this question is represented by Firey's classic study (1947) of the importance of sentiment and symbolism in the maintenance of Boston's Beacon Hill as a high status neighborhood in downtown Boston. Firey argued that historical, family, and aesthetic characteristics of the area made it attractive for high status persons. His explanation, by his own analysis, would seem to be subsidiary to other viewpoints since Firey recognizes that most downtown Boston neighborhoods have declined in status in a manner consistent with the Burgess perspective.

Consistent with the ecological perspective, differences in housing characteristics, particularly the quality and size of the housing, have been found to be very important in explaining differences in the residential distribution of white collar versus blue collar workers in 17 SMSA's (Guest, 1971). These results would suggest that income differences affect ability to purchase types of housing and lead to differences in residential distribution. But the results were not strong enough to exclude the importance of other factors. This analysis also found that the tendency of white collar workers to be decentralized in some SMSAs could be attributed to differences in the spatial distribution of types of housing. In some metropolitan areas, the land market leads to the peripheral distribution of spacious and high quality housing and, in turn, the decentralization of high status persons.

As pointed out earlier, the Chicago ecologists perceived racial and ethnic segregation as being primarily an aspect of social status segregation. They generally seemed to believe that the residential distribution of specific groups would become less distinctive as they moved upward to the social and economic structure. It now seems clear that individual differences in income and housing characteristics between members of specific racial-ethnic groups and base-line populations do not explain very adequately the degree of residential segregation which exists (Darroch and Marston, 1971; Lieberson, 1963; Taeuber and Taeuber, 1969). That is, high income blacks are highly segregard from all whites, high and low income. High income Poles are highly segregated from high income Germans. This finding should not be surprising since residential segregation by race and ethnicity seems to be at least as high, if not higher, than segregation by occupational status. Status explanations would seem to be particularly weak for black-white segregation, since high segregation is particularly characteristic of blacks, although segregation of first and second generation European ethnic groups is still relatively strong.

While individual differences in income and housing characteristics are not very adequate for explaining racial and ethnic segregation, group differences in social status do seem to be relatively important. That is, the overall average differences in residential segregation between Poles and Britons is approximately what one would expect on the basis of average differences (over the entire groups) in social status (Darroch and Marston, 1971; Guest and Weed, 1976). This suggests that members of individual ethnic and racial groups may be treated in the residential markets in terms of the attributes of their groups rather than individual characteristics. Thus, high income blacks may have trouble finding a home in high income white neighborhoods because they are treated in terms of their group's average status (relatively low for blacks) by gatekeepers, such as realtors, banks.

When individuals are treated in terms of the characteristics of their groups, other types of explanations for residential segregation besides the morphological must be used. Unfortunately, we do not know a great deal about the residential market experiences of a variety of ethnic groups. It is clear, though, that blacks have faced serious problems in the housing market due to discrimination both by individual home owners and by major institutional actors. The U.S. Civil Rights Commission (Lawson, 1971) concluded that even the passage of anti-discriminatory governmental legislation has not significantly affected the behavior of major institutional actors in the residential market. In recent years, major changes have occurred in the attitudes of whites on the right of blacks to live wherever desired (Campbell, 1971), and one could speculate that major changes may subsequently occur in patterns of residential segregation. Evidence from the 1960s suggests, though, that black-white segregation remained very high, with perhaps some slight declines (Sorensen et al., 1975). The importance of even these slight declines has been challenged by other research (Van Valey et al., 1977).

*Residential Decentralization*

Residential segregation may take many spatial forms, but the most attention has been devoted to patterns of centralization versus decentralization. Somewhat less research has been conducted on segregation in terms of sectors, perhaps because no one has ever adequately clarified how the existence of sectors could be measured across cities and time. Patterns of centralization and decentralization may be measured simply by calculating gradients of distribution in relationship to the metropolitan center. Issues of centralization and decentralization also seem to have more immediate policy relevance because the governmental structures of most metropolitan areas are bifurcated into a central city, on the one hand, and a myriad of smaller suburban municipalities, on the other hand. The absence or presence of various residential groups in central cities and suburbs may have important consequences for demands on city services and ability to pay the costs of government.

Studies of peripheral location of higher status groups have attracted the most attention, and much of the research has explicitly been related to the Burgess hypothesis. As noted earlier, Schnore (1965b:201-252) found that most suburban rings have been higher in status than their central cities during the post-World War II period, but a significant number of metropolitan areas have higher status central city residents. On a cross-sectional basis, the expected Burgess pattern is more often found in older rather than currently large metropolitan areas. These findings suggested the necessity of historical research to determine the major patterns behind the development of contemporary patterns of status distribution. In discussing this research, it should be noted that the tendency of status to increase with distance from the center is not very pronounced in most metropolitan areas (Guest, 1971, 1972b), meaning that only a small percentage of segregation can be explained on a central-peripheral basis, even in most of the oldest and largest metropolitan areas.

In searching for an explanation of cross-sectional patterns, Guest and Nelson (1978) analyzed changes in the central city versus suburban distribution of higher status persons between 1920 and 1950, and 1950 and 1970 across 204 metropolitan areas. Two contrasting patterns of change were evident.

They found that a pattern of higher status decentralization emerged during the 1920 to 1950 period in the oldest metropolitan areas. This occurred, they contended, because the oldest metropolitan areas had attained by 1920 the disagreeable centers which were predicted by the Burgess theory. With the diffusion of the automobile, higher status persons in these places particularly fled to the suburban rings. In the newer places, the centers had never developed the morphological characteristics found in the Burgess "large" city, and higher status workers had little reason to move away from the center, since it was still the primary site of their employment.

Between 1950 and 1970, almost all metropolitan areas had increases in suburban social status at the expense of the central city. The relationship between metropolitan age and the location of higher status persons remained approximately constant; what changed was the mean status over all metropolitan areas of suburban status relative to the central city. Guest and Nelson said that the post-World War II pattern could not be primarily attributable to the differential attractiveness of various central cities, since a higher status decentralization was almost universal. Rather, they claimed, higher status decentralization must be due to the universal pull of the suburbs. This period, of course, involved the mass subsidization of the suburban new housing market by the federal government.

The conventional wisdom has portrayed the suburbanization of higher status persons in the post-World War II period as a consequence of high status persons moving to the suburbs while low status persons moved into the central city. Actually, the process of change seems somewhat more complex. Evidence (Olsen and Guest, 1977) indicates that migrants to both central cities and suburban rings have been typically high in status. In some metropolitan areas, inmigrants to the central cities have been high in status in comparison to both suburban non-movers and suburban inmovers. The implication of these results is that the suburbanization of high status populations cannot be divorced from the general suburbanization of population. While suburban in-migrants have not always been high in status relative to central city in-migrants, there have been huge numbers of them and they have been high in status relative to all metropolitan dwellers. As a result, the sheer size of the suburban movement, in conjunction with the above-average status of suburban in-migrants (although not always higher than central in-migrants), has produced an increasing suburban relative to central city status. We badly need to know how the changing status of suburbs relative to their central cities has been related to changes in status of smaller areal units. According to the Burgess hypothesis, central neighborhoods would decline in average status over time while peripheral neighborhoods would increase in average status. Various evidence suggests that some change has occurred recently in the status of small areas, when they are arrayed in terms of their distances from the center or their ages (Guest, 1972b, 1974). However, what is most noteworthy is the relative persistence of social status in small areas, close and peripheral, new and old, during the post-World War II period.

How could total central cities become clearly differentiated from their suburban rings while changes in sub-areal status are less pronounced? One explanation, with some empirical documentation, is that the high status suburbs have particularly gained population growth during the period, and have driven upward the average status of the suburban ring by increasing their share of the total ring population (Guest, 1978). Thus, suburban ring status has changed primarily because the relative share of the population has shifted from low to high status suburbs, not because of strong sub-areal evolution. Unfortunately, we do not know much about the shifting location of population between high and low status areas in the central cities.

Recently, some indication of a high status revival in central cities has occurred. Newspaper and magazine articles report frequently that run-down central city neighborhoods have been invaded by higher status persons. Some have argued that this means the suburbs will become the slums while the central cities become the preserve of the rich (Peirce, 1977). Such visionary proclamations may be a little premature, although there is no reason why a limited market for high status housing might not be further encouraged in our central cities. Many high status persons work in the downtown areas, and they comprise a good market for inner city housing, particularly if they lack children. With the clearing of some land in the metropolitan center by such activities as urban renewal, the rehabilitation of older housing, and the relative decline of central land values, a potential site for high status housing has become available. In the future, the differentiation of central cities from suburbs in social status may become less pronounced. This is certainly suggested by census sample data from the 70s on the social status of white central city and suburban dwellers; very little change in relative status has occurred (U.S. Bureau of the Census, 1975: Table L).

In some sense, patterns of family composition provide strong support for traditional Burgess notions about the distribution of population groups, in that patterns of segregation are heavily explained by a central-peripheral location pattern (Guest, 1970, 1972a). However, unlike status distributions, patterns of centralization-decentralization by family composition seem to have less variation across metropolitan areas. One explanation of this second finding may be that childbearing families are primarily distributed in relationship to new, low density housing, a universal feature of the periphery of most metropolitan areas. In contrast, higher status persons are more frequently distributed in relationship to the quality and internal space of housing, factors which seem to vary more over metropolitan areas. While little research is available on this point, it does not appear that patterns of family distribution across metropolitan areas are strongly related to metropolitan growth, size or age attributes.

A major trend of the 60s was an apartment house boom in the suburbs (Neutze, 1968). In contrast, new housing in the 50s was disproportionately single-family and owner occupied. Some evidence suggests that the migrants to the suburbs in the 60s were less frequently in the childbearing stage than previously, but, on the whole, the familistic orientation of the suburban ring relative to central cities remained relatively strong (Long and Glick, 1976). This may have happened because the apartment house boom occurred in both central cities and suburbs. Thus, overall differences in types of housing remained relatively constant between center and periphery, producing little overall change in population composition.

The Chicago school perspective implied that suburbanization characterized ethnic groups as they moved upward in the social and economic structure. Yet, contemporary differences in suburbanization among various first and second generation ethnic groups (primarily European in origin) indicate that current differences in social status have only weak, predictive power (Guest, 1978a). However, current differences in suburbanization are closely related to historical differences in social status among ethnic groups. Those groups with relatively high status in the early 1900s are most suburbanized today (generally Northern and Western Europeans), while groups with relatively low status then are somewhat less suburbanized (generally from Southern and Eastern Europe and other continents). The distribution of low status groups in the early 1900s was probably influenced by a strong need to locate close to concentrations of low skill jobs and cheap housing around the center. These patterns have persisted over time, so that groups have changed their relative social positions but not their relative spatial positions.

Patterns of ethnic group suburbanization differ significantly across metropolitan areas, particularly for the Northern and Western European groups. In general, the Northern and Western Europeans tend to be centralized when high status persons are centralized, but suburbanized when high status persons also tend to assume that location.

Historically, most suburban rings in the United States have very small percentages of black population (Farley, 1970). In the post-World War II period, the black percentage of many central cities in large SMSAs has increased noticeably, while the black percentage in the suburban ring has shifted little (Guest, 1977d). In the South, many blacks lived, historically, in the suburban ring to serve occupational functions in the agriculturally-oriented economies. Over time, the black suburban ring population has decreased in percentage terms.

Even the limited nature of black suburbanization suggests little similarity with the Chicago school perspective. Black suburban populations are generally lower in status than the white populations living in the same community (Guest, 1977d). While almost as often apt to live in single-family homes as whites, they are somewhat less apt to be owners. In the past, black suburban populations have been lower in status than black central city populations, although this situation seems to be changing (U.S. Bureau of the Census, 1975: Table 9).

As discussed previously, one of the major trends of the post-World War II period has been the suburbanization of employment activity. The inter-relationship of this suburbanization with the population structure of parts of the metropolis is not well understood. Employment structure would seem to affect population structure in two major ways. First, different industries employ workers with varying social demographic characteristics; since employment location affects residential location, the distribution of types of employment may affect the distribution of population groups. Thus, a very high correlation exists between the social status, family, and ethnic composition of work-force and residential populations in large American suburbs (Guest, 1976a), primarily because so many persons work and live in the same community. It is also clear that suburbs with large amounts of manufacturing employment differ in population structure from suburbs with large amounts of service activity (Guest, 1977b). In particular, service-oriented suburbs are less familistic in their population structures, a finding which is consistent with what we know about the family structure of workers in the two different types of industries. Second, employment structure may also affect population structure through its environmental attractiveness. Manufacturing activity is well-known for its noxious odors, effluents, and unattractive appearance, and manufacturing suburbs have clearly lower status residential populations than service-oriented suburbs. Suburbanization of employment would have clear effects on the population structure of suburbia if some types of industries sub-urbanized more than others. Unfortunately, the question of whether industries are differentially suburbanizing is in some dispute, as we have already noted.

*Summary and Conclusion*

For several decades, the Burgess hypothesis provided the central paradigm of human ecology research on the city. It gave sociological research on the city a distinctive character which justified the ongoing separate existence of urban ecology. The viewpoint of this paper has been that the Burgess viewpoint has been extremely useful in understanding the development of cities in the pre-World War II period and for providing a central set of hypotheses and terminology. To the extent that the past influences the present, the Burgess theory is also valuable for understanding contemporary American cities. Yet, if human ecology perspectives on the city continue, new organizing themes and theories must be provided.

In the past few years, a growing number of sociologists have found the ideas of the human ecologists to be useful in understanding the development of cities. This research has been facilitated by the development of data sources and statistical techniques to investigate comparative and longitudinal patterns of urban structure. While the recent growth of empirical work is encouraging, I am often struck by the lack of anything more than routine and ritualistic thought. At the risk of superficial generalization, three major criticisms of many recent studies might be made. First, and most basically, work has been oriented toward a literal testing of the traditional Burgess–Chicago school theories of urban structure and has not actively tried to deal with the tech-nological-organizational revolutions in our cities. Thus, researchers frequently use metropolitan size or growth as a variable in analysis, but fail to ask how and why the relationship of growth to urban structure might have changed since the Burgess days. We need audacious studies, in both an empirical and theoretical sense, which help us account for and understand the major transformations of the post-World War II period. Second, work has been primarily descriptive and has not moved strongly toward the development of causal models. Thus, I have read several papers which present as the sole empirical analysis indices of residential dissimilarity among occupation, familial, and racial-ethnic groups, both cross-sectionally and over time. But there is little concern with testing theory to explain these patterns. We have still not begun, as a group, to introduce carefuly selected independent and dependent variables into multiple regression equations. Finally, too many studies analyze ecological patterns in only one metropolitan area, and then assume (falsely in my belief) that they apply to all areas. There are still significant differences in patterns of ecological structure across metropolitan areas, and comparative research is crucial for specifying the causal importances of the historical, technological, and organizational factors.

An adequate new paradigm for human ecology will have to deal with the following major facts: (a) accessibility does not continue to assume the importance in urban locations that it once did, (b) the center of the metropolis has simply become one (but still the major) among many nodal centers, (c) metropolitan population growth need not lead to functional differentiation, and (d) individual metropolitan areas develop out of the constraints imposed by an increasingly integrated and centralized national society.

In thinking about these "facts," I believe that human ecology perspectives on the city have possibly four futures. One is that we will find the new nodal structure amenable to analysis. That is, we will find that a hierarchy of nodal centers leads to some as yet unknown pattern of ecological relationships in the metropolis. Accessibility to these nodes will determine the new urban structure. Urbanites would presumably lead their lives within relatively autonomous sub-centers. The ingredients of a nodal theory will probably be much more complex than the Burgess theory. Techniques of mathematics, particularly geometry, will become crucial in analyzing spatial organization.

A second possibility is that the structure of metropolitan areas is increasingly organized in relationship to the corporate and political system. That is, to understand the emerging character of metropolitan America, we need to

focus on the way that decisions are made among major bureaucratic structures such as the governmental, corporate, educational, and financial bureaucracies. This seems to be an
important direction of research, but my feeling is that
analysis is still relatively primitive. We still seem to be
deciding who has power, and we really have not moved much in
the direction of studying the consequence of power. Furthermore, methodologies for these issues have not been clearly
formulated. This type of theoretical approach will take us
far away from the first future, because it places little
direct effect on the importance of accessibility in urban
location.

Another future for human ecology perspectives on the
city is that we will find the conventional metropolitan concentrations to be assuming an increasingly formless pattern.
That is, the decline in importance of accessibility factors
means that activities will increasingly be arranged in a
relative random pattern in relationship to other activities.
For those of us who make our bread and butter studying
cities, this possibility is distressing because variations
in urban structure will essentially be unaccountable. It is
hard to get articles published where the dependent variables
have little variation, and the independent variables explain
none of the variation.

A final possibility, not unrelated to the second, is
that human ecology must shift its level of analysis from
studying internal variation within the conventional metropolitan concentrations to a focus on the metropolitan
region. That is, the major patterns of spatial differentiation within the United States may be developing on the basis
of huge metropolitan regions, encompassing most of the
nation's territory and involving contrasts between the
regional core and periphery. It may even be necessary to
further develop a theory which will account for interrelationships among sets of metropolitan regions, a development
which has only begun.

I wish that I could tell you which future possibility is
correct. But, alas, I have only begun to comprehend these
possibilities, and only minimal evidence exists to suggest
which is correct. The Chicago ecologists gave us some nice
insights, hypotheses, and theories. With their foundation
and our empirically documented research, we can hopefully
move toward a new understanding of the "Growth of the City."
I appreciate the opportunity to propound some of my rudimentary ideas about where we have been and where we are going.
I hope that you will join me in the exciting research possibilities to determine the future of ecological perspectives
on the city.

# REFERENCES

Alihan, M. A. (1939). Social Ecology. New York: Columbia University Press.

Anderson, T., and J. A. Egeland (1961). "Spatial aspects of social area analysis." American Sociological Review 26 (June):392-393.

Berry, B. J. L. (1967). Commerical Structure and Commercial Flight. Research Paper No. 85. Department of Geography, University of Chicago.

Berry, B. J. L., C. A. Goodwin, R. W. Lake, and K. B. Smith (1976). "Attitudes toward integration: the role of status in community response to racial change." Pp. 221-265 in Barry Schwartz (ed.). The Changing Face of the Suburbs. Chicago: University of Chicago Press.

Birch, D. L. (1970). The Economic Future of City and Suburb. New York: Committee for Economic Development Supplementary Paper No. 30.

Brown, H. J. (1975). "Changes in workplace and residential locations." Journal of the American Institute of Planners 41 (January):32-39.

Burgess, E. W. (1925). "The growth of the city." Pp. 47-62 in R. E. Park, E. W. Burgess, and R. D. McKenzie (eds.), The City. Chicago: University of Chicago Press.

Campbell, A. (1971). White Attitudes towards Black People. Institute for Social Research, University of Michigan.

Carey, J. T. (1975). Sociology and Public Affairs. The Chicago School. Beverly Hills, CA.: Sage.

Catanese, A. J. (1970). "Commuting behavior: patterns of families." Traffic Quarterly 24 (July):429-457.

Clark, S. D. (1966). The Suburban Society. Toronto: University of Toronto Press.

Cressey, P. F. (1938). "Population succession in Chicago: 1898-1930." American Journal of Sociology 44 (July):56-68.

Darroch, A. G., and W. G. Marston (1971). "The social class basis of ethnic residential segregation: the Canadian case." American Journal of Sociology 77 (November):491-510.

Davie, M. (1938). "The pattern of urban growth." Pp. 133-161 in G. P. Murdock (ed.), Studies in the Science of Society. New Haven: Yale University Press.

Duncan, B., and O. D. Duncan (1955). "Residential distribution and occupational stratification." American Journal of Sociology 60 (March):493-503.

Duncan, O. D., and L. F. Schnore (1959). "Cultural, behavioral and ecological perspectives in the study of social organization." American Journal of Sociology 65 (September):132-146.

Farley, R. (1970). "The changing distribution of Negroes within metropolitan areas: the emergence of black suburbs." American Journal of Sociology 75 (January):512-529.

Feldman, A. S., and C. Tilly (1960). "The interaction of social and physical spaces." American Sociological Review 25 (December):877-884.

Firey, W. (1947). Land Use in Central Boston. Cambridge: Harvard University Press.

Form, W. H. (1954). "The place of social structure in the determination of land use." Social Forces 32 (May):317-323.

Ford, R. G. (1950). "Population succession in Chicago." American Journal of Sociology 56 (September):156-160.

Gans, H. (1967). The Levittowners: Ways of Life and Politics in a New Suburban Community. New York: Pantheon.

Greer, S. (1966). Urban Renewal and American Cities: The Dilemma of Democratic Intervention. Indianapolis: Bobbs-Merrill.

Guest, A. M. (1978a). "Suburban social status: evolution or persistence?" American Sociological Review 43 (April): 251- 264.

Guest, A. M. (1978b). "Suburban territorial differentiation." Sociology and Social Research 62 (July):523-536.

Guest, A. M. (1978c). "The suburbanization of ethnic groups." Unpublished paper, Center for Studies in Demography and Ecology, University of Washington.

Guest, A. M. (1977a). "Ecololigcal succession in the Puget Sound region." Journal of Urban History 3 (February): 181-210.

Guest, A. M. (1977b). "Employment and suburban residential character." Unpublished paper, Center for Studies in Demography and Ecology, University of Washington.

Guest, A. M. (1977c). "The functional re-organization of the metropolis." Pacific Sociological Review. 20 (October): 553-567.

Guest, A. M. (1977d). "The growth of black suburbs:1950-1970." Unpublished paper, Center for Studies in Demography and Ecology, University of Washington.

Guest, A. M. (1976a). "Nighttime and daytime populations of large American suburbs." Urban Affairs Quarterly 12 (July):57-82.

Guest, A. M. (1976b). "Occupation and the journey to work." Social Forces 55 (September):166-181.

318

Guest, A. M. (1976c). "Residential segregation in urban areas." Pp. 268-336 in K. Schwirian (ed.), Contemporary Topics in Urban Sociology. Morristown, NJ.: General Learning Press.

Guest, A. M. (1976d). "The function and growth of U.S. suburbs." Unpublished paper, Center for Studies in Demography and Ecology, University of Washington.

Guest, A. M. (1976e). "The location of workplaces in metropolitan areas." Unpublished paper, Center for Studies in Demography and Ecology, University of Washington.

Guest, A. M. (1976f). "Workplace and residential suburbanization." Unpublished paper, Center for Studies in Demography and Ecology, University of Washington.

Guest, A. M. (1975a). "Population suburbanization in American metropolitan areas, 1940-1970." Geographical Analysis 7 (July):267-283.

Guest, A. M. (1975b). "The journey to work: 1960-1970." Social Forces 54 (September):220-225.

Guest, A. M. (1974). "Neighborhood life cycles and social status." Economic Geography 50 (July):228-243.

Guest, A. M. (1973). "Urban growth and population densities." Demography 10 (February):53-69.

Guest, A. M. (1972a). "Patterns of family location." Demography 9 (February):159-170.

Guest, A. M. (1972b). "Urban history, population densities and higher status residential location." Economic Geography 48 (October):375-387.

Guest, A. M. (1971). "Retesting the Burgess zonal hypothesis: the location of white collar workers." American Journal of Sociology 76 (May):1094-1108.

Guest, A. M. (1970). Families and Housing in Cities. Unpublished Ph.D. dissertation. University of Wisconsin, Madison.

Guest, A. M., and C. Cluett (1974). "Metropolitan retail nucleation." Demography 11 (August):493-507.

Guest, A. M., and G. H. Nelson (1978). "Central city-suburban status differences: fifty years of change. "Sociological Quarterly 19 (Winter):7-25.

Guest, A. M., and J. A. Weed (1976). "Ethnic residential segregation: patterns of change." American Journal of Sociology 81 (March):1088-1111.

Guterbock, T. (1976). "The push hypothesis: Minority presence, crime, and urban deconcentration." Pp. 137-161 in B. Schwartz (ed.), The Changing Face of the Suburbs. Chicago: University of Chicago Press.

Hall, P. (1966). Van Thunen's Isolated State. London: Pergamon.

Harris, C. D., and E. L. Ullman (1945). "The nature of cities." Annals of the American Academy of Political and Social Science 242 (November):7-17.

Hawley, A. H. (1972). "Population density and the city." Demography 9 (November):521-529.

Hawley, A. H. (1950). Human Ecology: A Theory of Community Structure. New York: Ronald.

Hechter, M. (1971). "Toward a theory of ethnic change." Politics and Society 2 (Fall):21-45.

Hoover, E. M., and R. Vernon (1962). Anatomy of a Metropolis. New York: Doubleday Anchor.

Hoyt, H. (1939). The Structure and Growth of Residential Neighborhoods in the United States. Washington, D.C.: Federal Housing Administration.

Hunter, A. (1973)."Introduction," in L. S. Cottrell, Jr., A. Hunter, and J. F. Short, Jr. (eds.), E.W. Burgess on Community, Family, and Delinquency. Chicago: University of Chicago Press.

Jackson, K. T. (1975). "Urban deconcentration in the nineteenth century," in L. F. Schnore (ed.), The New Urban History. Princeton University Press.

Kasarda, J. D. (1972). "The theory of ecological expansion." Social Forces 51 (December):165-175.

Kaufman, I. R., and L. F. Schnore (1975). "Municipal annexations and suburbanization, 1960-1970." Center for Demography and Ecology Working Paper 75-4. Madison: University of Wisconsin.

Lawson, S. (1971). "Seven days in June: the great housing debate." City 5 (January):17-25.

Lieberson, S. (1963). Ethnic Patterns in American Cities. New York: Free Press.

Logan, J. R. (1976). "Industrialization and the stratification of cities in suburban regions." American Journal of Sociology 82 (September):333-348.

Long, L. H., and P. C. Glick (1976). "Family patterns in suburban areas: Recent trends," pp. 39-67 in Barry Schwartz (ed.), The Changing Face of the Suburbs. Chicago: University of Chicago Press.

McKenzie, R. D. (1933). The Metropolitan Community. New York: McGraw-Hill.

McKenzie, R. D. (1929). "Ecological succession in the Puget Sound region." Publications of the American Sociological Society: 60-80.

McKenzie, R. D. (1925). "The ecological approach to the study of the human community." Pp. 63-79 in R. E. Park, E. W. Burgess and R. D. McKenzie (eds.), The City. Chicago: University of Chicago Press.

Manners, G. (1974). "The office in metropolis: An opportunity for shaping metropolitan America." Economic Geography 50 (April):93-110.

Michelson, W. (1977). Environmental Choice, Human Behavior and Residential Satisfaction. New York: Oxford University Press.

Mills, E. S. (1972). Studies in the Structure of the Urban Economy. Baltimore: Johns Hopkins University Press.

Morrison, P. A. and J. P. Wheeler (1976). "Rural Renaissance in America?" Population Bulletin 31 (October):3-26.

Neutze, M.(1968). The Suburban Apartment Boom. Baltimore: Johns Hopkins University Press.

Olsen, R. A. and A. M. Guest (1977). "Migration and city-suburb status differences." Urban Affairs Quarterly 12 (June):523-532.

Pappenfort, D. M. (1959). "The ecological field and the metropolitan community: Manufacturing and management." American Journal of Sociology 64 (January):380-385.

Park, R. E. (1967). "The urban community as a spatial pattern and a moral order." Pp. 55-68 in R. H. Turner (ed.), Robert E. Park on Social Control and Collective Behavior. Chicago: University of Chicago Press.

Peirce, N. (1977). "Suburbs may be slums of future." Seattle Post-Intelligencer, July 18, p. 83.

Quinn, J. A. (1940). "The Burgess zonal hypothesis and its critics." American Sociological Review 5 (April):210-218.

Rossi, P. (1955). Why Families Move. New York: Free Press.

Sale, R. (1976). Seattle: Past and Present. Seattle: University of Washington Press.

Schmitt, R. C. (1956). "Suburbanization: statistical fallacy?" Land Economics 32 (February):85-87.

Schnore, L. F. (1965a). "On the spatial structure of cities in the two Americas." Pp. 347-398 in P.M. Hauser and L. F. Schnore (eds.), The Study of Urbanization. New York: Wiley.

Schnore, L. F. (1965b). The Urban Scene. New York: Free Press.

Schnore, L. F. and H. H. Winsborough (1972). "Functional classification and the residential location of social classes." Pp. 124-151 in B. J. L. Berry (ed.), City Classification Handbook: Methods and Applications. New York: Wiley.

Simmons, J. W. (1968). "Changing residence in the city: a review of intra-urban mobility." The Geographical Review 58 (October):622-651.

Sorensen, A., K. E. Taeuber, and L. Hollingsworth, Jr. (1975). "Indexes of racial residential segregation for 109 cities in the United States, 1940 to 1970." Sociological Focus 8 (April):125-142.

Speare, A. Jr., S. Goldstein, and W. H. Frey (1974). Residential Mobility, Migration, and Metropolitan Change. Cambridge MA.: Ballinger.

Stegman, M. (1969). "Accessibility models and residential location." Journal of the American Institute of Planners 55 (January):22-29.

Stein, M. (1960). The Eclipse of Community. New York: Harper Torchbooks.

Strauss, A. L. (1961). Images of the American City. New York: Free Press.

Taeuber, K. E., and A. F. Taeuber (1969). Negroes in Cities. New York: Atheneum.

Taylor, G. R. (1915). Satellite Cities: A Study of Industrial Suburbs. New York: Appleton.

Tobin, G. A. (1976). "Suburbanization and the development of motor transportation: transportation technology and the suburbanization process." Pp. 95-111 in B. Schwartz (ed.), The Changing Face of the Suburbs. Chicago: University of Chicago Press.

U.S. Bureau of the Census (1975) Current Population Reports, Series P-23, No. 55. Social and Economic Characteristics of the Metropolitan and Non-Metropolitan Population: 1974 and 1970. Washington: Government Printing Office.

U.S. Bureau of the Census (1971) U.S. Census of Population: 1970. Number of Inhabitants, Final Report PC(1)-A1. United States Summary. Washington: Government Printing Office.

Van Valey, T. L., W. C. Roof, and J. E. Wilcox (1977) "Trends in residential segregation: 1960-1970." American Journal of Sociology 82 (January):826-844.

Ward, D. (1971) Cities and Immigrants. New York: Oxford University Press.

Warner, S. B. (1972) The Urban Wilderness: A History of the American City. New York: Harper and Row.

Warner, S. B.(1962) Streetcar Suburbs. Cambridge: Harvard University Press.

Wilson, F. D. (1975) "The organizational components of expanding metropolitan systems." Working Paper 75-20. Madison: Center for Demography and Ecology, University of Wisconsin.

Winsborough, H. H. (1963) "An ecological approach to the theory of suburbanization." American Journal of Sociology 68 (March):565-570.

Yeates, M. (1965) "Some factors affecting the spatial distribution of Chicago land values." Economic Geography 41 (January):57-70.

Zimmer, B. G. (1975) "The urban centrifugal drift." Pp. 23-91 in A. Hawley and V. P. Rock (eds.), Metropolitan America in Contemporary Perspective. New York: Halsted.

Zimmer, B. G. (1964) Rebuilding Cities: The Effects of Displacement ·and Relocation on Small Business. Chicago: Quadrangle.

# 8
# Regional Ecology:
# A Macroscopic Analysis
# of Sustenance Organization

*Dudley L. Poston, Jr.*

## I. WHAT IS REGIONAL ECOLOGY?

This chapter is a position paper in the area of regional
ecology. It identifies the principal themes characterizing
this literature since 1950, and summarizes the basic
research contributions. Before embarking on these discussions, however, we will first set forth our understanding
of the scope and meaning of regional ecology.

1. *What is human ecology?* Otis Dudley Duncan once
wrote that a major difficulty in discussing the perspective
of human ecology is that "even a provisional statement of
(its) concerns will doubtless encounter strong objections
from one or another group of scientists and thinkers who
regard their studies of man as exemplifying the ecological
viewpoint" (1959:679). Even among sociologists and demographers, human ecology has different meanings. To some, it
involves the techniques for the study of spatial distributions through maps and related kinds of descriptions; to
others, ecological studies are analyses of any kinds of
phenomena in which the units of analysis are spatial rather
than individual entities (for example, factorial ecology);
to still others, ecological studies are "descriptions of the
physical features of specific natural areas along with the
social, economic, and demographic characteristics of their
inhabitants" (Kasarda, 1973:6). Examples of this genre range
from Zorbaugh's *The Gold Coast and the Slum* (1929),
Suttles' *The Social Order of the Slum* (1968) and *The*

323

*Social Construction of Communities* (1972). (Although this third description and examples are taken from Kasarda, [1973] this does not represent his conceptualization of human ecology.)

The above are only a few examples of studies and approaches considered by some to be illustrative of human ecology. And there are many others drawn from the social and natural sciences which could have been introduced, but have not because of space limitations (see Duncan, 1959:678-681). Many of these would tend to buttress Duncan's observation that "the term 'ecology' is sometimes applied rather casually--even irresponsibly. [Frequently,] studies adopting the label bear only a tenuous relationship to any systematic, scientific conception of the field" (1959:680).

In this chapter ecology is seen as a field of study grounded in four major (referential) constructs: population, organization, environment, and technology. The principal unit of analysis is a human population, circumscribed more or less in a territorial fashion. Major assumptions of human ecology are that human populations have unit character and integrity; and that properties and attributes of these populations do not necessarily involve the mere summation of their component parts. (See, in particular, Duncan, 1959.)

Human ecology may be characterized by its concern with the organizational aspects of human populations arising from their sustenance-producing activities. These activities are necessary for the collective existence of the populations and must be adapted to the changing conditions which confront them. Included here are an ever-changing and mediating environment, the technological repertoire at their disposal, and the size, composition and distribution of the populations themselves (see Duncan, 1959:678-684; Frisbie and Poston, 1978b, Chapter 2:13-14).

The major focus for human ecologists is the human population and its organizational forms, structures, attributes and characteristics deriving from its sustenance-producing activities. The conceptual and empirical literature to be highlighted in later sections of this chapter are in some way or another concerned with the determinants (and/or consequences) of the various configurations and characteristics of the sustenance organizations of human populations. This focus on sustenance organization is well within the mainstream of the major theoretical treatments of Hawley (1950, 1968), Duncan (1959, 1964), and Gibbs and Martin (1959).

2. *Is regional ecology "regional"?: The orientation and approaches of regional ecology.* Having dealt with the orientation and perspective of human ecology, attention is directed here to a consideration of regional ecology. In this chapter regional ecology refers to ecological investigations of regions, particularly the subareas of national populations. The topic may be distinguished from other kinds of ecological studies in which there is less (or greater) aggregation of the units of analysis. Rather than engaging in ecological studies of countries or neighborhoods, or other intra-urban population groupings such as census tracts or city blocks, for example, regional ecology studies the populations of a congeries of regions (i.e., the subareas of a national population), of which each has a specific location in physical space. Conceived in this manner, regional ecology has definite affinities with the study of population distribution, particularly as delimited by Bogue (1959).

Given the territory of a national population, "there is an infinite variety of ways in which it may be carved into subareas" or regions (Bogue, 1959:393) for the regional ecologist to study. Ecologists, demographers and geographers often delimit their universe of inquiry according to one or another of two criteria: homogeneity or nodality. Those adhering to the first criterion maintain that for maximum utility for scientific analysis, regions "should be of maximum internal homogeneity because data collected for homogeneous areas show a greater range of variation for phenomena and for factors selected as explanatory variables. Moreover each set of observations... tend(s) to be confounded with fewer other variables" (Bogue, 1959:393).

Those adhering to the second criterion for delimiting the universe of inquiry maintain that "modern economies [or ecological systems, in the sense of this paper] are highly organized divisions of labor, in which particular territories orient their activities toward nodal centers—in most cases, large metropolitan centers" (Bogue, 1959:394). The unit of analysis is the metropolitan area and its surrounding nonmetropolitan hinterland. Hinterlands are included with the metropolitan area depending upon the extent to which they are functionally interrelated with the metropolitan area regarding the flow of goods, services and related sustenance items and activities. Bogue notes that "internally, nodal regions are marked by diversity of characteristics rather than by homogeneity... Seemingly, one function of such nodes is to articulate and integrate the special needs of adjoining areas that are unlike each other" (1959:394). This particular way of thinking about regions

is, by the way, not at all at variance with the recommendations of the geographer Dickinson in his book *Regional
Ecology: The Study of Man's Environment* (1970). (However,
Dickinson's orientation to ecology is at some variance with
that of Hawley, Duncan, Martin, Gibbs, Schnore, Micklin and
other theorists who have written on the ecological approach.)

This review of the major research contributions in regional ecology since 1950 departs in a couple of instances
from the above decision to study as regions only the subareas of national populations (be they homogeneous or
nodal). For example, some of the major ecological research
on the division of labor has employed countries and nation-
states as units. These are conceived of as homogeneous, but
are (obviously) not national subareas. However, were these
investigations not included here, discussions of major
findings and conclusions on the particular topic would be
incomplete. In most instances, though, this chapter is
restricted to ecological studies conducted among subareas of
national populations.

3. *An outline.* The next sections of this chapter
focus on ecological studies in homogeneous populations
according to the following themes: the division of labor
(Section II), differentiation by ascription (Section III),
organizational change and demographic response (Section IV),
and other studies (Section V). The following three sections
on ecological studies of nodal populations are next addressed: the node and its immediate hinterland (Section VI),
systems of "cities" (or nodes) (Section VII), and studies of
single sustenance functions (Section VIII).

## II. HOMOGENEOUS POPULATIONS: THE DIVISION OF LABOR

One major theme in the human ecological literature since
1950 is the division of labor. Indeed until very recently,
the majority of work on ecological organization in homogeneous populations has concentrated on the division of
labor. There was good reason for such concentration of
interest, and the initial part of this section discusses its
rationale. In a later part, the major conceptual and
empirical research on the division of labor is reviewed and
analytical distinctions made.

1. *The division of labor and the Durkheimian legacy.*
The bulk of the work published since 1950 on ecological
organization in homogeneous populations has dealt primarily
with the division of labor. However, there is little in the
theoretical treatments of ecological organization which
would dictate such a concentration of attention. Hawley, for
example, notes that ecological organization "is the broad

and general term used to refer to the complex of functional interrelationships by which men live" (1950:178). Duncan observes that "the significant assumptions about organization [for the ecologist] are that it arises from sustenance producing activities, is a property of the population aggregate, is indispensable to the maintenance of collective life, and must be adapted to the conditions confronting a population—including the character of the environment, the size and composition of the population itself, and the repertory of techniques at its command" (1959: 682-683).

Despite these rather broad observations, most ecological inquiries concerned with the characteristics or attributes of sustenance organization in homogeneous populations have focused on the division of labor. While it is true that the division of labor, especially as discussed by Durkheim in Part II of his *Division of Labor in Society* (1893), involves two important attributes of sustenance organization—sustenance differentiation and functional interdependence—these are only two of a number of attributes which characterize sustenance organization. Why then the almost sole focus by ecologists since 1950 on the division of labor?

The full answer may never be known, and only some of the reasons which may be important for an understanding of this kind of concentration will be discussed here. If we place ourselves back in the early 1950s, human ecology as a field of study had barely survived more than a decade-and-a-half, or so, of rather scathing critiques of its concepts, generalizations, methodology and data. With the publication of Hawley's *Human Ecology* in 1950, the macro-sociological and morphological aspects of its approach were underlined. The discipline of sociology, however, had turned now in another direction. Kasarda has observed that "a perusal of the sociological literature... indicates that it was [during this period] that refined scaling and other psychometric techniques were having a substantial impact on social research; Bales and his colleagues were making their significant contributions on interpersonal dynamics of small groups, and even... Parsons had drifted into psychoanalytic and personality studies" (1973:17). What an inauspicious time for human ecology to attempt a re-entry into the sociological arena!

There was thus a real need to justify the entertainment of human ecological questions by sociologists. A series of apologetics were hence written in the late 1950s and early 1960s, principally by Duncan and Schnore (Schnore, 1958; 1961a; Duncan, 1961; Duncan and Schnore, 1959; Schnore and

Duncan, n.d.), intending to justify human ecology as a viable and honorable sociological specialization. These papers were powerfully written and argued, all leading to the statement that human ecology's concern for understanding the morphology of collective life is in the mainstream of the sociological enterprise. Indeed Schnore ended one of his essays by asking, "If human ecology is 'marginal' to sociology, what is central?" (1961a:139).

One of the major statements in this apologetic literature was Schnore's "Social Morphology and Human Ecology" (1958), in which he drew a number of parallels between Durkheim's morphological thinking and the structural concepts and perspective of contemporary human ecology. Durkheim's *Division of Labor,* he argued, was squarely within the ecological tradition, even though "Emile Durkheim, of course, was not himself a human ecologist" (1958:620). But here nevertheless was an essay in which it was compellingly demonstrated that a major publication of one of the two or three founding fathers and principal theorists in sociology focused on important elements or characteristics of ecological organization. What better way for sociologists to justify the study of ecological organization than to concentrate attention solely on those organizational attributes of the division of labor elucidated by Durkheim? This kind of concentration carried through the 1960s, and even into the early 1970s, in ecological analyses of organization in homogeneous populations.

2. *The conceptual and empirical literature on the division of labor.* The division of labor refers to differences among member of a population in their sustenance activities, i.e., specialization. It also refers to the exchange of goods and services among the same population members in their sustenance activities. Substantial, or even modest, amounts of exchange would appear to require a like amount of differentiation since population members can hardly produce a sufficient enough surplus to exchange with others without specializing in some type of sustenance activity (Gibbs and Poston, 1975:469; Lampard, 1955:86-92). Functional interdependence between, and differentiation of, sustenance activities are the principal considerations in the conceptualization of the division of labor.

The above thinking is fully congruent with Durkheim's discussions in *Division of Labor in Society* (1893). His principal concern was with the nature of social cohesion in complex societies, and a key element in its development was the division of labor. He was particularly interested in elucidating the conditions under which the division of labor is advanced in complex societies, and frequently employed the term globally. He never did present a concise and conceptually unencumbered definition of the division of labor. It is clear, however, that when he used the term he had in mind both the degree of differentiation in the sustenance functions of the society, as well as the intricate system of interdependence of the sustenance functions engendered principally through exchange. For that matter, he insisted that both features of the concept be utilized when he argued against Spencer's claim that differentiation alone leads to the division of labor. He noted that differentiation in the broad sense is a necessary but not a sufficient condition for the emergence of the division of labor since it must occur along with organization and interdependence. He wrote, "if these differences make possible the division of labor, they do not necessitate it. Because they are given, it does not follow that they are utilized" (1893 [1949]:265). (See Frisbie and Poston, 1978b: chapter 5.)

While most ecologists would not argue with a definition of the division of labor involving differentiation and functional interdependence, most empirical investigations of this concept among homogeneous populations have focused only on the differentiation dimension. Since adequate and comparable data are often not available on the volume of goods and services exchanged among and between the sustenance activities in a population, researchers often operationalize only the differentiation dimension assuming that it varies together with the interdependence dimension (Browning and Gibbs, 1971:234).

A related issue deals with the meaning of the differentiation dimension. Sustenance differentiation refers to the number of sustenance activities in a population (i.e., structural differentiation), and the uniformity of the distribution of the members of the population across the sustenance activities (i.e., distributive differentiation). Minimum structural differentiation obtains in a population if there is only one sustenance-producing activity. The greater the number of sustenance activities, the greater the structural differentiation. Low distributive differentiation is present in a population when most of its members are located in one sustenance activity, and a small number in each of the other activities. Maximum distributive differentiation obtains when each sustenance activity has the same number of persons, that is, the members are distributed evenly in the sustenance activities of the population (see Gibbs and Poston, 1975:470-471). Measures have been developed which attempt to specify one and both of these features of sustenance differentiation (Gibbs and Poston, 1975: esp. 471-474).

Ecologists have devoted significant amounts of time and attention to investigations of the determinants (and consequences) of the sustenance differentiation dimension of the division of labor. In the review to follow principal attention is given to those analyses focusing on its determinants.

A paper by Gibbs and Martin in 1958 is an introduction to this literature. They were concerned principally with evaluating the proposition that among large homogeneous populations (countries of the world prior to World War II), a direct relationship exists between the degree of urbanization and the "extent of the dispersion of its objects of consumption" (1958:270). They anticipated that countries consuming a great diversity of objects that are widely dispersed internally and internationally will have a large proportion of their populations living in cities. Both of these variables, they hasten to add, deal with the way populations have organized themselves to obtain a volume and diversity of sustenance. They found support for the expectation that variation in dispersion of objects of consumption is related with variation among countries in the extent of urbanization and metropolitanization (1958:270,276). (There is a companion paper by Martin [1962] testing with more recent data the dispersion-urbanization relationship.)

Implicit in the above paper (1958) is the realization that the degree of both technology and the division of labor underlies the relationship between urbanization and dispersion of objects of consumption. Gibbs and Martin thus wrote in 1962 that "it is only through the division of labor and an advanced technology that a population is able to bring material from great distances. It is in this particular connection that the relationship between urbanization and the spatial dispersion of objects of consumption can best be understood. For if large-scale urbanization requires that materials be brought from great distances, and if a high degree of division of labor and technological development are necessary for this, then the level of urbanization is contingent, at least in part, on the division of labor and technology" (1962:668). This thinking was tested with circa-1950 data across 41 countries of the world with considerable success. There was limited discussion of these findings a year later (Mehta, 1963:609-614; see also Gibbs and Martin, 1963:614-616), but for the most part the findings withstood the critical review.

A year later, the essentially processual reasoning of the above paper was tested with longitudinal data for the United States from 1900 to 1950. On the whole, the results were congruent with those of the earlier investigations at the international level (Labovitz and Gibbs, 1964:3-9).

Further work extended the above studies by introducing additional elements into the theoretical reasoning about the emergence of a complex division of labor. Gibbs and Browning found in 1966 that among selected countries in North and South America in the circa-1950 time period, the size of productive associations varied directly with two forms of the division of labor (among industries, and among occupations within industries). The division of labor variables were found to be more closely related "to indicators of technological efficiency than to estimated size of productive associations.[The authors concluded that this]"...differential relation suggests that large productive associations may only permit a high degree of division of labor; whether or not a high degree is realized depends upon technological efficiency" (1966:92). Seeking a further clarification of the relationship between size and the division of labor, Browning and Gibbs (1971) investigated the association between relative size of industry and intra-industry division of labor, and the results were mixed. They reasoned that "the relative size of an industry furthers the division of labor only insofar as the industry's labor force is territorially concentrated" (1971:244). Additional data were brought to bear on this hypothesis and the findings were generally as predicted.

Clemente and Sturgis (1972) continued this interest in the determinants of the division of labor by examining directly the extent to which population size, physical density, social density, and community age determine the degree of the division of labor. They developed hypotheses for each of these independent variables on the dependent variable drawing exclusively on Durkheim's observations. The hypotheses were examined in a sample of 600 urban places in circa-1960, and when holding constant the effects of the other variables, size, density (physical) and age were not found to be significantly associated with the division of labor. Only social density was reported to have an independent and significant effect on the dependent variable. According to Durkheim's reasoning and priorities, the social density variable should be the major determinant. The Clemente and Sturgis analysis at the very least provides support for this particular observation.

There are other ecological studies of the division of labor in homogeneous populations (Clemente and Sturgis, 1971; Webb, 1972; Miley and Micklin, 1972; Gibbs, 1974; Sly, 1972; Sly and Tayman, 1977; Frisbie and Poston, 1978a; 1978b: Chapter 5), but in most of these papers the division of labor is analyzed as influencing a host of dependent variables such as crime, suicide, and migration. Each of these analyses makes an important contribution to the general literature on the division of labor, but does not add directly to knowledge of its determinants. Further, the last four papers listed are discussed in a later section of this chapter under the heading "Organizational Change and Demographic Response."

### III. HOMOGENEOUS POPULATIONS: DIFFERENTIATION BY ASCRIBED STATUSES

Another research theme in the human ecological literature dealing with homogeneous populations asks: how do human populations use their members in sustenance activities? This section reviews some of the descriptive and analytical studies on this topic.

The extent to which human population differentiate by race and sex (and by age) in the allocation of their members to one sustenance activity or another has long been a topic of interest for ecologists. Hawley discusses these concerns in the first part of chapter 11 of *Human Ecology* on "Differentiation and Organization" (1950), and Durkheim's *Division of Labor in Society* (1893) also gives attention to this question. In the society based on mechanical solidarity, persons are very much "like" one another and, hence, the only differentiation is one based on sex and age. Many anthropologists and other social scientists have investigated differentiation by sex and age (and to some extent race) in the sustenance activities of primitive populations. The analyses of Brown (1970), Watson (1929), Schienfeld (1944), Herskovitz (1965), Holter (1970), North (1926) are of particular interest.

The utilization in sustenance activities of males and females, majority and minority race/ethnic group members, and the young and the old, has also been studied to some degree in the developed countries, particularly in the U.S., by human ecologists and other social scientists. Much of this literature is descriptive (Turner, 1951; Glenn, 1964; Gibbs, 1965; Gross, 1968; Price, 1968; Johansen, 1970; Johnson, 1972; Martin and Poston, 1972; Williams, 1972, 1976). Analyses have been conducted, however, where the variability in these forms of race (or sex, or age) differentiation is examined with ecological models, and they are discussed later.

Regarding the measurement of the phenomenon, most studies of differentiation by sex, race, or age, have relied on the index of dissimilarity (Duncan and Duncan, 1955; Taeuber and Taeuber, 1965; Cortese, et al., 1976). The studies generally report that sexual differentiation has experienced a modest decline in the U.S. since 1900 (Williams, 1976; see Gross, 1968, for another conclusion).

Moreover, measures of occupational differentiation by sex among SMSAs in the United States are related only on a very modest level with measures of occupational differentiation by race, suggesting that strategies for allocating sustenance roles to one ascribed status are not necessarily the same as the strategies for another. Some ecological communities show high differentiation by sex and by race, others show low differentiation by sex and high by race, while still others show low differentiation by both sex and race (Martin and Poston, 1972). Also, considerable variability exists among the metropolitan areas of the U.S. in 1960 in the extent to which they differentially allocate professional occupational positions to males and females (Johnson, 1972). And a similar observation has been made for variability in occupational differentiation by race among the states of the United States (Gibbs, 1965).

There are at least three explicitly ecological studies of occupational differentiation by sex and by race. One analysis attempted to account for variability in the degree of professional differentiation between males and females in the SMSAs of Arkansas, Louisiana, Oklahoma, and Texas (the West South Central division of the U.S.) in 1960. Variables measuring efficiency of sustenance organization and its size, level of living, and related items of ecological interest, collectively explained nearly 70 percent of the variation in differentiation (Poston and Johnson, 1971). Another investigation set out an ecological model of industrialization to account for occupational differentiation by race and occupational differentiation by sex in the 66 largest SMSAs of the United States in 1960. Even though differentiation by sex among these areas was not related at any other than a modest level with differentiation by race (see the preceding paragraph), the ecological model nevertheless accounted for over fifty percent of the variation in occupational differentiation by color, and more than forty percent of the variation in race (Martin and Poston, 1976:92).

A third study sought to explain the variation in professional differentiation by sex in the SMSAs of the United States in 1960 and 1970 by introducing as predictors four components of sustenance organization: wholesaling, retailing, manufacturing, and services. Together these four components accounted for nearly forty percent of the criterion variable in both 1960 and 1970 (Johnson, 1977).

All of these studies suggest the viability of ecological approaches to the analysis of racial and sexual differentiation in human populations. They also illustrate how differentiation variables may be conceptualized within the broader panorama of sustenance organization. In this brief review, we have not discussed the extensive literature on residential differentiation by race and the ecological models generated to account for its variation. Although patterns of residential differentiation or segregation may well be related to occupational differentiation (by race) (see Bahr and Gibbs, 1967; Roof and VanValey, 1972), these patterns are conceptually distinct from those dealing with the allocation of sustenance positions to the races.

## IV. HOMOGENEOUS POPULATIONS:
### ORGANIZATIONAL CHANGE AND DEMOGRAPHIC RESPONSE

Another principal research theme in the human ecological literature on homogeneous populations since 1950 is the relationship between changes in sustenance organization and the demographic processes. This interest is based on the fundamental tenet of human ecology that a population will tend to redistribute itself through the vital processes of fertility and mortality, as well as through migration, to achieve a balance or equilibrium between its size and life chances (Hawley, 1968:331). Duncan (1959:708) has emphasized the important ecological connections between organization and population size and this topic has long been of interest for ecologists. According to Hawley (1950), human populations will adjust their size through any of the demographic processes in order to maintain an equilibrium with their sustenance organization. Put another way, "demographic structure contains the possibilities and sets the limits of organized group life" (Hawley, 1950:78).

In this section of the paper, studies which focus on the relationship of organizational change and demographic responses occurring through migration, as well as overall population change, will be examined. In a second part, those concentrating on fertility, as well as overall vital change, will be presented.

1. *Organizational change and migration change (and overall population change)*. Before reviewing the major analyses focusing on sustenance organization change and migration, the basic thinking underlying this particular

relationship will be outlined. By pointing to the theoretical antecedents (drawn largely from Hawley, [1950], although the particular paragraphs which follow are also taken from statements in Poston and White, [1978]), we should be in a better position to evaluate the empirical investigations which follow. Finally, although the main focus here is on migration as a demographic response, some of the empirical studies evaluated later concentrate on overall demographic change. Since these demographic changes are investigated within the context of homogeneous populations which are largely nonmetropolitan, much of the demographic change is due to migration.

From the perspective of human ecology migration is the principal measure and mechanism of social change and adaptability for human populations. A basic premise is that a balance is maintained between a population's size and the resource base from which its sustenance is drawn. The level at which a population survives is a function of this balance, that is "...the ratio of numbers to the opportunities for living" (Hawley, 1950, p. 149).

One thus arrives at the proposition that there is a reciprocal relationship between population size and organization for sustenance which operates through the influence of each on a population's level of living. Therefore, treating population size as dependent and sustenance organization as independent, one can hypothesize that change in sustenance organization, to the extent that it produces change in the opportunities for living, will necessitate a change in population size. Insofar as migration becomes the agent for effecting the change in population size, it may be viewed as a demographic response attempting to preserve or attain the best possible living standard by re-establishing the balance between population size and organization.

The hypothesis usually investigated in ecological studies such as those cited below is that variation among populations in levels of net migration is a function of differentials in sustenance organization. As particular sustenance functions in a population expand, new positions (or niches) are created; these may be thought of as job opportunities. Conversely, the diminution of certain sustenance functions results in a contraction of the number of niches and, hence, a reduction generally in the opportunities for employment. The net result of these two developments, unless the effects of one cancel out the effects of the other, is a disturbance in the established equilibrium between population size and opportunities for living. Net migration is hence viewed as a population response, or a method of returning to the original condition of balance. Hawley's views are particularly instructive:

Readjustments to disequilibrium are effected primarily... through mobility. Population tends to distribute itself in relation to job opportunities, evacuating areas of diminishing opportunities and gravitating to areas of increasing opportunities (1950:167-168).

One of the initial tests of the relationship between organizational change and migration was Sly's study of southern Black migration from the "old cotton belt" a group of some 253 counties (with at least 25,000 acres in cotton as reported in the 1890 census) stretching in a belt from South Carolina to Texas. These migration patterns were hypothesized as responses to changes in organization, as well as in technology and environment. Sly writes:

Every population must adapt to its environment; and we assume that adaption is mediated through the population's organization and technology. The environment contains site and situation factors, both of which influence the population's sustenance organization. Site factors limit the sustenance organization because they dictate a population's activities. Furthermore, [the degree of]...land cultivation influences the size of the population which can be supported. Now assume some new technological breakthrough makes raw material available from another population; this time, however, the environment factor is a situation factor ... A larger sustenance organization...[becomes possible hence allowing] the support of a larger population. ... An imbalance exists [and] the population can alter itself through a demographic component of change--that is, a demographic response. (1972: 617-618).

This general reasoning was tested with data on Southern negro migration for the decades 1940-1950 and 1950-1960, and for the most part, support was adduced for the ecological model. In particular, Sly found that migration change during the decade could be viewed as a direct "demographic response to differences in sustenance organization" (1972:615), and furthermore, that ecological organization could be seen as mediating the effects of technology and environment on migration behavior.

Frisbie and Poston (1975) expanded upon these results by noting that while there may be an overall relationship between sustenance organization and demographic behavior, the relation will differ depending upon the particular kind of sustenance activity examined. They thus specified eight different components of sustenance organization for the non-metropolitan counties of the U.S. in the circa-1960 time period (general agriculture, commercial agriculture, manufacturing, minerals, wholesale services, retail services, educational services, and public administration services) and hypothesized that these would be related with population change in the counties between 1960 and 1970 in the following ways: "areas heavily dependent upon primary industry such as mining or agriculture (with the possible exception of large-scale agriculture) are likely to be population-decline areas; areas where services constitute the most significant form of sustenance activity are likely to be characterized by growing populations; areas dependent on transformation industry are expected to be intermediate in terms of growth potential" (1975:776). In general these hypotheses were upheld, and moreover, when the components were taken together, they accounted for nearly a quarter of the total variation in population change in the counties under investigation. Finally, this ecological interpretation of population change exceeded by several orders of magnitude the explanatory power of a number of alternative predictors.

In a follow-up analysis (1976), Frisbie and Poston were again concerned with the relation between sustenance organization and population growth and decline in nonmetropolitan America and hypothesized that the sustenance organizations of areas experiencing population growth in the 1960's should be more complex (i.e., be characterized by more sustenance functions) than those experiencing population loss. For the two types of population-change areas, principal components factor analyses with iteration and orthogonal rotation were executed. The sustenance configurations for the growing counties were found to be more complex than the structures for the losing counties.

They turned in another investigation to the relationship between sustenance organization components and sustenance differentiation, and migration behavior between 1960 and 1970 in the nonmetropolitan counties of the U.S. (Frisbie and Poston, 1978b). Drawing on the theoretical and empirical literature of human ecology, they hypothesized inverse relationships between relative net migration and sustenance components based on extractive functions including (1) small-scale agriculture, (2) land extensive agriculture, and (3) mineral industry. They predicted that positive associations would obtain between migration and (4) large-scale commercial agriculture and (5) land intensive agriculture.

They expected that counties dependent upon (6) transformation (i.e., manufacturing) industry would tend to show
growth through net migration. They further hypothesized that
positive relations would obtain between migration and each
of three types of service functions: (7) retail, (8) education, and (9) public administrative. An inverse relation was
predicted with regard to (10) wholesale services. With only
two exceptions, each of these hypotheses found support in
the data, and the sustenance organization components were
also shown to account for a substantial portion of the overall variation in net migration change. Finally, it was predicted, and demonstrated, that sustenance differentiation
would be directly related to migration change, as well as
show an effect independent of the effects of the ten components of sustenance organization (Frisbie and Poston,
1978b:61-64).

In another analysis, Frisbie and Poston (1978a) directly
addressed the relationship between the sustenance differentiation dimension of the division of labor and net migration
change in the nonmetropolitan counties of the U.S. As hypothesized, a positive relationship was reported between differentiation and migration, and moreover, the relationship
withstood the competition of alternative variables usually
employed as predictors of migration.

In reviewing these studies of sustenance organization
and migration change (and overall population change), it has
been suggested by Poston and White (1978) that an influential mediator of this relationship may have been overlooked:
the potential supply of labor already present in the population (or, the indigeneous labor force supply--see Pursell,
1972; Bradshaw, 1976; and Bowles, 1976, for earlier uses of
this concept). During a given period of time, they asserted,
younger age cohorts attain the usual age of labor force
entry, and older cohorts are removed from the labor force
through retirement (and death). It was hypothesized that the
sum of these positive and negative components should influence the degree of relationship between sustenance
organization and migration. It turns out that the indigenous
labor force supply variable does indeed have an effect on
migration independent of the other organization predictors,
and increases the overall amount of explained variation in
migration by nearly ten percentage points.

Another paper dealing with ecological approaches to
migration, particularly the impact of changes in sustenance
organization, is that of Sly and Tayman (1977) in which they
examined the migration patterns of all central cities of
SMSAs with at least thirty percent of their jobs in manufacturing; there are 90 such cities, 77 of which are located
in the industrialized northeast and northcentral states.

They found that the demographic responses of these populations through migration are not always a direct result of changes in sustenance organization. Environmental factors appear to be somewhat more influential than sustenance organization factors in determining whether a city will increase or decrease its population through migration (Sly and Tayman, 1977).

One should be cautious, however, before generalizing from this study of high-manufacturing cities to all cities. The fact that the authors demonstrated the primacy of environmental factors over sustenance organizational factors in accounting for migration change, does not necessarily mean that this finding applies to all cities. It is at least plausible to speculate that a reason for the failure of the sustenance variables to be uppermost in accounting for migration behavior in these manufacturing cities is the very fact that the units of analysis are characterized essentially by only one dominant sustenance function, viz., manufacturing. The full range of variation in sustenance organization components was excluded owing to the constraints imposed by the authors on the sample (see Eberstein, 1977).

The above studies, published since 1972, have empirically assessed the extent to which human populations adjust their size, through migration, to changes in sustenance organization, and to a more limited extent, to changes in technology, and in the physical and social environment. Although there are important differences among these various studies regarding the types of populations analyzed, the operationalization of some of the variables, and the particular focus of the dependent variable (migration versus overall population change), all demonstrate the viability of an ecological approach to the study of these types of demographic behavior. The focus on these particular studies has been selective. There are numerous analyses of demographic and migration change in which the phenomenon is implicitly conceptualized as responding to changes in ecological and economic organization (Gibbs, 1964; Fuguitt and Deeley, 1966; Stinner and DeJong, 1969; Kirschenbaum, 1971; Tarver, 1972; Brown, 1975; Beale, 1975; Fuguitt and Beale, 1976; and Wardwell, 1977, are representative examples of other studies of this genre). We turn now to the major findings in ecological research on homogeneous populations dealing with the relation between organizational change and fertility change (and vital change).

2. *Organizational change and fertility change (and vital change)*. Absent from most human ecological studies of demographic behavior are investigations focusing on

fertility change (or, more generally, vital change.) Most investigations of fertility behavior are conducted at the micro-level and are concerned with understanding the reasons why *persons* prefer, desire and have varying numbers of children. Important and convincing explanations have been developed (for incisive reviews of this impressive literature, see Hawthorne [1970] and Freedman [1975]). With only a few exceptions, human ecologists have not paid much attention to explaining demographic change occurring through decreases (or increases) in fertility. It is felt here, however, that human ecology may provide a viable theoretical approach to the study of macro-level fertility behavior. In the paragraphs below an ecological approach to the analysis of fertility is outlined, and then the basic studies which follow (more or less) this approach are reviewed.

An ecological approach to the explanation of fertility behavior could focus on the sustenance organization of human populations and ascertain the extent to which differences in their organizational forms or structures are related to differences in their fertility behavior, *ceteris paribus*.

For example, one could focus on the degree of *complexity* of sustenance organization, that is, the ways the members of the population are used in sustenance-producing activities and the range and type of sustenance activities. (For another use of complexity, see the above discussion of Frisbie and Poston, 1976.) A complex sustenance organization would fully utilize the members of the population; ascriptive criteria, for example, would not be as influential as achievement-based criteria in both the assignment and retention of workers in the sustenance-producing activities of the population. Furthermore, a population with a complex sustenance organization would be involved in a wide array of sustenance-producing activities. The kinds of sustenance produced, i.e., the goods and services, would be many, and working members of the population would be distributed rather evenly among the sustenance functions. (Clearly, there are other characteristics of sustenance organization in addition to its complexity that one could analyze, *viz.* its components, its efficiency, its productivity, etc. See the discussion in Section IX of this chapter.)

One way of viewing the relationship between sustenance organization complexity and fertility involves thinking of fertility behavior as a means of increasing (or decreasing) the population in much the same way that migration behavior is employed. For example, the population's sustenance organization becomes more complex and new positions (or niches in an ecological sense) are created. The population must respond in a demographic manner, i.e., provide members to fill these niches, so that the original equilibrium between population size and organization (which has now been disturbed through expansion) may be once again maintained.

Fertility behavior, however, is not the most efficient demographic response because, for one reason, there is a time lag involved between the creation of new members and their ultimate employment in sustenance activities. Sly has noted, that in "the short run, migration appears to be the most efficient response. It can increase (or decrease) population more rapidly than can changing fertility and is more efficient in that it can be more selective... [For example], let us assume that a population's sustenance activity depends as a result of a new technological discovery. To fill these niches by increasing fertility would require many years" (Sly, 1972:618).

It is probably the case that sustenance organization complexity works with (or influences) fertility behavior in a different manner from that discussed. Rather than the two being related directly with each other, they are probably related inversely. In the first place, a high fertility pattern is dysfunctional for an increasingly complex sustenance organization, since so much of the sustenance produced must be consumed directly by the members of the population. High fertility should curtail the absolute amount of noncommitted sustenance controlled by the population, thereby limiting its flexibility for adapting to environmental, technological and other type of changes and fluctuations. Conversely, low fertility should be congruent with respect to the needs and requirements of an expansive sustenance organization. Substantially greater amounts of sustenance would be available for investment back into the system in a low fertility population in contrast to a population where fertility is high. Large quantities of sustenance normally consumed by the familial and educational institutions in a high fertility population would be accessible as mobile or fluid resources in a low fertility population. Sustenance organization in this latter instance would thereby have the investment resources available for increasing complexity, given the requisite changes in the environment and technological system. One could thus hypothesize generally an inverse relation between organizational complexity and fertility behavior. (This thinking is not all that different from some of the descriptive interpretations of the transformations which occurred in European demographic patterns during the 19th century. Indeed a portion of demographic transition "theory" accounts for the fertility reductions by calling upon the organizational changes assumed by the societies through industrialization and urbanization. See Teitelbaum, 1975, for a general statement.)

One of the first investigators to examine the relationship between changes in sustenance organization and fertility behavior was Gibbs (1959). While not following exactly the reasoning just outlined, Gibbs was interested in ascertaining whether populations avoid an increase in mortality by reducing their fertility when they are confronted with organizational changes resulting in substantial decreases in the amounts of sustenance usually available to them. He examined changes in the crude birth and death rates for 45 countries in the circa 1921-1937 time period (the years of the worldwide economic depression), and his expectations are generally supported in the data.

A more direct test of the relation between organizational change and fertility behavior is Kasarda's (1971) comparative analysis of nations in the four periods between 1930 and 1969. Reasoning that the level of fertility in a society should be associated with its type of sustenance organization, he investigated the degree to which female labor force participation in nonagricultural occupations, the number of unpaid family workers, and the degree of youth labor force participation served as intervening variables between the background variables of industrialization, urbanization and education, and fertility. His findings suggested generally that the intermediate variables were related with fertility (with the exception of unpaid family workers). More importantly, with respect to an ecological approach to fertility, Kasarda was able to show that the background factors operated through the intermediate variables on fertility (Kasarda, 1971:314).

Another study is that of Poston and Clarke (1976), in which the variation in the fertility rates of the largest SMSAs of the U.S. in 1970 was examined with variables tapping the degree of sustenance complexity of the areas. Hypotheses expecting inverse relationships between the measures of complexity and fertility behavior were supported.

## V. HOMOGENEOUS POPULATIONS:  OTHER STUDIES

There are numerous ecological investigations of homogeneous populations which do not array themselves according to any of the three general research themes addressed in the preceding sections. There are general attempts at elaborating and expanding the ecological frame of reference, and there are efforts at specifying empirically the dimensions of key ecological concepts.

There are also studies concerned with ascertaining the form of the relationship between rubrics of the ecological complex, other than those examined in the earlier sections. Some attention has been directed, for example, to the relation between population size and ecological organization. Another group of studies has examined the relationship between characteristics of the physical and social environment and demographic and migration change. The sections below address these general areas.

1. *Conceptual and theoretical development*. The recent suggestions of Micklin (1973) for expanding the ecological frame of reference are particularly worthy of attention. Although to date there has been no systematic effort by him, or others, to specify empirically the dimensions of the model, he implies that the applicable units of investigation are homogeneous populations. Thus even though his work is presently without empirical substance, it shall be considered here since some of the issues he raises speak directly to questions of import for human ecology.

Micklin's representation of the human ecological system departs from those of Duncan (1959), and Gibbs and Martin (1959) in a number of ways. The technology rubric, a key element in earlier theoretical specification, is subsumed under one of four mechanisms of organizational adaptation. According to Micklin, a population's organization for sustenance need not focus primarily upon the collective arrangements obtained in the manner it uses its available technology for exploiting the natural and social environment; indeed he speaks of three additional mechanisms of adaptation. *Engineering* (particularly technology and science) mechanisms are instrumental agents, but also of interest are *symbolic, regulatory,* and *distributional* mechanisms. Symbolic mechanisms "include transmitted and created content and patterns of values, ideas, and other symbolic-meaningful systems as factors in the shaping of human behavior and the artifacts produced through behavior... It is through collectively recognized symbols that objective meanings are standardized, diffused, and transmitted from one generation to the next" (1973, pp. 9-10).

Regulatory "mechanisms reflect the political dimensions of social organization, i.e., those processes that serve to combine sub-units into a societal unit, to make out of parts a whole, and to guide societal action toward the realization of societal values as expressed via the political processes. Of central importance for understanding the capacity of a collectivity to regulate its internal organization, as well as its relationships with the external environment, is the concept of power..." (1973, p. 10).

Distributional mechanisms are composed of collective processes that result in the relocation of components of an ecological system in social and/or physical space. These processes may be a consequence of purposively calculated strategies or they may result from sub-social forces inherent in the on-going pattern of social organization" (1973, p. 11).

Micklin's scheme addresses many of the theoretical issues present in the ecological writings of Hawley, Duncan, Schnore, Martin, and Gibbs, but often they are organized and structured differently. Micklin and most other ecologists point to the central position of sustenance organization, but Micklin's conceptualization of organization is decidedly broader, and perhaps, more complex. Some of his organizational adaptive mechanisms are treated by other ecologists elsewhere in their representations of the ecological system. The distributional mechanism, for example, as it applies to populations, is a major feature of the ecological theory of migration as developed principally by Hawley and addressed here in an earlier section. Micklin's work gives major attention to system power as a manifestation of organizational adaptation. Furthermore he entertains the possibility that symbolic representations are important for ecological investigations because of their assumed certrality in organizational adaptation.

Attention is now directed to recent work on the conceptual and empirical elaboration of key ecological constructs. The work of Frisbie is particularly instructive. He has attempted to specify the conceptual and empirical dimensions of bureaucratization and of technology. His research on bureaucratization (1975) consisted firstly of providing theoretical reasoning for conceptualizing the construct in terms of four dimensions, and secondly, of operationalizing each of these dimensions with a series of empirical indicators; finally, he examined the individual relationships between and among the dimensions across 71 societies.

He argued in favor of four structural dimensions of bureaucratization grounding each element in sociological and ecological theory: hierarchical authority, structured communications, the division of labor, and requirement of thorough and expert training. Each of these dimensions was then operationalized with single variables following in many cases early bureaucratization research. In order then to provide some evidence of the reliability and internal consistency of the bureaucratization index, Frisbie gathered data on each of the four empirical indicators for 71 societies and carried out a factor analysis of the four variables. A single factor solution was obtained. Reliability of the index was assessed by means of the omega coefficient, its value in this case equalling .82, an acceptable reliability. He then examined the validity of the index by ascertaining its relation with the measure of technological development; a correlation of .82 was the result. This same strategy of conceptual elaboration and empirical operationalization was followed by Frisbie and Clarke 1979 in a recent paper on technology. Drawing on the work of Durkheim (1893), Ogburn (1951), Sjoberg (1965), Lenski (1970), Duncan (1959), Gibbs and Martin (1959) and Goldschmidt (1959), *inter alios,* the authors established the theoretical antecedents for an ecological study of technology. From these discussions, six technology dimensions emerged: energy, agriculture, manufacture, science, transporation, and communications. From two to seven per capita indicators were specified for each dimension, and these are appended in Figure 1. Data were gathered on each indicator for 66 countries, and the indicators for each dimension were combined by converting the raw data into standard scores and summing. The authors then factor analyzed the six technology components and a single factor solution was obtained. The authors assessed the reliability of the index with the omega coefficient, and the results were quite satisfactory. Validity of the index was next examined. The authors reasoned that the index of technology should correlate positively with measures of economic growth, urbanization, political modernization, bureaucratization and life expectancy, and negatively with fertility, infant mortality and the percent of all deaths due to contagious or infectious diseases. The results of these tests were most favorable and suggested the degree of theoretical consistency expected in this examination of index validity. We agree that "the index represents a logically consistent conceptualization of technology that augments predictive power and helps to specify the boundaries of a key sociological and we might add,[ecological] concept" (Frisbie and Clark, 1979, p. 610).

2. *Other studies relating rubrics of the ecological system.* In earlier sections, we have examined many analyses of homogeneous populations concerned with relating rubrics of the ecological system. However there are numerous investigations which do not fit into the general themes addressed. Some of these will be discussed in the paragraphs below.

A major theme addressed earlier related the effects of ecological organization on demographic change. It is not difficult to argue that such an endeavor is germane ecologically, particularly if we accept as one of the goals of

Figure 1.

MEASUREMENT OF THE DIMENSIONS OF TECHNOLOGY

| Dimensions | Indicators* |
|---|---|

**Energy**  Consumption of (in metric tons, coal equivalent)
1. coal          4. natural gas
2. lignite       5. hydro electricity
3. petroleum products  6. nuclear electricity

**Agriculture**  1. number of tractors   2. consumption of
                                         fertilizers (metric tons)

**Manufactures**  Consumption of          Production of
1. steel (metric tons)   3. cement (metric tons)
2. tin (metric tons)

**Science**  1. number of scientists,  Research and development
             engineers and            expenditures as:
             technicians              2. an average per scientist
                                          or engineer
                                       3. a percentage of the gross
                                          national product

**Transportation**  1. number of motor vehicles (passenger cars and
                       commercial vehicles
                    2. railroads (total net ton-kilometers)
                    3. shipping (international goods loaded and unloaded-
                       metric tons)
                    4. airplanes (total net ton-kilometers)

**Communications**  Number of               Use of
1. radios (receivers)    4. Newsprint (metric tons)
2. telephones            5. telegraph (domestic
3. televisions              telegrams)
   (receivers)           6. mail (domestic items sent
                            or received)
                         7. newspaper (circulation of
                            daily and non-daily)

*All values are per capita, except for
the research and development expenditure
indicators.

SOURCES: UNESCO Statistical Yearbook, 1973
         UN Statistical Yearbook, 1975

SOURCE OF FIGURE: Frisbie and Clarke, 1977

human ecology the establishment of "the consequences of the presence or absence of particular characteristics of sustenance organization in human populations" (Gibbs and Martin, 1959, p. 33). Indeed much of the demographic research informed by the perspective of human ecology follows this general form.

Another principal goal of human ecology is the explanation of "the presence or absence of particular characteristics of sustenance organization among human populations, i.e., [specifying the conditions]...under which a given characteristic will or will not appear" (Gibbs and Martin, 1959, p. 33). Much of the work on the division of labor, for example, has addressed this objective. There is also a study by Kasarda (1974) in which ecological organization is treated as dependent, and he examines the extent to which it is effected by demographic conditions. In short, he asks on what system levels does population size influence internal organization. Three levels are specified: institutional, communal, and societal. He hypothesizes that as each of these three system levels enlarge, there will be a disproportionate increase in the organizational positions whose primary function is to aid communication. In testing his hypothesis he gathered information at the institutional level on 178 school systems in the state of Colorado, at the communal level on 207 communities in the state of Wisconsin with populations less than 25,000, and at the societal level on the 43 nonagriculturally based nations "which have more than one-half their economically active population engaged in either secondary or tertiary activities" (Kasarda, 1974, p. 21).

The study found that "size has a pervasive influence on the internal organization of modern social systems... Large size promotes greater administrative intensity in institutions, communities, and industrialized societies... As institutions, communities and societies expand, substantially greater proportions of their personnel are devoted to communicative (clerical) functions. It may therefore be inferred that the major role of holding large social systems together rests with those whose primary function is facilitating communication" (Kasarda, 1974, p. 26).

One of the contributions of Kasarda's analysis lies in its examination of the structural implications of population size per se. Rather than treating the demographic component as process, and as dependent, he turns the hypothesis around the other way, confronting the historic question about the effects of population size on organization, one that has been asked so often by Durkheim, Spencer, Hawley and others.

His answers are compelling in scope, and his general work here should serve to remind ecologists that the population component in the ecological complex need not only be conceptualized in terms of process.

Another class of empirical research of interest involves relating various features of the physical and/or social environment with demographic change. This particular type of relationship has not been explored with the same intensity as relationships among some of the other ecological rubrics, but it is one which clearly needs empirical substance. There are numerous well-reasoned and empirically documented investigations concerned with the impact of the environment on population change, and four specific types will be addressed below. Each is concerned with a different aspect of the environment, and following Hawley, each of these environmental considerations is "external to and potentially influential upon a unit under study" (Hawley, 1973, p. 1198).

One investigation has asked whether county seat status is a factor in the demographic change of small towns (Fuguitt, 1965). County seats, by definition, are governmental centers. Moreover, often as a result of their political function, county seats "may be dominant trade and service centers in the local community." Although these latter attributes are somewhat difficult to entangle from the governmental function, together these characteristics suggest that county seats should be more likely to show demographic growth than other places. A test of this general hypothesis was undertaken with data for all nonmetropolitan places in the U.S. (outside New England) for the period 1940-1960. Although there was some regional variation in the general relationship, Fuguitt did demonstrate that particularly in the South, and to a lesser extent in the North, "county seats have tended to grow faster than other small towns-- between 1940 and 1960" (1965, p. 250). This analysis is suggestive of one characteristic of an area's environment, and also of the type of impact that such a factor may have on demographic change.

There has also been considerable interest in demographic investigations of nonmetropolitan and rural places with the relation between population growth and proximity to metropolitan areas. The closer the nonmetropolitan or rural area to a metropolitan area, the greater its chances for population increase, *ceteris paribus*. From an ecological point of view, the metropolitan area is conceptualized as an externality, an attribute of the environment, with the potential for influencing the growth patterns of the areas located about it. This hypothesis, when tested, has met with considerable success (Beale, 1962; Tarver and Beale, 1967; Fuguitt, 1971; Deare and Poston, 1973; *inter alios*).

The ecological meaning behind the relationship is clear. It is not so much that distance per se between the nonmetropolitan/rural area and the metropolitan area is important. Indeed few ecologists would make such an argument. Rather the reason for the relationship lies in the dominance and influence of the metropolitan area. The particular form of the nonmetropolitan area's sustenance organization, and perhaps the employment and income opportunities generated by that organization, is to a large extent influenced by the metropolitan area. Metropolitan dominance effects nonmetropolitan demographic change indirectly by impacting the nonmetropolitan organization structure (see Frisbie and Poston, 1978b:74). The location of a metropolitan area within the physical environment field of a nonmetropolitan area thus increases the latter's probabilities for population growth. The interpretation of this relationship, however, rests more with the functional integration of the sustenance structures of the areas than with distance and spatial location.

Two additional analyses of this genre are those dealing with the impact of military and college activities (Zuiches, 1970), and the presence of controlled access highways (Humphrey and Sell, 1975), on demographic and migration change. Zuiches' analysis dealt with migration into incorporated urban places of the nonmetropolitan U.S. counties between 1955 and 1960. He pointed to the positive relationship between levels of military and college activities, and net inmigration. The study by Humphrey and Sell showed that among nonmetropolitan places in Pennsylvania in the thirty years between 1940 and 1970, "high speed roads have augmented the demographic growth process of less densely settled territory within 25 miles of a metropolitan center" (Humphrey and Sell, 1975, p. 341). (See Gessaman and Sisler, 1976, for a related study.)

Hawley has noted that "a great deal of what is external to any entity is often overlooked in considerations of environment" (1973, p. 1198). The research themes discussed above employ a broad conceptualization of the environment, while providing important insights about some of the environmental determinants of demographic change. They illustrate well the kinds of environmental factors that may be brought to bear on investigations of demographic change, and they point to the significant impact that these environmental agents may have on demographic change. Ecologists have much to learn from these studies.

## VI. NODAL POPULATIONS:
## THE NODE AND ITS IMMEDIATE HINTERLAND

The regional ecological research reviewed and discussed to this point has been concerned generally with the investigation of ecological relationships in homogeneous populations (areas).

However, there is another perspective that may be assumed in the study of regional ecology. Rather than treating the regions as homogeneous, one would recognize that regions usually "orient their activities toward nodal centers—in most cases, large metropolitan centers... [Accordingly], the obvious units of analysis... [should be] metropolitan regions... Boundaries to such areas are determined not by homogeneity of characteristics but by functional interrelationships—lines of flow of goods and services and points at which competing nodes serve the hinterland areas" (Bogue, 1959, p. 394).

But even here there is more than one strategy for examining ecological relationships among nodal populations. There is an abundance of ecological studies pertaining to the form and structure of the relationship, and interrelationship, between the nodal area and its immediate hinterland. This topic has concerned human ecologists since the 1920s in Chicago, and others even earlier. Indeed, the concepts of central place theory have their basis in this general concern, and scholars beginning with Losch, von Thunen, and Christaller were long interested in this form of regionalization. (The modelling of Peter Haggett 1965 is particularly illustrative of contemporary geographical interest. See also Berry and Pred [1961].) This general area has also been one of continuing fascination for sociologists and human ecologists since 1950.

Another class of nodal studies also focuses on the relationship between the nodal area and the hinterland, but conceptualizes the hinterland more broadly, conceptually and spatially. Rather than defining it in terms of the immediate area around and about the node, the hinterland in this second class of investigations refers to the region which may be influenced by the node, and which itself may be influencing the node. The influence is almost always in terms of one or more features or characteristics of sustenance organization. This topic has not been as widely studied as the preceding one by human ecologists, especially in the earlier years. Since the important investigations in the mid-1950s, and in 1960, by Vance and by Duncan, and their colleagues, however, contemporary ecologists have given more attention to investigations involving an area's place in a larger hierarchy or system, and the directions and flows involved in this integration of sustenance activities.

Following somewhat from the preceding, a third group of analyses has dealt primarily with single sustenance functions, attempting to ascertain their respective positions and degree of integration in the larger (often national) network. Although inquiries of this type are not as numerous as the others, they have added substantially to our knowledge of the ecology of nodal populations, and we would be remiss if they were not paid their due.

In the balance of this section, we discuss the relations and interactions between nodal populations and their immediate hinterlands. The following two sections treat nodal populations and the national hierarchy, and studies of single sustenance functions. Any statement pretending to discuss the mechanisms of the relationship between a node and its hinterland must give some mention to the architects of central place theory, as well as to the writings of a few other scholars predating 1950. A brief discussion will thus set the stage for a more detailed presentation of research themes popular in this area since 1950.

Central place theory is an attempt to account for the locational patterns of cities. The first major statement of theoretical importance was von Thunen's observation in 1826 which "postulated an entirely uniform land surface and showed that under ideal conditions a city would develop in the center of this land area and concentric rings of land use would develop around the central city" (Ullman, 1941, p. 853). He discovered that these land use patterns changed with increasing distance from the city, and from these patterns a simple rent gradient could be derived (cf. Dickinson, 1970, p. 32).

Later thinking of Losch (1940 [1954]) on the concentration of populations and activities as a "punctiform agglomeration of nonagricultural locations--and an extended territory" (Duncan, et al., 1960, p. 40) and that of Christaller (1933) on the fact that "a certain amount of productive land supports an urban center" (Ullman, 1941, p. 855) provided the framework for developing a central place system. Ullman has observed that "as a working hypothesis one assumes that normally the larger the city, the larger its tributary area. Thus, there should be cities of varying size ranging from a small hamlet performing a few simple functions, such as providing a limited shopping and market center for a small contiguous area, up to a large city with a large tributary area composed of the service areas of many smaller towns and providing more complex

services, such as wholesaling, large scale banking, specialized retailing, and the like. Services performed purely for a surrounding area are termed 'central' functions by Christaller, and the settlements performing them 'central' places" (Ullman, 1941, pp. 855-856).
Ecological substance is given this model by Gras (1922) and by McKenzie (1933). After presenting an historical account for the emergence of a metropolitan economy, Gras stated that the one situational factor absolutely essential for a city to emerge as a metropolitan economy is its possession of a hinterland, "a tributary adjacent territory, rich in natural resources, accompanied by a productive population and accessible by means of transportation" (1922, p. 185).

In studying this organization we are inclined to emphasize the great metropolitan center; but to forget the large dependent district would be fatal to a correct understanding of the subject. Perhaps indeed it is somewhat incorrect to speak of the area as dependent upon the center, for though that is true, the center is also dependent upon the outlying area with its towns, villages, and scattered homesteads. Interdependence of parts is really the key to the whole thing" (Gras, 1922, pp. 186-187; quoted in Bogue, 1949 [1961, pp. 529-530].

Bogue has written that "the striking element about the metropolitan hypothesis as formulated by Gras is not that great cities exist, nor even that they dominate a broad expanse of territory, but that the metropolitan economy is the characteristic and dominant type of modern social and economic organization" (1949 [1961, p. 530]).
McKenzie arrived at essentially the same conclusion as Gras regarding the importance and organizing role of the metropolitan area (or the super-city or super-community, as he at times referred to it). He assembled a mass of demographic data on urbanization trends in the United States over time (see McKenzie, 1968, pp. 244-305). He concluded that "this new type of super community organized around a dominant focal point and comprising a multitude of differentiated centers of activity differs from the metropolitanism established by rail transportation in the complexity of its institutional division of labor and the mobility of its population. Its territorial scope is defined in terms of motor transportation and competition with other regions... It has become the communal unit of local relations throughout the entire nation" (McKenzie, 1933, p. 313).

There is another seminal piece of research written before 1950 that has informed much of the work to be discussed below on nodal populations and their hinterlands: Bogue's *The Structure of the Metropolitan Community* (1949 [1961]), a classic recognized as the "definitive study of metropolitan dominance" (Duncan, et al., 1960, p. 85). This study is an attempt to expand upon the work of Gras and McKenzie by developing and supporting the hypothesis "that a modern industrial society, as exemplified by the United States, is dominated by metropolises so that the entire nation is divided into a series of metropolitan communities, each dominated by a particular metropolis... [Ecological concepts are used] in analyzing the metropolis itself as a dominant, small cities as subdominants, rural nonfarm communities as influents, and rural farm communities as subinfluents, with each category based on the size of the area and the number of functions controlled" (Theodorson, 1961, pp. 511-512).

Bogue was principally concerned with the internal structure of the metropolitan community, the node and its immediate hinterland, and not with intermetropolitan aspects of dominance. Although his model implicitly assumed that "each metropolis provides all the dominance which may exist in its surrounding hinterland, this, of course, is not strictly true. Metropolitan influence... can extend completely across intervening metropolitan areas" (Bogue, 1949, p. 27—quoted in Duncan, et al., 1960, pp. 85-86). He was well aware that his approach could not specify this latter type of relationship.

We turn now to the principal themes dominant in this literature since 1950. It will be immediately apparent that the research just discussed, particularly that of Gras, McKenzie and Bogue, has influenced significantly the course of ecological study on this topic. In attempting to organize this literature, we have settled on the following themes: metropolitan growth and development; the node and its influences; the node influenced by the hinterland; differentials between the node and the hinterland.

a. *Metropolitan growth and development.* Following the initial leads of McKenzie (1933), many ecologists have described with empirical detail and quantitative sophistication the course of metropolitan growth and development. One statement by Schnore (1957b) attempted to illustrate the direction of metropolitan growth since 1900 and pointed in particular to the crucial role assumed by modern technology, particularly the new forms of transportation and communication, in bringing about this new form of urban supercommunity. He wrote that:

With the increased ease of travel... some of the larger subcenters underwent a significant transition. They lost their high degree of independence and fell under the dominating influence of the metropolis. For example, many establishments devoted to the provision of luxury goods abandoned operations in the subcenters, being unable to compete with the metropolis, which was now easily accessible to a wide market. At the same time, principles of mass production were increasingly adapted to distribution, and chains of retail outlets began to appear... During the same period, significant changes in communication came about with the development of the radio and the telephone. Instantaneous contact with a broad area now became possible, and the independence of subcenters was diminished accordingly (Schnore, 1957b, p. 174).

In an analysis five years later (1962), Schnore used data from the 1960 U.S. Census of Population and brought up to date the preceding work on decentralization (see, also, Berry and Kasarda, 1977, Part IV, esp. Chapters 8, 9, 12, 13).

Maintaining this interest in metropolitan growth and development, but following a strategy different from that of Schnore, other investigators have described the growth and morphological changes in nodes and their hinterlands. Duncan, et al., (1962) focused in particular on the role of residential construction in the redistribution of population in Los Angeles from the core city to the suburbs (see, also, Guest's 1973 study of Cleveland and Stokes' 1976 analysis of Chicago). Winsborough (1963) focused solely on suburban growth and concluded that the "state or process of suburbanization in a city is not a single thing but the result of changes in two elemental aspects of urban population distribution, concentration and congestion. The parameters of the distribution of population over the urban aggregate provide well-defined and empirically productive measures of the state of concentration and congestion of the city" (1963, p. 570). Berry, et al., (1963), dealt more with the extent of population density in large cities, focusing upon the city size--compactness relationships by concentrating on the interactions between socioeconomic patterns and transportation. Finally, a recent analysis by Edmonston (1975) has not only generated intriguing procedures for measuring population concentration while describing changes in the major U.S. metropolitan centers since 1970, but has also analyzed principal features causally related to concentration. This volume is another example of the high level of methodological and theoretical sophistication typical of much of the current research in human ecology.

b. *The node and its influences.* One way of ascertaining the extent of nodal influence is to inquire about the degree to which the nodal area, often the central city or core city of a metropolitan area, is an organizational agent for the hinterland by providing integrating services. Developing this hypothesis from the work of Gras, Carroll (1963) expected that "certain cities, adapting to particular conditions, perform services for a hinterland to a much greater degree than other cities of a similar size, and thereby integrate (dominate) the activities in the hinterland to a greater degree than do the other cities." He examined the extent to which the city performs integrative functions both at the local and regional levels, and showed that "only 30 of the 168 central cities perform integrative activities above the average for both local and regional types of dominance, and that 41 central cities perform well below the average... [He concluded that these data provided] a strong negative answer to the taxonomic question of whether or not all central cities of Standard Metropolitan Areas should be included in a special metropolitan city classification" (1963, pp. 169-172).

Other investigators have examined the influence of the node on income levels (Lincoln and Friedland, 1977) and on fertility (Slesinger, 1974). With data on 2,610 incorporated urban places located outside SMSAs in 1960, Lincoln and Friedland demonstrated that certain industries and occupational functions, indicative of metropolitan influence, are highly related with income levels (1977, p. 304). Focusing on the urban-rural fertility differential, Slesinger asked if it was "due to the effect of metropolitan dominance, or... to the distribution of characteristics of the individuals living in the rural and urban areas" (1974, p. 350). With regard to the immediate cause of the differential, she concluded that it was "less a matter of metropolitan dominance ... and more the characteristics of the population residing in these areas" (1974, p. 360). However, she did not completely dismiss the potential effects of metropolitan dominance on the differential. Indeed, she left with the suggestion that dominance theory might be involved in the answer to why older women who are married longer and who have more children live in the rural rather than the urban areas.

Finally, Mark and Schwirian (1967) were interested in knowing the extent to which the central place functions of the nodes have an effect on population growth. They examined data for the period of regional industrialization in Iowa and concluded that "central place function was no longer a significant community-building activity. The population growth that characterized most of the towns was a result of other expansions of the local economic base" (1967, p. 40). Martin, too, was interested in the degree to which changes in the satellite rural areas were related to nodal dominance and the node-hinterland relationship. After reviewing a number of studies, he concluded that changes in the "satellite rural areas conform consistently with the gradient principle of urbanization" (1957, p. 183). The ecological and demographic changes taking place in the hinterland "are directly related to changes in the dynamic relationship between the rural and urban sectors of the industrializing society" (1957, p. 183).

c. *The node influenced by the hinterland.* In his discussions of the relationship between the node and its immediate hinterland, Gras noted that "perhaps indeed it is somewhat incorrect to speak of the... [hinterland] as dependent upon the center the node, for though that is true, the center is also dependent upon the outlying area with its towns, villages and scattered homesteads" (1922, pp. 186-187). The complementary nature of the node-hinterland relationship is itself a topic of ecological research, and there has been considerable attention directed by scholars specifically to the degree of influence that the hinterland has upon the node.

A statement by Zimmer and Hawley (1956) concentrated on individual responses of fringe and central city residents in Flint regarding the degree to which they favored "some kind of joint action of city and fringe in the approach to fringe problems" (1956, p. 268). This particular investigation recognized the interdependencies involved in providing services to nodal and interland areas. Although essentially a micro-study of a single area, it was the precursor of ecological studies conducted by Kasarda and others in the 1970s.

In one analysis, Kasarda examined the impact of suburban population growth on central city service functions by focusing on 168 SMSAs. He concluded that the degree of suburban (hinterland) influence has been underestimated. By engaging in both "cross-sectional and longitudinal analysis he demonstrated... that the suburban population has a large impact on central city retail trade, wholesale trade, business and repair services, and public services provided by central city governments... The suburban population in general, and the commuting population in particular, exerts strong effects on police, fire, highway, sanitation, recreation, and general administrative functions performed in the central cities. [This impact...] remains strong when controls are introduced..." (Kasarda, 1972a, p. 1123). In a related analysis (1972b), he tests the ecological theory of expansion that increases in the size of hinterland areas "will be matched with a development of organizational functions in their centers to insure integration and coordination of activities and relationships throughout the enlarged units" (1972b, p. 165). Aside from the fact that these state-ments advance our knowledge of the kinds of influence the hinterland has over the node, they are also tests of the relationship between the ecological rubrics of population and organization. Recall our earlier discussion of Kasarda's 1974 analysis of the structural implications of social system size, another test of the relationship between population size and organization. The contribution of these studies is, thus, apparent on at least two grounds.

d. *Differentials between the node and the hinterland*. Most of these analyses of differentials rest on distinctions made earlier on the ecological and demographic structure of the hinterland, particularly the suburban areas. Both Schnore (1957a, 1957c) and Martin (1956) focused initially on suburban classification and definitions, and then turned to detailed descriptions of these interland areas. Having developed the empirical foundation, attention was then turned to differentials, particularly with regard to status, between cities (nodes) and suburbs (hinterlands, narrowly speaking).

In two influential investigations, Schnore (1963, 1964) questioned the impression that suburbs are inhabited by populations of higher socioeconomic status than those living in the nearby cities. He showed that this impression is an overstatement because it is only the "older urbanized areas ... [that] possess peripheral populations of higher socio-economic standing than found in the central cities themselves. In contrast, newer cities tend to contain populations ranking higher on education, occupation, and income than their respective suburbs" (1963, p. 80).

This section has examined selected ecological literature on four specific topics under the general heading of the node and its immediate hinterland. The writings of Losch and Christaller, and then Gras, McKenzie and Bogue, were first reviewed before addressing the more recent ecological literature. The limitations of space have precluded consideration of all important themes. The journey to work, for example, has been an area of interest for human ecological research (Schnore, 1954; B. Duncan, 1957; Sheldon and Hoermann, 1964; Poston, 1972; Guest, 1975; *inter alios*) because, for one reason, it is an integrating force between the node and the hinterland. It has not been given attention here, and the same applies for other topics. However, the preceding reviews do illustrate the range of interests shown by ecologists since 1950 in their investigations of the node and its immediate hinterland.

## VII. NODAL POPULATIONS: THE NODE AND THE HIERARCHY

...[N]early every city has a more or less standard repertoire of functions performed for its own inhabitants and for its immediate continuous "hinterland"-- comprising the area which it serves and upon which it depends most closely... But many cities have highly distinctive functions that make up important parts of their economic base and that involve them in ramified relationships with a variety of types of "regions"... (Duncan, et al., 1960, p. 5).

The above remarks served as an introduction to *the* definitive statement on nodal populations and the hierarchy. It serves the same utility here as we begin to review this basic literature. Unlike most of the research areas already investigated, the explicitly ecological literature on this topic is sparse. In organizing these materials for presentation, they have been grouped into four sections: development of the hierarchy; metropolitan organization of the South; occupational composition and the hierarchy; other uses of the hierarchy.

1. *Development of the hierarchy. Metropolis and Region* was published in 1960 under the authorship of O. D. Duncan, W. R. Scott, S. Lieberson, B. Duncan and H. H. Winsborough. Three tasks were set out early by the authors: (1) "... to bring into juxtaposition some of the leading ideas which have been propounded on the nature of the metropolis, its role in the national economy, and its relation to the regional differentiation of the economy...; (2) to test the cogency of ideas and formulations distilled from the literature. [They thus attempted to develop] a comprehensive outline of the major structural characteristics of the United States metropolitan economy as of about 1950...; (3) to provide a systematic survey of the industrial composition and regional relationships of the larger cities of the United States--those most likely to manifest distinctively metropolitan characteristics" (1960, p. 2).

*Metropolis and Region* is comprised of four parts; the first provided a comprehensive conceptual introduction to metropolitanism, the basic literature, criteria and types of statistical data for studying the issues. Part II focused on metropolitan dominance. "Metropolitan influence or dominance is not conceived as flowing to each hinterland areal unit from a single metropolitan center. Instead, each... [area] is considered to occupy a position in a generalized 'ecological field' as indexed by a global measure of accessibility, population potential... [T]he association of hinterland economic activity is studied with this indicator of generalized accessibility and with distance to nearest metropolis" (1960, pp. 11-12). This general procedure was followed in studies of hinterland manufacturing activity and resource-extracting activities: coal mining and agriculture. The materials in Part II showed that "metropolitan influences broadly classified under the heading of 'dominance' actually occur in a variety of ways. Most important is the discovery that a somewhat diffused kind of dominance--that reflected in an index of generalized accessibility--must be taken into account in order to interpret any specific influences of a particular metropolis in a given region" (1960, p. 14).

Parts III and IV, the authors urged, should be thought of as one unit. Part III discussed in detail the methodology followed in generating Part IV, and also included "a summary of the salient conclusions derived from a compara- tive study of the reports on individual metropolitan centers contained in Part IV" (1960, p. 14). Throughout both Parts, the authors were concerned with the following questions: "In what terms should the entire industry structure of a large city be described in order to bring out the relative importance of distinctively 'metropolitan' functions and to reveal relationships with 'regions'? Where metropolitan characteristics clearly are in evidence and where basic metropolis-region input-output relationships are found, what locational factors can be adduced to explain these characteristics and relationships? Is it possible to construct an outline of major features of metropolitan structure in mid-century America, the headings of which will be both fairly generalized and reasonably realistic?" (1960, p. 14).

The authors thus dealt with a number of indicators of metropolitan function for Standard Metropolitan Areas (SMAs) with a population of at least 300,000 or more in 1950. They developed a seven-fold quasi-hierarchical classification of metropolises which showed "concretely how cities are differentiated in terms of metropolitan functions and regional relationships" (1960, p. 260). This classification, long familiar to human ecologists, is presented here as Table 1.

Measures of manufacturing, financial and commercial functions provided the major basis for its development, although the authors observed that a broader interpretive base was also employed. As initial coordinates for classification, they relied on a single manufacturing variable and a single commercial variable (per capita value added by manufacturing, and per capita wholesale sales, respectively). The SMA values were examined on these two variables and two subgroups clearly emerged: *Specialized Manufacturing Centers* (high on value added and low on wholesale sales), and Special Cases (low on both variables but otherwise heterogeneous in characteristics). The sub-group of *National Metropolises* was determined by selecting the five largest SMAs, and the remaining four sub-groups, *Regional Metropolises, Regional Capitals, Submetropolitan, Diversified Manufacturing with Metropolitan Functions, and Diversified Manufacturing with Few Metropolitan Functions*, were developed by using the previous characteristics and others such as per capita commercial and financial measures of business service receipts, nonlocal commercial loans, and demand deposits. The size of cities also played a role, and if two SMAs were "otherwise similar, the larger... was assumed to be the more important" (1960, p. 260). It was also noted that the "relative weights and particular combinations of variables regarded as crucial shift somewhat from category to category... This is only to concede that impressionism and judgment have been allowed to play a role" (1960, p. 266).

As noted earlier, this study is the definitive statement on hierarchical systems. Aside from developing the scheme presented here in Table 1, the authors provided extensive statements in Part IV on the individual SMAs included in the analysis. These studies presented "rich materials for a critique of the concepts of hinterland and of nodal regions. ... [R]ecurring themes in the SMA reports provide an inductive basis for identifying general patterns of metropolis-region relationships and for suggesting a heuristic classification of the larger SMAs in the United States" (1960, pp. 16-17). Since its publication in 1960, there has been nothing to rival it in terms of breadth, scope, and methodology. Of all the ecological materials that have been published since 1950, *Metropolis and Region* is the classic.

In 1972, Bean, Poston and Winsborough re-examined the *Metropolis and Region* variables with multiple discriminant analysis to assess the extent to which they account for the classification. That is, rather than working toward a classification with a metropolitan size variable and a number of indicators of metropolitan function, they took the classification as given and ascertained the adequacy of the

Table 1.

The <u>Metropolis and Region</u> Classification

<u>National Metropolises</u>
New York
Chicago
Los Angeles
Philadelphia
Detroit

Diversified Manufacturing
<u>with Metropolitan Functions</u>
Boston
Pittsburg
St.Louis
Cleveland
Buffalo
Cincinnati

Diversified Manufacturing
with Few Metropolitan
<u>Functions</u>
Baltimore
Milwaukee
Toledo
Hartford
Syracuse

<u>Specialized Manufacturing</u>
Providence
Dayton
Akron
Rochester

<u>Special Cases</u>
Washington
San Diego
San Antonio
Miami
Norfolk-Portsmouth
Wilkes-Barre-Hazleton
Tampa-St.Petersburg
Knoxville
Phoenix

<u>Regional Metropolises</u>
San Francisco
Minneapolis-St.Paul
Kansas City
Seattle
Portland
Atlanta
Dallas
Denver

Regional Capital, Sub-
<u>Metropolitan</u>
Houston
New Orleans
Louisville
Birmingham
Indianapolis
Columbus
Memphis
Omaha
Fort Worth
Richmond
Oklahoma City
Nashville
Jacksonville

SOURCE: O.D. Duncan, et al., Metropolis and Region. Baltimore:
The Johns Hopkins Press, 1960, p. 271.

variables. This was done for both 1950 (the *Metropolis and Region* period) and for 1960. Bean and his colleagues found that "the variables most important in defining the significant discriminant functions for both the earlier and later time periods... substantiate [d] the heavy reliance in *Metropolis and Region* upon certain variables as initial bases of classification" (1972, p. 31).

The initial classification, as already noted, reflected distinctions with regard both to size and metropolitan characteristics. On the basis of the a *posteriori* discriminant analyses executed by Bean, Poston and Winsborough, however, two outcomes emerged which the authors of *Metropolis and Region* could not have anticipated in their a *priori* investigation. First, "given the quantitative indicators employed, the dimensions characterized mostly by size on the one hand and functional specialization on the other are linearly independent, thus providing evidence that the classification reflects differences among cities that cannot be conceptualized solely in terms of size. Secondly, the discriminant analysis suggests that the differences among the types of cities with respect to their performance of metropolitan functions may be depicted by a single dimension instead of two or more dimensions, if emphasis is given to the notion of metropolitan specialization as opposed to gross level of metropolitanism per se" (1972, p. 32).

2. *Metropolitan organization of the South.* A few years prior to the publication of *Metropolis and Region,* Rupert B. Vance of the University of North Carolina inquired about the patterns of metropolitan dominance and integration in the South because "except for their recent rapid growth, they are unremarkable cities [and] human ecologists and students of urbanism in the United States have had little reason to study them" (Vance and Smith, 1954 [1957, p. 103]). He and a student Sara Smith (Sutker), thus set out to ascertain the numerous inter-relationships among Southern cities extending from the smallest villages through the large cities to the supercities lying outside of the South. Following the earlier statements of Gras, McKenzie and Bogue (see the discussions in Section VII above), Vance and Smith also recognized that there was more to metropolitanism than large size. They wrote that "whereas urbanization may refer to any aspect of population agglomeration, metropolitanism should be reserved for the organizational component that great cities impose upon the urbanization process. Any city with a large population is usually referred to as a metropolis, but it may be well to point out that, while all metropolises are large cities, not all large cities are metropolises. Population size is a concomitant; function is the keynote" (1954 [1957, pp. 103-104]).

After tracing the development of urban and metropolitan growth in the South and, less specifically, in the United States, the authors posed the question: "How much and what kind of metropolitan development may one expect in the South of 1950 [and]... which of the larger [cities in the South] ... may be considered metropolises... and how do they rank in the dominance they exert?" (1954 [1957, pp. 110-111]).

In order to rank southern cities on their metropolitan function, Vance and Smith selected six indices: wholesale sales, business service receipts, number of branch offices, retail sales, bank clearings, and value added by manufacturing. The first three factors were an attempt by the authors to measure "high-level distribution, specialization, and control... [and these ] are weighted two to one... the last three indices [except for bank clearings ] reflect the gross underpinnings a city has for building its market and amassing wealth" (1954 [1957, p. 113]).

These indexes were constructed, combined, and manipulated for the 29 metropolitan areas of the South with central cities over 100,000 in 1950. The ranks and scores of these cities are listed on the left half of Table 2. The authors concluded that "Atlanta and Dallas with similar scores on metropolitan function stand head and shoulders above the other cities. There is no doubt about their being the regional capitals... [They] have been classified as Second Order Metropolises, with the idea that the First Order Metropolis has a nation-wide sphere of influence," and there were none in the South in 1950. They discussed in some detail the various rankings and the remaining three subgroups and then addressed the fact that "metropolitan regionalism involves more than the relation of dominance and subdominance among great cities. In the organization of its hinterland, the metropolis extends its way through subdominant centers to the smallest hamlet and rural homestead within its orbit. In the new South as elsewhere, the metropolis is related to its region in the way it integrates communities of different size, position and function. Here, each center plays a distinct and necessary role and the region itself can be thought of as a constellation of communities" (1954 [1957, p. 117] ). The authors never did approach empirically the notion of inter-metropolitan, or node-hinterland, integration. However, they did recognize the importance of conceptualizing metropolitan dominance as extending beyond the immediate hinterland of the node and, in this sense, their work differed from that of Gras, McKenzie, Bogue, and the others who maintained their conceptualizations strictly at the level of the immediate hinterland.

Table 2.

CITIES OF OVER 100,000 IN THE SOUTH,
RANKED BY METROPOLITAN FUNCTION:1950

| The Vance and Smith Ranking System | | The Galle and Stern Ranking System | |
|---|---|---|---|
| City | Rank Score | Z-Score | City |

| | | SECOND ORDER METROPOLISES | | |
|---|---|---|---|
| Atlanta | 9.91 | 16.47 | Dallas |
| Dallas | 9.71 | 15.21 | Houston |
| | | 14.29 | Atlanta |

| | | THIRD ORDER METROPOLISES | |
|---|---|---|---|
| Houston | 8.10 | 7.68 | New Orleans |
| New Orleans | 7.36 | 7.49 | Louisville |
| Memphis | 6.62 | 6.05 | Memphis |
| Louisville | 6.43 | 4.31 | Miami |
| Birmingham | 5.94 | 3.25 | Birmingham |

| | | SUB-DOMINANTS WITH METROPOLITAN CHARACTERISTICS | |
|---|---|---|---|
| Richmond | 5.34 | .44 | Fort Worth |
| Fort Worth | 5.24 | .31 | Richmond |
| Oklahoma City | 5.02 | - .36 | San Antonio |
| Miami | 4.90 | - .53 | Oklahoma City |
| Charlotte | 4.80 | - .88 | Tampa-St.Petersburg |
| Jacksonville | 4.79 | -1.42 | Tulsa |
| Tulsa | 4.60 | -1.62 | Nashville |
| Nashville | 4.59 | -2.24 | Charlotte |
| Little Rock | 4.54 | -2.26 | Jacksonville |
| San Antonio | 4.48 | -2.37 | Norfolk-Portsmouth |
| Norfolk-Portsmouth | 4.42 | -3.45 | Chattanooga |
| El Paso | 4.38 | -3.56 | Knoxville |

| | | SUBDOMINANTS | |
|---|---|---|---|
| Tampa-St.Petersburg | 4.18 | -5.75 | Little Rock |
| Chattanooga | 4.11 | -6.13 | Mobile |
| Knoxville | 3.84 | -6.37 | Shreveport |
| Shreveport | 3.62 | -7.06 | Savannah |
| Mobile | 3.54 | -7.11 | El Paso |
| Savannah | 3.46 | -7.30 | Corpus Christi |
| Corpus Christi | 3.30 | -7.55 | Baton Rouge |
| Montgomery | 3.25 | -7.44 | Montgomery |
| Baton Rouge | 3.25 | -7.81 | Austin |
| Austin | 3.19 | | |

SOURCE: Galle and Stern, 1976

Galle and Stern (1976) took this classic statement of Vance and Smith and extended it to 1970. They first expanded upon the methodological procedures of Vance and Smith, but these produced only minor adjustments in the original Vance and Smith rankings. For a comparison, see their 1950 rankings on the right side of Table 2. In the extension of the analysis to 1970 (see Table 3), the authors observed "that despite a relatively simple methodology, the delineation of an urban system in the South as of 1950... has shown a remarkable robustness. Further, as one looks toward the present, the dominating theme of urban growth from 1950 to 1970 has been the 'inertia' of the system—that is, the fact that the urban system today looks very much like it did over 20 years ago" (1976, p. 1). They did point to a number of important deviations from the 1950 delineation of Vance and Smith. The differences would appear to suggest an increasing integration with the metropolitan system of the United States, including the emergence of at least one National Metropolis (Houston).

3. *Occupational composition and the hierarchy.* This section on research published since 1950 on the general topic of the node and the hierarchy concentrates on those efforts relating the notion of hierarchical structure with elements of occupational composition. Winsborough (1960), for example, asked whether metropolitan dominance has effects separate from those predicted solely from central place theory. If this were not the case, he reasoned, the orderly variation across cities in occupational composition "may be merely the result of variation in industrial composition." If the gradients in occupational employment could be "accounted for by central place theory, we could eschew the interpretation of these gradients as evidence for a dominance gradient with city size and thereby simplify our set of explanatory concepts" (1960, p. 894). His investigation demonstrated that the "variation of occupational composition with city size cannot be explained solely by variation in industrial composition" (1960, p. 897), suggesting the applicability of a dominance interpretation.

Galle (1963) was concerned with the degree to which the occupational composition of large metropolitan areas was a function of the inter-metropolitan division of labor. He demonstrated that "variations in the occupational composition... can be attributed primarily to the occupational structure of their profile industries [i.e.] , those city-building industries in which the city specializes" (1963, p. 260). This analysis points directly to the pervasiveness of hierarchical location in that "the differing occupational

Table 3.

CHANGES IN THE METROPOLITAN SYSTEM IN THE SOUTH:  1950-1970
THE ORIGINAL 29 CITIES FROM 1950 (NEW RANKINGS)

| City | Z-score in 1950 | Z-score in 1970 | City |
|---|---|---|---|
| | SECOND ORDER METROPOLISES | | |
| Dallas | 16.47 | 21.03 | Houston |
| Houston | 15.21 | 17.64 | Dallas |
| Atlanta | 14.29 | 15.45 | Atlanta |
| | | 11.23 | Miami |
| | THIRD ORDER METROPOLISES | | |
| New Orleans | 7.68 | 3.95 | New Orleans |
| Louisville | 7.49 | 2.89 | Louisville |
| Memphis | 6.05 | 2.89 | Memphis |
| Miami | 4.31 | 2.20 | Tampa-St.Petersburg |
| Birmingham | 3.25 | | |
| | SUBDOMINANTS WITH METROPOLITAN CHARACTERISTICS | | |
| Fort Worth | .44 | .23 | Birmingham |
| Richmond | .31 | .18 | Fort Worth |
| San Antonio | -.36 | -.01 | Charlotte |
| Oklahoma City | -.53 | -1.17 | Richmond |
| Tampa-St.Petersburg | -.88 | -1.21 | Oklahoma City |
| Tulsa | -1.42 | -1.27 | Jacksonville |
| Nashville | -1.62 | -1.52 | Nashville |
| Charlotte | -2.24 | -1.85 | San Antonio |
| Jacksonville | -2.26 | -2.24 | Tulsa |
| Norfolk-Portsmouth | -2.37 | | |
| Chattanooga | -3.45 | | |
| Knoxville | -3.56 | | |
| | SUBDOMINANTS | | |
| Little Rock | -5.75 | -4.09 | Norfolk-Portsmouth |
| Mobile | -6.13 | -4.28 | Chattanooga |
| Shreveport | -6.37 | -4.75 | Knoxville |
| Savannah | -7.06 | -5.36 | Little Rock |
| El Paso | -7.11 | -5.51 | Mobile |
| Corpus Christi | -7.30 | -5.90 | Baton Rouge |
| Montgomery | -7.44 | -5.99 | El Paso |
| Baton Rouge | -7.55 | -6.06 | Shreveport |
| Austin | -7.81 | -6.37 | Austin |
| | | -6.44 | Corpus Christi |
| | | -6.82 | Montgomery |
| | | -6.88 | Savannah |

SOURCE:  Galle and Stern, 1976

structures of large metropolitan communities are accounted for in large part by the specialized tasks these communities perform in the national economy" (1963, p. 267).

There are many additional analyses drawing upon the system of cities framework as an aid for interpreting changes and adjustments in metropolitan structure. One study (Beckham, 1973) asked whether, within a system of cities, there is increasing or decreasing functional differentiation among them over time. It was shown that "communities tended to become more alike over time, and those closer together tended to be more alike than communities farther apart" (1973, p. 462). However, a later study by the same author (1975) suggested increasing differentiation when the examination was based on occupational differentiation within industries. Additional work is needed before a more definite answer on this issue is known.

Surprisingly, there has not been an abundance of studies using the hierarchy as predictors of other kinds of phenomena. Few ecologists have concerned themselves with the consequences or effects of variations in hierarchical locations among cities, despite the fact that hierarchical position may be argued as a major dimension of sustenance organization (see the discussion in Section IX). There may be more to its influence than many have thought, especially if the recent study of Lincoln (1976) is any indication. He conducted an ecological study of community decision-making in which policy outputs were viewed as the result of the sequence of causes having their origination in the city's functional role in the national metropolitan hierarchy. City size and function were shown to influence a "chain of events of urban structure which have distinct consequences for local policy-making... [It was also demonstrated] that the scope of city government is... an important intervening variable, conveying some of the impact of ecological structure on policy outputs" (1976, p. 13). This is only one example of any number of investigations where ecological position might serve as a viable influence and predictor.

## VIII. NODAL POPULATIONS:
### INTERREGIONAL STUDIES OF SINGLE SUSTENANCE FUNCTIONS

Ecological studies of nodal populations are not restricted to investigations of populations and their hinterlands, and to systems of "cities." Although not receiving as much emphasis as these first two types of nodal studies, interregional studies of single sustenance functions have received attention in the literature.

One of the earlier analyses (since 1950) of single sustenance functions is Lieberson's study of banking (1961). Using data from a survey conducted in October, 1955, by the Federal Reserve System, he examined the relationship between size of bank and function, and bank size and borrower. The study for the most part focused on banks in the Seventh Federal Reserve District. Large banks generally were found to engage primarily in lending money to large business borrowers, whereas small banks in the same cities were primarily engaged in lending to small businesses. However, small and medium-sized banks in cities without large banks were found to make more non-local loans and larger loans than small and medium-sized banks in the major financial centers (p. 494). From these results, Lieberson argues that a greater division of labor exists in the large financial centers than in other places.

Regarding the relationship between bank size and borrower he shows that "banks in a class of a given size are more similar to banks of the same size in other cities than they are to banks of a different size in their own city" (p. 495). Hence, he notes that, with respect to the industrial distributions of borrowers, the large Chicago and Detroit banks better resembled one another than they did the smaller and medium-sized banks in their own or other cities. His analysis is a representative illustration of the insights that may be gained by applying the ecological framework to the study of institutional organization.

An equally influential study, one published two years before Lieberson's, is Pappenfort's analysis of manufacturing (1959). He concentrated for the most part on locating "operating combinations," i.e., the units engaged in production and the units in administration. The production units of manufacturing were found to be spatially separated from their administrative counterparts. In Illinois, he found a strong tendency for the factories to be farther from Chicago's center than the home offices. And the same general pattern was found to obtain within Chicago, and within the nonmetropolitan counties in Illinois, when these were examined independently of one another. He then related these and other findings with the general positions of Chicago in the national system of cities, suggesting that the patterns observed regarding manufacturing and management "may reflect general principles of ecological organization on the national level" (p. 385) that one would miss if interpretation were based solely on local factors.

Perhaps the most extensive collection to date of inter-regional investigations of single sustenance functions is Duncan and Lieberson's *Metropolis and Region in Transition* (1970). The sustenance functions of manufacturing and banking are the principal topics of this book. Manufacturing is addressed in three of the chapters (5, 10, and 14), and national-level analyses of banking are covered in three chapters (6, 11, and 12). Related to these banking studies are two additional chapters dealing with banking studies on explicitly regional levels: Chapter 16 on the rise and development of the financial network in the Texas region, and Chapter 17 on the same topic particularly bank corres-pondents in Florida.

The studies of the manufacturing sustenance activity are particularly intriguing not only because of the historical perspective assumed, but also because of the conceptual and quantitative precision employed. The ecological system of manufacturing centers is described in detail from 1900 to 1960 through location quotients and related kinds of in-dexes. Profiles are prepared for the major centers and manufacturing specialization changes are discussed. A por-tion of the investigation breaks the manufacturing function down into the state of resource use (first stage, second stage, indirect), and the type of market (nonfinal, final). The shifting of centers from one to another of the manufac-turing subactivities is discussed. In some centers, new specialties are shown to emerge between 1900 and 1960. Indeed, the authors argued that centers breaking into the hierarchy since 1900 gained this national prominence pre-cisely because they had relatively more specialties in new lines of industry than did the older centers.

Having delineated the manufacturing profiles for the major metropolitan centers, illustrating their growth and change over time, the authors then focus on twenty-five pro-duction areas, "each including one or more metropolitan areas" (p. 226), and identify the destinations of manu-facturing sustenance from these areas. After tracing the flows of manufacturing from these production areas, the authors conclude that there "is ample evidence of a terri-torial division of labor within the manufacturing sector that extends beyond the differentiation of metropolitan from nonmetropolitan territory. Not only do metropolitan centers differ with respect to their manufacturing specialties [ as they have amply demonstrated in chapter 10] , but they provide for one another important markets for the outputs of the key industries. If the nation is conceived as a mosaic of metro- politan regions, the interregional trade flows are more vital than intraregional trade flows in the marketing of manufactured goods" (p. 242).

The sustenance activity of banking is also discussed in detail. Duncan and Lieberson first address the extent to which shifts in the relative positions of the nation's major centers have occurred in the financial network. They examine reserve-status information from the Federal Reserve System, but illustrate that these data series do not really reveal shifts in the positions of the major centers because most of the centers "held reserve status when the Federal Reserve System was established and each has maintained its special status" (p. 185). To determine changes in the financial prominence of the major centers, they decided to rely primarily upon "the selection of their [the major centers'] financial institutions as underwriters of municipal bond issues and correspondent banks" (p. 185).

The authors reviewed various municipal bond issues over time and, particularly, for 1964. Over time, Cincinnati diminished considerably as a center. In 1900 "underwriters of municipals were more likely to be found in Cincinnati than in any other major center... [By] 1964, Cincinnati firms served as underwriters for 4 percent of the municipal issues, as compared with 38 percent for New York firms and 22 percent for Chicago firms. In fact, thirteen of the major centers were found to have concentrations of underwriters greater than the Cincinnati concentration" (pp. 190-191). The prominence of New York and Chicago is especially apparent. The authors note that one way of looking at their importance is that if "one were to select a major offering from any region, the chances are high that New York City and Chicago firms would be prominent and that some major cities in the region would be particularly active. The participation of underwriters headquartered in centers outside the region probably would be minimal, aside from New York or Chicago firms... The participation of New York and Chicago... has the effect of linking the various regional underwriters into the national money market" (p. 198).

The second procedure for assessing prominence, and changes in prominence, of the major centers in the financial network is through the selection of their institutions as correspondent banks. The authors thus examined a sample of banks in 1900, 1940, and 1965, classifying each bank by its geographic region, and noting each major center in which the bank had a principal correspondent. "The proportions of banks selecting a correspondent in a given center at the three dates offer a basis for assessing change in the prominence of that center in the financial network" (p. 201). The interdependencies existing between the major centers in 1965, as measured by whether a center has a correspondent in another center, is extremely complex. "Fewer than 25 percent of New York's banks selected a correspondent in any other major center, but New York was selected as a correspondent location by more than 25 percent of the banks in each other major center. Chicago's only choice was New York, but it, in turn, was selected by sixteen major centers... Boston and Dallas chose only New York, although they were chosen by seven and eight other centers, respectively. The intercenter relations become much less clearly structured when the remaining linkages are examined, however" (p. 213). In summary, these studies which have received here only selective and cursory review point to the variability among some centers and to the stability among others with regard to their positions of prominence in the national hierarchy on particular sustenance functions, and on the full range of sustenance organization. These studies indicate well the presence of a territorial division of labor in manufacturing and banking, while also illustrating that the more prominent centers in these hierarchies are among the more prominent ones in the national system of cities.

## IX. FUTURE RESEARCH

Future research on sustenance organization would appear to be threefold. In the first place, considerable work needs to be devoted toward operationalizing the sustenance organization dimensions and identifying and operationalizing the components (see the taxonomy developed in Chapter 3 of this volume). There has been already some attention along these lines (Gibbs and Poston, 1975; Frisbie and Poston, 1975; Frisbie, 1975), but these efforts have in no way exhausted the possibilities. Secondly, having initiated work in the operationalization of the sustenance dimensions and components, human ecologists would be in a better position to begin developing an understanding of the structure and form of sustenance organization. How do the various dimensions relate with one another? How do the component-specific sustenance dimensions vary with one another? Although it appears that the seven sustenance dimensions delineated in Chapter 3 are conceptually distinct from one another, it could turn out that, empirically, one may be the image of another. And this may indeed be the case when the seven sustenance dimensions are examined in their component-specific forms.

Thirdly, having initiated research in the direction of describing the dimensions and components of sustenance organization, and identifying the linkages whereby they relate with one another, ecologists should then turn to the question of accounting for the variability in sustenance organization among human populations. We should seek "to explain the presence and absence of particular characteristics of sustenance organization..., i.e., to state the conditions under which a given characteristic will or will not appear" (Gibbs and Martin, 1959, p. 33). Employing only a portion of the taxonomy of sustenance organization presented in Chapter 3 of this book provides considerable information on the sustenance organizations of the populations. We should also seek "to establish the consequences of the presence or absence of particular characteristics of sustenance organization" (Gibbs and Martin, 1959, p. 33). Only in so doing will we ever be able to pretend to possess an even elementary understanding of the structure and form of sustenance organization and the dynamics of ecological change.

REFERENCES

Allen, R. F. (1957). Technology and Social Change. New York: Appleton–Century–Croft.

Bahr, H. M., and J. P. Gibbs. (1967). "Racial differentiation in American metropolitan areas." Social Forces 45 (June):521–532.

Beale, C. L. (1962). "The causes of population growth in rapidly growing rural countries." Paper presented at the annual meeting of the Rural Sociological Society, Washington, D.C., August.

Beale, C. L. (1975). "The revival of population growth in nonmetropolitan America." USDA Economic Research Service, ERS–605.

Bean, F. D., D. L. Poston, Jr., and H. H. Winsborough. (1972). "Size, functional specialization and the classification of cities." Social Science Quarterly 53 (June):20–32.

Beckham, B. (1973). "Some temporal and spatial aspects of interurban industrial differentiation." Social Forces 51 (June):462–470.

Beckham, B. (1975). "A new analytic approach to urban differentiation: occupational differentiation within industries." Sociological Focus 8 (October):297–308.

Berry, B.J.L. (1965). "Internal structure of the city." Law and Contemporary Problems 30 (Winter):111–119.

Berry, B.J.L., and J. D. Kasarda. (1977). Contemporary Urban Ecology. New York: Macmillan.

Berry, B.J.L., and A. Pred. (1961). Central Place Studies: A Bibliography of Theory and Applications. Philadelphia: Regional Science Institute.

Berry, B.J.L., J. W. Simmons, and R. J. Tennant. (1963). "Urban population densities: structure and change." Geographical Rev. 53 (July):389–405.

Bogue, D. J. (1949). The Structure of the Metropolitan Community. Portions reprinted on pp. 524–538 of G. A. Theodorson (ed.), Studies in Human Ecology (1961). Evanston: Harper and Row.

Bogue, D. J. (1959). "Population distribution." Pp. 383–394 in P. M. Hauser and O. D. Duncan (eds.), The Study of Population: An Inventory and Appraisal. Chicago: University of Chicago Press.

Bowles, G. K. (1976). Potential change in the labor force in the 1970–1980 decade for metropolitan and nonmetropolitan counties in the United States. Phylon 37 (3):263–269.

Bradshaw, B. S. (1976). Potential labor force supply, replacement, and migration of Mexican American and other males in the Texas-Mexico border region. International Migration Review 10 (Spring):29-45.

Brown, D. L. (1975). "Socioeconomic characteristics of growing and declining nonmetropolitan counties, 1970." USDA Economic Research Service, ERS-306.

Brown, J. K. (1970). "A note on the division of labor by sex." American Anthropologist 72 (October):1074-1078.

Browning, H. L., and J. P. Gibbs. (1971). "Intra-industry division of labor: the states of Mexico." Demography 8 (May):233-245.

Carroll, R. L. (1963). "The metropolitan influence of the 168 Standard Metropolitan Area central cities." Social Forces (December):166-173.

Christaller, W. (1933). Die Zentralen Orte in Suddeutschland. Jena.

Clemente, F., and R. Sturgis. (1971). "Population size and industrial diversification." Urban Studies 8 (February):65-68.

Clemente, F., and R. Sturgis. (1972). "The division of labor in America: an ecological analysis." Social Forces 51 (December):176-182.

Cortese, C. F., R. F. Falk, and J. K. Cohen. (1976). "Further considerations on the methodological analysis of segregation indices." American Sociological Review 41 (August):630-637.

Deare, D., and D. L. Poston, Jr. (1973). "Texas population in 1970: trends and variations in the population of nonmetropolitan towns." Texas Business Review 47 (January):1-6.

Dickinson, R. E. (1970). Regional Ecology: The Study of Man's Environment. New York: Wiley.

Duncan, B. (1957). "Intra-urban population movement." Pp. 297-309 in P. K. Hatt and A. J. Reiss (eds.), Cities and Society: The Revised Reader in Urban Sociology. New York: Free Press.

Duncan, B., and S. Lieberson. (1970). Metropolis and Region in Transition. Beverly Hills: Sage.

Duncan, B., G. Sabagh, and M. D. Van Arsdol, Jr. (1962). "Patterns of city growth." American Journal of Sociology 68 (January):418-429.

Duncan, O. D. (1959). "Human ecology and population studies." Pp. 678-716 in P. M. Hauser and O. D. Duncan (eds.), The Study of Population. Chicago: University of Chicago Press.

Duncan, O. D. (1961). "From social system to ecosystem." Sociological Inquiry 31 (Spring):140-149.

Duncan, O. D. (1964). "Social organization and the eco-system." Pp. 36-82 in R. E. L. Faris (ed.), Handbook of Modern Sociology. Chicago: Rand McNally.

Duncan, O. D., and B. Duncan. (1955). "A methodological analysis of segregation indexes." American Sociological Review 20 (April):210-217.

Duncan, O. D., and L. F. Schnore. (1959). "Cultural, behavioral, and ecological perspectives in the study of social organization." American Journal of Sociology 65 (September): 132-162.

Duncan, O. D., W. R. Scott, S. Lieberson, B. Duncan, and H. H. Winsborough. (1960). Metropolis and Region. Baltimore: Johns Hopkins University Press.

Durkheim, E. (1893). The Division of Labor in Society. New York: Free Press, 1949.

Easterlin, R. A. (1971). "Does human fertility adjust to the environment?" American Economic Review LXI (May):399-407.

Eberstein, I. W. (1977). "Organization and environmental influences on migration." The University of Texas at Austin. Unpublished paper.

Edmonston, B. (1975). Population Distribution in American Cities. Lexington, MA.: Lexington Books.

Freedman, R. (1975). The Sociology of Human Fertility: An Annotated Bibliography. New York: Irvington.

Frisbie, W. P. (1975). "Measuring the degree of bureaucratization at the societal level." Social Forces 53 (June): 563-573.

Frisbie, W. P., and C. J. Clarke. (1977). "Technology in evaluationary and ecological perspective: theory and measurement at the societal level." Social Forces 58 (December):591-613.

Frisbie, W. P. and D. L. Poston, Jr. (1975). "Components of sustenance organization and nonmetropolitan population change: a human ecological investigation." American Sociological Review 40 (December):773-784.

Frisbie, W. P., and D. L. Poston, Jr. (1976). "The structure of sustenance organization and population change in nonmetropolitan America." Rural Sociology 41 (Fall):354-370.

Frisbie, W. P., and D. L. Poston, Jr. (1978a). "Sustenance differentiation and population redistribution." Social Forces 57 (September):42-56.

Frisbie, W. P., and D. L. Poston, Jr. (1978b). Sustenance Organization and Migration in Nonmetropolitan America. Iowa City: Iowa Urban Community Research Center, University of Iowa Press.

Fuguitt, G. V., (1965). "County seat status as a factor in small town growth and decline." Social Forces 44 (December):245-251.

Fuguitt, G. V., (1971). "The places left behind: population trends and policy for rural America." Rural Sociology 36 (December):449-470.

Fuguitt, G. V., and C. L. Beale (1976). "Population change in nonmetropolitan cities and towns." USDA Economic Research Service, AER-323.

Fuguitt, G. V., and N. A. Deeley (1966). "Retail service patterns and small town population change: a replication of Hassinger's study." Rural Sociology 31 (March):53-63.

Galle, O. (1963). "Occupational composition and metropolitan hierarchy: the inter- and intra-metropolitan division of labor." American Journal of Sociology 69 (November): 260-269.

Galle, O., and R. N. Stern (1976). "Metropolitan dominance and integration in the South: continuity and change." Paper presented at the annual meeting of the Southern Regional Demographic Group, New Orleans, LA. (October).

Gessman, P. H., and D. G. Sisler (1976). "Highways, changing land use, and impacts on rural life." Growth and Change 7 (April):3-8.

Gibbs, J. P. (1959). "Demographic adjustment to a decrease in sustenance." Pacific Sociological Review 2 (Fall): 61-66.

Gibbs, J. P. (1964). "A note on industry changes and migration." American Sociological Review 29 (April):266-270.

Gibbs, J. P. (1965). "Occupational differentiation of Negroes and whites in the United States." Social Forces 44 (December):159-165.

Gibbs, J. P. (1974). "Intra-industry division of labor and the growth of industries." Pacific Sociological Review 17 (October):457-477.

Gibbs, J. P., and H. L. Browning (1966). "The division of labor, technology and the organization of production in twelve countries." American Sociological Review 31 (February):81-92.

Gibbs, J. P., and W. T. Martin (1958). "Urbanization and natural resources: a study in organizational ecology." American Sociological Review 23 (June):266-277.

Gibbs, J. P., and W. T. Martin (1959). "Toward a theoretical system of human ecology." Pacific Sociological Review 2 (Spring):29-36.

Gibbs, J. P., and W. T. Martin (1962). "Urbanization, technology and the division of labor: international patterns." American Sociological Review 27 (October):667-677.

Gibbs, J. P., and W. T. Martin (1963). "Reply to Mehta." American Sociological Review 28 (August):614-616.

Gibbs, J. P., and D. L. Poston, Jr. (1975). "The division of labor: conceptualization and related measures." Social Forces 53 (March):468-476.

Glenn, N. D. (1964). "Some changes in the relative status of American nonwhites." Phylon 24 (Summer):109-122.

Goldschmidt, W. (1959). Man's Way. New York: Holt.

Gras, N.S.B. (1922). An Introduction to Economic History. New York: Harper and Brothers.

Gross, E. (1968). "Plus ca change...? The Sexual structure of occupations over time." Social Problems 16 (Fall): 198-208.

Guest, A. M. (1973). "Urban growth and population densities." Demography 10 (February):53-69.

Guest, A. M. (1975). "The journey to work: 1960-1970." Social Forces 54 (September):220-225.

Haggett, P. (1966). Locational Analysis in Human Geography. New York: St. Martin's Press.

Hawley, A. H. (1950). Human Ecology. New York: Ronald Press.

Hawley, A. H. (1968). "Human ecology." Pp. 323-332 in D. L. Sills (ed.) International Encyclopedia of the Social Sciences. New York: Crowell, Collier and Macmillan.

Hawley, A. H. (1973). "Ecology and population." Science 179 (23 March):1196-2001.

Hawthorne, G. (1970). The Sociology of Fertility. London: Collier-Macmillan.

Herskovits, M. J. (1965). Economic Anthropology: The Economic Life of Primitive Peoples. New York: W. W. Norton and Company.

Holter, H. (1970). Sex Roles and Social Structure. Oslo, Norway: Universitetsforlaget.

Humphrey, C. R., and R. R. Sell (1975). "The impact of controlled access highways on population growth in Pennsylvania nonmetropolitan communities, 1940-1970." Rural Sociology 40 (Fall):332-343.

Johansen, E. J. (1970). The Sexual Basis of the Division of Labor: Interstate Variation in Labor Force Participation Rates by Sex in the United States. Austin: The University of Texas at Austin, Department of Sociology. Unpublished Ph.D. dissertation.

Johnson, G. C. (1972). Professional Differentiation by Sex in the Metropolitan United States: A Descriptive and Methodological Study. Austin: The University of Texas at Austin, Department of Sociology. Unpublished M.A. thesis.

Johnson, G. C. (1977). Metropolitan Sustenance Organization and Professional Sexual Differentiation: An Ecological Study. Austin: The University of Texas at Austin, Department of Sociology. Unpublished Ph.D. dissertation.

Kasarda, J. (1971). "Economic structure and fertility: a comparative analysis." Demography 8 (August):307-317.

Kasarda, J. (1972a). "The impact of suburban population growth on central city service functions." American Journal of Sociology 77 (May):111-1124.

Kasarda, J. (1972b). "The theory of ecological expansion: an empirical test." Social Forces 51 (December):165-175.

Kasarda, J. (1973). "The ecological approach in sociology." Paper presented at the annual meeting of the Southwestern Sociological Association. Dallas, TX. (April).

Kasarda, J. (1974). "The structural implications of social system size: a three-level analysis." American Sociological Review 39 (February):19-28.

Kirschenbaum, A. (1971). "Patterns of migration from metropolitan to nonmetropolitan areas: changing ecological factors affecting family mobility." Rural Sociology 36 (September):315-325.

Labovitz, S., and J. P. Gibbs (1964). "Urbanization, technology, and the division of labor: further evidence." Pacific Sociological Review 7 (Spring):3-9.

Lampard, E. E. (1955). "The history of cities in the economically advanced areas." Economic Development and Cultural Change 3 (January):81-136.

Lenski, G. E. (1970). Human Societies. New York: McGraw-Hill.

Lieberson, S. (1961). "The division of labor in banking." American Journal of Sociology 66 (March):491-496.

Lincoln, J. R. (1976). "Power mobilization in the urban community: reconsidering the ecological approach." American Sociological Review (February):1-15.

Lincoln, J. R., and R. Friedland (1977). "Metropolitan dominance and income levels in nonmetropolitan cities." Sociology and Social Research 61:304-319.

Losch, A. (1940). The Economics of Location. Translated by W. H. Woglom (1954). New Haven: Yale University Press.

McKenzie, R. D. (1933). The Metropolitan Community. New York: McGraw-Hill.

McKenzie, R. D. (1968). "The rise of metropolitan communities." Pp. 244-305 in A. H. Hawley (ed.), R. D. McKenzie on Human Ecology. Chicago: University of Chicago Press.

Mark, H., and K. P. Schwirian (1967). "Ecological position, urban central place function, and community population growth." American Journal of Sociology 73 (July):30-41.

Martin, W. T. (1956). "The structuring of social relationships engendered by suburban residence." American Sociological Review 21 (August):446-453.

Martin, W. T. (1957). "Ecological change in satellite rural areas." American Sociological Review (April):173-183.

Martin, W. T. (1962). "Urbanization and national power to requisition external resources." Pacific Sociological Review 5 (Fall):93-97.

Martin, W. T., and D. L. Poston, Jr. (1972). "The occupational composition of white females: sexism, racism and occupational differentiation." Social Forces 50 (March):349-355.

Martin, W. T., and D. L. Poston, Jr. (1976). "Industrialization and occupational differentiation: an ecological analysis." Pacific Sociological Review 19 (January):82-97.

Mehta, S. K. (1963). "The correlates of urbanization." American Sociological Review 28 (August):609-614.

Micklin, M. (1973). "Introduction: a framework for the study of human ecology." Pp. 2-19 in M. Micklin (ed.) Population, Environment, and Social Organization: Current Issues in Human Ecology. Hinsdale, IL.: Dryden.

Miley, J. D., and M. Micklin (1972). "Structural change and the Durkheimian legacy: a macrosocial analysis of suicide rates." American Journal of Sociology 78 (November): 657-673.

North, C. C. (1926). Social Differentiation. Chapel Hill, NC.: University of North Carolina Press.

Ogburn, W. F. (1951). "Population, private ownership, technology and the standard of living." American Journal of Sociology 56 (September):314-319.

Pappenfort, D. (1959). "The ecological field and the metropolitan community: manufacturing and management." American Journal of Sociology 64 (January):380-385.

Poston, D. L., Jr. (1972). "Socioeconomic status and work-residence separation in metropolitan America." Pacific Sociological Review 15 (July):367-380.

Poston, D. L., and C. J. Clarke (1976). "Sustenance organization complexity and fertility behavior in metropolitan America." Paper read at the annual meeting of the Southern Regional Demographic Group, New Orleans, LA. (October).

Poston, D. L., Jr., and G. C. Johnson (1971). "Industrialization and professional differentiation by sex in the metropolitan Southwest." Social Science Quarterly 52 (September):331-348.

380

Poston, D. L., Jr., and R. White (1978). "Indigenous labor supply, sustenance organization, and population redistribution in nonmetropolitan America: an extension of the ecological theory of migration." Demography 15 (November): 637-641.

Price, D. O. (1968). "Occupational changes among whites and nonwhites, with projections for 1970." Social Science Quarterly 49 (December):563-572.

Pursell, D. E. (1972). "Determinants of male labor mobility." Demography 9 (May):257-281.

Roof, W. C., and T. L. Van Valey (1972). "Residential segregation and social differentiation in American urban units." Social Forces 51 (September):87-91.

Schienfeld, A. (1944). Women and Men. New York: Harcourt, Brace and Company.

Schnore, L. F. (1954). "The separation of home and work: a problem for human ecology." Social Forces 32 (May):336-343.

Schnore, L. F. (1957a). "The growth of metropolitan suburbs." American Sociological Review 22 (April):165-173.

Schnore, L. F. (1975b). "Metropolitan growth and decentralization." American Journal of Sociology 63 (September):171-180.

Schnore, L. F. (1957c). "Satellites and suburbs." Social Forces 36 (December):121-127.

Schnore, L. F. (1958). "Social morphology and human ecology." American Journal of Sociology 63 (May):620-634.

Schnore, L. F. (1961a). "The myth of human ecology." Sociological Inquiry 31 (Spring):128-139.

Schnore, L. F. (1961b). "Social mobility in demographic perspective." American Sociological Review 26 (June):407-423.

Schnore, L. F. (1962). "Municipal annexations and decentralization, 1952-1960." American Journal of Sociology 67 (January):406-417.

Schnore, L. F. (1963). "The socioeconomic status of cities and suburbs." American Sociological Review 28 (February):76-85.

Schnore, L. F. (1964). "Urban structure and suburban selectivity." Demography 1:164-176.

Schnore, L. F., and O. D. Duncan (n.d.). "A review of the recent critical literature in human ecology." Unpublished paper.

Sheldon, H. D., and S. A. Hoermann (1964). "Metropolitan structure and commutation." Demography 1:186-193.

Sjoberg, G. (1965). "Cities in developing and in industrial societies: a cross-cultural analysis." Pp. 213-263 in P. M. Hauser and L. F. Schnore (eds.), The Study of Urbanization. New York: Wiley.

Slesinger, D. P. (1974). "The relationship of fertility to measures of metropolitan dominance: a new look." Rural Sociology 39 (Fall):350-361.

Sly, D. F. (1972). "Migration and the ecological complex." American Sociological Review 37 (October):615-628.

Sly, D. F., and D. Tayman (1977). "The ecological approach to migration reexamined." American Sociological Review 42 (October):783-795.

Stinner, W. R., and G. F. DeJong (1969). "Southern Negro migration: social and economic components of an ecological model." Demography 5:455-473.

Stokes, E. D. (1976). Racial Components of Urban Population Density: Growth Patterns in Chicago, 1930 to 1970. Unpublished M.A. thesis, Department of Sociology, The University of Texas at Austin.

Suttles, G. D. (1968). The Social Order of the Slum. Chicago: University of Chicago Press.

Suttles, G. D. (1972). The Social Construction of Communities. Chicago: University of Chicago Press.

Taeuber, K. E., and A. F. Taeuber (1965). Negroes in Cities. Chicago: Aldine.

Tarver, J. (1972). "Patterns of population change among southern nonmetropolitan towns: 1950-1970." Rural Sociology 37 (March):53-72.

Tarver, J. D., and C. L. Beale (1967). "Population trends of southern nonmetropolitan towns, 1950-1960." Rural Sociology 33 (March):19-29.

Teitelbaum, M. S. (1975). "Relevance of demographic transition theory for developing countries." Science 188 (May):420-425.

Theodorson, G. A. (1961). "Introduction to Part V: regional studies." Pp. 509-515 of G. A. Theodorson (ed.), Studies in Human Ecology. Evanston: Harper and Row.

Turner, R. H. (1951). "The nonwhite female in the labor force." American Journal of Sociology 56 (March):438-447.

Ullman, E. (1941). "A theory of location for cities." American Journal of Sociology 46 (May):853-865.

Vance, F. B., and S. Smith (1954). "Metropolitan dominance and integration." In R. V. Vance and N. J. Demerath (eds.), The Urban South. Chapel Hill: University of North Carolina Press. Reprinted in P. K. Hatt and A. J. Reiss (eds.), Cities and Society. New York: Free Press of Glencoe, (1957).

Wanner, R. A. (1977). "The dimensionality of the urban functional system." Demography 14 (November):519-537.

Wardwell, J. M. (1977). "Equilibrium and change in nonmetropolitan growth." Rural Sociology 42 (Summer):156-179.

Watson, W. T. (1929). "A new census and an old theory: division of labor in the preliterate world." American Journal of Sociology 34 (January):632-652.

Webb, S. D. (1972). "Crime and the division of labor: testing a Durkheimian model." American Journal of Sociology 78 (November):643-656.

Williams, J. G. (1972). Occupational Differentiation by Sex in the United States Labor Force: 1900 to 1960. Austin: The University of Texas at Austin, Department of Sociology. Unpublished Ph.D dissertation.

Williams, J. G. (1976). "Trends in occupational differentiation by sex." Sociology of Work and Occupations 3 (February):38-62.

Winsborough, H. H. (1960). "Occupational composition and the urban hierarchy." American Sociological Review 25 (December):894-897.

Winsborough, H. H. (1963). "An ecological approach to the theory of suburbanization." American Journal of Sociology 68 (March):565-570.

Zimmer, B. G., and A. H. Hawley (1956). "Approaches to the solution of fringe problems: preferences of residents in the Flint metropolitan area." Public Administration Review 16 (Fall):258-268.

Zorbaugh, H. W. (1929). The Gold Coast and the Slum. Chicago: University of Chicago Press.

Zuiches, J. J. (1970). "In-migration and growth of nonmetropolitan urban places." Rural Sociology 35 (September): 410-420.

# Part III

---

# THE APPLICATION
# OF ECOLOGICAL KNOWLEDGE

# Introduction

*the Editors*

In this final chapter, William Catton's discussion both resembles and differs from those of his fellow authors. Addressing the question of how and why sociological human ecology may be useful, he extends some themes set forth in the previous chapters. For example, like Paul Siegel, he argues that human ecology should draw more directly upon the strengths of general ecology. Disapprovingly, Catton shows the limited overlap in vocabularies between human ecology and bio-ecology, noting that the latter field offers a number of powerful concepts which should be applicable in the study of humans in ecological systems. Sociologists are simply failing to use these potentially illuminating ideas. On the other hand, Catton also scolds ecological sociologists for sometimes using ecological concepts incorrectly by distoring or not appreciating their theoretical assumptions.

Catton's chapter is unique in the volume, representing a different tone, an urgency, a passionate appeal, unlike the other contributions. Readers will readily detect Catton's environmentalism. He displays a deep concern about food and energy in the world's future. He is critical of American culture, suggesting that it advocates economic growth and high levels of consumption, leading in dangerous directions. Thus, Catton is also critical of the United States' political system insofar as it encourages or permits the exploitation of natural resources and fails to insure conservation. Indeed, at points, he arrives at conclusions which will strike at least some readers as quite radical.

Catton accepts a major challenge, to propose an applied field of human ecology. He asserts that sociological human ecology has a great deal to offer the policy sciences. Since the beginnings of human ecology, sociologists have examined "real world" problems, analyzing rural and urban communities, examining migration and social change, studying the impacts of technological change; all these processes being major concerns of their times. But Catton implies that the ecological sociologists have stood too far from the field of action. He suggests that it would be more helpful and effective to develop a direct method of applying human ecological knowledge. Catton posits a new role, the ecologist as clinician, therapist, advisor, or consultant. In this role ecologists must interact effectively with decision-makers, all the way up to the highest levels of government. The ecologist could help policy-makers analyze problems by offering alternative courses of action and by pointing out various kinds of consequences--social and political, long-range as well as short-run--of the possible choices. At one point Catton uses the physician as a model of the ecologist-as-clinician, while at others his active ecologist resembles a member of the President's Council of Economic Advisors or a political candidate's media and polling consultant, providing expertise to the political actor. In other words, Catton argues that the applied human ecologist should have confidence that ecological theory and research, or at least an ecological approach, will provide superior intellectual tools to aid in decision-making, tools more powerful than conventional wisdom.

# 9
# Human Ecology and Social Policy

*William R. Catton, Jr.*

## Urban Ecology and Change

In the final chapter of their new textbook, *Contemporary Urban Ecology*, Berry and Kasarda (1977:429) speak of a spreading "awareness that we have the ability to strive and deliberately contrive change"--implying a conviction that human ecologists might tend to welcome opportunities to influence the future's unfolding rather than just to forecast it or explain it.

Applied ecology has as much right to be considered a "policy science" as does the study of national defense strategy, or national monetary policy, or the analysis of foreign policy (Caldwell, 1966:525). It transcends the boundaries of both biology and sociology. But the effectiveness of an applied science depends not only on the validity of its knowledge but also on the circumstances in which efforts to apply that knowledge to policy-making take place (Caldwell, 1966:526). Some types of institutional arrangements are more compatible than others with an ecological orientation, and it ought to be possible, according to Caldwell, to identify the factors in existing institutions that make them resistive to ecological reasoning. American institutions at the present time do tend to be resistive to ecological understanding of the human situation (Marx, 1970), and later in this paper I shall consider such resistance and some possible tactics for coping with it.

An ecological orientation may predispose us toward truly major policy changes. Two biological scientists who wrote a small book on urban ecology—without citing any of the leading sociological human ecologists' work—expressed the view that "One of our major enemies may be our notion that you can patch up society with paper tape" (George and McKinley, 1974:110). Then, as if to imply that urban problems may sometimes reach a point where they become essentially irremediable, these biologists cited the presence of 100,000 heroin addicts in New York City and noted the occurrence there in 1969 of 900 drug-abuse-caused fatalities. They described this as an example of "one of the things that people do to themselves to make city life livable."

Sociological human ecologists have generally been much more inclined to accept urbanism as a viable mode of human sustenance organization. Sociologists have sometimes sought to contribute to programs of urban change, reform, or improvement, but more often they have taken it upon themselves to *study* urban structures, processes, and trends—as scholars rather than interventionists. Occasionally their studies have been aimed at assessing the impact of ostensibly ambitious reform programs, such as "urban renewal." This federally sponsored patching effort has, according to Greer (1967:185), lacked the powers it would have needed "to fulfill its radical aims. It also lacks the precedents that could create legitimacy for those aims. It is hemmed in by laws which support the individual's choice of residence and land use, which leave building to the market place in real estate, which leave action to the local public agency. But its most important limits are, simply, the limits of our knowledge." In an effort to contribute needed knowledge, sociologists have sometimes felt constrained to violate or stretch the canons of scientific rigor by indulging in deliberate over-generalization from a case or two they may have studied intensively. (See, for example, Rossi and Dentler, 1961:275-292, who offer some general propositions about the indispensability and limited utility of "citizen participation" in urban renewal projects.)

Careful research using standard demographic procedures and acceptable to the most scholarly has also been possible. For example, Hawley (1963) showed that the higher the

ratio of proprietors, managers, and officials to the total
employed labor force in a city, the less likely that city
was to have advanced to the execution stage in an urban
renewal program. For the federal sponsor of urban renewal,
the Housing and Home Finance Agency, Hawley suggested that
this meant its investments were more likely to achieve success if directed to cities with high concentration of power.
For his academic colleagues, he used the study to shed light
on the meaning of "power" in a human ecology framework.

Throughout the last several decades, Hawley has been a
recognized leading contributor and shaper of sociological
human ecology. And he has repeatedly undertaken inquiries
that have contributed to the policy potential of this field.
Hawley and Zimmer (1970), for example, were convinced that
urban problems could only be solved if metropolitan organization could be reformed, so they surveyed six metropolitan
areas to find out what objections people tend to have toward
governmental consolidation. It happened that all six areas
they studied were in northern states in the East and Midwest, whereas eight of the nine successful instances of
city-county consolidations during three postwar decades had
occurred in the South. Kasarda (1975) therefore suggested
that the Hawley-Zimmer study would have been improved had it
taken into account the different "ecological and political
structures" of metropolitan areas in the different regions.
He further suggested that attitudes should have been surveyed among residents of one or two successfully consolidated metropolitan areas.

Nevertheless, Kasarda acknowledged, the Hawley-Zimmer
study was a source of useful information with public policy
implications. It showed, first of all, that despite the
manifest difficulties arising from metropolitan "balkaniza-
tion," continued citizen resistance to metropolitan governmental consolidation could be expected. Second, it implied
that as a means of overcoming such resistance it would be
important to increase citizen awareness of problems and in-
efficiencies arising from political fragmentation. Third,
the findings made it seem advisable to seek alternative
mechanisms for offsetting the ills of fragmented political
jurisdictions. These alternatives might include creation of
special service and taxing authorities that would be metropolitan in scope but would stop short of full-scale governmental consolidation. Or, they might include creation of
metropolitan service commissions comprising elected officials from the several municipalities in an area, brought
together to exercise combined responsibility for regional
planning and provision of certain metropolitan services.
Still another alternative might be creation of federal or

state offices of metropolitan affairs in each area; such an agency could help coordinate service efforts of local governments. Extension of federal and state grants-in-aid and revenue-sharing programs to assist local jurisdictions was another possibility.

The knowledge, perspectives, and skills of the sociological human ecologist have been recognized for their policy potential. Hawley was a member of a social science panel created to analyze the significance of community in the metropolitan environment for an advisory committee to the Department of Housing and Urban Development. (See, National Academy of Sciences—National Academy of Engineering, 1974).

Other pertinent work has been done under non-university auspices. At The Rand Corporation, for example, Peter Morrison has written a series of papers pointing out policy implications of metropolitan demographic changes, redistribution of population, cessation of growth, etc. He has shown, for instance, how Congress might be advised to anticipate impacts such changes may bring for Social Security, retirement programs, educational financing, revenue-sharing, welfare, food stamp, or Medicare programs (Morrison, 1978). In a statement prepared at the request of the House Subcommittee on Housing and Community Development (Morrison, 1975b), he reviewed the onset of population decline in many metropolitan rings and the revival of population growth in areas remote from metropolitan development, and discussed fiscal and other adaptations these changes would entail. Earlier, Morrison (1973) had suggested that population redistribution could be deliberately influenced by policies designed to enhance potential migrants' preferences for some distinations and reduce their attraction to other places.

Describing the influence of cultural predispositions, migratory preferences, and government activities and programs upon the national system of urban settlement, Morrison (1975a) suggested that efforts to intervene and modify the system must begin with an assessment of "hidden" policies. By this term he meant the (possibly unintended, generally unacknowledged) population distributional effects of highway construction programs, defense contract allocation, location of federal installations, etc. In the same paper he suggested the importance of understanding "cultural geography" such as the concentration of retired persons in Arizona, Mormons in Utah, and environmentally concerned persons in Oregon.

More recently, Morrison (1977a) has begun to analyze emerging conflicts between "the right to migrate" and "less well-defined rights of the population already living where migrants decide to go." Such conflicts have become apparent in such places as "energy boomtowns" (e.g., Gillette, Wyoming, and Colstrip, Montana) and in "growth-limiting communities" (e.g., Petaluma, California, and Boulder, Colorado). Morrison (1977b) has also argued that the approach of the United States to a condition of zero population growth will not eliminate the impact of rapid population growth in particular localities. Local population declines, too, will imply problems of community organizational adjustment. Migration will increasingly alter political and fiscal relationships.

Revival or acceleration of population growth in non-metropolitan areas can affect the population composition in those areas, and can affect their economic situation. As McCarthy and Morrison (1978) have pointed out, population redistribution can be expected to result from (1) increasing accessibility of nonmetropolitan areas to the national metropolitan economy due to changes in transportation; (2) decentralization of manufacturing, expansion of energy extraction, and energy-related industrial development--e.g., in the Rocky Mountain states; (3) changes in American life style, such as earlier retirement and, among all age groups, rise of a leisure activity orientation, attracting people to amenity-rich areas. Population redistribution has important implications for the use of fuel. If heating could be supplied centrally to whole districts, instead of by individual heating devices in separate dwellings, fuel consumption could be significantly reduced (Karkheck, et al., 1977).

It has been recognized that changes in U.S. population distribution, from colonial times until the present, occurred in response partly to the changing availability, types, and costs of energy (Lee, 1977). These factors contributed to development of different means of transportation. They also played a major part in reducing the fraction of the population working the land and they increased per acre productivity. But Lee (1977:13) wrongly calls this "an unparalleled conservation of natural resources [that] is largely a triumph of petroleum." The word "conservation" is surely a misnomer, when some estimates indicate that we now invest several calories of fossil fuel energy in the production, processing, and transportation of each calorie of food (Perelman, 1972). As depletion of reserves raises the monetary costs of fuel, the ability of modern agriculture to feed the world's burgeoning population will become more visibly precarious. It has been estimated that to provide a world population of four billion with an average American diet, using American agricultural technology, energy equivalent to 488 billion gallons of fuel annually would be required (Pimentel, et al., 1973:448). That is roughly equal to the *total* amount of energy used annually for *all* purposes by the United States, and the United States uses about one-third of all the energy used by all of mankind (Ehrlich, et al., 1973:65).

*Focus of this Paper*

Recognizing with Kenneth Watt (1968:17) that energy is going to become for human populations in the near future "the coin of the realm," I propose to focus on a truly monumental policy question now facing mankind. I want to assess the competence of sociological human ecologists to come to grips with that question, account historically for the shortfall in that competence as I see it, propose what seems to me the only feasible remedy for that shortfall, and then raise questions regarding the likely impact on policy of ideally trained human ecologists. Throughout the rest of this paper I shall therefore assume that most of us would hope our influence on social policy might be wielded in some larger arena than simply providing empirical guidance for "locational decisions" by, say, businesses, churches, residence-buying families, or public service agencies in search of an optimum market. Some of us may have larger aspirations than just advising urban or regional planning authorities.

Before going further I should state my agreement with Berry and Kasarda (1977:417-418) that "It is a mischaracterization to think of research as merely providing data or information...." I agree with these authors that the most important policy influence of research "is perceptual, through its effect on the way that policy makers look at the world." I hope Berry and Kasarda are right in claiming research can influence what policy makers "regard as fact or fiction; the problems they see and do not see; the interpretations they regard as plausible or nonsensical; the judgments they make as to whether a policy is potentially effective, irrelevant, or worse." I am sure they are right in suggesting "Much of this influence may occur before a specific policy issue arises, in how people are educated before they become policy makers."

*At the Turning Point*

Whether we recognize it or not, we are in the midst of a policy-making episode of the first magnitude. Sociological human ecologists ought to be contributing to public understanding of the policy-making process by clarifying the concepts by which this episode gets debated. There is no certainty that a national policy realistically suited to actual circumstances is going to emerge from the deliberative process that was launched in the third week of April 1977, when the world's most colossal users of fossil energy were called upon by their president to face the need for, to understand the philosophy behind, and to consider soberly and wisely the components of a comprehensive energy policy. President Carter and Energy Secretary Schlesinger have sought to rechannel public thinking according to a new definition of the situation confronting mankind in general and America in particular.

In apparent recognition of the physical impossibility of continuing the past pattern of escalating energy use, emphasis in their proposed policy has been placed on energy conservation. It was going to take Congress more than a year to enact energy legislation that was much weaker in controlling American energy appetites than the measures the president had requested. It would become apparent that belated passage of this watered down policy legislation was barely a first step in humanity's initiation into a new era of deprivation and reduced aspirations.

Much of what the president said on three occasions during that pivotal week in the spring of 1977 was meant to persuade skeptics that the energy shortage was real, not just a contrivance of oil companies or of some other groups somehow able to profit from an illusory problem. By traditional American standards, the president's speeches on this topic were radical (Carter, 1977). That is, they called for some basic changes from customary American practices. The president sought no applause from Congress but tried to make it clear not only to members of the House and Senate but also to the television public that American problems were part of a global pattern. Early in the 1980's, he said, "even foreign oil will become increasingly scarce." But he lapsed into less-than-ecological thoughtways when he went on to speak of increasing overseas trade deficits as if *they* were the essence of our predicament (rather than mere ledger-book symptoms of the real problem).

The real problem is that our technological civilization has overshot the carrying capacity of our habitat. This is reflected in the fact that, as the president said, "We imported more than $35 billion worth of oil last year, and we will spend much more than that this year." But when he added, "The time has come to draw the line," he *seemed* for the moment to be calling again for something like President Nixon's "Project Independence." Congress and the public were thus permitted to persist in the old-style notion that trade deficits from increased oil imports were the source of national vulnerability. What needed to be conveyed by an ecologically sophisticated national leader to an orientation-seeking constituency was that further crowding of an already overloaded world will make us all more implacably competitive, and competition for the world's remaining fuels is just a piece of that monumental problem.

However, it was clear that the president's thinking and planning had *begun* to be shaped by a genuinely ecological perspective. His repeated emphasis on the need to be "fair" in the ways we apportion sacrifices showed he sensed something like a Hobbesian threat of rampant competitiveness as the besetting condition of our future. That competitive condition appeared to be the background social dimension of the "catastrophe" he indicated a national energy policy was meant to ward off.

But the transitional, rather than altogether ecologically enlightened, nature of the president's thinking was apparent when he explained that "Along with conservation, our second major strategy is production and rational pricing." He was ecologically realistic in pointing out that "We can never increase our production of oil and natural gas by enough to meet our demand," but his continued use of the customary word "production" to refer to *extraction* of fossil fuels reflected lingering commitment to a pre-ecological worldview (Catton, 1973). He called for a sensible system of fuel prices that would discourage waste and encourage "new production," not yet recognizing that the real meaning of "new production" was hastened draw-down of the planet's finite savings deposits. Encouraging "new production" thus means further reliance on the method of *illusory enlargement of carrying capacity* that brought us into our present grave predicament. The coal and oil we have already "produced" gave us seductive but inherently temporary increments of carrying capacity, and we expanded both our numbers and our standard of living to levels that were not permanently feasible.

President Carter's plan to shift from dependence on scarce oil and natural gas to "abundant" coal has to be, at best, a merely transitional remedy. Coal does exist in the world (and under American soil) in greater quantity than petroleum, but it is just as truly a finite remnant of the photosynthetic productivity of ancient vegetation and using it as fuel to prolong our high-energy way of life is just as truly living off of savings rather than contemporary income as if we were to try to remain a nation that runs on oil. Any policy that seeks to perpetuate energy abundance by accelerating "production" of *any* of the fossil fuels merely aggravates our commitment to living at the expense of our own posterity.

## Persistence of an Obsolete Worldview

The important glimmerings of ecological realism in the president's policy proposals were underscored by the way others clung more steadfastly to traditional cornucopian assumptions. The minority leader in the Senate, Howard Baker of Tennessee, said, for example, in an interview on ABC television immediately after the joint session addressed by President Carter, that he was really bothered by one thing:

> ... it seems to me that we're *giving up*. We're giving up on the idea that we can produce ourselves out of this problem. And you know that's the traditional American way, that you *can* find new reserves of oil and gas, you can find new techniques to fuel the energy requirements of this country, and I'm not willing to give up. I'm not willing to allocate this shortage, and I'm not willing now to say that we've got to impose a huge tax on fuel oil or the equivalent of that tax on natural gas or gasoline in order to meet our requirements. There —in the oil and gas field, for instance—the last geological survey I saw by the government in 1975 indicated that there's as much oil probably yet undiscovered as we've ever found or used in the United States. And I find nothing in this proposal that creates any incentive for anyone to explore and develop those reserves.

Senator Baker was obviously *not* thinking in ecological terms. First of all, he was overlooking the fact that our rate of using petroleum had so accelerated that discovery of new supplies equal to all that we had ever used before would only supply us for an additional 19 years at present rates of consumption. But a much more fundamental oversight than this was the fact that he did not see that efforts to provide incentives "to explore and develop" yet undiscovered deposits of fossil fuels would be efforts to continue the deeply prodigal hunting and gathering way of life to which the industrial revolution had so firmly bound us. We have arrived at a point in history where it is perilous to remain blind to the fact that the high-sounding words "exploration" and "development" are euphemisms for *hunting* and *gathering*. The Senate minority leader's glib hope of continuing to "find" the substances we have learned to need neglects some enormously important ecological considerations. Ecologically, a modern industrial society is a society of colossal hunters and gatherers, as dependent in their own prodigious way as their pre-Neolithic ancestors were upon unmanaged processes of nature to put into their environment the sustenance materials upon which their lives and activities depend.

Appeals like Senator Baker's to "the traditional American way" reflect non-recognition that life is now being lived under circumstances very different from those in which our exuberant traditions were formed. Leaders of the political opposition remain less able than President Carter or his first Energy Secretary to see the seriousness of the situation now confronting humanity. They persist in supposing options are still open that really are not.[1] They just do not seem to comprehend what it means for mankind to have already overshot the permanent human carrying capacity of a world or a continent and to have been already so prodigal in drawing down finite resources. They mean to insist on more of the same. They still suppose we can permanently enjoy a carrying capacity surplus like the one with which pioneer settlers of "the New World" were blessed as they began exploiting by European methods and with advancing technology a previously "virgin" hemisphere. They do not see the ecological implications of the kind of economic progress our more recent forebearers made by industrializing. Industrialization escalated not only our use of, but also our appetites for, the earth's deposits of non-renewable resources. With the resources depleted, persistence of the appetites constitutes a momentous example of cultural lag.

---

[1] *For indications that this supposition may be endemic to the Republican party, see Dunlap and Gale, 1974; Caldwell, 1975:85-95; and Dunlap and Allen, 1976.*

*To Be or Not to be Ecological*

Before going any farther, I should try to make clear just what I mean by "ecology" and "ecological." I hope it is already apparent that I have taken seriously Amos Hawley's (1944:405) claim that human ecology can hardly be autonomous among the sciences because no science is likely really to be autonomous. Every science has relevance for every other science. I have come to believe, moreover, that there was profound truth in the concluding sentence of his paper on "Ecology and Human Ecology," that "human ecology might well be regarded as the basic social science." But I believe there has arisen again an urgent need to reiterate Hawley's lament (1944:399) that sociological human ecology was beset with difficulties traceable "to the isolation of the subject from the mainstream of ecological thought."[2]

I share Hawley's (1950:66) view that human ecology is part of general ecology. I would go farther and assert that human ecology will contribute more to our understanding of human social organization and the efforts of human societies to survive and prosper if we conceive it as a specialty within general ecology than if we conceive it more parochially as a specialty within sociology. The latter discipline has confined its attention to just the human species in isolation from a larger biotic context. It is of fundamental importance that mankind be seen as inescapably involved in the biosphere, that all human groups be recognized as components of biotic communities. Human activities, at least at a macro level, are very importantly shaped by biogeochemical constraints which sociologists have learned to neglect. Ecologists have studied such constraints in considerable depth and detail. But sociological neglect of such matters is quite unnecessary. The core idea of sociology, it seems to me, has long been that people behave as they do not merely because of what they are, but because of what they are part of. To escape the stifling effects of past sociological anthropocentrism, sociological human ecologists need

---

[2]*That idea was boldly put forth by Hawley during a period when others were criticizing human ecology on quite different grounds, either contending it was too analogical, too theoretical, or too unsophisticated methodologically. See Theodorson, 1961:5-7, 77-122; Bailey and Mulcahy, 1972; Murdock and Sutton, 1974.*

only acknowledge that people always are part of a system
that comprises not only other people but also other species
and entails interactions also with inanimate components of
nature.

Sad to say, sociological human ecology has stubbornly
continued to cripple itself, it seems to me, by largely dis-
regarding mainstream ecology. With a few notable exceptions, sociologists have been too often and too strongly
tempted to suppose that Homo sapiens as a culture-building
and culture-dependent creature is so unlike other animals
that the analysis and explanation of human behavior can have
no useful connection to any branch of biological theory. So
it is as important today as it was over three decades ago to
reaffirm Hawley's conviction that "the only conceivable
justification for a human ecology must derive from the
intrinsic utility of ecological theory as such" (Hawley
1944:399).[3]

Mine is hardly the first reaffirmation of that stance
since Hawley stated it so plainly. Just six years after
publication of his trenchant paper in *Social Forces*,
Hawley's own textbook-length development of "a full and
coherent theory of human ecology" (1950:v) constituted a
profound personal implementation of the premise that principles of general ecology have human application. Sociological
human ecologists, however, continued too generally to ignore
mainstream ecology, and nine years later it was again
necessary for someone to urge reconsideration of human
ecology's fundamental problem. Gibbs and Martin (1959) took
up the challenge in a paper in which they argued cogently
that human ecologists should pursue two goals: (1) "to explain the presence and absence of particular characteristics
of sustenance organization among human populations" by ascertaining "the conditions under which a given characteristic will or will not appear," and (2) "to establish the
consequences of the presence or absence of particular
characteristics of sustenance organization in human populations."

---

[3]*Hawley also said (1944:402) that there was "no basis..
for calling a study human ecology, if it was not ecological." A legitimate alternative to making sociological
"human ecology" more genuinely ecological, then, might
simply be to re-name it; call some of it "urbanology" and
some of it "spatial sociology," and stop calling these
topics "human ecology."*

If that were what sociological human ecologists had been doing all these years we would have a great deal to say that would be relevant to current deliberations over a national energy policy. Moreover, we would have recognized what solid foundations had been laid by Cottrell's *Energy and Society* (1955) for a sociological theory of the energetics of ecosystems involving humans. Pursuit of such a theory would have paralleled and could have benefitted from and contributed to studies of energetics by mainstream ecologists. But in a significant footnote to this paper, Gibbs and Martin reported finding by a review of the literature that human ecology seemed to be viewed by sociologists either as a mere method or as a field concerned only with the spatial distribution of social phenomena. Gibbs himself, with various collaborators, did try to press on with a program of research on sustenance organization (Gibbs, 1959; Gibbs and Schnore, 1960; Gibbs and Martin, 1962; Labovitz and Gibbs, 1964; Gibbs and Browning, 1966; Gibbs, 1968), but it is my strong impression that even though current literature (e.g., Berry and Kasarda, 1977) speaks of things like sustenance organization, symbiosis, and commensalism, the vast majority of sociologists continue even now to perceive human ecology as a sociological specialty concerned primarily with the spatial structure of cities and perhaps incidentally with spatial dimensions of other human aggregates. (See, e.g., Blau, 1977:155-184.)

Duncan and Schnore (1959) were also compelled to note how easily the ecological viewpoint can be deflected in sociological research into strictly geographic studies of environment or into demographic exercises. As a corrective, they tried to focus attention on "the ecological complex," comprising four classes of variables--population, environment, organization, and technology--and emphasized their reciprocal interrelations. The ecologist's sociologically relevant task, they said, was "to account for the forms that social organization assumes in response to varying demographic, technological, and environmental pressures." They also noted the cross-disciplinary character of ecological inquiry.

Five years later, in his chapter in the *Handbook of Modern Sociology*, Duncan (1964) took a giant step toward articulating principles from general ecology as foundations for sociological human ecology. He justified this by concurring explicitly with Hawley's earlier claim that the mainstream of ecological thought was (as Duncan put it) "a concern with generic features of the problem of organization as experienced by populations constrained to cope with the exigencies of their environments..." and he described his own effort as "primarily an extension of some of the elements in Hawley's work."

In my own teaching of human ecology within a sociology curriculum, I have tried to follow these valuable leads. For several years I have had students read both the 1950 volume by Hawley and a more recent biological treatment of the ecology of man, currently Arthur Boughey's *Man and the Environment* (1975) which incorporates much worthwhile material from ecological anthropology and archeology. I have considered it remarkable (and salient testimony to the validity of what Hawley said in 1944) that his 1950 book has remained so long in print. Nevertheless, I finally decided to replace it with the more recent text, *Contemporary Urban Ecology* by Berry and Kasarda (1977).

With mixed feelings I have noted that among books recently published with titles containing a phrase like "human ecology," "ecology and man," or "man and environment," many seem to have come from authors who are in biology or a kindred science, rather than from sociologists (e.g., Ehrlich, et al., 1973; Vann and Rogers, 1974; Sargent, 1974; Wagner, 1974). I simply do not know whether publication of books like these by biologist authors will help to persuade sociological human ecologists in greater numbers to accept at last the idea that concepts and principles from mainstream ecology are relevant to our concerns. I fear sometimes that we may react instead by imagining a need to claim a distinct intellectual niche for ourselves by the expedient of increased detachment from the mainstream.

I would hope the balance might have been tipped toward integration of sociological human ecology into mainstream ecology by our careful scrutiny of two books written by the two ecologist sons of the late eminent sociologist, Howard Washington Odum. Howard Thomas Odum's *Environment, Power, and Society* (1971), sets forth some of the principles we ought to be contributing to contemporary energy policy discussions. Eugene P. Odum's (1975) paperback in the Modern Biology Series by Holt, Rinehart and Winston, has a subtitle that should be thought-provoking to sociological human ecologists. It is called, *Ecology: The Link Between the Natural and the Social Sciences.* (See also E. P. Odum, 1977) Although I have not employed either of these Odum Books as course texts, I have made much use of especially the latter one in developing my own presentation of ecological concepts and principles.

*Sociological   Human   Ecology   and   Mainstream   Ecology:*
*Vocabulary Comparisons*

Mainstream ecology has a rich vocabulary that is largely
unfamiliar to sociologists. To help acquaint students with
important ecological concepts, I begin my course by distributing a dittoed list of 97 terms that will occur in my lec-
tures. Most of them commonly appear in ecological literature, though a few are special words or phrases denoting
concepts of my own devising. I have recently used this list
as an instrument for assessing just how much of a conceptual
gulf currently separates sociological human ecology from
mainstream ecology. I compared the list with the subject
indexes in Berry and Kasarda (1977), and Odum (1975). Four-
teen of my terms appeared jointly in the Odum and the Berry
and Kasarda indexes: community, competition, culture, dominance, ecosystem, mortality, natality (or fertility), niche,
pollution, resources, succession, symbiosis, technology, and
territoriality.

If we take the total of 57 items from my list that appeared in Odum's index as our standard of comparison, and
call them "mainstream concepts," then the Berry and Kasarda
version of sociological human ecology appears to be only 25
percent in the mainstream.

The 43 terms from my list that appeared in the Odum
index but *not* in the Berry and Kasarda index provide some
indication of the (75 percent) disparity between contemporary sociological human ecology (as influenced by geography)
and mainstream ecology. The terms present in Odum but not
listed in Berry and Kasarda were: abiotic substance, anti-
biotic, autotroph, biogeochemical cycles, biomass, biosphere, bloom, carnivore, carrying capacity, competitive
exclusion, conservation, decomposers, detritovore, detritus,
energy, eutrophication, extrametabolites, food chain, fossil
fuels, gradient, green revolution, habitat, herbivore,
heterotroph, homeostasis, irruption, limiting factors,
metabolism, mutualism, natural selection, nutrients, photosynthesis, predation, production, recycling, respiration,
seral stages, sere, speciation, species, species diversity,
standing crop, and trophic level.

There are also some simple words that are too much a
part of ordinary everyday English for me to have put them
into my class hand-out but which turn out to differentiate
sociological human ecology as represented by Berry and
Kasarda's index from bio-ecology as represented by the Odum
index. If the prescriptions for sound human ecology put
forth by Hawley, by Gibbs and Martin, and by Duncan and

Schnore, had prevailed, so that contemporary sociological human ecology were indeed the study of sustenance organization, one would expect to find terms like "food" and "fuel" appearing with numerous citations in the indexes. "Food" does appear in the biologist's index but not in the sociological human ecology index. "Fossil fuel" appears in the biologist's index but not in the sociological human ecology index. "Energy" appears in the Odum index but not in the Berry and Kasarda index. So do "coal," "gasoline," and "power."

On the other hand, three terms appearing in Berry and Kasarda but not in Odum reflect the spatial interests that so long passed for "ecological" among sociologists: centralization, segregation, and natural areas.

Clearly there is room for doubt that sociological human ecologists are studying their subject-matter with a truly ecological conceptual framework.

*Redefinition*

If ecology is the study of systems of interactions among organisms and between them and the non-living components of their environment--or, more succinctly, the study of ecosystems--then "human ecology" should presumably denote simply the study of ecosystems that involve human beings.

Ecosystems that involve human beings may be tremendously varied, and human ecology might be expected to consider three broad categories. First, there are ecosystems in which man is a very dependent part; the study of environmental influences on human behavior and social institutions in such ecosystems has been a concern of ecological anthropology. Second, there are ecosystems that humans dominate--in varying degrees. I am suggesting that human ecology (even as pursued by sociologists) ought to concern itself with the full range of this variation, seeking to ascertain both the causes and the consequences of variations in human dominance. Third, there may be ecosystems (or fragments of ecosystems, such as cities) so strongly dominated by human activities that they give the illusion of human autonomy. It seems to me that sociological human ecology has been impoverished by concentrating almost exclusively upon this category. By studying urban complexes, for example, with little regard for the non-human or non-manmade ecosystem components other than, say, topography, we have *seemed* to support the notion that humans, collectively if not individually, are exempt from ecological principles that apply to other types of organisms.

*Ecological Principles*

To rectify that mistaken impression, therefore, let us consider some ideas from mainstream ecology that ought to be recognizable as germane for human ecologists. First: speciation, the separation of organisms into distinct noninterbreeding types, has ecological significance largely as an indication of "occupational" differentiation, rather than differentiation of form. Among the higher forms of life, however, increasingly elaborate symbiotic relationships can emerge *within* species. Conspecifics can sometimes *behave* enough differently from each other so that they make somewhat different demands on the environment. The human species in particular is capable of becoming so behaviorally differentiated that it is *as if* it were divided into many species. Interactions between human roles, or between different labor-force occupations, are functionally equivalent to the interactions between diverse species (Stephan, 1970). Insofar as each role has a distinctive configuration of symbiotic and competitive relationships to organisms occupying other roles, many ecological principles that describe relationships between species should be expected to prove useful in understanding relationships between functionally differentiated human categories. In short, the enormous capacity of Homo sapiens for behavioral differentiation may turn up many ecological principles as principles of sociology.

As was pointed out by Sumner (1896), the ratio between a population and the available quantity of an essential resource is an important determinant of the intensity of competition among members of that population. Insofar as the population's members make identical demands on their environment, their relationship to each other tends to be competitive. As population increases, competition has to be intensified.

Competition may apply not only to resource acquisition but to waste disposal as well. Not only does every organic species take substances from its habitat in the process of living; it also puts transformed substances into the habitat. The life processes of many organisms put into their habitat certain chemical compounds whose presence affects the life processes of these and other organisms sharing the same habitat. Such "extrametabolites" may act either as inhibitors of growth, or as promotors of growth, depending on their chemical properties. When these chemical by-products of the life processes of one species (or occupational group) are harmful to another species, the relationship of the two species or groups to each other is "antagonistic." Increased population density increases the probability of antagonistic interactions.

In the ecological context, antagonism is quite impersonal. The word does not have the emotional connotations it would have in reference to human conflict. There is neither animosity nor vituperation between the people of Los Angeles, for example, and the Ponderosa Pine trees miles away which are killed by the smog that city generates, or between the penicillium mold and the bacteria its extrametabolite (penicillin) stifles. Antagonism in ecology merely means that fulfillment of one organism's needs is antithetical to maintenance of environmental conditions suitable for fulfilling the needs of another organism.

Among human beings, however, animosity can perhaps be aroused by mutual interference between groups even when the interference is indirect and unintended. An age of overpopulation can thus become an age of human conflict. Similarly, as population increase intensifies competition for finite resources (including space), the probability that competitive interactions can turn into conflict may be increased.

Differentiated organisms which influence each other adapt collectively to the life-supporting conditions of their shared habitat, forming thereby a "community"--a more or less self-sufficient and localized web of life. The roles in a community are performed by many different species of living things, both plants and animals, so it is appropriately termed a "biotic community." If the most significant roles are performed by plants, it is properly called a "plant community." When animals play a more conspicuous part in the collective adaptation, the association of diverse organisms can be called an "animal community," without meaning that animals only are involved. Similarly, when man, through his own extensive differentiation on social and occupational lines, plays so many of the roles that it appears the community is mostly under human control, we call it a "human community." But man cannot be self-sufficient; the term "human community" should never be construed as implying independence from other species. Human communities are biotic communities in which non-human components remain indispensible even if unconspicuous.

Frederic Clements (1916) recognized that the kind of biotic community which can thrive in a given habitat depends on that environment's characteristics; they act upon the organisms that make up the community. But he also saw that organisms, in the process of living, *react* upon their habitat. Soils are changed by the plants that grow in them. Sites are made suitable for shade-tolerant species by tall, shade-giving species. Plants requiring stable conditions of moisture cannot become established on some sites until other plants have provided a moisture-holding ground cover. Clements realized that the reaction of a community upon its habitat was central to the process of ecological succession. Pioneer communities alter their environment and foster their own replacement by quite different communities in subsequent seral stages.

A few sociologists such as Park and Burgess (1921:525-527) began almost immediately to use ideas from ecology in their efforts to understand human experience. But when they talked of succession, this key insight into its nature was easily lost. Perhaps because there was still an almost unquestioned belief that technological advances were both inevitable and beneficial, students of Ernest W. Burgess came to regard succession in human communities not as a product of adverse site-modification resulting inexorably from normal use, but essentially as a process of aggression. Invaders were imagined to be succession's driving force (Burgess, 1928), rather than recognized as beneficiaries of what prior occupants did to a site in the course of using it. Missing was the basic insight that users of an environment may make it unsuitable for themselves by using it, an idea that is sorely needed today for understanding such problems as underlie the current quest for an energy policy.

To summarize: Within human populations there arises a division of labor that is ecologically similar to species differences in biotic communities. But since some of our sustenance needs remain essentially similar throughout the human species, as our numbers increase relative to environmental resources, competition has to be intensified. Antagonism (of an impersonal, ecological sort) increases also as population presses upon an environment's capacity to absorb and recycle products of metabolism, and ecological antagonism may stimulate conscious animosity. Human dependence on other species remains ineluctably a fact of life, and a human community like any other biotic community alters its habitat by using it, fostering its own replacement by a later seral stage.

*Spotlight on the Human Predicament*

Current policy deliberations could be greatly illuminated by recognition that mankind may be involved in a global process of succession. An industrial civilization based on enormous inputs of fossil energy cannot be a climax community for it necessarily undermines its own existence by what it does to its resource base (and by exuding autotoxic extrametabolites, too--i.e., pollution). But sociological human ecologists cannot contribute to this illumination of man's current predicament if we go on misusing the word "succession" to mean merely such events as ethnic replacement in residential neighborhoods (e.g., Aldrich, 1975; Aldrich and Reiss, 1976) and fail to recognize the essence of the concept as used in mainstream ecology (Kormondy, 1969:158). The concept of succession, and especially the component of the process that ecologists call "reaction"--site-modification by users, often adverse to themselves--can be tremendously helpful in enabling us to recognize the significance of industrial societies' precarious dependence on nature's dwindling legacy of non-renewable resources. No community whose dominant members depend on non-renewable resources can be self-perpetuating. As modern man draws down nature's finite legacy, we subject ourselves to the constraints of a changed environment, and the relationships between some of our major forms of sustenance organization (corporations, nations, cartels, etc.) become more competitive and more antagonistic. Efforts to formulate policies to cope either with resource shortages or with the activities of such organizations need to be based on clear understanding of the relations of one to the other.

That kind of understanding is impeded by assumptions about the world that are deeply entrenched in our culture, based on the historic experience of a people who found themselves blessed just a few centuries ago with a vast (and therefore seemingly inexhaustible) increment of carrying capacity when an additional hemisphere of colonizable territory became known. As Leo Marx, a Professor of English and American Studies, pointed out several years ago, the perspective of ecology is "in the purest meaning of the word, radical" when contrasted with the merely "pragmatic and meliorist" thought of conservationism (Marx, 1970:946). He went on to say to members of the American Association for the Advancement of Science that:

> The relative popularity of the conservation movement helps to explain why troubled scientists, many of whom foresaw the scope and gravity of the environmental crisis a long while ago, have had such a difficult time arousing their countrymen. As early as 1864 George Perkins Marsh, sometimes said to be the father of American ecology, warned that the earth was 'fast becoming an unfit home for its noblest inhabitant,' and that unless men changed their ways it would be reduced 'to such a condition of impoverished productiveness, of shattered surface, of climatic excess, as to threaten the depravation, barbarism, and perhaps even extinction of

the species.' No one was listening to Marsh in
1864, and some 80 years later, according to a distinguished naturalist who tried to convey a similar
warning, most Americans still were not listening.
'It is amazing,' wrote Fairfield Osborn in 1948,
'how far one has to travel to find a person, even
among the widely informed, who is aware of the processes of mounting destruction that we are inflicting upon our life sources.

The language of these men is chosen more for vivid
imagery than for theoretical rigor, but it expresses important ecological ideas even so. As I have written elsewhere (Catton, 1976:263):

...in a high-energy industrial civilization the
differently specialized organisms of our global
community (including differently specialized human
groups) cannot cause the mutually offsetting reactions upon the environment that would characterize
a climax.

One indication of the size of the gap between
industrialism and climax is the imbalance in the
carbon cycle. Organic fixation by photosynthesis no
longer equals the return of oxidized carbon to the
atmosphere by respiration plus combustion. This imbalance is inescapably fostered by man's efforts as
a tool-making species to do on a grand scale the
very kinds of things for which he has evolved
special aptitudes. The worldwide ratio of man-
caused oxidation to man-managed fixation is now at
least 10 to 1 (Jensen, 1970:83), rather than the 1
to 1 ratio of P/R in a climax community. This can
be taken as an indication of our involvement in a
process of heterotrophic succession; it is a
measure of our commitment to using temporary carrying capacity....

If we are to see where we are headed, therefore, we must
have a clear understanding of the differences between climax
communities and communities undergoing succession. We need
to see the human significance of such measures as the ratio
between fixation and oxidation of carbon in an ecosystem in
which we are involved. We must understand the causes and
consequences of succession accurately, and not content ourselves with crudely metaphorical and sometimes distorted
usages of words that have important technical meanings in
mainstream ecology. We even need to know the circumstances

that result in heterotrophic succession as distinct from autotrophic succession, and we need to recognize just what special kind of heterotroph Homo sapiens has become by virtue of the colossal technology now employed by humans. Otherwise we shall continue to suppose technology can always be depended upon to "mediate" population-environment relationships in a favorable direction (enlarging carrying capacity as needed) and will fail to see that the mediation is often deleterious (because it shrinks carrying capacity by enlarging per capita resource appetites).[4]

A "human ecology" that neglects these matters scarcely merits the name. The sociologist's professional phobia about "reductionism" has excused such neglect too long.

When any niche in an ecosystem becomes overfilled (either by population increase or by resource depletion), there is pressure toward niche diversification. Among non-human organisms, this leads eventually to the emergence of new species. Among humans, through sociocultural processes, it leads to the emergence of new occupations (Durkheim, 1933). But neither impersonal nature nor human foresight can provide any guarantee that new niches or occupations will automatically be already available at the right time and in the right quantity to absorb whatever surplus population may have been crowded out of an older niche. Nor is there any guarantee of pre-adaptation of surplus individuals to new niches.

In nature, overfilling of old niches can result in heightened mortality. Among human organisms, when old niches become obsolete, we can ostensibly retrain ourselves for new roles, so mortality increase may be an *avoidable* result of niche saturation. But retraining for new niches can be traumatic. The classic study of Polish emigrants by Thomas and Znaniecki (1918) showed how unlikely it is even among members of the relatively flexible and plastic human species that re-adaptation to new niches (as old ones close up) will occur easily or automatically. People who had come to the "land of opportunity" after absorbing the folkways of their native Poland were faced with the necessity of adapting to unfamiliar circumstances. Old ways of behaving and thinking

---

[4]*For indications that even the most ecologically-minded sociologist can backslide into making unwarranted assumptions that the mediating effects of technology will necessarily (or usually) enlarge carrying capacity, see Hawley, 1973, and Hawley, 1975:1-17.*

were not easily abandoned; new ways were learned or accepted only with difficulty. Thomas and Znaniecki generalized from the immigrant's situation that *an accustomed way of behaving* (or thinking) *tends to persist as long as circumstances allow.*

Any event that makes old ways unworkable and new ways mandatory can inflict upon humans the trauma of reorientation. Half a century after the *Polish Peasant in Europe and America* was published, Alvin Toffler (1970) coined and popularized the phrase "future shock," an illuminating variant of the term "culture shock" which was already in use to denote the bewilderment and disorientation even a casual tourist can feel when he travels abroad and is surrounded by an alien culture. Toffler's phrase helped make it clear that forced adjustment to *new* ways can be as traumatic as forced adjustment to *foreign* ways.

The kind of foot-dragging about unavoidable policy changes that is reflected in obstinate American desires to "produce our way out" of present resource problems may be as symptomatic of future shock as it is of the persistence of a pre-ecological worldview. In fact, what human ecologists should be able to see better than anyone is that the persistence of pre-ecological perspectives is part of the reason people are shocked by the future that is now befalling them. Certain resources have now already been drawn down to a point where the non-climax character of industrialized human communities is making itself felt in our lives. People are experiencing the process of "heterotrophic succession" and even without knowing what the phrase means they can feel that it is a trend in a direction they don't like.

The impact of changed circumstances is the impact of an arrived "future" that very few people were taught to anticipate. Insofar as the future shock now being felt results from changes that are irreversible, it can be ameliorated only by so enlightening those who suffer from it that they *understand* the irreversibility and the real reasons for the unavoidable modifications in their lives. But this will not be easy.

## Human Ecologists as Consultants

The idea of alleviating stress by revealing its basis and nurturing acceptance of reality reminds us, of course, of psychoanalysis. If future-shocked policy makers begin turning to human ecologists as consultants, human ecologists will need not only to understand clearly the roots of the problems that bring such clients to them, and the nature of their clients' aspirations; human ecologist consultants to

policy makers will also need some of the special skills of
the clinician. Care, and keen awareness of social (as well
as ecological) reality, will be required for three tasks:
(1) structuring the client-consultant relationship; (2) attempting a prognosis; and (3) managing the client's resistance to insight.

As an aid to understanding these tasks, consider what
transpires when a patient presents himself for psychotherapy
(Taylor and Catton, 1963:36; Cf. Sussman, 1966), a situation
significantly parallel to that of the counsel-seeking
future-shocked policy maker:

> The patient may say that he is anxious and
> disturbed; he may feel that he needs training in
> 'becoming adjusted'; he may suffer from psychoso-
> matic problems--the symptoms are as many as there
> are cases. The clinician listens, aware that the
> presenting symptoms are often only indirectly re-
> lated to the real problems. He knows that the
> patient has other motivations for coming and he
> must be alert to these. He knows that the patient
> is apt to have magical hopes and expectations about
> treatment--a 'cure' may be expected after two
> visits, or the patient may hope somehow to become
> impossibly effective and perfect, or the therapist
> may be expected to prove that the patient's prob-
> lems are 'normal' and so should be disregarded. It
> is not uncommon for the patient to try to enlist
> his therapist in a power struggle, hoping for a
> powerful ally to defeat a spouse, a parent, or a
> boss. To all of these needs and maneuvers the
> therapist must remain sensitive and--usually--
> apart, patiently explaining the conditions and
> limitations of treatment.

While description of the patient-clinician relationship
is not meant to suggest that policy makers who come to human
ecologists are "sick" or need "therapy," policy makers may
be expected to consult human ecologists only when they are

faced with a problem they suppose the human ecologist's expertise can help solve.[5] The policy maker will have his own prior conceptualization of the problem; often he will see it as a problem of social control, supposing that what is needed is expert advice on how to redirect the behavior of others. It may be supposed by the policy maker that this can be accomplished by obtaining evidence from the expert consultant which will prove to these others that some preconceived plan of the policy maker is, after all, correct and effective, so that they should dutifully acquiesce in it. Sociological human ecologists need to be wary of becoming cast in the role of purveyor of opposition-squelching Scientific Proof of the Rightness of the Preordained Plan. (I trust I am not expressing excessive cynicism when I venture the hypothesis that this may be precisely the kind of role thrust upon many of those who become engaged in writing environmental impact assessments under provisions of Section 102, paragraph 2C, of the National Environmental Policy Act of 1969.)

Policy makers may be expected, of course, to view their own preferences ethnocentrically, in terms of their own values and professional or partisan norms. It is unlikely that findings from properly conducted research or general principles from human ecology will conclusively confirm their ethnocentrically preferred definitions of otherwise vexing situations. Ecological situations and processes are unlikely to be as simple, nor policy outcomes as benign, as they are ordinarily portrayed by partisan ideologies (Goodman, 1970). Because of this, however, the human ecologist consultant must expect to be berated for a time by his client when it becomes apparent that he does not accept the client's simplistic definitions. To *serve* the client, and especially to serve both truth and the larger human community of which the policy maker client is presumably an agent, it may be necessary to endure a temporarily hostile phase in the client-consultant relationship. Avoiding client wrath by accepting (or seeming to accept) unsound client definitions of the problem(s) about which one is being consulted is likely to result in larger difficulties later.

---

[5]*Some human ecologists may not be willing to wait for policy makers to request their services as consultants, but may wish to play an activist role. Few human ecologists are actually likely to attain public office, however, and if activism merely consists of agitation, I have doubts whether its efficacy would exceed that of the consultant in the long run. Therefore I shall limit my discussion in this paper to the consultant role.*

The policy maker may easily imagine that many others would support his preferred plan if only they "really understood" it, which usually means the policy maker wishes others would attribute the same wisdom and good intentions to him that he imputes to himself. In that case there is the risk that the consultant will be pressed into the role of legitimator of the client.

Assuming that such problems of structuring the relationship between client and consultant are solved, it becomes necessary for the consulting human ecologist to discourage in his client any unrealistic expectations of potential results and encourage realistic ones, just as the psychotherapist has an ethical responsibility of estimating his potential services to a prospective patient. It should be almost self-evident that a consulting human ecologist can hardly expect to help a policy maker client who seeks magical answers and will accept nothing short of all-encompassing solutions—and wants them instantly. Nor can he help one who comes to the relationship with a closed mind, unwilling to consider alternative perspectives, unfamiliar evidence, or the possibility of having to abandon some cherished scheme as unworkable. In short, what needs to be assessed by the human ecologist if he is to be useful in a consulting role is the client's receptivity to new knowledge and new concepts. (And again I trust it is not mere cynicism to offer the hypothesis that most policy makers can be expected to be at least as resistive as most average citizens to the kind of knowledge and reconceptualization provided by ecological expertise.)

No prospective client is likely to be *totally unresistive* to new insight. So even when a consulting relationship has been established with mutual understanding of its limits and reasonable expectations of effectiveness, it remains for the consultant to exercise persuasive skills in fulfilling his role obligations. Substantive knowledge will not suffice. Just as the psychotherapist knows the futility of sitting a patient down and bluntly telling him "this is what's wrong, and this is what you must do," the consulting human ecologist must have the forebearance to match his investigation of the client's problem and his efforts to enlighten the client to the client's ability to absorb new information and adopt new perspectives. That ability can be expected to increase as the consulting relationship moves along, but concern with timing is essential. Attempts to impart more new knowledge than the client is prepared to accept will arouse resistance. Such attempts would be as useless as writing an irate letter to Senator Baker, denouncing him as an ignoramus for wishing to aggravate the plight of our hunting and gathering society.

In the end, however, the consulting human ecologist must be able to cope with frustrations in himself, for he is likely to encounter *some* policy makers for whom it turns out that there is *no* pace of enlightenment gradual enough to assuage resistance and achieve fresh insight. It may just be that some minds are constitutionally incapable of accepting an ecological perspective and therefore cannot comprehend ecological principles. Hopefully there are no such inflexible minds among those sociologists who have chosen to consider themselves human ecologists.

## A Scenario

To explore further what might be involved in availing ourselves of wished-for opportunities to shape public policy on vital issues for which principles of human ecology have relevance, let us suppose we had been engaged as consultants by Senator Baker. He put the challenge to us somewhat like this: "I know," he said, "that our country has a problem. We are bigger, more powerful, and more productive than ever before, but there are tensions among our people in spite of advances we have recently made in social justice, there are threats to the quality of our environment that take some of the joy out of this century's gains in the American standard of living, and we are becoming too dependent on foreign sources for some of the resources that are vital to our industry and to the maintenance of that standard of living. Furthermore, inflation has been eating away not only a major fraction of our gains in affluence but has been wiping out the savings of our retired people and seriously undermining the well-being of those Americans who have to live on fixed incomes. The president has outlined some policies he wants Congress to legislate. He calls them 'the moral equivalent of war,' and says we face catastrophe if we don't change our ways, if we keep on trying to live higher and higher on the hog. I admire his courage in offering comprehensive programs, but I think he's giving up too easily in the face of adversity and abandoning the American 'can do' tradition. So I come to you for your advice as a human ecologist. How can you help me develop legislation that will more fittingly take this nation into a brighter future?"

How should we begin the ecological education of a Howard Baker? Surely not in "Peanuts" comic strip fashion by blurting out a Lucy-like aphorism, offering a five-cent antidote to heterotrophic succession! He'd expect more and he'd not be ready for even that much.

rapidly as possible. Americans are habituated to unrecognized prodigality, and that winter they seemed bent on hastening the day when none of these materials would be left for our descendants.

Can any significant number of policy makers or their constituents learn to recognize at last the inescapable intricacy of any non-detritovorous relationship between the human species and its habitat? Is it possible for a politician to realize, as did the forester Aldo Leopold (1933), that if a civilization is to endure it has to be a system of "mutual and interdependent cooperation between human animals, other animals, plants, and soils"?

Can political leaders ever candidly acknowledge that general affluence simply cannot last in the face of a carrying capacity deficit? Amid Congressional debate of the administration's energy policy proposals there occurred expressions of public yearning to believe that curtailed use of energy need not entail reduction of the traditionally high American standard of living. In an admonitory (and possibly wistful) way, some spokesmen for reduced energy consumption have noted that affluence of an American level somehow prevails in Sweden and in West Germany despite their using only about half as much energy per capita as Americans use. But how likely is it that any really heroic program of efficiency measures would be willingly undertaken and fully implemented by American industry and American consumers? And if, as Ross and Williams (1977) acknowledged after proposing an elaborate list of energy-saving changes to achieve a 40 percent reduction of gross energy use, this large a saving would merely buy us 17 years' postponement of the ultimate consequences of our colossal commitment to draw-down, what then? Will we accept with any grace an involuntary but unavoidable return to a simpler life, or will we kick and scream our way into it, imagining we could always have everything we wanted if only those people in Washington weren't taxing it or forbidding it? It seems improbable that mankind on any large scale will adapt gracefully to "de-development." At present the urge toward worldwide development remains potent and prevalent. We are long out of tune with the mores of asceticism.

Is there any chance at all that Americans can learn to practice such mandatory austerity unless we can first be freed of the widespread, deliberate badgering of people into wanting more, more, more? With a truly ecological way of perceiving relationships we should begin to recognize the increasingly antisocial ramifications of advertising. But how could we realistically hope to discredit and wind down this want-multiplying industry? Is there any prospect of legally suppressing it? In an overpopulated and resource-depleted world, an industry fundamentally devoted to making people dissatisfied with what they have is an industry dedicated to augmenting human frustration. Given enough rope it may foster the resentful attitudes that could turn inescapable competition into destructive conflict.

It should not be inconceivable that a civilized people could do without such badgering. Freedom to exhort people to hasten exhaustive draw-down of nonrenewable resources was not what the authors of the American Bill of Rights presumably intended to establish, yet a great deal of modern, jealously protected "communication" now fosters the self-destruction of our hunting and gathering industrial economy. Make no mistake, though—freeing ourselves from such pressures toward self-destruction would entail truly revolutionary changes. Drastic reorganization of American radio and television broadcasting would be required. Magazine and newspaper publishing would have to change greatly, getting by on sources of revenue other than advertising. These changes would be vehemently resisted. Even suggesting them would be denounced as "unrealistic." Reinterpretation (if not alteration) of the First Amendment provision for unabridged freedom of speech and press would be a necessary constitutional step. Is any reform less probable?

*Other Options*

There are, of course, various other paths that might be chosen by sociological human ecologists who want the policy relevance of their work to be felt. We can continue developing knowledge that is useful to city planners (Kligman, 1945; Gillette, 1957; Peterson, 1967; Dorney, 1973; Salter, 1974). We might branch out, join forces with rural sociologists, and contribute to the knowledge base for regional planning in rural areas (Boskoff, 1949; Young and Larson, 1970; Lassey, 1977). In doing so, we might develop renewed awareness of the unremitting dependence of cities upon rural hinterlands. This might lead to increasing recognition of the sociological relevance of concepts and principles developed by bio-ecologists. It might stimulate us to read with new appreciation some of the works of one of the sociological pioneers of human ecology who, without yet knowing the term "ecosystem," saw Homo sapiens as inescapably part of a multi-species web of life and a system embracing soil, moisture, and climate (Mukerjee, 1930; 1938).

Probably we would begin by commending our client for having the wisdom to seek further knowledge. But then we'd have to suggest quickly that the issues he raises are quite as involved ecologically as they are complex politically and therefore require careful and time-consuming study. He would probably acknowledge that he was not expecting definitive answers "overnight." From his own political experience he would probably recognize a need for cutting the pattern to fit the cloth, so we might soon get him to temper his expectations even further and agree that in perhaps two years of consulting we could be expected to provide him with "some guidance" on "no more than half" of the serious matters that led him to seek our assistance. It would be important also to persuade him that our initial sessions with him would be entirely devoted to exploring the dimensions of the problem and would provide no policy recommendations at all. We would need to be alert for signs of impatience and ever ready to remind him that "Rome wasn't built in a day," or that no ship is seaworthy the day its keel is laid.

Somehow, then, we might hope to begin laying the keel, perhaps engaging him in a series of Socratic dialogues, or in some other way, leading him to understand the following kinds of ecological propositions.

We might ease into our first dialogue with a leading question: Don't you agree, sir, that everything people do requires an expenditure of energy? ("Expenditure" would be a less accurate word ecologically than "conversion" of energy, but we should start out using his language, working into ours only gradually. No need to fret about laws of thermodynamics yet.) With his assent to this opening proposition we could go on to discuss the fact that human communities once relied almost entirely on organic sources of energy—plant fuels and animal muscle power. These were supplemented very modestly by the equally renewable energy of moving air and flowing water. All of these energy sources were derived from on-going solar income. (Getting the Senator, a non-ecologist, to see that this is true would be a small but important step toward getting him to perceive familiar processes ecologically.)

Locally, forested land might have been over-harvested. Green pastures might have been overgrazed. Local changes of climate might sometimes compel human communities to migrate. But always there used to be resources available *somewhere* that could support the activities of the human population then in existence. Primitive man lived within the earth's "current income" (hopefully a persuasive metaphor for a budget-minded Senator)—not necessarily from wisdom but from ignorance of the buried treasure yet to be discovered.

Then the earth's savings (fossil fuels) began to be discovered as new ways of using them were gradually devised.
Admiring this expanding technology, man committed himself to
the fatal error of supposing that life could thenceforth be
lived on a scale commensurate with the rate at which
treasure was discovered and unearthed. (To give our client
an idea of *how much* larger this scale of living was than
the one based on current energy income, we might show him a
table included in Duncan's *Handbook* chapter (1964:63)
which shows changes in annual work output per capita in the
United States, by source of energy. From 1850 to 1950, use
of *renewable* energy per capita remained constant, but
*total* energy use per capita increased tenfold. In 1850,
the largest share of the renewable energy was obtained from
work animals; in 1950 more than three-fourths was hydro-
electric. Energy from *exhaustible* sources in 1850 amounted
to little more than half the energy obtained from the
muscles of human workers; by 1950, coal, petroleum, and
natural gas were supplying energy equivalent to the muscle
power of about 96 workers per capita.)

Time after time, as industrial expansion forged ahead,
the rate of withdrawal of savings deposits was mistaken for
a rise in income. Because the Carboniferous energy legacy
was huge, no regard for its total size, or for the rate at
which nature might still be storing carbon away, seemed
necessary.

At this point in the dialogue, the political relevance
of ecological perspectives could begin to be made apparent.
Pre-ecological misunderstanding of what mankind was actually
doing to the future, we could point out, was epitomized by
that venerable loophole in the corporate income tax laws of
the United States, the oil depletion allowance. (The dero-
gatory word "loophole" might arouse resistance in our
Republican client.) This measure permitted so-called oil
"producers" to offset taxable revenue by a generous percentage on the pretext that their earnings reflected depletion of "their" crude oil reserves. (Continuing resistance
expressed by Senator shifting position in his chair.) Even
though it was nature, not the oil companies, that had put
the oil into the earth, this tax write-off was rationalized
as an incentive to "production." (Good words, incentive and
production. Resistance somewhat assuaged. Now for an end run
around client's mental barrier, using socially acceptable
metaphor.) Since "production" really meant *extraction,*
this was like paying someone interest on each withdrawal of
savings rather than on the principal left in the bank. It

was a government subsidy, in fact, for diminishing the legacy to our grandchildren. (Here the consultation should be recessed until another day. The client has been subjected to some ideas that are unorthodox enough that time must be allowed for them to "take.")

Next session. The essence of the draw-down method of supplementing carrying capacity is this: man began to spend nature's legacy as if it were income. (Pause to define carrying capacity.) Temporarily this made possible a dramatic increase in the quantity of energy per capita per year by which human beings could do the various things they wanted to do. This increase led among other things to reduced manpower requirements in agriculture. It also led to the development of many new occupational niches for increasingly diversified human beings. (Pause to define niche, discuss analogy between species and occupation, discuss processes of social differentiation as distinct from genetic sources of trait variation.) Because the new niches depended on spending the withdrawn savings, they were niches in what amounted to a "detritus ecosystem." Detritus, an accumulation of dead organic matter, provides some kinds of creatures with a one-time burst of sustenance. Energy from such an accumulation affords an opportunity for lavish living *for a short time*. When the legacy is gone, the niches must collapse. The social ramifications of that collapse are unpleasant to contemplate. (Consultation recessed again; this is a large idea to swallow, people and their machines being detritus consumers.)

Detritus ecosystems flourish and collapse because they lack the life-sustaining biogeochemical circularity of other kinds of ecosystems. They are nature's own example of communities that flourish briefly by the draw-down method, and industrial civilization based on drawing down fossil energy reserves is basically similar.

Most people, of course, have never heard the phrase "detritus ecosystem." (This flatters the client, who now knows some esoterica still unknown to most of his constituents.) "Bloom" and "crash" cycles are common among organisms that depend on exhaustible accumulations of dead organic matter for their sustenance. Bloom and crash are a special kind of sere (pause to define); certain kinds of populations in certain kinds of circumstances typically experience these two seral stages—irruption followed by die-off. (Frequent stops in this session to define terms and reassure client of need for "all this jargon.")

Crash can be thought of as an abrupt instance of "succession with no apparent successor." Just as in cases of ordinary succession, the biotic community changes its habitat by using it, and finds itself (much) less viable in the

changed surroundings. Sometimes after crash the environment
can recover from resource depletion by that species. Then a
new increase of numbers may make that species "its own successor." Accordingly, among species as different as rodents,
insects, and algae, there are *cycles* of irruption and die-
off. But some of the resources we use cannot recover. They
are non-renewable. (Momentous thought, hard to take; time to
retreat into less threatening and therefore more convincing
example.)

When yeast cells are introduced into a wine vat, they
find their "New World"--the moist, sugar-laden fruit mash--
abundantly endowed with the resources they need for exuberant growth. Their population responds explosively to this
magnificent circumstance, but as a consequence the accumulation of their own fermentation products makes life for them
increasingly difficult. Eventually the microscopic inhabitants of this artificially contrived detritus ecosystem all
die from the alcohol and carbon dioxide they have produced;
they die of self-made pollution.

A similar fate happens to organisms in a pond when its
plant and animal inhabitants fill it up with organic debris.
This turns it eventually into a meadow, in which aquatic
creatures can no longer live.

(If not presented very carefully, this bundle of ideas
might provoke any intelligent non-ecologist into asking
petulantly, "Who cares about such episodes?" the answer
should be a sympathetic "We all *need* to.") We need to see
what a common occurrence it is for organisms using their
habitat to end up unavoidably reducing its capacity to support their kind by what they necessarily do to it in the
process of living. Sometimes, in making their habitat less
suitable for themselves, organisms make it more suitable for
another species or group of species. If the other types are
available to move in, we have succession.

Like the yeast, we humans have been inflicting serious
damage upon *our* habitat's capacity to support *our*
species. Nature had treated mankind as winemakers treat the
yeast cells, by endowing our world as theirs is initially
with abundant but exhaustible resources. When the earth's
deposits of fossil fuels and mineral resources were being
laid down, Homo sapiens had not yet been prepared by evolution to take advantage of them. But later, when our species
had developed and had been equipped by innovations in technology, we eagerly took on the role of detritovore, a consumer of buried remains of prehistoric vegetation. Using
coal, oil, and natural gas, our industrial civilization

bloomed, and now we must expect to undergo crash as the natural sequel unless we earnestly set about phasing out activities that depend so heavily on lavish spending of this exhaustible legacy.

Our client heaves a pensive sigh. We fall silent.

## Facing the Big Questions

Is it conceivable that by patiently but persistently allowing him to "work through" to new insights at his own pace we could actually render a leader of the loyal opposition so ecologically perceptive that he would turn the debate about how to cope with the future toward questions of greater profundity than merely arguing over whether to "give up" or "provide incentives" and try to "produce" our way out of trouble?

Could a politician be led to consider the question, What kind of role are human beings going to play in their own impending crash?[6] Could he be made to wonder how much our efforts to avoid the unavoidable might make it worse?

Men who continue to perceive today's human predicament in pre-ecological terms just will not recognize limits imposed by the world's finiteness. Their assumptions require them to suppose that only machinations of antagonists can thwart our attainment of long-sought goals. Can such men be induced, by reorientation to an ecological way of viewing the world, to ask whether we might actually begin to make ourselves less detritovorous? That is, can they begin to consider *phasing out our use of "fossil fuels" as combustible sources of energy?* Could they learn to think seriously about winding down our use of oil and natural gas *and* coal as fuels? Will policy makers ever believe that far more drastic change is require of us to escape the fate of other detritovores than merely shifting from scarce oil to "abundant" coal, and supplementing both with nuclear power, as proposed by President Carter?

During the harsh winter of 1977, our initial response to the energy pinch was to increase efforts to extract the earth's Carboniferous legacy. Not only a culprit-seeking Congress and the scandal-hungry news media but even the conservationist Secretary of the Interior, Cecil Andrus, felt obliged to berate oil and gas companies for "withholding" some of nature's finite legacy rather than "producing" it as

---

[6]*For some indications of the kind of role humans might fall into playing in their own impending crash, see Catton, 1976, and the references cited therein.*

We might join forces with the architectural profession (Zeisel, 1975; Michelson, 1977). Even this might eventually involve us with a somewhat more biologically-implicated branch, landscape architecture, which again might serve to remind us that ecological concepts are biological (Hackett, 1963; Herbert, 1967).

We might discover that there are human ecologists who are more or less innocent of any sociological training or affiliations, and that they have already pre-empted the job of providing useful knowledge for such fields as public health (Hinkle, 1965; Lee, 1965) and the conservation of resources (Callison, 1967; Jordan, 1968).

Sooner or later, I suspect, sociological human ecologists would be compelled to discover that they had lost something important when they drifted out of the ecological mainstream. Worthy as these other options all are, how are we to avoid acquiring a reputation for being intellectually trivial unless at least some sociological human ecologists attempt to provide conceptual and informational inputs to the on-going public debate over a really fundamental question—whether human dominance over a global ecosystem has to be curtailed to perpetuate that ecosystem's human carrying capacity?

*Radical?*

If it seems absurdly visionary to imagine persuading a Republican Senator to consider that kind of issue, what about those minds who profess to be "radical" or "revolutionary"? Do they actually penetrate much closer than "establishment" politicians to the real root of the human predicament? They, too, work from an obsolete paradigm. In their pre-ecological worldview, the myth of limitlessness persists. It pervades their rhetoric. The editor of a recently published compilation of excerpts from the writings of Marx and Engels that purports to show them off as pioneers of ecology has attributed to Marx views that are as unecological as the assumptions implicit in Senator Baker's objections to President Carter's energy plan (Parsons, 1977: 206). In a concluding section of selections in which Marx expounds upon "The Transformation of Man's Relation to Nature Under Communism," Marx is said to have shown how to open the way "for a real material basis for wealth and for the true wealth of human fulfillment." Capitalism, of course, has obstructed such fulfillment, but "Marx...foresaw in a grand and lyrical vision how labor can become liberating 'as an activity regulating all the forces of nature'" under communism. (Clearly, man was not expected by Marx to relinquish the role of an ecological dominant.) But Marx, we are told, foresaw "how, under socialist control and direction of society, and under man's rational cooperation with nature, all people might be released from backbreaking labor and the oppressions of the ruling class, and pass at last from the burdensome necessity of the past to true human freedom."

As human *ecologists* we are obliged to ask what is radical about proposing merely to get rid of capitalist procedures for providing economic progress to burgeoning populations by means of accelerated draw-down if they are just to be replaced with socialist procedures for providing economic progress to burgeoning populations, also by means of accelerated draw-down? In an ecological sense, this ostensibly revolutionary scheme would leave the problem intact. Both the Marxist and the capitalist versions of sustenance organization amount to variations on a single theme. Capitalists advocate achieving progress by ever more extravagant indulgence in "finding" and "producing" oil, gas, minerals, etc. for mass consumption. Socialist revolutionaries urge what they regard as a more equitably arranged system of consumption, but it would still be based on avid hunting and gathering of non-renewable resources.

As long as each side diagnoses the world's ills by concepts derived from a pre-ecological paradigm, both remain blind to the principle that human society is part of a global biotic community in which excessive dominance by one species (equipped with powerful technology) is self-destructive. Let us, as human ecologists, seek to replace blindness with clear vision.

The public debate launched by President Carter's energy policy messages in 1977 is ultimately a debate over whether to curtail human dominance. It will continue far beyond the sessions of the 95th Congress. Its outcome may be a decision *not* to halt the self-destructive activities of our detritus-based national (and world) economy, especially if no group of scholars comes forth to make it clear that that is what the debate is about.

REFERENCES

Aldrich, H. (1975). "Ecological succession in racially changing neighborhoods: a review of the literature." Urban Affairs Quarterly, 10 (March):327-348.

Aldrich, H., and A. J. Reiss, Jr. (1976). "Continuities in the study of ecological succession: changes in the race composition of neighborhoods and their businesses." American Journal of Sociology, 81 (January):846-867.

Bailey, K. D., and P. Mulcahy (1972). "Sociocultural versus neoclassical ecology: a contribution to the problem of scope in sociology." Sociological Quarterly, 13 (Winter): 37-48.

Berry, B. J. L., and J. D. Kasarda (1977). Contemporary Urban Ecology. New York: Macmillan.

Blau, P. M. (1977). Inequality and Heterogeneity: A Primitive Theory of Social Structure. New York: Free Press.

Boskoff, A. (1949). "An ecological approach to rural society." Rural Sociology, 14 (December):306-316.

Boughey, A. S. (1975). Man and the Environment (2nd ed.). New York: Macmillan.

Burgess, E. W. (1928). "Residential segregation in American cities." Annals of the American Academy of Political and Social Science, 140 (November):105-115.

Caldwell, L. K. (1966). "Problems of applied ecology." BioScience, 16 (August):524-527.

Caldwell, L. K. (1975). Man and His Environment: Policy and Administration. New York: Harper and Row.

Callison, C. H. (ed.) (1967). America's Natural Resources (revised printing). New York: Ronald.

Carter, L. J. (1977). "Carter energy message: how stiff a prescription?" Science, 196 (6 May):630-632.

Catton, W. R., Jr. (1973). "Extensional orientation and the energy problem." ETC.: A Review of General Semantics, 30 (December):344-356.

Catton, W. R., Jr. (1976). "Can irrupting man remain human?" BioScience, 26 (April):262-267.

Clements, F. E. (1916). Plant Succession: An Analysis of the Development of Vegetation. Washington, D.C.: Carnegie Institution.

Cottrell, F. (1955). Energy and Society. New York: McGraw-Hill.

Dorney, R. S. (1973). "Role of ecologists as consultants in urban planning and design." Human Ecology, 1 (March): 183-200.

Duncan, O. D. (1964). "Social organization and the ecosystem." Pp. 36-82 in R. E. L. Faris (ed.), Handbook of Modern Sociology, Chicago: Rand McNally.

Duncan, O. D., and L. F. Schnore (1959). "Cultural, behavioral, and ecological perspectives in the study of social organization." American Journal of Sociology, 65 (September):132-146.

Dunlap, R. E., and M. P. Allen (1976). "Partisan differences on environmental issues: a congressional roll-call analysis." Western Political Quarterly, 29 (September): 384-397.

Dunlap, R. E., and R. P. Gale (1974). "Party membership and environmental politics: a legislative roll-call analysis." Social Science Quarterly, 55 (December):670-690.

Durkheim, E. (1933). The Division of Labor in Society (Transl. by G. Simpson). New York: Macmillan.

Ehrlich, P. R., A. H. Ehrlich, and J. P. Holdren (1973). Human Ecology: Problems and Solutions. San Francisco: W. H. Freeman.

George, C. J., and D. McKinley (1974). Urban Ecology: In Search of an Asphalt Rose. New York: McGraw-Hill.

Gibbs, J. P. (1959). "Demographic adjustment to a decrease in sustenance." Pacific Sociological Review, 2 (Fall):61-66.

Gibbs, J. P. (1968). "Change in industry structure: international comparisons." Pacific Sociological Review, 11 (Spring):38-48.

Gibbs, J. P., and H. L. Browning (1966). "The division of labor, technology, and the organization of production in twelve countries." American Sociological Review, 31 (Feb.): 81-92.

Gibbs, J. P., and W. T. Martin (1959). "Toward a theoretical system of human ecology." Pacific Sociological Review, 2 (Spring):29-36.

Gibbs, J. P., and W. T. Martin (1962). "Urbanization, technology, and the division of labor: international patterns." American Sociological Review, 27 (October):667-677.

Gibbs, J. P., and L. F. Schnore (1960). "Metropolitan growth: an international study." American Journal of Sociology, 66 (September):160-170.

Gillette, T. L. (1957). "A study of the effects of Negro invasion on real estate values." The American Journal of Economics and Sociology, 16 (January):151-162.

Goodman, D. (1970). "Ideology and ecological irrationality." BioScience, 20 (December):1247-1252.

Hackett, B. (1963). "Ecological approach to design." Landscape Architecture, 53 (January):123-126.

Hawley, A. H. (1944). "Ecology and human ecology." Social Forces, 22 (May):398-405.

Hawley, A. H. (1950). Human Ecology: A Theory of Community Structure. New York: Ronald.

Hawley, A. H. (1963). "Community power and urban renewal success." American Journal of Sociology, 68 (January):422-431.

Hawley, A. H. (1973). "Ecology and population." Science, 179 (23 March):1196-1201.

Hawley, A. H. (1975). Man and Environment. New York: New York Times Company.

Hawley, A. H., and B. Zimmer (1970). The Metropolitan Community: Its People and Government. Beverly Hills, CA.: Sage Publications.

Herbert, J. R. (1967). "Ecology and environmental design." Pp.241-253 in J. M. Lambert (ed.), The Teaching of Ecology. Oxford and Edinburgh: Blackwell Scientific Publications.

Hinkle, L. E., Jr. (1965). "Studies of human ecology in relation to health and behavior." BioScience, 15 (August): 517-520.

Jensen, W. G. (1970). Energy and the Economy of Nations. Henley-on-Thames: G.T. Foulis & Co.

Jordon, P. A. (1968). "Ecology, conservation, and human behavior." BioScience, 18 (November):1023-1029.

Karkheck, J., J. Powell, and E. Beardsworth (1977). "Prospects for district heating in the United States." Science, 195 (11 March):948-955.

Kasarda, J. D. (1975). "Policy change and grassroots inertia: the case of metropolitan services." Pp. 45-55 in N. J. Demarath, III, O. N. Larsen, and K. F. Schuessler (eds.), Social Policy and Sociology. New York: Academic Press.

Kligman, M. (1945). "Human ecology and the city planning movement." Social Forces, 24 (October):89-95.

Kormondy, E. J. (1969). Concepts of Ecology. Englewood Cliffs, NJ: Prentice-Hall.

Labovitz, S., and J. P. Gibbs (1964). "Urbanization, technology, and the division of labor: further evidence." Pacific Sociological Review, 7 (Spring):3-9.

Lassey, W. R. (1977). Planning in Rural Environments. New York: McGraw-Hill.

Lee, D. H. K. (1965). "An ecological approach to environmental health sciences." BioScience, 15 (August): 524-526.

Lee, E. (1977). "Energy and the distribution of population." Paper presented at the annual meetings of the American Association for the Advancement of Science, Denver, 24 February.

Leopold, A. (1933). "The conservation ethic." Journal of Forestry, 31 (October):634-643.

Marx, L. (1970). "American institutions and ecological ideals." Science, 170 (27 November):945-952.

McCarthy, K. F., and P. A. Morrison (1978). "The changing demographic and economic structure of nonmetropolitan areas in the 1970s." Santa Monica, CA.: The Rand Corporation (The Rand Paper Series, P-6062), January.

Michelson, W. (1977). Environmental Choice, Human Behavior, and Residential Satisfaction. New York: Oxford University Press.

Morrison, P. A. (1973). "A demographic assessment of new cities and growth centers as population redistribution strategies." Public Policy, 21 (Summer):367-382.

Morrison, P. A. (1975a). "Toward a policy planner's view of the urban settlement system." Santa Monica, CA.: The Rand Corporation (The Rand Paper Series, P-5357), January.

Morrison, P. A. (1975b). "The current demographic context of national growth and development." Santa Monica, CA.: The Rand Corporation (The Rand Paper Series, P-5514) September.

Morrison, P. A. (1977a). "Migration and rights of access: new public concerns of the 1970s." Santa Monica, CA.: The Rand Corporation (The Rand Paper Series, P-5785), March.

Morrison, P. A. (1977b). "Emerging public concerns over U.S. population movements in an era of slowing growth." Santa Monica, CA.: The Rand Corporation (The Rand Paper Series, P-5873), October.

Morrison, P. A. (1978). "How demographers can help members of congress." Santa Monica, CA.: The Rand Corporation (The Rand Paper Series, P-6079), March.

Mukerjee, R. (1930). "Ecological contributions to sociology." Sociological Review, 22 (October):281-291.

Mukerjee, R. (1938). The Regional Balance of Man: An Ecological Theory of Population. Madras: University of Madras.

Murdock, S., and W. A. Sutton, Jr. (1974). "The new ecology and community theory: similarities, differences, and convergencies." Rural Sociology, 39 (Fall):319-333.

National Academy of Sciences--National Academy of Engineering (1974). Toward an Understanding of Metropolitan America. San Francisco: Canfield.

Odum, E. P. (1975). Ecology: The Link Between the Natural and the Social Sciences (2nd ed.). New York: Holt, Rinehart and Winston.

Odum, E. P. (1977). "The emergence of ecology as a new integrative discipline." Science, 195 (25 March):1289-1293.

Odum, H. T. (1971). Environment, Power, and Society. New York: Wiley-Interscience.

Park, R. E., and E. W. Burgess (1921). Introduction to the Science of Sociology. Chicago: University of Chicago Press.

Parsons, H. L. (ed.) (1977). Marx and Engels on Ecology. Westport, CT.: Greenwood.

Perelman, M. J. (1972). "Farming with petroleum." Environment, 14 (October):8-13.

Petersen, W. (1967). "On some meanings of 'planning.'" Pp. 176-196 in S. V. Ciriacy-Wantrup and J. J. Parsons (eds.), Natural Resources: Quality and Quantity. Berkeley and Los Angeles: University of California Press.

Pimentel, D., L. E. Hurd, A. C. Bellotti, M. J. Forster, I. N. Oka, O. D. Sholes, and R. J. Whitman (1973). "Food production and the energy crisis." Science, 182 (2 November): 443-449.

Ross, M. H., and R. H. Williams (1977). "The potential for fuel conservation." Technology Review, 79(February): 49-57.

Rossi, P., and R. A. Dentler (1961). The Politics of Urban Renewal. New York: Free Press.

Salter, P. S. (1974). "Toward an ecology of the urban environment." Pp.238-263 in W. H. Johnson and W. C. Steers (eds.), The Environmental Challenge. New York: Holt, Rinehart and Winston.

Sargent, F. II, (ed.) (1974). Human Ecology. New York: Elsevier.

Stephan, G. E. (1970). "The concept of community in human ecology." Pacific Sociological Review, 13 (Fall): 218-228.

Sumner, W. G. (1896). "Earth hunger or the philosophy of land grabbing." Pp. 31-64 in A. G. Keller (ed.), Earth-Hunger and Other Essays. New Haven: Yale University Press, 1913.

Sussman, M. B. (1966). "The sociologist as a tool of social action." Pp.3-12 in A.B. Shostak (ed.), Sociology in Action. Homewood, IL.: Dorsey.

Taylor, J. B., and W. R. Catton, Jr. (1963). "Problems of interpretation in clinical sociology." Sociological Inquiry, 33 (Winter):34-44.

Theodorson, G. A. (ed.) (1961). Studies in Human Ecology. New York: Harper and Row.

Thomas, W. I. and F. Znaniecki (1918). The Polish Peasant in Europe and America (5 vols.). Chicago: University of Chicago Press.

Toffler, A. (1970). Future Shock. New York: Random House.

426

Vann, A., and P. Rogers (eds.) (1974). Human Ecology and World Development. London: Plenum.

Wagner, R. H. (1974). Environment and Man (2nd ed.). New York: W. W. Norton.

Watt, K. E. F. (1968). Ecology and Resource Management: A Quantitative Approach. New York: McGraw-Hill.

Young, R. C. and O. F. Larson (1970). "The social ecology of a rural community." Rural Sociology, 35 (September): 337-353.

Zeisel, J. (1975). Sociology and Architectural Design. New York: Russell Sage Foundation.

# EPILOGUE
# Research and Policy Issues in Sociological Human Ecology: An Agenda for the Future

*Michael Micklin*
*Harvey M. Choldin*

This Epilogue suggests directions for further work in sociological human ecology. Necessarily, though, the issues raised sometimes transcend purely sociological concerns because of ecology's multidisciplinary perspective. This discussion emphasizes questions about the field that require additional thought and investigation, and about which there is a lack of consensus among ecologists from sociology as well as other disciplines.

---

*This discussion draws upon several sources. First, there are the issues raised in the preceding chapters. Second, the Battelle Conference on Sociological Human Ecology, at which these papers were first presented, included a panel discussion on current issues in human ecology (by John W. Bennett, William R. Burch, Walter T. Martin, and Leo F. Schnore) as well as a number of open discussions involving all the participants. Finally, following the conference the editors asked each participant to prepare a brief summary of his reactions to the conference presentations and discussions. In this regard, the comments prepared by William R. Catton, Jr. were particularly useful.*

427

The issues raised are organized around five general topics. *Conceptual issues* include questions about the scope and organization of human ecosystems, and about how this reality can be represented in a sociological frame of reference. *Theoretical issues* reflect concerns over the ordering of cause and effect relationships, and over the potential of the ecological approach to advance prediction and explanation of variations in social structure and social process. *Methodological issues* center on the adequacy of current operational measures of key ecological concepts and of the research designs and statistical procedures used to test hypotheses generated by ecological theories. *Substantive issues* involve questions about the proper subject matter for human ecological research and about the most productive topics for further investigation. Finally, *practical issues* concern the bearing of ecological knowledge on policies and programs designed to eliminate or reduce societal problems. For a variety of reasons, only some of which will be mentioned here, the issues to be discussed are not distributed evenly among the five topical areas. Stated otherwise, sociological human ecologists have given considerable thought to some issues relevant to development of their field of inquiry while neglecting others.

## CONCEPTUAL ISSUES

In recent years some conceptualizations of sociological human ecology have reemphasized connections with the parent field of bioecology. Many of the preceding chapters advocated building bridges to general ecology. Nonetheless, there is still considerable debate over the extent of the conceptual gap between the two fields and whether it can be bridged without violating the integrity of both fields. The fundamental paradigm for organizing bioecological phenomena is the ecosystem model. However, it is not clear whether this model should be defined to include the subject matter of human ecology (as Siegel and Catton advocate) or, alternatively, whether social systems should be analyzed on their own terms and treated as merely analogous to ecosystems. If the first of these approaches is adopted, we may lose sight of those characteristics that are unique to human social systems. To follow the second approach may lead us to use ecosystem concepts that have no counterpart in human societies. The fundamental issue, then, is the degree to which the organization of human populations follows the same principles that guide the organization of nonhuman populations.

A second conceptual issue involves the relationship between sociological human ecology and the ecological approaches developed in other social sciences. For example, while there is considerable overlap between sociological and anthropological versions of human ecology, there are some critical differences. The two disciplines differ radically in that anthropologists emphasize culture, material and non-material, while ecological sociologists' tend to exclude symbolic phenomena from their domain of inquiry. Few, if any, sociologists would deny the importance of non-material culture in structuring the organization of human societies. But is it necessary for answering questions about ecological organization? Similarly, we may ask whether the fundamental concepts that distinguish geography, political science, economics and other disciplinary approaches to human ecology are redundant or superfluous when applied to the concerns of sociological human ecology? Alternatively, is it possible to enhance the predictive and explanatory power of the sociological approach by incorporating selected assumptions and concepts from these other disciplines?

Related to these first two issues is the question of whether the ecological perspective's scope is so comprehensive that there is no way to define the boundaries of the field. Any science that claims to be capable of addressing all or even most of the substantive problems of societal organization is immediately suspect and reminiscent, perhaps, of Spencer's imperial sociology as the queen of sciences. The test of such a global perspective is its ability to predict and/or explain a wide range of sustantive phenomena. To date, no version of sociological or any other human ecology has demonstrated these abilities. Thus we need to specify more clearly the strengths and weaknesses of the ecological perspective as an approach to the study of social organization.

There are also several problematic issues surrounding the use of particular concepts in sociological human ecology. For example, what is the utility of the equilibrium concept for the study of human ecological systems? The equilibrium assumption characterized sociological and anthropological functionalism a generation ago and gave rise to vigorous attacks from those who view societies as strife-ridden, full of internal conflicts, and continually undergoing structural change. Why, then, should human ecological systems be characterized by equilibrium, except to serve as a benchmark for comparing deviations from that state?

Another key concept in many of the dominant approaches to sociological human ecology is sustenance organization. While there can be little doubt that all human societies are organized, at least in part, to provide for the material needs of members, the questions of how patterns of sustenance organization originate and why they change have yet to be answered satisfactorily. Should sustenance organization be viewed as enacted or emergent? That is, is it the result of purposeful actions by human groups or is it created through the interaction of more or less random events? Moreover, how is sustenance organization related to social organization conceived more broadly?

Symbiosis, or interdependence, is a generic assumption of bioecological models which has been incorporated into most ecological approaches in sociology. However, this assumption raises problems in terms of defining units of analysis. Sociological human ecologists have typically concentrated on spatially bounded and somewhat artificially defined aggregates such as neighborhoods, communities, counties, or societies and have treated them as though they were closed systems. However, apart from truly isolated "primitive" societies of the ethnographic past, we know that the analyst's imposition of artificial boundaries ignores a variety of influences on the ecological system. A more realistic approach would treat human aggregates--"communities, etc.--as open systems. But, taken to its logical extreme, the adoption of an open system perspective would suggest that the entire solar system, if not the universe, should comprise the unit of analysis. Considered more realistically, the assumption of interdependence would require that a comprehensive study of the ecological organization of a community in Kansas take into account relationships with the rest of the United States and many other nations of the world. In short, the implications and limitations of the interdependence concept need to be reconsidered.

The final issue to be considered here has to do with the distinction between evolution and expansion (or growth) and the significance of these concepts for understanding ecosystem development. Typically, social scientists have viewed societal evolution as a long-range process by which more complex societies emerge from their simpler predecessors. New societal forms are hypothesized to be "selected" for survival on the basis of their superior adaptability to the possibilities and constraints of the environment. Societal expansion, on the other hand, posits an increasing network of interdependence among key groups or institutions, and hypothesizes the gradual spread of societal influence and control to surrounding areas and their constituent populations. At the moment, evolution and expansion may be viewed as competing theories of social change. The issue is which of these models best fits the developmental process characteristic of human ecosystems.

# THEORETICAL ISSUES

As suggested in earlier chapters, a few theoretical orientations have dominated sociological human ecology in recent decades, particularly Hawley's theory of expansion, the ecological complex (as an analytical framework), and the sustenance organization model. However, each of these models undoubtedly requires further specification. For example, their underlying assumptions are not always well-defined, questions of causation are frequently ignored and, with a few notable exceptions, testable hypotheses have not been deduced formally. In other words, while recent research in sociological human ecology has frequently been guided by one or another of the dominant theoretical frameworks, insufficient attention has been given to elaboration of the theoretical infrastructure.

The apparent lack of continuity between theory and research is paradoxical. Given the existence of these theoretical orientations and the widespread adherence to them among sociologists who call themselves ecologists, why is so much of the empirical work in the field descriptive? Are there difficulties inherent in the subject matter of sociological human ecology which preclude an emphasis on prediction and/or explanation?

Another issue that should be addressed has to do with the generalization of ecological theories in sociology. Human ecology deals with territorially-circumscribed populations which are usually defined in terms of political or cultural criteria. Both political and cultural distinctions typically imply normative differences, but the dominant approaches in sociological human ecology ignore such variables. Thus, for example, how could ecologists deal with different forms of sustenance organization in Japan and the United States or different forms of metropolitan organization in Mexico and Canada? The question is, should human ecological theories be stated relativistically in order to capture normative variations among the populations studied, or are the ecological regularities we seek unaffected by these differences?

There is some concern that theories in sociological human ecology are overly concerned with structural relations while neglecting the processes that underlie human ecosystems. The foremost exception to this criticism is the work of Amos Hawley and his students on the expansion process. Generally, though, sociological human ecologists have given scant theoretical attention to mechanisms through which societal and more limited ecosystems are generated, maintained and changed.

Perhaps the most evident example of theoretical neglect of a basic ecological process is with regard to "adaptation." The concept of adaptation in human ecological theory has not been elaborated sufficiently by sociologists. Anthropologists, studying small communities closely and directly involved with the environment and its plant and animal species, have analyzed adaptation in terms of explicit ecosystem energy flows. This body of research may offer some models applicable to larger social units.

Our last question about ecological theory regards the cumulation of knowledge. One of the principal functions of theory is to provide a framework within which knowledge can be organized, examined, and added to. Any field of inquiry that fails to emphasize knowledge accumulation is unlikely to contribute to the solution of empirical problems. Are research findings from sociological human ecology growing additively, or are we merely increasing the number of unrelated empirical observations?

## METHODOLOGICAL ISSUES

Is there a "proper" unit of analysis for human ecological studies in sociology? This question has been addressed, implicitly and explicitly, for many years. Early work in the field centered on the community, variously defined. In recent years attention has shifted to the societal level of analysis. The chapters in Part II of this volume show that ecologists now study phenomena at several levels, ranging from formal organizations to subnational regions. Sociological ecologists have yet to respond to world-systems models arising from various quarters, some of which emphasize ecological variables such as population and resources. Do these concerns fall within the scope of sociological ecology? The issue is whether sociological human ecology's basic concepts and theories are more appropriate for some units of analysis rather than others.

Measurement of ecological concepts is of course a central issue. Concepts that cannot be operationalized, even if only approximately, are of little use in scientific inquiry. Sociological human ecologists continue to experience difficulty in measuring a number of key concepts. An uneven development of measurement techniques is apparent. Thus demographic processes, particularly of mortality and fertility, can be measured very precisely. Some other phenomena, notably spatial segregation and the division of labor in occupational structures, have elaborate methodological tools and extensive research literatures. On the other hand there are basic ecological concepts which have not been operationalized. What are the crucial dimensions of environment and how should they be measured? How are adaptation and interdependence to be measured?

Incorporating time into ecological analysis continues to challenge researchers. Some believe that growth and evolution occur in cycles or rhythmatic patterns. Time frames must be investigated in order to specify important points of measurement. Even if meaningful patterns cannot be discerned, we must identify appropriate time intervals in which lagged effects might be observed.

Finally, there is the issue of replication. Many of the early generalizations in sociological human ecology were derived from single studies of individual communities or regions. The question is, how much replication is required before we have confidence that a particular hypothesis is supported or not?

## SUBSTANTIVE ISSUES

Since its inception, sociological human ecology has emphasized urban organization, process, and change. Should this tradition be continued? Is metropolitan growth still the principal substantive problem for the field? What is the utility of research focused on urban growth models, particularly that proposed by E. W. Burgess? Have researchers neglected the ecological organization of nonmetropolitan areas?

Another issue has to do with the tendency of sociological human ecologists to concentrate on industrialized societies. Some students of international development have suggested that the major problems facing the less developed nations of the world are essentially ecological. Are sociologists missing an important opportunity by avoiding the ecology of development?

In recent years conceptualizations of human ecology have highlighted the role of energy in the ecosystem. Nonetheless, sociologists have not looked carefully at ecological aspects of energy supply, conversion processes, and conservation. In short, the study of energetics requires further development from a sociological perspective.

Another current emphasis, particularly at the macroscopic level, is on interdependence. Localities and regions exchange materials and information within as well as between nations. What are the ecological consequences of growing interdependence? In this connection, how much attention should be given to the redistributive processes that necessarily accompany interdependence?

Finally, there is little doubt that the human species has assumed an increasingly dominant role in the ecosystem. Human decisions are likely to determine the quality of life on the planet in the future, which in turn will depend largely on the degree to which the ecosystem is disrupted. It is therefore important to examine more closely the role of political decision-making and social power relationships in ecological processes.

## PRACTICAL ISSUES

Over the years, sociological human ecologists have not devoted much attention to the application of ecological knowledge to societal problems. We have concentrated on developing the epistemological basis of the field—its concepts, theories, and methodology—and on producing a wide range of empirical studies. Only rarely have we asked ourselves how this information can be used to improve human welfare and to prevent continuing deterioration of the ecosystem.

Before we can contribute to the policy sciences we must first develop a dialogue with policymakers and program implementors. Usually, social scientists fail to inquire about the kinds of information practitioners find useful. We need to know more about the ways in which policymakers use social information, and to let them know what we can provide. We need to distinguish between findings that merely clarify the nature of problems and those that actually contribute to workable solutions. We must be able to separate abstract indicators that exist only in the minds of social scientists from concrete conditions that can be acted upon through political decisions and policy initiatives. In short, we must become more relevant.

There are many aspects of ecological research in sociology that can be useful to policymakers. One of the most obvious contributions we can make is to help policymakers think ecologically, i.e., to recognize the interdependence between human collectivities and their environments. Societal welfare depends in large part on maintaining the balance of nature, though one might have great difficulty recognizing this premise in the policies of most of the world's nations.

Another basic contribution the human ecologist can make to policy decisions is to examine the environmental and organizational consequences of prolonged rapid population growth or drastic shifts in the distribution or composition of a population. Such studies have, of course, been conducted, but few have been set in an ecological frame of reference.

Likewise, current trends in the consumption of materials, energy, and information are natural concerns of both the human ecologist and the policymaker. A better understanding of the causes and consequences of these trends can be attained through the application of ecological principles developed in sociology as well as other social science disciplines.

## CONCLUSION

We have raised a number of issues pertaining to the further development of sociological human ecology. While the range of issues covered is in no way comprehensive, this discussion does suggest that the field can benefit from conceptual and theoretical clarification, greater methodological precision, additional substantive exploration, and increased attention to practical applications. The vitality of sociological human ecology will depend on how we deal with the issues before us. We hope the essays presented in this volume have provided insights into how we can proceed most productively.

# Author Index

Abrahamson, M., 142
Abrams, P., 37
Abu-Lughod, T.T., 135
Adams, R.N., 19, 59, 75, 76, 84
Aigner, D.J., 163
Aldrich, H.E., 11, 194, 404
Alexandersson, G., 141
Alihan, M., 126, 286
Alker, H.R., 151, 152, 157
Alland, A., 60, 61
Allardt, E., 151
Allee, W.C., 22
Allen, M.P., 394
Anderson, J.N., 68, 69
Anderson, T.R., 133, 151, 252, 298
Andrews, F.M., 159
Armer, J.M., 147
Arney, W.R., 164

Bahr, H.M., 334
Bailey, K.D., 395
Barker, R.G., 63
Barrows, H.H., 51, 78
Bateson, G., 25
Beale, C.L., 157, 339, 348
Bean, F.D., 103, 360-362
Beckham, B., 367
Bell, W., 134, 242, 258, 265
Bennett, J.W., 27, 61, 68, 70, 71, 72-73, 75, 82, 84
Berger, B., 251, 257
Berry, B.J.L., 64, 79, 80, 97, 99, 126, 127, 133, 135, 142, 144, 165, 183, 248, 295, 301, 350, 354, 385, 390, 397, 398, 399
Berube, M.R., 264
Bidwell, C.E., 11, 96, 97, 101, 102, 104, 179
Biehe, K., 150
Birch, D.C., 295, 296

Blalock, H.M., Jr., 105, 145, 151, 162
Blau, P.M., 146, 185, 397
Blauner, R., 264
Bogue, D.J., 139-140, 142, 145, 150, 153, 154, 155, 156, 325, 350, 342, 353
Bogue, E.J., 145, 150, 153, 154, 155, 156
Booth, A., 249
Borgatta, E.F., 103
Boserup, E., 35
Boskoff, A., 413
Bott, E., 255
Boughey, A.S., 398
Boulding, K.E., 63, 134
Bowen, S., 38
Bowles, G.K., 338
Bradburn, N.M., 239, 258
Bradshaw, B.S., 338
Brown, D.J., 143
Brown, D.L., 339
Brown, H.J., 302
Brown, J.K., 332
Browning, H.L., 115, 116, 129, 130, 132, 143, 165, 329, 331, 397
Bruhn, J.G., 84
Buckley, W., 58
Burch, W.R., Jr., 68
Burchell, R.W., 256
Burgess, E.W., 5, 64, 132, 133, 157, 180, 239, 240, 243, 244, 277, 278, 279, 280-286, 287, 288, 289, 290, 292, 293, 294, 297, 403
Burns, T.R., 184

Cain, S.A., 84
Caldwell, L.K., 81, 385, 394n
Callison, C.H., 419
Campbell, D.T., 24, 159, 160

Caplow, T., 133, 184
Carpenter, N., 241
Carrey, J.T., 277
Carroll, R.L., 355
Carter, L.J., 391
Cassel, J., 249
Catanese, A.J., 291
Catton, W.R., Jr., 26, 54, 59, 392, 405, 408, 418
Caughley, G., 37
Chandler, A.D., Jr., 206, 228n
Cherstein, I.W., 103, 109, 115
Choldin, H.M., 136, 179-180, 253, 279
Chorley, R.J., 79
Christaller, W., 351
Clark, C., 35, 133, 165
Clark, P.J., 40
Clark, S.D., 301
Clarke, C.J., 96, 100-101, 100n, 103, 342, 345
Clarkson, J.D., 79
Clemence, T.G., 137
Clemente, F., 115, 129, 130, 132, 331, 402
Cluett, C., 295
Cohen, D., 32
Cohen, E., 73
Cohen, Y.A., 56, 60, 73, 74
Colinvaux, P., 29
Connell, J.H., 43
Cortese, C.F., 138, 333
Costner, H.L., 105
Cottrell, F., 397
Cowgill, D.D., 136
Cowgill, M.S., 136
Craven, P., 238, 255
Cuzzort, R.P., 125
Cyert, R.M., 185, 186, 187

Daly, H.E., 63
Davie, M.R., 126, 133, 279, 282, 288
Davies, V., 130
Davis, B., 151
Davis, J.A., 146, 154, 165
Deare, D., 348

DeChiara, J., 254
Deeley, N.A., 339
DeJong, G.F., 339
Dentler, R.A., 263, 386
DeVore, I., 34
Dice, L.R., 53, 56, 246
Dickinson, R.E., 326, 351
Dogan, M., 81
Dorney, R.S., 413
DuBick, M.A., 142
Dubin, R., 184
Duis, P., 252
Dumond, D.E., 34
Duncan, B., 110, 125, 133, 136, 137, 138, 333, 358
Duncan, O.D., 4, 19, 30, 37, 42, 54, 63, 66-67, 96-97, 100n, 101-103, 105-106, 116, 125-128, 136-143, 150-151, 154, 158, 160, 179, 183, 190, 239, 242, 245, 248, 258, 261, 279, 305, 323-324, 326-327, 333-334, 343, 345, 350-351, 353-354, 358-362, 369, 397, 415
Dunlap, R.E., 394n
Durbin, J., 163
Durkheim, E., 21, 80, 108, 114, 115, 180, 327, 329, 331, 345, 406

Eberstein, I.W., 339
Edmonston, B., 354
Ehrhardt, A.A., 26
Ehrlich, P.R., 390, 398
Elton, C.S., 40
Emery, F.E., 63
Emlen, J.M., 28
Emmell, T.C., 53
England, J.A., 133, 252, 288
Erickson, M.L., 142
Etizoni, A., 185
Evan, W.M., 211n

Farkas, G., 148
Farley, R., 137, 252, 256, 312

Farnsworth, E.G., 39
Fava, S.F., 238, 242, 257
Feldman, A.S., 306
Felson, M., 258
Ferkiss, V., 81, 82
Firebaugh, G., 151, 154
Firey, W., 68, 105, 126, 133, 279, 286, 287, 305, 306
Fischer, C.S., 242, 251
Fitch, J.M., 249
Foley, D.L., 238, 244
Form, W.H., 133, 238, 240, 243, 293
Frake, C.D., 69
Freedman, R., 340
Freeman, J.H., 23, 25, 26, 28, 143, 144, 149, 161, 191
Friedland, R., 355
Frisbie, W.P., 96, 100, 100n, 103, 104, 106, 108-111, 115, 116, 129, 131, 134, 324, 329, 331, 336-338, 340, 345
Fuguitt, G.V., 157, 161, 256, 258, 339, 348
Furez, M., 240, 252

Gale, R.P., 294n
Galle, O.R., 110, 141, 146, 365
Gans, H., 238, 239, 241, 242, 251, 256, 259, 261, 263, 301
Garrison, W.L., 142
Geertz, C., 69
Gehlke, C.E., 150
Geisel, T.S., 29
George, C.J., 386
Gessaman, P.H., 349
Gibbs, J.P., 19, 67, 96, 105-110, 115, 116, 126, 128-132, 143, 145, 165, 248, 324, 326, 328-334, 339, 342, 343, 345, 347, 371, 372, 397
Gillette, T.L., 414
Gilmore, H.W., 133
Glass, R., 238, 240, 244
Glenn, N.D., 332
Glick, P.C., 311

Godelier, M., 34
Goldschmidt, W., 345
Golley, F.B., 39
Goodman, D., 409
Goodman, L.A., 151, 153-155
Gras, N.S.B., 352, 255, 355
Greenwood, J.M., 162
Greer, S., 241, 297, 386
Gross, E., 332, 333
Guest, A.M., 136, 180, 256, 286, 289, 290, 294, 295-297, 299-313, 354, 358
Gusfield, J.R., 245
Guterbock, T., 301

Hackett, B., 419
Hadden, J.K., 102
Hage, J., 158
Hagerstrand, T., 79
Haggarty, L.J., 133, 157
Haggett, P., 350
Hall, P., 281
Hall, R.H., 185
Hammond, J.L., Jr., 147, 150, 151, 153
Hannan, M.T., 23, 25, 26, 28, 143, 145, 149, 160, 162, 163-165, 191
Hansen, L.K., 144, 158, 159, 161, 162
Hardin, G., 33, 37
Harris, C.D., 132, 287
Harris, M., 76-78, 83
Haswell, M.R., 35
Hatt, P.K., 238, 240
Hauser, P.M., 26, 147, 148, 149, 240
Hawley, A.H., 3, 21-23, 28-31, 35, 63-67, 73, 84, 92-97, 100-102, 105, 107, 108, 115, 117, 126, 127, 132, 136, 140, 143, 152, 157, 179, 183, 195, 200, 215, 216n, 238, 242, 245-247, 250, 261, 279, 282, 297, 324, 326, 327, 334, 335, 348, 349, 356, 386, 387, 395, 396, 406n

440

Hawthorne, G., 340
Heatwole, H., 41
Hechter, M., 287
Heise, D.R., 160, 162, 166
Helm, J., 63
Henry, S.M., 39
Herbert, J.R., 419
Herskovitz, M.J., 332
Hettner, A., 51
Hibbs, N.A., Jr., 162, 163, 164
Hillery, G.A., 245
Hinkle, L.E., 419
Hobson, B.T., 79
Hoerman, S.A., 358
Holter, H., 332
Hoover, E.M., 300
Horn, H.S., 43
Howell, N., 34
Hoyt, H., 132, 279, 287
Humphrey, C.R., 249
Hunter, A., 135, 157, 238, 239, 240, 243-245, 261, 267, 277
Hutchinson, G.E., 29

Indik, B., 251
Insel, M., 63
Isard, W., 38

Jackson, K.T., 298
Janowitz, M., 238, 245, 260, 267, 268
Johansen, E.J., 332
John, J.A., 136
Johnson, G.C., 115, 332-335
Johnston, J., 135, 162, 163
Jordan, P.A., 419

Kahn, R.L., 184
Kantrowitz, N., 252
Karkheck, J., 389
Kasarda, J.D., 8, 11, 64, 66, 79, 80, 96, 97, 99-102, 104, 126, 133, 144, 161, 165, 179, 238, 245, 248, 267, 296, 323, 324, 327, 342,

347, 354, 356-357, 385, 387, 390, 397-399
Kass, R., 103, 141, 142
Katz, D., 185
Katz, E., 255, 268
Kaufman, I.R., 299
Keller, S., 238, 241
Kemper, T.D., 143
Kirschenbaum, A., 339
Klausner, S.Z., 68, 157
Kligman, M., 413
Koppelman, L., 254
Kormondy, E.J., 404
Kornblum, W., 238, 240, 241, 252, 262
Kotler, M., 260
Kroeber, A.L., 51
Kronenfeld, J.E., 161
Kruskal, J.B., 143
Kuhn, S., 57
Kuhn, T., 91

Labovitz, S., 115, 116, 330
Lachenmeyer, C., 58
Lampard, E.E., 115, 328
Langenheim, J.H., 53
Larson, O.F., 413
Lassey, W.R., 413
Lawrence, P.R., 185, 187
Lawson, S., 307
Lazarsfeld, P., 268
Lee, D.H.K., 419
Lee, E., 389
Lee, R.B., 34
Lenski, G.E., 8, 59, 100, 345
Lenski, J., 59
Leopold, A., 412
Levin, S.A., 39
Levine, S., 211n
Levins, R., 27, 28, 32, 39, 41, 43
Lewontin, R.C., 24, 32
Lieberson, S., 4, 103, 110, 143, 144, 158, 159, 161, 162, 307, 358, 368, 369
Lincoln, J.R., 355, 367

Linz, J., 146
Logan, J.R., 303
Long, L.H., 311
Lorsch, J.W., 185, 187
Losch, A., 351
Lotka, A.J., 36, 38, 39, 43
Lynch, K., 244

MacArthur, R.H., 28, 36–37, 40, 41
McCarthy, K.F., 389
McCay, B., 61, 73
McClenahan, B.A., 241, 243, 251, 254, 258
McFarland, D.D., 143
McKay, H.D., 260
McKenzie, R.D., 4, 157, 165, 238, 241, 243, 251, 254, 258, 277, 278, 280, 285, 292, 352, 353
McKinley, D., 386
McLauren, I.A., 31
Manners, G., 295
March, J.G., 185, 186, 187
Mark, H., 356
Marston, W.G., 307
Martin, W.T., 67, 96, 106, 107, 109, 115, 116, 126, 129, 130, 132, 165, 248, 324, 326, 330, 332, 333, 343, 345, 347, 356, 357, 372
Maruyama, M., 26
Marx, L., 386, 404
Masering, C.H., 61
Mason, L.H., 53
Masterman, M., 57
Matre, M., 134, 135
May, R.M., 31, 32, 39, 40
Mayer, T.F., 164
Mayo, E., 184
Mayr, E., 28
Mehta, S.K., 330
Meier, R.L., 245
Menzel, H., 152
Meyer, M.W., 185
Michelson, W.H., 83, 98, 99, 103, 143, 246, 257, 258, 302, 419

Micklin, M., 23, 61, 68, 104, 115, 143, 157, 326, 331, 343–345
Miley, J.D., 115, 331
Miller, A.D., 162
Mills, C.W., 9
Mills, E.S., 299
Mohr, C.O., 246
Molotch, H., 240, 241, 252, 264
Money, J., 26
Moore, W., Jr., 259
Moos, R.H., 63
Morrison, P.A., 251, 301, 388–389
Mukerjee, R., 413
Mulcahy, P., 395n
Muller, P.O., 243, 259
Murdock, S., 395n

Nakamura, A.O., 163
Nelson, G.H., 309
Nelson, H.J., 102, 141
Nett, R., 57
Neutze, M., 311
Newman, O., 257
Nolan, P.D., 161
North, C.C., 332
Notestein, F.W., 8

Odum, E.P., 11, 22, 42, 398, 399
Odum, H.P., 39, 42, 52, 54, 56, 58
Odum, H.T., 398
Ogburn, W.F., 101, 345
Olsen, R.A., 309
Orians, G.H., 25
Oster, G.F., 31

Pahl, R.E., 79
Pampel, F.C., 136, 253
Pappenfort, D.M., 4, 297, 368
Park, R.E., 1n, 51, 64, 241, 251, 254, 259, 277–280, 403
Park, R.K., 157
Parsons, H.L., 419

Patrick, R., 40
Pearl, R., 31
Pedersen, P.O., 135
Peirce, N., 310
Pelz, C.D., 159
Perelman, M.J., 389
Perrow, C., 185, 187
Peterson, W., 413
Pfeffer, J., 11
Pigeon, R.F., 39
Pimentel, D., 390
Pomeroy, L.R., 42
Popenoe, D., 256
Poston, D.L., Jr., 99, 100,
  104, 106-111, 114-116,
  129-132, 134, 145, 180,
  181, 279, 324, 328, 329,
  331, 332, 333, 335-340,
  342, 348, 349, 358,
  360-362
Pred, A., 350
Preston, R.E., 103
Price, D.O., 100, 332
Pringle, J.W.S., 24
Pursell, D.E., 338

Quinn, J.A., 63, 282, 288

Rainwater, L., 249, 258
Rapoport, A., 25
Rappaport, R.A., 74, 75, 83,
  84
Reed, H.H., 253
Reed, L.J., 31
Rees, P.H., 135, 258
Reichelle, D.E., 42
Reid, L., 53, 55
Reiss, A.J., 102, 141, 404
Robinson, W.S., 147, 151-153
Roethlisberger, F.J., 184
Rogers, E.S., 63
Rogers, P., 398
Rokkan, S., 81
Roof, W.C., 139, 145, 334
Roper, M.W., 244
Rose, H.M., 252
Rossi, P.H., 263, 301, 386
Roughgarden, J., 37, 39

Rozelle, R.M., 160
Rubinson, R., 4
Rushing, W.A., 130
Russett, B.M., 81
Ryder, N.B., 53

Sahlins, M.D., 34, 59, 71
Sale, R., 295
Salins, P.D., 133, 134
Salter, P.S., 413
Sargent, F., 398
Scheuch, E.K., 144-146, 166
Schienfeld, A., 332
Schluter, D., 51
Schmitt, R.C., 298
Schnore, L.F., 66-67, 78, 98,
  101, 107, 126, 150, 157,
  165, 183, 189-190, 245,
  247, 253, 279, 282, 286-
  287, 290, 298-300, 303,
  308, 326-328, 353-354,
  357, 358, 397
Schoenherr, R., 185
Schorr, A.L., 249
Schrödinger, E., 189
Schuessler, K., 155
Schultz, A.M., 38
Schuman, H., 261
Schwirian, K.P., 132-135,
  165, 356
Scott, W.R., 358
Sell, R.R., 349
Service, E.R., 59, 71
Sewell, W., 147
Shaw, C.R., 260
Sheldon, H.D., 358
Shevky, E., 134, 332
Shively, W.P., 151, 154
Simkus, A.A., 136, 258
Simmie, J.M., 63
Simmons, J.W., 301, 305
Simon, H.A., 40, 185-187
Sisler, D.G., 349
Sjoberg, G., 57, 101, 250,
  345
Slayter, R.O., 43
Slesinger, D.P., 355
Slobodkin, L.B., 25, 36

Sly, D.F., 100, 103, 115, 143, 331, 336, 338-339, 341
Smith, D.L., 131
Smith, J., 4
Snow, R.E., 131
Sofer, C., 184
Sorensen, A., 137, 252, 308
South, S.J., 115
Spear, A.H., 252
Speare, A., Jr., 159, 305
Spodek, H., 135
Spooner, B., 35
Sprout, H., 80
Sprout, M., 80
Stalker, G.M., 185
Stegman, M., 302
Stein, M., 278
Stephan, G.E., 401
Stern, R.N., 365
Sternlieb, G., 251, 256
Steward, J., 68-69
Stinchcombe, A.L., 194, 201
Stinner, W.R., 339
Stoddart, D.R., 79-80
Strauss, A.L., 286
Sturgis, R.B., 129-130, 132, 331
Sumner, W.G., 401
Sussman, M.B., 408
Sutker, S.S., 103, 142, 362, 363
Suttles, G.D., 238, 242, 252, 256, 258-260, 262, 267, 323
Sutton, W.A., 395
Sweetser, F.L., 135, 238, 241, 242
Sykes, M.M., 100

Tabovitz, S., 129
Taeuber, A.F., 136-139, 145, 252, 307, 333
Taeuber, K.E., 136-139, 145, 252, 307, 333
Tarver, J.D., 339, 348
Taub, R.P., 258, 261
Tax, S., 263
Taylor, F.W., 184
Taylor, G.R., 294

Taylor, J.B., 408
Tayman, D., 100, 104, 115, 331, 338-339
Teitelbaum, M.S., 342
Terreberry, S., 211n
Theodorson, G.A., 64, 353, 395n
Thomas, E.N., 151
Thomas, W.I., 406
Thompson, J.D., 185, 187, 200, 211n, 218n
Thompson, W.S., 8
Tilly, C., 306
Tilly, L., 245
Timms, D.W.G., 258
Tobin, G.A., 290, 291
Toffler, A., 407
Trager, W., 39
Trist, E.L., 63
Tuma, N.B., 165
Tunnard, C., 253
Turk, H., 4
Turner, R.H., 332

Ullman, D.R., 30, 132, 287, 351, 352

Valkonen, T., 151
Vance, F.B., 350
Vance, R.B., 4, 103, 142, 352-363
Vandermeer, J.H., 29
Vann, A., 398
Van Valey, T.L., 137, 139, 145, 308, 334
Verhulst, P.F., 31
Vernon, R., 300

Wagner, L., 63
Wagner, R.H., 398
Wallace, A.F.C., 256
Wallerstein, I., 4
Wanner, R.A., 103, 116, 142
Ward, D., 288, 290
Wardwell, J.M., 339
Warner, S.B., 243, 294
Warren, D.I., 262
Warren, R.L., 4, 259

Watson, G.S., 163
Watson, W.T., 332
Watt, K., 390
Webb, S.D., 331
Webber, M.M., 238, 256
Weber, M., 184
Weed, J.A., 286, 307
Wellman, B., 238, 255-256
Wheeler, J.P., 302
White, L., 8
White, P.E., 211n
White, R., 99, 335, 338
Whittaker, R.H., 39
Whyte, W.H., 261
Williams, B.J., 34
Williams, G.C., 33
Williams, J.G., 332, 333
Williams, R.H., 412
Williamson, O.E., 206, 207
Wilner, D.M., 249
Wilson, E.O., 206, 207
Wilson, F.D., 298

Winsborough, H.H., 103, 288,
  290, 299, 354, 358, 360,
  365
Winship, P.C., 138, 139
Winter, S.G., 23
Wirth, L., 146, 238, 240-241,
  251-252
Wolff, K.H., 189
Woodward, J., 185, 187
Wynne-Edwards, V.C., 33-34

Yeates, M., 291, 297
Young, A.A., 162-164
Young, R.C., 413

Zeisel, J., 419
Zelinsky, W., 80, 84
Zimmer, B.G., 291-293, 256, 287
Znaniecki, F., 406
Zorbaugh, H., 237, 240, 259,
  323
Zuiches, J.J., 256, 258, 349

# Subject Index

Abundance, relative. *See*
    Carrying capacity
Accessibility, 282, 291
    index of, 359
Accumulation, 67
Activity patterns, 88, 192
    *See also* Organizational
    structure
Adaptation, 2, 5-6, 22, 28,
    56-57, 72-73, 84, 99
    biological versus socio-
    cultural, 60-61, 76
    in cultural materialism, 78
    definitions of, 23-26
    diachronic analysis of, 157
    in environmental orientation
    theory, 74
    macrolevel analysis of,
    126-127
    measurement of, 61-62
    organizational, 25, 66-67,
    104, 127, 183-184, 343-
    344
    in political science, 80
    variations in, 56-57
Adaptive mechanisms, 26-27,
    42, 61
    *See also* Adaptive processes;
    Adaptive strategies
Adaptive processes, 27, 72
    ecological succession, 25
    natural selection, 24
    *See also* Adaptation;
    Adaptive mechanisms;
    Adaptive strategies
Adaptive strategies, 62, 75
    learning, 24
    specialization, 205
    *See also* Adaptation
Adaptive systems, 70
Aggregate analysis, 152-153
    *See also* Ecological
    concepts, measurement of
Aggregation bias, 152-154

    *See also* Ecological con-
    cepts, measurement of
Aggression, 403
Autocorrelation, 162-165

Behavioral theory of the firm,
    186
Bias
    in cross-national analysis,
    165-166
    levels, change score and
    simultaneity, 160-162
Bioecological models, 430
Bioecology, 3, 22-23, 383,
    399-400
Biotic communities
    human groups in, 395
    *See also* Ecosystems
Boundaries
    permeability of, 100
Bureaucratization
    dimensions of, 344
    index, 344
Burgess hypothesis, 280-294
    criticism of, 286-288
    historical relevance of,
    288-293

Carrying capacity, 207-208,
    213, 223, 225
    deficit, political
    implications of, 412
    and energy, 70-71, 392
    of environment, 30, 32,
    207-208
    illusory enlargement of,
    392
    supplementing of, 416
    and survival, 61
Causal inference, 159-160.
    *See also* Ecological con-
    cepts, measurement of
Central Business District
    (DBD), 283, 294, 295

Central city, 355. See also
Cities, systems of;
Nodality; Subcommunities
Central place theory, 351, 352
effects of occupational
composition on, 365
See also Cities;
Metropolises; Metropolitan
dominance
Chicago School of Sociology,
277-280
Cities, 237-238
central, and migration
patterns, 338. See also
Central Place Theory
industrial composition
and regional relationships
of, 358
problems of comparisons
between, 138
systems of 367-372
See also Central City;
Community; Metropolises;
Metropolitan areas;
Regional ecology
Climax communities, 56, 59,
405
Closed-system theory, 184-189
limitations of, 185
Collective actions
symbiotic and commensalistic,
93
See also Interdependence,
hierarchy of
Collective life
morphology of, 328
See also Community
Commensalistic relations in
communities. See
Interdependence,
hierarchy of
Communications, electronic.
See Technology
Community, 53
Competition within, 93
human ecology of, 248
interdependence within, 93
local, transitions of, 250-
265
metropolitan, 247
non-human components of,
402
as principal unit of
ecological organization,
65
as shared habitat, 402
trophic structure of, 41
Community area. See Sub-
communities
Community organization
models, 40-43
Community structure, 279
theory of, 93
Conflict resolution, 187
Conservation, 404
Consultants
human ecologists as,
407-413
Contextual analysis, 145-150
See also Ecological con-
cepts, measurement of
Contextual fallacy, 147-148
See also Ecological con-
cepts, measurement of
Control-System theory; 188-
189, 192
Cross-level analysis, 150-
156
inference of, 154-156
methodological bias,
151-153
See also Ecological con-
cepts, measurement of
Cross-national analysis,
165-166
See also Ecological con-
cepts, measurement of
Cross-temporal analysis.
See Diachronic analysis;
Ecological concepts,
measurement of
Cultural ecology, 68-71, 74.

See also Ethnoecology;
Human ecology; Sociological
human ecology
Cultural evolution, 71
Cultural materialism, 76-77
Cultural patterns, 95
Cumulative change, 2, 8, 66,
94-95

Decentralization, 354
Demographic change
and physical and social
environment, 348
Demographic structure
age, 252-253
differential population
growth, 289. See also
Population density
ethnicity, 252
morphological charac-
teristics, 305-308
motor vehicle, effect on,
289
population composition, 303
race, 252, 312-313
segregation, effect on,
304-308
of subcommunities, 251-265
technology, effect on, 212
since World War II, 294
See also Population
Demography and sustenance
organization. See
Sustenance organization,
demography of
Diachronic analysis, 157-167
autocorrelation in, 162-165
causal priority, 158
use in determining direction,
158
See also Ecological con-
cepts, measurement of
Differential population
growth. See Demographic
Structure, differential
population growth

Differentiation, 65, 284, 297
by ascribed status, 332-334
behavioral, 401
occupational, by race and
sex, 333
structural, 329
sustenance, 329
Disaggregation bias, 153-154.
See also Ecological con-
cepts, measurement of
Discrete analysis
at different levels, 144-
145. See also Ecological
concepts, measurement of
Dissimilarity
index of, 136, 333. See
also Ecological concepts,
measurement of
Distributional mechanisms of
organizational adapta-
tion. See Adaptation,
organizational
Division of labor, 129-132,
326-332
distributive differentia-
tion in, 132
functional interdependence
of, 132
interindustry dispersion in,
132
population characteristics,
331
structural differentiation
in, 131
Dominance
as a principle of
ecological organization,
66
variations in, 400
See also Metropolitan
dominance

Ecological analysis, 94
comparison of approaches,
82-84
See also Ecological rela-
tionships

Ecological anthropology. See Human ecology
Ecological change, 55-56, 66, 71, 74, 76, 94
Ecological complex, 66-67, 92, 95, 97-101, 102-106, 397, 431
Ecological concepts
applicability for social sciences, 59
biological basis, 419
definition of population, 41
measurement of, 127-128, 144-167, 432
Ecological fallacy, 150-156
Ecological institutionalization, 73
Ecological issues
conceptual approach to, 428-430
methodological approach to, 432-433. See also Ecological concepts, measurement of
substantive approach to, 433-434
theoretical approach to, 428, 431-432
Ecological niche. See Niches
Ecological organization, 65, 94, 98, 104
and population, 93, 343
Ecological perspective
political relevance of, 81-82, 385-422
Ecological processes, 83
antagonism, 402
competition, 401
Ecological relationships, 144-156. See also Ecological analysis
Ecological Succession, See Adaptive processes
Ecological theory. See Human ecology

Ecological theory of social change. See Social change, ecological theory of
Ecology
definition, 22, 52-55; of populations, 41
descriptive versus analytical, 126
factorial, 133-135
mainstream, 396
as policy science, 385-386
political, 80-82
regional. See Regional ecology
systems, 69-70
See also Ecosystems; Environment; Human ecology; Urban ecology
Economy
regional differentiation of, 358
Ecosystems, 11, 42
change. See Ecological change
commodity flow in, 100n
crash cycle of, 416-417
detritus, 416
and environmental policy, 81. See also Policy making
relations of species within, 54-55, 60
social relationships in, 96
See also Biotic communities; Human ecology
Ecosystem theory, 97
Energy, 76, 389
policy, 390-391, 398. See also Ecology, as policy science; Policy making
resources, 404, 415
shortage, 391
in technology, 101
Engineering as an adaptive mechanism. See Adaptation, organizational
Entrophy, 189

Environment, 3, 6
  biotic community,
    characteristics of, 402
  definition of, 53, 65, 97
  institutional, 222-224
  of organizations, 200
  of populations, 98
  relationship of systems, 2-9
  social and physical
    components of, 62, 76
  variation in, 27
  See also Ecological complex;
    Ecosystems
Environmental determinism, 79
Environmental model of migration. See Migration,
  environmental model
Environmental policy, 81. See
  also Policy making
Environmental properties,
  202-214
  carrying capacity of. See
    Carrying capacity, of
    environment
  generalizability of, 206-
    210
  perturbation of, 210-214,
    219, 221
  scope of, 202-207
  See also Input-output
    axiom
Equilibrium, 58-59, 69, 71,
  429
Ethnoecology, 69. See also
  Cultural ecology; Human
  ecology; Sociological
  human ecology
Evolution, 98, 430
Expansion, 66-67, 95, 430-431
Extrametabolites, 401

Feedback, 224-229
Fertility, 339-342
  sustenance organization,
    role of. See Sustenance
    organizations and
    fertility

Functional integration
  in interurban organization,
    141-143

Gini index, 136. See also
  Ecological concepts,
  measurement of

Habitat. See Human ecology
  of an organism. See
  Environment
Hinterland. See Nodal areas
  and hinterland
Homeostasis. See Equilibrium
Homogeneity. See Populations,
  homogeneous; Regional
  ecology
Housing, 248-249. See also
  Neighborhood
Human ecology, 2, 9-10, 183-
  184, 189, 190, 192, 193,
  237, 239, 245-250, 277,
  279, 295, 304, 395, 400
  anthropology's role in, 63,
    68-78, 82
  bioecology, relationship to,
    22
  date in, 125
  definition, 400
  genre range, 324
  geography's role in, 63,
    78-80, 82
  methodology in, 125
  as morphology of human
    communities, 93
  of organizations, 191-194
  political science's role in,
    63, 83
  social science's role in,
    51-52, 81-82
  and sociology, 12-13
  subcommunity as unit of
    analysis, 245-247
  vocabulary of, 383, 399-
    400
  See also Cultural ecology;
    Ethnoecology; Sociological
    human ecology

Information and technology.
   See Technology, and information
Information flows, 103
Infrastructural determinism,
   76-77
Input-output axiom, 193-216.
   See also Environmental
   properties
Input-output relationships,
   359
Insomorphism, 66
Interdependence
   and exchange flows, 103
   functional, 108, 114-115
   hierarchy of, 93, 102
   systemic, 65, 102
Interpopulation competition,
   35, 40-41. See also
   Demography; Population
Interpopulation models, 35,
   39, 40
   and community organization,
   29
Interurban organization, 132-
   141

Key functions, 214-224
   as a principle of ecological
   organization, 65
   and productivity, 216-224

Labor
   potential supply of, 338.
   See also Division of
   labor; Population,
   organizational structure
   of
Law of Limited Variety, 188-
   189, 193, 229
Local area. See Subcommunities

Measurement of ecological
   concepts. See Ecological
   concepts, measurement of
Metropolises
   commercial variable in, 360

   hierarchical classification
      of, 359-362
   manufacturing variable in,
      360
   national economy, role in
      358
   regional relationships,
      360-361
Metropolitan areas
   characteristics of, 462
   demography, policy implica-
      tions of, 388
   dominance and influence of,
      348-349, 353-354
   government, consolidation of,
      387
   growth patterns of, 348, 353.
      See also South, metropol-
      itan organization of
   historical emergence, 352
   occupational composition,
      365
   organizational reform, 387
   organizing role of, 352
Metropolitan community. See
   Community, metropolitan
Metropolitan dominance, 353,
   358, 365
Microcommunity. See Sub-
   communities
Migration
   and demographic change, 335
   differentiation, relation-
      ship to, 338
   environmental model, 104
   military and college
      activities, impact on,
      349
   and organizational change,
      334-339
   and service functions, 338
   sociological conflicts
      arising from, 389
   See also Mobility
Mobility
   and equilibrium, 336
   of subcommunities, 251

Monetary flows, 103
Multilevel analysis, 144. See
    also Ecological concepts,
    measurement of
Mutualism
    models of 35, 39, 40-41
    See also Interpopulation
    models

National economy
    role of metropolises in.
    See Metropolises, national
    economy, role in
National energy policy. See
    Ecology, as policy
    science; Energy policy
National hierarchy, 351. See
    also Regional ecology
Natural areas. See Neighbor-
    hood; Subcommunities
Natural geographic region.
    See Regional ecology
Natural selection, 24, 28
Neighborhood, 241-245. See
    also Subcommunities
Niches, 190, 196, 202-204,
    207, 406
    administrative, 216
    diversification of, 406
    environment of, 200
    production, 216, 218
Nodal areas
    fertility in, 355
    hierarchy of, 358-367
    and hinterland, 350-372
    income levels of, 355
Nodal centers
    functional interrelation-
    ships, 350
    populations, 351
    See also Cities, systems of;
    Metropolises; Regional
    Ecology
Nonmetropolitan areas
    population growth and
    decline, 337. See also
    Metropolitan areas

Open-system theory, 185-192
Organizational adaptation.
    See Adaptation, organi-
    zational
Organizational structure,
    126-127, 183, 192-233
    change, demographic response
    to, 334-342
Organizations, 65, 100
    as closed systems, 183-188
    as control systems, 186-189
    and environment, 200-202
    and technology, 197-200
    See also Ecological complex

Policymaking, 407-413
    ecological approach, 80-81,
    82
    prime mover, 184-185
Population, 6-7, 94, 99, 102
    definition of, 53
    density, 300
    and environment, 65
    gradient, 298
    growth and competition,
    29-31
    growth and equilibrium,
    31-35, 39
    human, 29, 324, 428
    organizational structure
    of, 106-107
    redistribution, 354, 389
    regulation, by predators,
    parasites and disease, 33
    social limits on, 33
    and zero population growth,
    389
    See also Demography;
    Ecological complex
Population, organizational, 29,
    195-202
    demography of, 196
    and environment, 200-202
    and technology, 197-200
Population composition. See
    Demographic structure,
    population composition

Population distribution. See
    Demographic structure,
    Population, density
Population genetics, 23-25,
    28
Population models, 31-35
Populations
    homogeneous, 326-349
    interacting, 40
    interbreeding of, 28-29
    number of, 40
    sympatric and synchronic,
        29
Population size
    and central place function,
        356
    growth and decline of, 337
    structural implications of,
        347
    sustenance organization,
    role of. See Sustenance
        organization, and popula-
        tion size
    and system level, 347
Predator-prey models, 35,
    37-38, 40-41. See also
    Interpopulation models
Prime mover, 184-185
Production
    efficiency of, 116
    Productive associations,
        331

Regional ecology, 2-5, 323-372
Regulatory mechanisms of
    organizational adaptation.
    See Adaptation, organi-
    zational
Reorientation, trauma of, 407
Replacement index, 138. See
    also Ecological concepts,
    measurement of
Residential areas. See
    Community; Subcommunities
Residential decentralization,
    308-314
    role of status in, 309-313

Segregation
    causes of, 139
    cross-sectional, 137
    longitudinal, 137
    residential, 136-137
Segregation indexes, 136
Self-modification. See
    Adaptation
Settlement
    density of, 140-141
    See also Metropolises;
        Regional ecology
Simultaneity bias, 160-162
Site modification, 403
Social area. See Sub-
    communities
Social change
    ecological theory of, 95
Social Organization, 23, 70-71
    urban, 102
    See also Organizations
Social structure
    and ecological analysis, 94
    evolution of, 75
Societal evolution. See
    Ecological change
Sociological human ecology,
    63-68, 92-96, 296-297,
    396-403
    mainstream ecology, integra-
        tion into, 398
    social sciences, relation-
        ship to, 429
    See also Cultural ecology;
        Ethnoecology; Human
        ecology
Sociological intervention, 386
South
    metropolitan organization
        of, 362-367
    See also Metropolises;
        Metropolitan areas, growth
        patterns
Spatial analysis, 278, 280,
    281, 287
Specialization, 328. See also
    Differentiation; Division

of Labor; Sustenance activities

Specification, 401

Structural-functional analysis, 146. See also Ecological concepts, measurement of

Subcommunities, 237-269
  definition and measurement of, 239-245
  ecological approach to, 245-247
  environment of, 256-257
  formal organization of, 259-265
  social organization of, 257-265
  stratification of, 258-259
  sustenance functions of, 248-250
  See also Community; Neighborhood

Suburbs. See Community; Subcommunities

Suburbanization, 296, 301-303

Succession community, 25, 403, 404, 405, 406, 417

Survival
  and adaptation, 61, 68
  collective, 61
  of human populations, 93, 96
  as production of sustained yields, 61

Sustenance activities, 93, 324, 328

Sustenance differentiation, 107, 114-115, 329

Sustenance functions, 108-109, 110
  in banking, 369-371
  interdependence of, 329
  in manufacturing, 368

Sustenance involvement, 116

Sustenance organization, 67, 95, 431
  bureaucratization, 108, 115
  complexity, 340-341

components of, 337, 339
concept of, 107
demography of, 336
efficiency of, 109
and fertility, 341
hierarchical location, 116
in human ecology, 128-129
and population size, 335, 339
taxonomy of, 111-114
technological changes in, 339
and urbanization. See Urbanization and sustenance organization

Sustenance organization model, 92, 106-114

Sustenance productivity, 116

Sustenance roles
  allocation by ascribed status, 333

Symbiotic relations within a community. See Interdependence, hierarchy of

Taylorism, 184

Technology, 70-71, 100-101
  demographic structure, impact of, 253-256
  and information, 101
  measurement of, 346
  in organizations, 197-200
  See also Ecological complex

Territorially based systems. See Regional ecology

Trade flows, 103

Transiency. See Mobility

Upward mobility. See Mobility

Urban ecology, 385-390
  land use in, 133

Urbanization, 94, 330
  index of, 137-138
  and population distribution, 354
  and sustenance organization, 386

454

Urban renewal, 387
Urban settlement
  national system of, 388
Urban social organization. See
  Intraurban organization;
  Social organization, urban
Urban structure, 132–143

Vital change. See Fertility

Work force. See Population,
  organizational
Workplace
  importance of, 302

# About the Book and Editors

## Sociological Human Ecology:
## Contemporary Issues and Applications
### edited by Michael Micklin
### and Harvey M. Choldin

A comprehensive review and synthesis of sociological human ecology, emphasizing advances in the field since 1950, this text addresses the fundamental question of how human populations survive within the constraints of a limited and changing environment. Leading scholars in the field examine in detail spatial and temporal variations in the forms of social organization that evolve as populations adapt to environmental constraints and exploit environmental opportunities. They cover conceptual, theoretical, and methodological issues; synthesize recent ecological research findings applicable to varying levels of social organization, ranging from formal organizations to subnational regions; and address the policy implications of research on the ecology of human societies. The book also contains a prologue that traces the historical development of the ecological paradigm in sociology and an epilogue that raises a number of questions for future work in the field.

Although addressed primarily to sociologists, *Sociological Human Ecology* will be of interest to students and practitioners of other disciplines as well, including anthropology, political science, economics, and geography. The book provides a perspective for understanding many of the central problems faced by contemporary societies: rapid population growth, environmental deterioration, urban expansion, and the depletion of natural resources.

MICHAEL MICKLIN is co-director of the Population and Development Policy Program at the Battelle Human Affairs Research Centers, Washington, D.C. He is the editor of *Population, Environment, and Social Organization: Current Issues in Human Ecology* (1973) and he is the co-editor of *Handbook of Applied Sociology: Frontiers of Contemporary Research* (1981) and *Village and Household Availability of Contraceptives: Africa/West Asia* (1977).

HARVEY M. CHOLDIN is professor of sociology at the University of Illinois, Urbana. He is the author of *Cities and Suburbs* (forthcoming, 1984) and numerous articles in sociological and demographic journals.

## Other Titles of Interest from Westview Press

*The Ecosystem Concept in Anthropology*, edited by Emilio F. Moran

*\*Human Adaptability: An Introduction to Ecological Anthropology*, Emilio F. Moran

*Rethinking Human Adaptation: Biological and Cultural Models*, Rada Dyson-Hudson and Michael A. Little

*\*Biology and the Social Sciences: An Emerging Revolution*, edited by Thomas C. Wiegele

*Applied Social Science for Environmental Planning*, edited by William Millsap

*Demographic Responses to Development: Sources of Declining Fertility in the Philippines*, Robert A. Hackenberg and Henry F. Magalit

*Urban Migrants in Developing Nations: Patterns and Problems of Adjustment*, edited by Calvin Goldscheider

*Aging from Birth to Death: Interdisciplinary Perspectives*, edited by Matilda White Riley

*Aging from Birth to Death, Volume 2: Sociotemporal Perspectives*, edited by Matilda White Riley, Ronald P. Abeles, and Michael S. Teitelbaum

*Demographic Behavior: Interdisciplinary Perspectives on Decision-Making*, edited by Thomas K. Burch

*\*Prisoners of Space?: Exploring the Geographical Experience of Older People*, Graham D. Rowles

*The Impact of Population Change on Business Activity in Rural America*, Kenneth M. Johnson

*Available in hardcover and paperback.

# Sociological Human Ecology:
## Contemporary Issues and Applications
### edited by Michael Micklin
### and Harvey M. Choldin

A comprehensive review and synthesis of sociological human ecology, emphasizing advances in the field since 1950, this text addresses the fundamental question of how human populations survive within the constraints of a limited and changing environment. Leading scholars in the field examine in detail spatial and temporal variations in the forms of social organization that evolve as populations adapt to environmental constraints and exploit environmental opportunities. They cover conceptual, theoretical, and methodological issues; synthesize recent ecological research findings applicable to varying levels of social organization, ranging from formal organizations to subnational regions; and address the policy implications of research on the ecology of human societies. The book also contains a prologue that traces the historical development of the ecological paradigm in sociology and an epilogue that raises a number of questions for future work in the field.

Although addressed primarily to sociologists, *Sociological Human Ecology* will be of interest to students and practitioners of other disciplines as well, including anthropology, political science, economics, and geography. The book provides a perspective for understanding many of the central problems faced by contemporary societies: rapid population growth, environmental deterioration, urban expansion, and the depletion of natural resources.

**Michael Micklin** is co-director of the Population and Development Policy Program at the Battelle Human Affairs Research Centers, Washington, D.C. He is the editor of *Population, Environment, and Social Organization: Current Issues in Human Ecology* (1973) and he is the co-editor of *Handbook of Applied Sociology: Frontiers of Contemporary Research* (1981) and *Village and Household Availability of Contraceptives: Africa/West Asia* (1977).

**Harvey M. Choldin** is professor of sociology at the University of Illinois, Urbana. He is the author of *Cities and Suburbs* (forthcoming, 1984) and numerous articles in sociological and demographic journals.

ISBN 0-86531-671-6

Cover design: Anita Meyer

# Date Due